EVOLUTION
AND
LEARNING

EVOLUTION AND LEARNING

Edited by
ROBERT C. BOLLES
MICHAEL D. BEECHER
University of Washington

LEA
LAWRENCE ERLBAUM ASSOCIATES, PUBLISHERS
1988   Hillsdale, New Jersey   London

Lawrence Erlbaum Associates, Inc., Publishers
365 Broadway
Hillsdale, New Jersey 07642

Library of Congress Cataloging-in-Publication Data

Evolution and learning.

  Includes bibliographies and indexes.
  1. Learning in animals. 2. Learning, Psychology of.
3. Behavior evolution. I. Bolles, Robert C.
II. Beecher, Michael D.
QL785.E96   1988   591.51   87-22361
ISBN 0-89859-542-8

Printed in the United States of America
10 9 8 7 6 5 4 3 2

Contents

Preface

Evolutionary theory and learning theory have for a long time developed in quite separate traditions. The two traditions have been built by different scholars who publish in different journals, typically are concerned with different questions, and who have often been quite separated geographically. Even with this separation, however, there have been some cross currents, some bits of influence. Commonly these have taken the form that advances in one of the traditions have been seen as having implications for the other. For example, Darwin made a number of implicit assumptions about the place of learning in the overall scheme of things. He did not know much about learning as a formal discipline for the very good reason that it was not a formal discipline at that time. But the implications were clearly there for the discipline that was to come along later.

These cross currents have moved in both directions. Thus, Hull was a prominent learning theorist who from time to time drew important implications from evolutionary theory. At one point Hull noted that avoidance behavior might be remarkably slow to extinguish because of the biological importance of animals not lapsing in their avoidance of predators. The exchange of these ideas and implications has probably been fairly even in the two directions.

One evidence of the separation of the two traditions is that when, for example, a psychologist includes evolutionary considerations in his or her learning theory, the evolution people usually pay very little attention. The various cross currents have generally had the character that to solve some problem in one discipline, assumptions, implications, and sometimes mere guesses have been made about the other discipline. Workers in the other discipline may well see the assumption or implication as uninformed or ill-considered. Unfortunately, it has often been the case that these borrowings from the other tradition, what someone has called "promissory notes," were pretty bad debts. Both sides, both learning theorists and evolutionary theorists have been guilty of making uninformed assumptions about the other tradition. The ethologists who developed the concept of the search image, which was a psychological idea if ever there was one, a borrowing from the other tradition, rarely concerned themselves with whether such a concept was feasible from the psychologist's viewpoint. More recently we have seen the development of optimal foraging theory, which for a time at least appeared to place a great psychological burden on the foraging animal in the sense that it required the creature to integrate energy intake over time much more effectively than was psychologically plausible.

But the times are changing. Certainly since the time learning theorists became excited about the so-called biological boundaries movement in the 1970s, the pace of interaction between the two long-separated traditions has picked up. The cross currents are not just occasional, they are occurring continually. Zoologists are now well aware of the psychological problems in optimal foraging models. There is much more informed consideration. One way to think about what is happening is to suppose that all sorts of phenomena are getting ever more complicated, and that there is growing recognition on both sides that a lot of phenomena are multiply determined. Thus, learning can now be seen as an adaptation; it is a behavioral characteristic that really does have a place in evolution. And in psychology the evidence of species differences and specificities has now become overwhelming. So the two disciplines, so long separated, can now much more meaningfully mingle.

Perhaps the most exciting recent development is the new people who have come upon the scene. There are people who are much better informed in both traditions. There are people who do not write promissory notes. There are people now who, while they are convinced that selection is the ultimate explanatory principle, put their energies into searching for the mediating mechanisms. They want to find the immediate cause of this or that phenomenon. And, of course, that is the only way in which all those promissory notes can finally be settled. The purpose of this book is partly to celebrate these new developments by displaying some of the work of this new breed of scholar. We also hope that we can encourage others to look more carefully at the mechanisms that make learning an evolutionary consideration and evolution a learning theory consideration.

Robert C. Bolles
Michael D. Beecher
University of Washington

EVOLUTION
AND
LEARNING

1 Nativism, Naturalism, and Niches

Robert C. Bolles
University of Washington

THE EMPIRICIST BACKGROUND

The empiricist position is that we are entirely the result of our experience. Our knowledge, personality, behavior, our entire psychological makeup is the product of our experience. Psychologists have always been favorably disposed toward the empiricist position. Sometimes we go for it wholeheartedly, and at least we tend to find it appealing. For example, if someone were to propose that there is a natural, inevitable set of stages the human child goes through in development, most psychologists would immediately begin to think of empiricist alternatives. According to the empiricist viewpoint, the theory of stages is culture-bound. The stages are not immutable but should be altered with appropriate training. Empiricists suspect that if the right kind of conditions were set up, they could bypass this stage or accelerate that one. The concept of stages would dissolve in an adequate analysis of the data, they might say. In short, empiricists rebel at the idea of fixed stages of development. Such an idea violates their empiricistic expectations. It challenges their empiricistic bias.

The empiricist bias has always been a basic part of psychology; it was so long before psychology became a science. When addressing old philosophical questions, psychologists, then as now, almost always like the empiricist position. For example, long ago John Locke (1690) observed that the idea of God cannot be innate because there is no evidence for the idea in children and "savages." Thus, such an idea has to be gained through experience. His argument tends to appeal to psychologists, both past and present. We tend to regard Locke, the first whole-hearted advocate of the empiricist position, as one of us. That shows our bias.

1

Empiricism has changed shape considerably over the years. Originally, it was a theory of knowledge, but about a century ago it became a theory of perception, and subsequently, it has become a theory of behavior. Learning is now the empiricist's territory. Originally, Locke argued that experience rather than authority was our prime source of knowledge. He was suspicious of the different forms of authority, such as the church, the sovereign, and the universities, all are suspect; one cannot believe what the Church says about God, what the King says about sovereignty, or what the universities say about philosophy. Locke's suspicions were no doubt well-founded, so some approach, such as his empiricist philosophy, was much needed as an alternative to authority as a source of knowledge.

The pursuit of knowledge became more secure in the 18th century, however, and the concern with authority less imperative, so the few empiricists turned their attention to other matters. For example, Hume (1739) pursued epistemological questions. If all knowledge comes from experience, he asked, and is ultimately derived from the senses, then is not all our knowledge necessarily limited to sensory data? In particular, how can one know anything about the physical world apart from our own perception of it? How can one know anything about the relationships between things, such as the cause-effect relationship? Hume's doubts about the limits of knowledge raised an uproar in psychological circles. Other philosophers felt that he was carrying empiricism too far, beyond all reason. There had to be knowledge, common sense if nothing else, that transcended sensory data. There was no satisfactory answer to Hume's challenge, however, until an alternative doctrine, which we now call nativism, was developed by Kant in 1781. Nativism provided the opposition to empiricism; it established a polarity. Kant's insight on Hume's dilemma also provides the beginning of this story.

NATIVISM

Kant conceded most of Hume's points. Knowledge does come from experience, through one's own senses. Thus, one can have direct contact with one's own sensory impressions, but not with things, objects, as they really are. Nor is it possible to know for certain anything about causation or other relationships between things. As Hume had said, causation must forever remain an inference that people make. All these points were conceded. But then Kant saw something Hume had missed. He posed a simple, brilliant question: Why do we infer causation? We all do it, but the inference itself does not arise from experience. Why do people make it? His answer was that people are obliged to: It is a psychological imperative. People infer causality because there is something about the human mind that requires them to do so. Kant maintained that certain other categories have the same sort of imperative control over our experience and our thoughts. Space is such a category. People are obliged to think of things as located spatially. For example, things are located behind, above, and so on. The linear time dimension is another example. People think in terms of what occurred before, and what will happen later.

Kant's primary concern was to move on from this point and confront Hume's skepticism. He suggested that there is knowledge that does not derive from the senses. The discovery that humans naturally think in terms of cause and effect constitutes an important bit of knowledge derived from pure reason rather than from the senses. But psychologists are not very concerned with such epistemological issues; they are wrapped up in the empiricist position and in the nativist opposition to it. That is why psychologists have taken note of Kant. Kant maintained that the mind has a structure to it, a framework into which experience is fitted. This structure is like a set of pigeonholes into which people must sort their sensory impressions.

So, the empiricism-nativism issue began to take shape 200 years ago. Is the mind a passive, amorphous thing? Is it just a long sequence of sensory impressions, a meaningless stream of events, each of which is itself uncertain, undependable, and meaningless? That is the empiricist position as Hume developed it. On the other hand, nativists were asking, does the mind have a structure? Does the sensory data fit into categories and thus acquire meaning? Is there an inherent structure to the kinds of things one learns, a framework into which we place information from our experience?

One point, perhaps, needs emphasis. The nativist might argue that experience does not count at all, that everything is based on structure, or that everything is inherited. However, this position is rarely defended by psychologists or by other scholars. An intermediate or compromise position is generally taken. Consider again the nature of Kant's argument. He did not suppose that people are exempt from experience, or even that knowledge does not come from experience. His position was that experience cannot be the sole source of knowledge because experience has to fit into an a priori structure. Thus, the empiricism-nativism issue reveals an interesting asymmetry. The empiricist takes a nothing but position: All knowledge comes from experience. The nativist argues, more modestly, that there is something else: Knowledge also depends on something else. I will take the something-else approach here and apply it to learning. I will grant that animals learn through experience about events in their environment. However, I argue that animal learning must also fit into a structure. Further, that structure is determined genetically through evolutionary selection pressures. An animal learns through experience, but some sequences of events are more readily learned than others, because each animal has inherited a structure into which its experience is obliged to fit.

The nativist-empiricist issue has had a long, complex history. One may note that Kant by no means settled it. Many of the questions he raised, such as whether people innately organize events into cause and effect relationships, have been pursued both philosophically and experimentally. Another question that has aroused considerable interest is the innateness of the spatial sense—a much debated issue which I will not pursue. Note, however, that new questions keep arising from the old issues. For example, a current question is whether women are intrinsically different from men. The nativist would say that there is a difference. The thorough-going empiricist would disagree: Men and women are only living different roles, meeting different expectations, and being exposed to different circumstances. Men and women simply learn to behave and think and look differently. Each person is equally the product of his or her own experience.

Furthermore, the controversy is not without its sociopolitical implications. Empiricists are inherently liberal. Locke was a raging radical in his day. So was Hume. But Kant was the stodgy old professor, a classic authoritarian personality. His writings reveal his faith in scripture, country, and human nature. One wonders whether one's own conversion to the nativist position might just be the result of advancing professional recognition, and years, and taxes. One wonders whether the peculiarly fertile soil on which psychology has prospered in America has had anything to do with the social value of individual achievement, of the pioneering spirit, and the idea of engineering a better world for all. These are all empiricist, liberal, and American ideas. Is that why psychology flourished here while it failed to catch hold in most other cultures? And is that also why American psychology is so empiricist?

LEARNING THEORY

Rather than following up these interesting issues, this chapter moves to a discussion of learning theory, which has seen the major impact of empiricism, and hence the major challenge to nativism, in recent times.

Learning theory attained a dominant position in the 1920s. A musician playing a piece on the violin? That is just a complex set of conditioned reflexes, Pavlov said. A bird building its species-specific nest? The same explanation holds (Pavlov, 1927). An animal avoiding predation? Simple conditioning, according to Hull (1929). Psychiatric problems? These are corrected by applying conditioning principles (Watson & Rayner, 1920). At its peak, there were no limits to what empiricism could accomplish, or at least conceive of accomplishing, with the laws of learning. An animal's genes mattered not a whit. It made no difference whether the subject was a human, a rat, or some other creature, it was shaped by the laws of conditioning. By the 1920s nativism had virtually disappeared and there were no conceptual limits to the empiricist position.

Nativism does not necessarily mean, and does not logically imply, genetic determinants, as opposed to experiential determinants of behavior. But if one seeks to limit the impact of experience and sets boundaries for the empiricist position, then genetic determinants are essentially all that can be used. Even though everyone recognizes its futility, the nature-nurture debate continues because there does not seem to be any other alternatives. Even in psychology, which is a predominantly empiricist discipline, there are experimental results that cannot be explained in purely empirical terms.

For example, it has been known since the turn of the century that rats are better able to learn mazes than humans are. Small (1901), builder of the first rat maze, anticipated such an outcome, and explained it in functional terms. Even Thorndike in his earliest report of instrumental learning (Thorndike, 1898) noted that while cats in a puzzle box could learn manipulative, manual responses in order to obtain food, they did not learn to groom themselves. They did not learn a simply body care response to produce the same reinforcer. So the nativist position was presented and argued for right at the beginning of the study of learning. But no one paid any attention. All interest was centered upon the learning mechanism itself and upon the associative process. The functionalist, nativist viewpoint almost died by the 1920s.

The view of learning that has prevailed throughout the 20th century is that animals that learn have a great adaptive advantage over those that do not. Learning enables them to adjust to the arbitrary arrangements of circumstances that arise in the world. The world is conceived to be fickle and unpredictable. One of the ways to adjust appropriately to such a state of chaos is to be able to learn about local conditions. The animal that can learn is able to adjust to arbitrary arrangements of events in the environment. That is how it survives.

I now propose the nativist alternative. I argue that there is much to be gained by assuming that there is some structure to the events an animal learns about, and that there is a corresponding structure in the organism that does the learning. I argue that the world is not arranged in arbitrary ways, but in a more or less systematic manner. The way for an organism to succeed is to be able to learn what needs to be learned. This involves not the random learning ability of the empiricist, but the genetically programmed learning ability of the nativist.

The empiricist position states that in order to solve a problem, one must learn how one event or thing is related to another. The nativistic alternative presented here is that one may be able to recognize that one thing stands for another. The recognition might be innate, as it no doubt is in organisms with simple nervous systems. And the recognition can result from learning in those who possess complex nervous systems. But whether an organism is simple or complex, it does not necessarily adjust to arbitrary arrangements of events in the world. Instead, animals adjust well to the arrangements that prevail in the particular niche that they occupy in the world, and in which, by and large, they have evolved.

It might be thought that the laboratory situation provides an arbitrary format. In the laboratory the experimenter is free to pick a stimulus, choose a reinforcer, and select the criterion response. But it turns out that the laboratory situation is not totally arbitrary either. For one thing, experimental procedures themselves have an evolutionary history. The Skinner box does not require the animal to make an *arbitrary* response. It is, rather, a response that emerged because it provided consistent data as Skinner manipulated other variables (Skinner, 1956). It is clear that laboratory situations have evolutionary histories as much as subjects do. Gradually psychologists find out how to build the apparatus so as to get replicable data. They gradually learn to use and then to depend on certain stimuli because they get good results. And psychologists settle upon certain species, the rat and the pigeon, because they have learned a lot about these animals and know how to get them to perform as wanted. Thus, events in the laboratory are not arbitrary. In nature what is learned is a function of what has happened over preceding generations. In the laboratory what happens is a function of what has resulted from prior experiments.

Referring again to the old-time empiricists, it may be noted that learning was originally proposed for two quite different purposes. For Locke it was necessary to learn to associate the different sensory qualities of an object, to combine the elements, in order to have the idea of the object. Locke's atomism led him to believe that one does not perceive things as such. Rather, one experiences sensory qualities, a color here, a sense of extension or size there. It is only when these different primary and secondary sensory qualities are united in the mind that one can have some idea of the object that possesses those properties. Thus, for Locke, the essential function of learning was to put together the different parts of experience into meaningful wholes. This atomist position has a long and noble tradition in psychology. It is seen in the analytic attitude of Wundt and Titchener and again in Watson's behaviorism. Watson's was atomism with a vengence: All those little twitches added up to human thought! In the later behaviorisms of Hull and Skinner one can still see the Lockean principle of combining meaningless elements through association to produce a meaningful whole. This doctrine might be labeled atomistic empiricism.

But there was also a quite different approach, that of Hume, which might be designated as sequential empiricism. Hume was fascinated with the question of what led to what. That is how he got into the cause and effect problem. If one has learned about a cause and effect relationship, then, when the cause occurs again, one is led to expect the effect. The perception or idea of an object leads to the idea of that which in the past has followed it. If one has presented an animal with a number of trials in which a tone has preceded food, then one can suppose that the next time the animal encounters the tone it will expect food. That seems like a modern idea, since the notion of expectancy was introduced by Tolman (1932), but we need to keep things in their place. When Tolman used the term expectancy to describe learning he was reviving it. It had been current in Hume's time, but then it had gradually passed from use in the 20th century as the mechanists (e.g., Watson) banned all psychological terms that smacked of mentalism. Tolman introduced the mentalistic word deliberately to strike some sort of balance with the strongly mechanistic atmosphere of the 1920s. From Hume (1739) to Dickinson (1980) empiricists, and associationists, seem to be comfortable talking about expectancies.

I argue that this matter of language aside, Tolman was, in fact, a nativist. Moreover he was exerting a nativistic influence at just that time when psychology really needed it. Empiricism had taken over, as I've already indicated. Instinct, which might have served as an organizing or *something-else* principle, was dead in the 1920s. Genes did not count for anything; recall Watson's bold claim of what he could do with a bunch of healthy babies. Comparative psychology was degenerating into rat psychology. Learning, whether by conditioning or by reinforcement, was the only thing that mattered. But there were two ways in which Tolman countered the empiricist bias. For one thing, Tolman saw learning as having a structure. The white rat did not just learn willy-nilly whatever responses were required of it. Quite the contrary, the rat was busy learning maps, by integrating spatial information. Or it was learning places (rather than responses), or it was learning about the valences (values) of things in the situation. Thus, the rat seemed to have its own agenda for assembling information. The whole thrust of Tolman's research was that responses do not get passively connected to prevailing stimuli. That is nativism at its best.

The second important way in which Tolman was a nativist was in his treatment of motivation. In Tolman's system, motivation played an organization role; it was something else. At that time, the prevailing theories of learning were those of Watson and Guthrie, which contained no motivation concept. Indeed, no learning theorist prior to Tolman had paid any attention to motivation. Motivation for Guthrie was simply the persistence of a "maintaining stimulus," some internal stimulus to which food obtaining behavior become conditioned. Early psychologists (for example, Watson, 1919) and physiologists (Cannon, 1929) maintained that motivation was merely another stimulus, another piece of the empiricist matrix.

Tolman saw, quite rightly, that this view was inadequate. Motivation acts as a vital determinant of the animal's behavior, by providing a framework for learning. For Tolman, instrumental behavior was flexible, but it was always focused on a goal. As early as 1923 Tolman had emphasized that behavior occurs in episodes. These episodes have instinctive endpoints, so it was the instinct (or, later, the drive) that directed behavior and provided the structural format within which learning occurred. The early latent-learning studies and later place-response studies demonstrated that learning is not necessarily reflected in behavior. Only a transfer test can reveal what has been learned. Furthermore, there is a necessary prior condition. The animal has to be properly motivated. Guthrie (1935) had made a clear statement of the all-out empiricist position; he said that the animal learns whatever response it happens to make. Tolman showed that such a position was simply wrong. There was, in fact, something besides experience—a structure, perhaps motivational, perhaps instinctive—that had to be considered. Tolman did not move very far in the nativist direction, not as far as the gestaltists did, but he was surely moving in the right direction.

NATURALISM

This chapter turns now from ancient and profound issues to rather secondary issues with a much shorter history. The story also becomes more personal. When Lewis Petrinovich and I were graduate students, we had occasion to run rats that were either hungry or thirsty in a maze. We discovered that the hungry animals were much more variable in their choice behavior than the thirsty ones (Petrinovich & Bolles, 1954). That was not altogether surprising. Whether we had anticipated such a finding or whether our understanding of it was completely ad hoc is hard to say; I cannot remember. However, it seemed entirely plausible to us that while the rat's sources of water in nature tend to be in fixed locations, food is more likely to be found in uncertain and unpredictable places. For other species (the gerbil, for example) the circumstances might be reversed. But for the rat, adapted to a wide variety of environmental circumstances, it seemed entirely plausible that it should enter our laboratory learning situation with a bias.

Was I rejecting empiricism? Not really. The animals had to learn where food was, and they certainly were capable of such learning. They showed a learning curve. But while they were capable of learning to approach food, they also made numerous errors. The large number of errors proved more interesting than the expected finding that errors disappeared over trials. So we believed in learning, but we also believed there was something else. We believed that learning serves some function and that the function should be interpreted in terms of the animal's habits and its *natural* problems. Certainly both of us believed, as have Locke and all psychologists of the last 2 centuries, that knowledge is based on experience. But some kinds of knowledge may be easier to come by than others. And, some kinds of learning make more sense than others in view of an animal's evolutionary position.

As I look back now, it is apparent that I have always been some sort of nativist. Whereas I believed learning was a very basic adaptive process, I have never subscribed to the idea that learning could provide a sufficient account of behavior. There has always been something else, other factors, motivation for one, and the animal's own naturalistic biases for another, to be considered. So I believed in learning, but I also believed in something else, something that moderated and limited the all-embracing grasp of empiricism. And to that extent, I was unknowingly a nativist.

When I was at Berkeley, I had the privilege of being the teaching assistant for J.J. Gibson's perception class when he was visiting us one year. I played a very active part in the class, not only grading papers and putting on demonstrations, I was also in the front of the room, next to him, where he could keep me in my prescribed role. He made me the empiricist, the voice of Helmholtz, in any discussion. Gibson, of course, did his best for his own fiercely nativistic position. I cannot speak for the students in the class, but it was a great intellectual adventure for me. I remember, though, being rather uncomfortable in my role. By that time I was already rejecting any thoroughgoing empiricism. I do not now know where my skepticism and rebellion may have come from. Graduate students were reading Tinbergen's *The study of instinct* (1951), perhaps that was it. Or was it Gibson? Or Tolman himself? Or Brunswik? We had all been much impressed by Egon Brunswik's ideas, and maybe he was the native nativist. Brunswik was a "functionalist," and perhaps that is a good way to think of what was brewing at Berkeley in those days. We believed that learning was important, but not just because it "assembled" bits of behavior to form coordinated action, but because it had a purpose. It served a function. And we believed that the function of learning was best revealed in how an animal solved the problems that arose in its natural environment. If we think of the laboratory situation as it ought to be, as a sort of model of the animal's natural habitat, then of course hungry rats display variability. That is part of what I mean by naturalism.

This ill-defined concept of naturalism is illustrated by other methodological trends in some of my early research. About 1960 I started watching rats in their home cages. I had spent a lot of time watching rats in different kinds of apparatus, so it seemed reasonable to watch them at home. Not too facetiously, one might suppose that the natural habitat of the laboratory animal is its living cage. As we watched them, we observed that rats spend a large part of their waking hours grooming themselves. One does not think of a rat as a fastidious beast, but it is; it spends 2 hours or more a day washing, grooming, combing, scratching, and generally keeping its fur and skin in order (Bolles, 1960). Note that Kant, the first nativist, had said psychological experiments were impossible and thus he encouraged noninvasive, "anthropological" techniques.

At about the same time I got involved in a psychophysical problem: Can we scale the discriminability of different intensities of hunger, I asked. It occurred to me that delicate discrimination threshold determinations in animals would likely be impaired if the animals were disturbed by the experimenter coming in each day, picking them up, removing them from their home cage, putting them in the apparatus, and so on. To obviate this problem we used an apparatus that enabled the animal to live at the choice point. Once a day the doors of its living compartment opened and it could then discriminate in a low-stress context. No handling, no jostling, no intrusion of the experimenter, just the opening of the doors. (The idea was not entirely new with me; it had been proposed much earlier for quite different reasons at Berkeley). I got the discrimination and the threshhold measurements I was looking for (Bolles, 1962). We pursued the idea of Kantian nonintervention, or unobtrusive observational techniques, and looked at animals in their home cages to assess the effects of deprivation on general activity (Bolles, 1963). And we examined the ontogeny of behavior in infant rats in the same way (Bolles & Woods, 1964).

There is a third aspect of this naturalistic approach that in retrospect I can see in some of my early research. When I first became interested in defensive behavior, escape and avoidance, I bemoaned the fact that almost the entire literature was based on shock as the aversive stimulus—shock is a very unnatural stimulus. But I soon discovered why shock was such a popular US; it is the only aversive stimulus that produced appreciable levels of either discriminated or free-operant avoidance behavior. Nothing else produces much responding either with Mowrer's or Sidman's procedures. That told me that if the behavior depends on using an unnatural stimulus, then the behavior must be unnatural. Fear as it had been studied in the laboratory (as the motivation for avoidance behavior) could not be very relevant to fear and defensive behavior as they have evolved in the field (nor to fear as it is known in the clinic). In our first attempt to get at the problem we used loud noise as an aversive stimulus (Bolles & Seelbach, 1964). A white noise of 94 dB is not a naturally occurring threat, either, of course, but it seemed preferable to shock for our purposes. The use of a noise US required us to go to an escape paradigm, but we settled for that. One other element of my Berkeley heritage was incorporated in this study. It occurred to me that an animal might be quite capable of learning *what leads to what* in an aversive situation and yet not be able to perform the particular response that was required as an index of the learning. Motivational systems can produce response biases. The frightened animal might have a biologically determined commitment to some sort of behavioral expression and be quite handicapped if required to express itself in some other, arbitrary way. Therefore, we ran three groups of animals that were required to make three different responses to escape the noice, plus three more groups in a punishment paradigm. For each response requirement, we chose one that was part of the rat's natural repertoire, such as poking its nose in a hole or rearing on its hind legs. We did not want to complicate the indices of learning of what leads to what with the additional learning of some arbitrary motor skill, so we chose to look at what we took to be the simplest and most natural responses in the rat's repertoire, those it normally uses to explore its environment.

The results were stunning; it was clear that some of these *natural* responses were learnable under escape conditions and that a different subset were learnable under punishment conditions. Here we really had something for the empiricists to worry about.

In the avoidance literature the same problem existed, but on a larger scale. While some avoidance responses were very readily learned, others could only be acquired, at best, with considerable difficulty. Rats can readily learn to run back and forth to avoid shock. But they find it extraordinarily difficult to press a bar to avoid shock. Similarly, it was widely recognized that it was easy to teach the rat to press a bar to obtain food, but teaching a rat to press a bar to avert a negative consequence was a quite different matter. The literature was full of such anomalies. Pigeons, which are so adept at making subtle sensory discriminations in pecking a key to obtain food, had never been reported to solve its other biological problem in the same way. Somewhat earlier, E. J. Gibson (1952) had reported that while it was possible to classically condition leg withdrawal in a frightened animal it was extraordinarily difficult to condition the same response using an instrumental paradigm. Thus it appeared that while fear might elicit a withdrawal reaction that was conditionable, it was quite another matter to establish and strengthen the same response with reinforcement.

We were about at the same point Tolman had been. Learning of some sort, perhaps just fear conditioning, has occurred, but there were constraints and restrictions on the kind of behavior that can occur. Learning occurs, but it is not quite what we supposed it would be when we started the experiment. There is a basic dilemma here. We set up a situation in which biologically important events occur, where the frightened animal is permitted to obtain freedom from shock, but it appears unable to learn about that. It learns something else. The dilemma is that the animal ought to solve the problem, at least according to all contemporary theories of learning and their underlying empiricist presuppositions, but the animal does not solve the problem. Its behavior is not adaptive. But how can this be? Had our naturalistic tendencies led us astray? No, on the contrary, we had not pursued them far enough. If the rat survies dangers in nature using its own successful strategies, perhaps it persists in using them in our experiments even though they are no longer effective. The answer was clear; the rat's strategy is to use fixed patterns of behavior to protect itself, what I called species-specific defense reactions (Bolles, 1970). There just is very little flexibility in the response itself; the animal mainly only learns about stimuli; it learns which stimuli are dangerous and which are safe.

There was precedence for such an interpretation in the imprinting literature. Imprinting had been dimly seen a century earlier (Spalding, 1873) and brought into focus by Lorenz (1935). Its impact on American psychology was that it was recognized as learning, but it was a very peculiar kind of learning. By the 1950s almost everyone subscribed to the proposition that all learning was response learning. The animal learned a response when, if, and because that particular behavior was reinforced. In the case of imprinting, there was evidently learning, but it was not response learning. The response was set, fixed ahead of time. We know a priori what the imprinted animal will do, it will follow the imprinting stimulus. Later, it may display other social behavior and even sexual behavior toward the stimulus. So the learning is essentially just stimulus learning, i.e., learning about the functional significance of some stimulus. In effect, the bird learns who or what its mother is. Once mother is identified the young bird reacts to ''her'' in highly predictable ways, such as following her, and approaching her when distressed. It was much like an animal avoiding dangers by learning what was dangerous and then reacting with a fixed set of SSDRs.

The idea that an animal could learn about an arbitrary stimulus and yet react to it in predetermined (nativist) ways violated everything holy in the empiricist tradition. It also violated everything in the S–R reinforcement tradition. Nevertheless, the nativist possibility seemed all the more appealing as the diehard empiricists began to invent new ways to deal with the imprinting anomaly in terms of their conventional learning paradigms. There were the fear-reduction possibility, the arousal possibility, the optimum stimulation hypothesis, and so on. The prevailing paradigm might have to be bent beyond all recognition, but imprinting was, for a time, forced to accommodate to the empiricist bias.

NICHES

The remarkable discoveries of John Garcia (this volume) nicely complemented my own work on avoidance behavior. While I had focused mainly on failures of learning, Garcia and Koelling (1966) found extraordinary facilitations of learning that occur under seemingly impossible conditions. Yet from a naturalistic point of view, it all made sense. Since the rat is a small omnivore, a generalized eater that samples a great variety of foods, it should be capable of learning about the ill consequences of ingesting a bad food even though those consequences may be delayed for several hours. Here, in the late 1960s, was sudden undeniable evidence for the nativist view in learning. It was denied, of course (see Revusky, 1977), but the phenomenon remained. The interpretation was childishly simple and impossible to refute. If rats were not capable of learning about illness following the consumption of a novel food, there simply could not be any rats. They could not occupy their niche. Garcia was right, and the empiricistic position in its extreme form had to be wrong.

Note that while the naturalistic approach necessarily requires one to think in terms of species specificities, these developments during the late 1960s made this orientation quite explicit and gave it emphasis. For example, one should expect, and can test for, quite different conditioned taste aversion phenomena in different kinds of animals (e.g., Garcia, Hankins, & Coil, 1977). As factors of eating style and dietary selection enter the picture, the functional significance of food-aversion learning will alter, and the species' ability for such learning should be altered too. In the same way, an animal's defensive behaviors have to be adapted to its niche. Among small rodents, a gerbil must defend itself differently from the house mouse because it lives in a different world, runs different risks, has different predators, and so on. Different animals are also obliged to have quite different defenses because they differ so much in size, weapons, and the like. The niche, how a species relates to other species, is the thing.

Thus, animals have an obligation, an imperative, to learn this and to not learn that depending upon their niche and how they fit into the overall scheme of things. We should expect some kinds of experience to be reflected in learning, and some not. A rat readily learns to anticipate food given regularly once a day, but it fails to learn anything about electric shock given once a day (Bolles, Riley, Cantor, & Duncan, 1974). A learning task which violates an animal's a priori biological commitments to its niche, can be expected to produce anomalous behavior. A learning task which capitalizes on an animal's a priori predisposition to behave in certain ways is likely to be a glowing success. That is the niche argument.

One might think that the niche argument is empirically empty, a tautology, or perhaps just a bunch of ad hoc fables. Perhaps we suspect that rats live in tunnels because we know they are good at mazes. But this is not the case. We knew about the rat's subterranean habitat first. That rats might be good at mazes was a conjecture, one that happened to be confirmed when the appropriate comparative experiments were carried out (Small, 1901). Sometimes, though, conjectures from an animal's life style are not confirmed. One might anticipate that because of their eating habits, persistent and indiscriminant browsing, cattle would not show conditioned taste aversions. But in fact they do (Zahorik & Houpt, 1977).

Even I have been wrong. At one point I was convinced that defensive behavior was totally inflexible on the response side, and that all learning in the frightened animal was stimulus learning. When we ran a punishment experiment to check this possibility we found rapid and robust learning about specific response topographies (Bolles, Holtz, Dunn, & Hill, 1980). More recently, naturalistic speculation led me to expect that because the rat is an omnivore and an opportunistic feeder, it ought to acquire taste preferences on the basis of the caloric content of small meals that had distinctive tastes. But the data (Bolles, Hayward, & Crandall, 1981) disproved the conjecture. Although the picture is not yet entirely clear, it appears that taste-preference learning is based on several mechanisms, but these do not include the taste of a small, high caloric meal.

Thus the problem for the niche argument is not one of testability. It is rather that the empiricists' position keeps changing. The underlying form of the bias is still recognizable, but its substance, the proclaimed principles of conditioning, keep changing. The battle lines were much clearer, and more advantageous for the nativist, when the empiricists were committed to empiricism *and* to an S–R conception of learning. That was because the S–R concept was so hopelessly inadequate. Nativists in general opposed S–R psychology. But now we need to regroup because, having won a lot of territory, we have new battles to engage in. For a variety of reasons that need not be detailed, the S–R view has fallen out of fashion. Contemporarily, learning is S–S (stimulus–stimulus). The modern empiricist model is essentially S–S: A stimulus A is followed by stimulus B. When A and B occur together a few times, because of environmental circumstances, or because of the experimenter's whim, the animal learns an *association* between A and B. In its experience, B always follows A. Consequently, whenever A occurs the animal will have a *central representation* of B. After the A–B correlation, presentation of A will elicit the idea of B. This is Hume's model all over again! There is nothing in most of these modern models to indicate that it makes a particle of difference what A and B are, or what the animal is thinking about, or how its ongoing behavior is motivated, or even what kind of animal it is.

Philosophically, modern associationists are every bit as empiricist as Watson and Guthrie were. If two events occur, one after the other, then they become associated. The animal does not matter. Why animals learn in the first place, does not matter. Some "inhomogeneities" are sometimes noted. Thus, some unions of particular A's and B's are learned more readily than others. But the empiricist's concern is usually limited to whether the difference is associative, that is, really a difference in learning, or whether it merely reflects motivational factors or other kinds of artifacts.

There are still conflicts and compromises to be worked out. Perhaps the next significant new direction has been signaled by Collier (1982). Collier's main concern was with the inadequacy of our traditional homeostatic reinforcement view of motivation and learning, a point well taken. But he also observed that animals do not learn specific and arbitrary associations. Animals are obliged to learn certain kinds of things, the nature of which depends on what kind of animal they are. They have to find how much food there is, where it is, and what kind of predators are around, and where the boundaries of their territories are. They have to learn local landmarks so that they can go and come without getting lost. Some animals have to learn social hierarchies, some who their mothers are, and others where the potential escape routes and hiding places are. In other words, there are a variety of schemata to be filled in with detail. And Collier observes that imprinting is a typical form of learning not a bizarre type, in spite of the fact that the response is fixed so that the animal has only to learn the significance of the stimulus. The structure of what the animal must learn to survive is determined by where it lives, how it lives, what kind of animal it is, how its social system works, what its reproductive strategy is, in short, by its manner of solving its various biological problems. That is how it is; it cannot be any other way.

REFERENCES

Bolles, R. C. (1960). Grooming behavior in the rat. *Journal of Comparative and Physiological Psychology, 53,* 306–310.

Bolles, R. C. (1962). A psychophysical study of hunger in the rat. *Journal of Experimental Psychology, 63,* 387–390.

Bolles, R. C. (1963). Effect of food deprivation upon the rat's behavior in its home cage. *Journal of Comparative and Physiological Psychology, 56,* 456–460.

Bolles, R. C. (1970). Species-specific defense reactions and avoidance learning. *Psychology Review, 77,* 32–48.

Bolles, R. C., Hayward, L. & Crandall, C. (1981). Conditioned taste preferences based on caloric density. *Journal of Experimental Psychology: Animal Behavior Processes, 7,* 59–69.

Bolles, R. C., Holtz, R., Dunn, T., & Hill, W. (1980). Comparisons of stimulus learning and response learning in a punishment situation. *Learning and Motivation, 11,* 78–96.

Bolles, R. C., Riley, A. L., Cantor, M. B., & Duncan, P. M. (1974). The rat's failure to anticipate regularly scheduled daily shock. *Behavioral Biology, 11,* 365–372.

Bolles, R. C., & Seelbach, S. E. (1964). Punishing and reinforcing effects of noise onset and termination for different responses. *Journal of Comparative and Physiological Psychology, 48,* 127–131.

Bolles, R. C., & Woods, P. J. (1964). The ontogeny of behaviour in the albino rat. *Animal Behaviour, 12,* 427–441.

Cannon, W. B. (1929). *Bodily changes in pain, hunger, fear and rage.* New York: Appleton.

Collier, G. H. (1982). Determinants of choice. In D. J. Bernstein (Ed.), *The Nebraska Symposium on Motivation.* Lincoln: University of Nebraska Press.

Dickinson, A. (1980). *Contemporary animal learning theory.* England: Cambridge University Press.

Garcia, J., & Koelling, R. A. (1966). Relation of cue to consequence in avoidance learning. *Psychonomic Science, 4,* 123–124.

Garcia, J., Hankins, W. G., & Coil, J. D. (1977). Koalas, men, and other conditioned gastronomes. In N. Milgram, L. Krames, & T. Alloway (Eds.), *Food aversion learning.* New York: Plenum.

Gibson, E. J. (1952). The role of shock in reinforcement. *Journal of Comparative and Physiological Psychology, 45,* 18–30.

Guthrie, E. R. (1935). *The psychology of learning.* New York: Harper Row

Hull, C. L. (1929). A functional interpretation of the conditioned reflex. *Psychological Review, 36,* 498–511.

Hume, D. (1739). *A treatise of human nature.*

Kant, I. (1781). *Critique of pure reason.*

Locke, J. (1690). *Essay concerning the human understanding.*

Lorenz, K. (1935). Der Kumpans in der Umwelt des Vogels. Journal of Ornithology, 83, 137–213.

Pavlov, I. P. (1927). *Conditioned reflexes.* Trans. by G. V. Anrep. New York: Oxford University Press.

Petrinovich, L., & Bolles, R. C. (1954). Deprivation state and behavioral attributes. *Journal of Comparative and Physiological Psychology, 47,* 35, 450–453.

Revusky, R. (1977). Interference with progress by the scientific establishment: Examples from flavor aversion learning. In N. Milgram, L. Krames, & T. Alloway (Eds.), *Food aversion learning.* New York: Plenum.

Skinner, B. F. (1956). A case history in scientific method. *American Psychologist, 11,* 221–231.

Small, W. S. (1901). An experimental study of the mental processes of the while rat. II. *American Journal of Psychology, 12,* 206–239.

Spalding, D. A. (1873). Instinct: With original observations on young animals. *Macmillans Magazine, 27,* 282–293.

Thorndike, E. L. (1898). Animal intelligence: An experimental study of the associative processes in animals. *Psychological Review Monograph, 2.* (Whole No. 8)

Tinbergen, N. (1951). *The study of instinct.* New York: Oxford University Press.

Tolman, E. C. (1923). The nature of instinct. *Psychological Bulletin, 20,* 200–218.

Tolman, E. C. (1932). *Purposive behavior in animals and men.* New York: Appleton.

Watson, J. B. (1919). *Psychology from the standpoint of a behaviorist.* Philadelphia: Lippincott.

Watson, J. B., & Rayner, R. (1920). Conditioned emotional reactions. *Journal of Experimental Psychology, 3,* 1–14.

Zahorik, D. M., & Houpt, K. A. (1977). The concept of nutritional wisdom: Applicability of laboratory learning models to large herbivores. In L. Barker, M. Best, & M. Domjan (Eds.), *Learning mechanisms in food selection.* Waco, TX: Baylor University Press.

2 Darwin was a Learning Theorist

Rodrigo Garcia y Robertson
Villanova University

John Garcia
University of California, Los Angeles

Charles Robert Darwin (1809–1882) was a learning theorist well-versed in the associationistic explanations of empirical philosophy and mental chemistry. Explicit and implicit appeals to associative learning permeate the *Origin of Species* (1859) and the *Descent of Man* (1871). Observations of flowering plants and their insect pollinators provided him with numerous examples of animals responding to contingencies between visual signals and sweet rewards according to the law of association by contiguity. In one crucial case, which we discuss below, Darwin appealed to association by causality and similarity in order to buttress his theory of natural selection. In other cases, he employed a flexible theory of habit to explain evolutionary change. Usually the causal current ran from inherited structure to acquired habits but it also ran the opposite way. More often than not, according to Darwin, the causal influences between structure and habit ran in both directions simultaneously.

Of course, evolution did not spring, fully clothed, from Darwin's brow. It was but one explanation, albeit a brilliant one, to account for the enormous variety of life forms. For ages, theorists have devised purposive schemes around which to organize the bewildering mass of empirical biological observations. One thought has occurred and reoccurred in many cultures throughout history. Perhaps, an infinitely more powerful and enduring Supreme-Organism simply created all this diversity for mysterious reasons of its own, much as a talented master creates an imaginary world out of pigment and clay. Many scientists subscribed to this static contrivance. At Harvard, Louis J. R. Agassiz (1807–1873), renown professor of comparative zoology, believed that each species, even each human race, was created as a separate immutable entity (Gould, 1980, p. 170). Such creation theories inevitably lead to endless speculations concerning the power and purpose of the Creator, whose ways and means are, usually by a priori postulation, unknowable.

During the 16th century, European explorers of the western hemisphere returned with evidence of an even greater diversity of life forms, under whose combined weight, Noah's Ark sank forever. Many students then set out to catalogue the biological diversity and to analyze the geological records in order to determine what the Creator had in mind. Others simply sought to specify the common principles of life and to classify the various life forms. Carolus Linnaeus (1707–1778), a Swedish botanist, was a great taxonomist, as was the French anatomist, Georges Leopold Cuvier (1769–1832) who emphasized the catastrophic extinction of species. A dimension of complexity became obvious to all; organisms range from single-celled entities to large differentiated organizations of many cells, tissues, and organs. In the fossil records, the deep ancient layers of the earth reveal no life at all, the next layers reveal primordial forms of life consisting of small simple organisms. The upper layers, laid down most recently, provide abundant evidence for the larger more complex organisms.

While many Christians cling to the belief in a single immutable creation of all life forms, other mystics believe that the purpose of creation is to produce ever higher and more perfect forms of life through gradual evolutionary change. Progressive perfection often appears in religions proclaiming reincarnation as fundamental dogma. The idea also appears in biological thought without the assumption of spiritual continuity. Jean Baptiste de Lamarck (1744–1826) was the great biological theorist of progressive evolution.

In the Western world another idea occurred early on; perhaps there is no general purpose to life at all. In a footnote to the very first page of the historic preface to the *Origin of Species,* Darwin (1859) cites Aristotle (384–322 B.C.) foreshadowing a mechanistic notion of natural selection after dispensing with illusory purpose.

Aristotle . . . after remarking that rain does not fall in order to make corn grow, any more than it falls to spoil the farmer's corn when threshed out of doors, applies the same argument to organisation; and adds. . . . "So what hinders the different parts (of the body) from having this merely accidental relation in nature? As the teeth, for example, grow by necessity, the front ones sharp, adapted for dividing, and the grinders flat, and serviceable for masticating the food; since they were not made for the sake of this, but it was the result of accident. And in a like manner as to the other parts in which there appears to exist an adaptation to an end . . . like as if they were made for the sake of something, these were preserved, having been appropriately constituted by an internal spontaneity; and whatsoever things were not thus constituted, perished, and still perish. (p. 3)

Darwin was generous in crediting others. He was the one who verified and established evolution through natural selection as the only systematic theory in biology. As the result of his formulation, creation, and purpose are now gratuitous concepts in biology. Variation of form by internal spontaneity is the essence of life. Variant forms, fortuitously serving some adaptive end, survive and reproduce; forms, not doing so, perish.

Darwin admired Lamarck's evolutionary theory but rejected the progressive aspect because his own monumental studies on transitional varieties revealed progress to be an illusion. To the contrary, many variations serving adaptation appeared to be regressive, but only in a superficial sense, as in the case of some lizards adaptively shedding their legs, the marks of a "higher" animal, to slither more effectively through thickets like the "lowly" worms. Some mammals returned to the sea, as seals for example, assuming once again the gross "fishlike" form of their lobe-finned ancestors but retaining their mammalian lungs. Tapeworms have "lost" limbs, musculature and practically all structure, to lie in the guts of large animals absorbing the food of their hosts and manufacturing eggs. These changes are neither regressive nor progressive, only adaptive.

Confusion can arise out of abstract concepts such as progression and regression because they are value judgments implying some future ideal form of life. Confusion lies in theoretical abstractions as well. For example, evolution can be *explained* by a random generator of variance and future selection of the more efficient variant forms of life. Such a scheme cannot predict very well unless the future is specified. Furthermore, since a random generator can produce systematic runs, natural selection appears to be gratuitous if not fallacious. For example, the scoring of points when tossing dice is essentially random in an honest game, yet *runs* are often produced favoring the financial survival of a *lucky* gambler and the demise of the *unlucky* ones. The same can be said to be true of the natural random generator of biological variation, it might produce runs of *lucky* species without benefit of natural selection. Natural selection would seem to be a post hoc explanation like the gambler's fallacy of a *hot streak*. This confusion arises when random variation is reified as a *fact* of life. Random variation is not an empirical fact, it is a simplifying assumption for dealing with innumerable causal events "of which we are quite ignorant" (Darwin, 1859, p. 102). Which goes to prove that theories stripped of empirical observations and mediating mechanisms, are mere abstract skeletons on which bizarre trapping can be hung. Credit belongs to Darwin for clothing the conceptual skeleton of evolution with the fiber, sap, and leaves of plants and the bone, blood, muscle, and nerve of animals.

Darwin exerted a powerful influence upon the two great proponents of modern learning theory. Ivan Petrovich Pavlov (1849–1936) using salivation as a paradigm stressed the inherent adaptive features of the unconditioned reflex (UR) to the unconditioned stimulus (US). Classical conditioning is a learning process by which adaptive salivation to a food US is extended to environmental cues associated with feeding. When a neutral cue consistently preceeds US–UR salivation, it becomes a conditioned stimulus (CS) and evokes a conditioned response (CR) anticipating the impact of the food US. The new CS–CR sequence is adaptive. Edward Lee Thorndike (1874–1949) theorized selective acquisition of fortuitous associations as a function of survival value. He deprived the animal of some necessity and placed the vital requirement beyond a barrier of space and time. He noted that the animal became restless, spontaneously generating various responses; the responses which lead to the goal were retained and those which did not, were eliminated. Thus, a new species of habit evolved by trial and success.

DARWIN'S LAMARCKIAN THEORY OF HABIT

Fame is often a chancy fleeting thing of dubious parentage. Take the case of Lamarck's giraffe. Textbooks rarely mention Lamarck without relating the most famous, or infamous, example of "Lamarckianism"; generation after generation of giraffes elongating the neck of the species by stretching to eat the leaves of tall trees. Lamarck (1809) describes the process as follows:

> It is interesting to observe the result of habit in the peculiar shape and size of the giraffe (Camelo-pardalis): this animal . . . is obliged to browse on the leaves of trees and to make constant efforts to reach them. From this habit long maintained in all its race, it has resulted that the animal's fore-legs have become longer than its hind legs, and that its neck is lengthened. . . . (p. 122)

The belief that characteristics acquired during the parent's lifetime can be passed on to its offspring became known as "Lamarckism." This notion, now deemed an error because it runs counter to modern genetic theory, is considered to be the hallmark of Lamarck's "incorrect" theory of evolution distinguishing it from Darwin's "correct" version.

Few people now read Lamarck's *Philosophie Zoologique* (1809), hence the giraffe's fame probably comes from its inclusion in the second paragraph of Darwin's historic preface to the *Origin of Species*. Darwin begins his own work with a discussion of the evolutionists who came before him selecting Lamarck as the one "who first did the eminent service of arousing attention to the probability of all change in the organic, as well as the inorganic world, being the result of law, and not of miraculous interposition." There follows a short complimentary sketch of "this justly-celebrated naturalist" and his work (Darwin, 1859, pp. 3–4). As always, Darwin is so complimentary that it is somewhat difficult to tell exactly where he disagrees with Lamarck, though it is now generally believed that Darwin disagreed with Lamarck's hypothesis on the hereditary effects of habitual use of organs.

However, a careful reading of the *Origin of Species* shows that this is not the case. When Darwin (1859) tackled the question of the giraffe he wrote:

That the individuals of the same species often differ slightly in the relative lengths of all their parts may be seen in many works of natural history, in which careful measurements are given. These slight proportional differences, due to the laws of growth and variation, are not of the slightest use or importance to most species. But it will have been otherwise with the nascent giraffe, considering its probable habits of life; for those individuals which had some one part or several parts of their bodies rather more elongated than usual, would generally have survived. (p. 161)

This is the *correct* explanation, (so far as it goes). That is to say, it is a good brief example of the theory of natural selection not inconsistent with modern genetic theory. The genes influencing the tall stature of a giraffe are not affected by the feeding habits of the parents; such genes are passed on to their offspring in a fortuitous manner. As a result, some of the next generation are taller than others, so when famine strikes, the taller ones survive by browsing on tall trees and pass their genes on to the next generation. The shorter ones starve, taking their genes out of the giraffe gene pool, thus long necks and fore limbs evolve in the species by natural selection.

The problem occurs in the next paragraph when Darwin (1859) throws in Lamarck's explanation as well:

By this process long-continued, which exactly corresponds with what I have called unconscious selection by man, combined no doubt in a most important manner with the inherited effects of the increased use of parts, it seems to me almost certan that an ordinary hoofed quadruped might be converted into a giraffe. (p. 161)

History is never as neat as it should be. This is not an isolated case, throughout the *Origin of Species,* Darwin continues to use Lamarck's explanation. Take the case of the flatfish. Lamarck (1809) originally put it this way:

But such fishes as are forced by their habits to be constantly approaching the shore and especially slightly inclined or greatly sloping beaches, have been compelled to swim on their flattened surfaces in order to make a close approach to the water's edge. In this position, they receive more light from above than below and stand in special need of paying constant attention to what is passing above them; this requirement has forced one of their eyes to undergo a sort of displacement, and to assume the very remarkable position found in the soles, turbots, dabs, etc. (p. 120)

On this point, Darwin (1859) is more "Lamarckian" than Lamarck.

The first stages of the transit of the eye from one side of the head to the other . . . may be attributed to the habit, no doubt beneficial to the individual and to the species, of endeavouring to look upwards with both eyes, whilst resting on one side of the bottom. We may also attribute to the inherited effects of use the fact of the mouth in several kinds of flat-fish being bent towards the lower surface, with the jawbones stronger and more effective on this the eyeless side of the head, than on the other, for the sake . . . of feeding with ease on the ground. Disuse, on the other hand, will account for the less developed condition of the whole inferior half of the body. . . . (p. 169)

It must be remembered that Lamarck, writing in the early 19th century, and Darwin writing 50 years later, did not make the modern distinction between somatic and germ plasm. Darwin was apparently unaware of the work of a contemporary biologist, Gregor Johann Mendel (1865) who was working in a flower garden in Moravia establishing the principles of genetics, although they were both studying plant fertilization. While Darwin (1859, p. vi) was writing "On the Various Contrivances by Which Orchids are Fertilized by Insects" (1862), Mendel (1865) was describing his "Experiments in Plant Hybridization." Apparently, there was no meeting between these two great minds. The sharp distinction between the organism's genes and its somatic tissues is a post-Darwinian theoretical development that was appended to Darwin's theory *ex post facto*. The rather strange notion that somatic habits could change the genes directly was not Lamarck's idea, it was appended to him *ex post facto*. In fact, neither Lamarck nor Darwin made a grievous error on use and disuse of organs. Habitual use of somatic structures can be transferred from one generation to the next generation through imprinting, imitation, and parental guidance.

Neither Lamarck nor Darwin made habitual use and disuse of organs the centerpiece of their respective theories; it was a secondary principle for both. For Lamarck (1809), evolution was progressive, as follows:

It will in fact become clear that the state in which we find any animal is, on the one hand, the result of the increasing complexity of organization tending to form a regular gradation; and, on the other hand, of the influence of a multitude of various conditions ever tending to destroy the regularity in the radiation of the increasing complexity of organization. (p. 107)

Clearly, the driving force in evolution is increasing complexity of organization in Lamarck's formulation. As we mentioned earlier, the geological record supports the notion that the range of organismic complexity has increased enormously over time due to adaptive radiation, as for example, when Archyaeopteryx established a new niche for avian species by taking to the trees and evolving feathers from reptillian scales to glide from tree to tree and ultimately to fly. Lamarck (1809, p. 21) believed that, were it not for environmental effects, each species would form a continuous historic spectrum of increasing complexity of organization; this process is distorted when the environment creates specialized needs within any organism. The new habits evoked by these needs often cause regressive structural changes through disuse of parts thus accounting the *simplification* of some organisms such as snakes, seals, and tapeworms. Thus, habitual use and disuse of organs actually *hampers* Lamarck's first principle of progression.

On the other hand, in the *Descent of Man,* Darwin (1871) discusses this personal commitment to Natural Selection as the first principle while agreeing with Lamarck's secondary principle;

> I had two distinct objects in view; firstly to shew that species had not been separately created, and secondly, that natural selection had been the chief agent of change, though largely aided by the inherited effects of habit, and slightly by the direct action of the surrounding conditions. (p. 442)

Darwin (1859) did not disagree strenuously with Lamarck on the seemingly progressive course of evolution, but he did put a limitation on progression reducing it to a corollary of competition;

> Natural selection tends only to make each organic being as perfect as, or slightly more perfect than, the other inhabitants of the same country with which it comes into competition . . . this is the standard of perfection attained under nature. The endemic productions of New Zealand, for instance, are perfect one compared with another; but they are now rapidly yielding before the advancing legions of plants and animals introduced from Europe. (p. 149)

Darwin also agrees with Lamarck on two other important points; "the gradual change of the species" and the usefulness of "the analogy of domestic production" of hybrids by animal breeders in explaining natural selection. However, Darwin does point out the greatest difficulty for Lamarck's Law of Progressive Development: What accounts for the existence at the present day of so many simple organisms? Lamarck "maintains that such forms are now spontaneously generated" (Darwin, 1859, p. 4). Thus far, the evidence does not support Lamarck on the current spontaneous generation of life, though it must have happened at least once at the very beginning of life.

At one point, Darwin (1859) rejects the modern notion that biological variation is "due to chance" saying, "This, of course, is a wholly incorrect impression, but it serves to acknowledge our ignorance of the cause of each particular variation". He goes on to say that, "variability is generally related to the conditions of life to which each species has been exposed during several successive generations." He described some direct effects that were fairly clear, "size from the amount of food, colour from the nature of food, thickness of the skin and hair from the climate. .." (pp. 101–102).

Darwin was a naturalist rather than an experimentalist, therefore it is little wonder he concluded that an organism's behavior and the conditions of its life would affect its offspring. With careful control, near-perfect Mendelian ratios may be obtained in a laboratory or a hot house, but they are unlikely to be observed in nature. A naturalist deals with populations subject to very different pressures from those found in the laboratory. To take the simplest case, anyone attempting to study purely genetic variation would hold nutrition constant. In the field, food intake is by no means constant. Variation at birth can easily result from differential nourishment, stress, disease, or parasitization. All of these conditions of life provide ample opportunity for the organism's habits and for local environmental vagaries to modify the developmental outcomes of any *original* genetic blueprints. But, in the final analysis, Darwin wisely left the question open for future scientists to answer:

> Again, innumerable instances are known to every naturalist, of species keeping true, or not varying at all, although living under the most opposite climates. Such considerations as these incline me to lay less weight on the direct action of the surrounding conditions, than on a tendency to vary, due to causes of which we are quite ignorant. (p. 102)

CORPOREAL STRUCTURES, INSTINCTS AND HABITS

At times, Darwin is a mechanist rejecting psychological assumptions. He castigates the critics who objected that natural selection implies "conscious choice" in organisms and who argued that, as plants have no volition, natural selection is not applicable to them. The problem appears to be surplus meaning in the word "selection" according to Darwin (1859). "In the literal sense of the word, no doubt, natural selection is a false term; but who ever objected to chemists speaking of the elective affinities of the various elements?—and yet an acid cannot strictly be said to elect the base with which it in preference combines" (p. 64). At the very beginning of the *Origin,* he emphatically points out that learning is not a necessary condition for adaptation:

> In the case of the mistletoe, which draws it nurishment from certain trees, which has seeds that must be transported by certain birds, and which has flowers with separate sexes absolutely requiring the agency of certain insects to bring pollen from one flower to the other, it is equally preposterous to account for the structure of this parasite, with its relations to several distinct organic beings, by the effects of external conditions, or of habit, or the volition of the plant itself. (p. 12)

At other times, Darwin appealed to psychological factors as sufficient conditions for adaptive change. Volitional habits in animals might easily turn small anatomical variations into the critical margin of survival. It must have been so for the "nascent giraffe" with a habitual taste for the leaves of tall trees. The feeding habit set up a competition wherein variation in neck length, generated by internal spontaneity, lead to differential survival.

Conditioned Taste Aversion research points to the mechanisms for this dynamic explanation of the giraffe's peculiar habit of dining. When the flavor of a food, such as leaves, is followed by nutritious satisfaction, that flavor will be more palatable when it is encountered again. The neurological mechanisms for this change in palatability have been clearly established. Taste receptors send afferent fibers to the relay stations in the brain stem. Visceral monitors of food digestion send afferent fibers to the same relay stations via the vagus nerve. As food is absorbed, the monitors of circulating blood products in the area postrema report to the same stations. The afferents carrying the taste information and the feedback from digestion proceed rostrally via the parabrachial area to the anterior insular neocortex and the limbic system. This is a *learning system* which adjusts the palatability of ingested substances in accordance with the effect of the ingesta upon internal homeostasis. Thus, the giraffe may acquire the leaf-browsing habit, as well as the flora and fauna in its gut, enabling it to utilize leaves as food (Garcia, Hankins, & Rusiniak, 1974; Garcia, Lasiter, Bermudez-Rattoni, & Deems, 1985; Garcia, Rusiniak, Kiefer, & Bermudez-Rattoni, 1982).

Although most studies of acquired food tastes employed poisons, hence the designation "conditioned taste aversions," there is a substantial literature on positive effects as well. Arbitrary flavors paired with recuperation from an emetic drug injection are preferred by laboratory rats. This positive *medicine* effect is approximately equal to the negative *poison* effect induced by pairing the arbitrary flavors with nausea from the same injection (Green & Garcia, 1971). More to the point of the giraffe story, arbitrary flavors paired with nutrients gain in palatability. For example, hungry rats acquire a preference for flavors paired with caloric intubations (Sherman, Hickis, Rice, Rusiniak, & Garcia, 1983). Similarly, humans report that glucose tastes better when their blood sugar is low (Cabanac, 1979). Thiamine-deprived rats acquire a positive preference for flavors paired with thiamine injections (Garcia, Ervin, Koelling, & Yorke, 1967; Zahorik, 1977). Furthermore, these same mechanisms act upon the giraffe's nursing offspring. The mammalian mother's diet imparts its specific flavor to her nutritious milk so that the infant is positively conditioned to her diet. Galef and Sherry (1973) have demonstrated this mother-infant interaction in the rat. By this mechanism, combined no doubt in an important manner by the tendency of the young to imitate their parents (Galef, 1977) it seems almost certain that the habit of dining on the leaves of tall trees is passed on to succeeding generations of giraffes.

Darwin was well aware that feeding habits played an important role in exploiting new niches in the environment. In a sense, animals actively *invent* new niches and Darwin (1859) explains how invention comes about.

We can clearly discern this in the case of animals with simple habits. Take the case of a carnivorous quadruped, of which the number that can be supported in any country has long ago arrived at its full average. If its natural power of increase be allowed to act, it can succeed in increasing (the country not undergoing any change in conditions) only by its varying descendents seizing on places at present occupied by other animals: Some of them, for instance, being enabled to feed on new kinds of prey, either dead or alive; some inhabiting new stations, climbing trees, frequenting water, and some perhaps becoming less carnivorous. The more diversified in habits and structure the descendents of our carnivorous animals become, the more places they will be enabled to occupy. (pp. 84–85)

Again and again, Darwin appeals to feeding habits to illustrate the dynamic principle of evolution through adaptive radiation. This was a wise choice, for feeding is a universal process in the animal kingdom and analogous processes are evident everywhere in the plant kingdom. Furthermore, recent research in learning has demonstrated that insects, molluscs, fish, amphibians, reptiles, birds, and mammals have the capacity to efficiently exploit new foods by associating food cues with food effects (Barker, Best, & Domjan, 1977).

Recently Strum (1975, 1981) reported a new feeding habit where one animal appears to be seizing a niche formerly occupied by another animal. In this case, the country (East Africa) is undergoing a change in conditions. Stockmen are killing off all the large carnivores, such as lions and leopards, preying upon domestic animals. In the past, these large cats also preyed upon baboons forcing them to move across the open veldt in tight convoys with large male baboons serving as defensive screens to protect their females and young. As this threat disappeared, the baboon troop ranges more freely, foraging for vegetable food. Occasionally, an adult male encounters an infant gazelle, kills it and eats it. Once the baboon tastes the flesh and receives the nutrient feedback from flesh in the gut, it acquires a taste for flesh. Changes in social behavior soon follow. Normally baboons do not share food because harvesting and gleening bits of vegetation requires many hands. But efficient hunting requires many baboons, and the kill represents a mass of nutritious food, more than one baboon can eat and defend, so social patterns appear to be changing. If this situation were to continue for ages, the new way of life would favor structural changes. Cooperative hunting and food-sharing habits would be acquired. Canine teeth, now used for defense and threat, would become adapted to killing prey. Fingernails would evolve into claws for seizing and holding prey. In short, a new carnivorous sabre-tooth primate would evolve. In this case, it is a new feeding habit which initiates the evolution of corporeal change. The same would be true for Darwin's carnivorous quadrupeds.

Which came first for Charles Darwin, the new habit or the corporeal variation? Darwin chooses the woodpecker to illustrate his answer. This bird, according to Darwin, is strikingly adapted for a single mode of life, climbing trees and seizing insects in the chinks of the bark. Yet in the wild, woodpeckers have become accustomed to other forms of feeding. Some chase insects on the wing, others eat fruit; the insectivores have longer wings than the frugivores. In the treeless plains of La Plata, woodpeckers dwell in mudbanks and are beginning to lose their characteristic stiff tail feathers, used to prop themselves against tree trunks, and their strong straight beaks, used for chiselling wood and extracting larva. Though these examples strongly imply that habits changed first, Darwin (1859) is equivocal on this point:

> It would be easy for natural selection to adapt the structure of the animal to its changed habits, or exclusively to one of its several habits. It is however, difficult to decide, and immaterial for us, whether habits generally change first and structure afterwards; or whether slight modifications of structure lead to changed habits; both probably often occurring almost simultaneously. (pp. 130–131)

Darwin mentions a number of instances where "habits have changed without a corresponding change in structure" (p. 132). These could be cases of variation waiting to happen. However Darwin linked his theory of habit to the principle of use and disuse. Presumably, the habit of not using a structure would already be reducing it while the changed habits would be enlarging and developing other structures.

Darwin treated instincts as he treated habits and corporeal structures; all three classes are products of natural selection. He had a problem defining "instinct". After starting a paragraph with the statement "I will not attempt any definition of instinct," Darwin (1859) writes:

> An action . . . when performed by an animal, more especially by a very young one, without experience, and when performed by many individuals in the same way, without their knowing for what purpose it is performed, is usually said to be instinctive. But I could show that none of these characters are universal. *A little dose of judgement or reason* . . . often comes into play, even with animals low in the scale of nature (italics added) (p. 184)

Then Darwin provides us with examples of his favorite instincts, seemingly contradicting himself on the psychological components in these instinctual patterns.

> It can be clearly shown that the most wonderful instincts with which we are acquainted, namely, those of the hive-bee and of many ants, could not possibly have been acquired by habit. (pp. 184–185)

Darwin's definition may seem vague and unsatisfactory but it is fairly accurate. Subsequent research (Gould, 1975; Lindauer, 1961; von Frisch, 1967) demonstrates that some judgment or reason seems to come into play in the most wonderful instinct of the hive-bee. The housekeeping bee patrols the hive and seems to *judge* what is needed and communicates this to the foraging bee with her enthusiastic reaction to the delivery of the needed commodity. When the forager finds a source of the required substance, she uses the sun as a reference point, communicating her acquired information to her sisters by performing her species-specific dance; but she *judges* the lapsed time to allow for the sun's movement and she compensates for the wind's drift on her own flight path to *reason* the true heading according to the sun compass. Of course, reason and judgment seem to be rather fanciful when applied to a lowly insect, but these are the best words we have to describe the complex performance of the hive-bee, and these words serve to acknowledge our ignorance of the decision-making mechanisms in the brain of the bee.

As Lehrman (1953) argues, it is impossible to eliminate experiential components from instinctive patterns. Even Lorenz and Tinbergen (1939) suggest that fixed action patterns (FAP) contain plastic components enabling the organism to adjust its species-specific pattern to local conditions. To put it the other way, learning is an adjustment of a FAP (Garcia, Forthman Quick, & White, 1983). Thus our modern distinction between *species-specific behavior,* as opposed to *learned behavior,* is no clearer than Darwin's distinction between instinct and habit. This means that the distinctions among corporeal structure, instincts and habits may be semantic illusions and it is greatly to Darwin's credit, that he treats habit, instinct and corporeal structures in exactly the same way. Darwin (1859) states:

> It will be universally admitted that instincts are as important as corporeal structures for the welfare of each species, under its present conditions of life. Under changed conditions of life, it is at least possible that slight modifications of instinct might be profitable to a species; and if it can be shown that instincts do vary ever so little, than I can see no difficulty in natural selection preserving and continually accumulating variations of instinct to any extent that was profitable. It is thus, as I believe, that all the most complex and wonderful instincts have originated. As modifications of corporeal structure arise from, and are increased by, use or habit, and are diminished or lost be disuse, so I do not doubt it has been with instincts. But I believe that the effects of habit are in many cases of subordinate importance to the effects of the natural selection of what may be called spontaneous variations of instincts;—that is of variations produced by the same unknown causes which produce slight deviations of bodily structure. (p. 185)

It is apparent that Darwin viewed *instinct* as corporeal structure in action, and *habit* as the brain in action. Moreover, Darwin's habits could become instincts and instincts could become habits, and either one could become corporeal structure as dictated by natural selection:

> I am, however, very far from wishing to deny that instinctive actions may lose their fixed and untaught character, and be replaced by others performed by the aid of free will. On the other hand, some intelligent actions, after being performed during

several generations, become converted into instincts and are inherited, as when birds on oceanic islands learn to avoid man. (p. 447)

THE DARWIN–WALLACE CONDITIONING THEORY

Strangely enough, it was A. R. Wallace, not Darwin, who suggested an explicit associative hypothesis integrating learning theory with natural selection. In a paper entitled "On the Origin of Food Aversion Paradigms," Garcia and Hankins (1977) present the case for a Darwin–Wallace conditioning theory initiated in 1866 and experimentally verified by 1887. Their theory was actively generating research 2 decades before Pavlov began his studies on classical conditioning, and 3 decades before Thorndike presented his thesis on instrumental conditioning. This pioneer effort culminated in today's research area, narrowly labeled "conditioned taste aversion." More broadly considered, this paradigm is representative of homestatic conditioning which Tolman (1949) called "cathexis"; when responding to survival needs, organisms come to cherish one particular type of food and drink, or one given type of mate, and to abhor others. Here, we only summarize the first 2 decades of research on the Darwin–Wallace hypothesis.

Wallace did not always agree with Darwin, particularly on sexual selection and the evolution of the brain but in this case he came to Darwin's rescue. In an argument with St. George Mivart, Darwin (1859) held that predation would tend to produce insects which blended into their environment.

> Insects are preyed on by birds and other enemies, whose sight is probably sharper than ours, and every grade in resemblance which aided an insect to escape notice or detection, would tend toward its preservation; and the more perfect the resemblance so much the better for the insect. (p. 165)

Darwin was disturbed by the multitude of gaudy caterpillars flaunting their colorful patterns so as to catch the eye of every passing predator. For a sexually active adult butterfly, advertisement pays; mates are attracted so the adult is well-compensated for the higher predation risk. But a caterpillar is a "sexless embryo" with no need for sexual advertisement. Darwin turned to Wallace who, he said, had an innate genius for solving evolutionary problems. He describes Wallace's response as follows:

> Mr. Wallace thought it probable that conspicuously coloured caterpillars were protected by having a nauseous taste; but as their skin is extremely tender . . . a slight peck from the beak of a bird would be . . . fatal. . . . Hence . . . distastefullness alone would be insufficient to protect a caterpillar unless some outward sign indicated to its would-be destroyer that its prey was a disgusting morsel. Under these circumstances it would be highly advantageous to a caterpillar to be instantaneously and certainly recognized as unpalatable by all birds and other animals. (p. 668)

Observations indicated that birds, lizards and frogs rejected brightly colored caterpillars in favor of green and camouflaged varieties. Commenting on the reactions of birds to noxious larva, Darwin (1871) said:

> When the birds rejected a caterpillar, they plainly shewed, by shaking their heads, and cleansing their beaks, that they were disgusted by the taste. . . . Thus the probability of Mr. Wallace's view is confirmed, namely, that certain caterpillars have been made conspicuous for their own good, so as to be easily recognised by their enemies, on nearly the same principle that poisons are sold in coloured bottles by druggists for the good of man. (p. 669)

Twenty years later, E. B. Poulton (1887) published a comprehensive review entitled, "The Experimental Proof of the Protective Value of Color and Markings in Insects in Reference to their Vertebrate Enemies." Garcia and Hankins (1977) list four propositions firmly established by this remarkable paper. They are as follows:

1. *Food Aversion Learning:* Acceptable food becomes aversive when followed by illness. Poulton recounts observations indicating that recently hatched chickens peck at insects which they afterward learn to avoid without trial. Furthermore, chickens ate chickweed readily enough on the first trial, then became ill as a consequence vomiting freely; when the same plant was offered to them on a second trial, the chickens refused to touch it.

2. *Food Preference Learning:* Unattractive food becomes more palatable if it is followed by general repletion of hunger. Poulton theorizes that if a vertebrate predator was driven to eat an insect in spite of its unpleasant taste, it would soon acquire a relish for that insect, and the insect would be in danger of extermination due to its warning coloration. In this case, a nasty taste is not enough, the taste must be periodically followed by toxicosis to maintain its aversive property.

3. *Flavor Mediation:* Visual avoidances are mediated by aversive flavors. Poulton (1887) describes his own observations on lizards. A lizard will seize a colorful insect with great vigor and it is only when the larva is injured beyond hope, that the lizard will recognize its unpleasant taste and release it. In contrast, a very hungry lizard will approach a highly colored larva, which it knows to be distasteful, in a reluctant and hesitating way. He also describes similar observations by others. At first, birds will taste noxious larva, but subsequently they avoid the same larval species on sight.

4. *Generalization:* The aversive effect spreads to non-toxic insects bearing color patterns similar to the toxic species according to Poulton (1887):

> If there is a superficial resemblance between the colors employed by very different insects . . . even a similarity of pattern . . . a comparatively few unpleasant experiences are sufficient to create a prejudice against any insect with colours and

patterns at all resembling the nauseous forms which have already produced so indelible an impression on memory. (p. 226)

Thus, Darwin started from his consideration of natural selection by noting the importance of the feeding behavior, and rightly so, for all organisms are bound together in a vast "feeding web." Before an organism can reproduce, it must eat or absorb nutrients to grow and gain energy for reproduction. It must also avoid being eaten prematurely. After reproducing and aging, the organism is inevitably eaten or absorbed by other organisms. Darwin observed that a common defense against predation is concealment and cryptic coloration and form. Poison reverses the cryptic role offering a dramatic example of the subtle power of natural selection. Poisonous organisms advertise their presence and harmless organisms often mimic the advertisements of poisonous ones. For example, a fly *(Zonosemata vittigera)* looks just like a poisonous jumping spider from the rear. The spider's eyes are *painted* on the caudal end of the fly's abdomen and the spider's legs are *painted* on the fly's wings. Tom Eisner, the authority on chemical defenses in insects, reports that the fly also mimics the quick erratic movements of a jumping spider, and displays itself in the same bold fashion as the poisonous one, thus warning predators that it may be difficult and dangerous to attack this harmless fly from the rear.[1]

Such fraudulent displays, calculated to strike fear in predators through association by similarity to dangerous organisms, are a widespread and intriguing phenomenon of natural selection. Darwin and other evolutionists were drawn to the problems of toxiphobia and the acquisition of fear responses. For example, Spencer (1892, Vol. 1, p. 409) rates a moth low on intelligence because, he speculated, it cannot associate the light from a flame with the pain of burning, though the same insect can associate the sweetness of honey with the "odour of a flower." In a similar way, Spencer cites the example of a child who is able to associate the Brightly colored berry with a pleasant taste but not with the possibility of poison. Later, Spencer changed his mind in deference to Darwin; if the berry were poisonous, the child's first trial might be its last so there is little opportunity for learning. Spencer concluded that through natural selection, species could acquire taste aversions that a single individual could never acquire with repeated trials. But in fact, Darwin did not believe that natural selection was always necessary for toxiphobia, noting that many apes avoided poisonous fruits; he suggested that perhaps they learned this aversion either by experience or by imitation of their parents (Darwin 1871, p. 446). Since then, research on taste aversions has demonstrated that most vertebrates acquire aversions in all three ways: They instinctively reject bitter, the natural sign for poison. They learn an aversion after a single taste-illness experience. They are favorably influenced by their parent's food selections (Garcia & Hankins, 1975, 1977).

---

[1]Photo by Tom Eisner: Consumer Fraud: The Natural Moment (1984). *Natural History, 93,* November,112.

Darwin discusses another puzzling effect of predation. Veteran hunters are convinced that game animals become wary during the hunting season. Moreover, male deer and antelope, which can be legally taken, are more wary than females, which cannot legally be killed. Such animal targets tend to be much tamer even during the hunting season in national parks where hunting is not allowed. It is not clear how animals acquire this adaptive fear since wounds caused by guns are often fatal amd most of the wary survivers have never felt a wound. Animals soon habituate to mere noise without pain; birds are often a nuisance on runways despite the tremendous roar of jet planes. Nevertheless, Darwin (1859) was convinced that game animals acquired their fear of the hunter by associative learning:

> The fear of man is slowly acquired as I have elsewhere shown, by the various animals which inhabit desert islands; and we see an instance of this even in England, in the greater wildness of all our large birds in comparison with our smaller birds; for the large birds have been most persecuted by man. We may safely attribute the greater wildness of our large birds to this cause; for in uninhabited islands large birds are not more fearful than small; and the magpie, so wary in England, is tame in Norway, as is the hooded crow in Egypt. (p. 187)

PAVLOV, THORNDIKE AND THE LATTER-DAY ADAPTIVISTS

The naturalists who examined the problem of the gaudy caterpillars were not as rigorous in their observations as modern experimental psychologists would have liked. Furthermore, they were mainly concerned with developing plausible mechanisms of natural selection. Therefore, they approached the problem from the point of view of the caterpillar, a passive victim carrying the colorful warning signals and the naseous effect; it was the predators who learned to select and reject on the basis of the association between signal and effect. The predator shaped the color and pattern of caterpillars as surely as the pigeon breeder shaped the form and functions of the domestic pigeon.

Pavlov (1903) was a rigorous experimenter focusing upon the dog as a learner of arbitrary associations. But he also was a adaptive functionalist. In his classical series of experiments, Pavlov examined the mechanism that underlies the simple act of salivation. He showed how the afferent neurones that controlled the salivary glands reacted differentially to a wide range of stimuli. Dry food stimulates more saliva than wet food. Nonedible irritants evokes a thin watery saliva suitable for flushing the mouth, while food induces a thick mucin to lubricate the bolus for swallowing. The same material can produce different effects depending on its form; a smooth pebble will produce only a little saliva, but that same pebble ground into sand evokes much more saliva.

The sound of a bell will not elicit saliva from a naive dog indicating that the auditory system does not directly control the salivary reflex. However, after a few conditional pairings of bell and food, the sound of the bell alone will evoke the salivary reflex. The acquisition of this associative habit indicated to Pavlov that a new temporary pathway between the auditory analyzer and the salivary center had been established in the dog's brain. Pavlov dedicated himself to studying the formation of associative mechanisms in the brain and so have the neurophysiologists following his lead. The naturalists have focused on how such habits shaped the evolution of the dog.

Thorndike's (1911) early work spanned both the natural and mechanistic approach to learning as he extended the learning sequence beyond Pavlov's consummatory phase forward into the instrumental phase. In the naturalist tradition, he assumed that:

> The satisfiers for any animal in a given condition cannot be determined with precision and surety save by observation. Food when hungry, society when lonesome, sleep when fatigued, relief from pain, are samples of the common occurrence that what favors the life of a species satisfies its individual members. . . .

Unlike Darwin, Thorndike was careful to test his belief with specific experiments and to postulate specific neural mechanisms. Darwin (1871), for example, was puzzled by the way human behavior often ran counter to his Victorian notions of what was good for the species (pp. 489, 491). Thorndike (1911) pointed out that behavior was directly controlled by the nervous system and only indirectly influenced by natural selection. In the mechanistic tradition, he argued:

> Upon examination it appears that the pernicious states of affairs which an animal welcomes are not pernicious *at the time to the neurones*. We learn many bad habits, such as morphinism, because there is incomplete adaptation of all the instincts of the body state to the temporary interests of its ruling class, the neurones. . . .

"Incomplete adaptation" is a concept which must be treated with care—it has a theological ring to it. Presumably in Thorndike's example, adaptation to morphine usage has not progressed far enough, that is, natural selection has not yet exerted an evolutionary pressure sufficient to cause complete adaptation to the narcotic drug. Given sufficient time, natural selection should produce a race whose neurones are annoyed with the euphoric effects or whose bodies tolerate the toxic effects.

"Incomplete adaptation" is also exhibited by the rat in a field of ionizing radiation. We discussed the paradoxical effects of X-rays recently stressing historical and psychological ramifications of radiation exposure elsewhere (Garcia y Robertson & Garcia, 1984). Here, we summarize these effects from an evolutionary perspective. When a rat is subjected to X-rays, the radiation produces two effects: First, the rat immediately senses the onset of the exposure via its olfactory receptors. Like other sensory processes, this olfactory stimulus is a function of the intensity of the X-ray. X-ray acts as a "neutral" stimulus; when it is novel, X-ray arouses the rat, when it is familiar, the rat does not arouse or orient overtly. However, a tiny exposure, such as that used in a dental X-ray, is an excellent olfactory signal for foot-shock in an avoidance task (Garcia & Koelling, 1970). Second, ionizing rays have a delayed aversive effect which mimics a slow nauseous poison. This toxic effect is a function of the total accumulated dose independent of intensity. As the radiation continues, the rat becomes nauseous; gastric-stasis, lassitude, and death will follow. If a drink of saccharin water is followed by a longer exposure, such as that used to combat cancer in humans, the rat will develop a strong saccharin aversion. Serum from irradiated donners will also induce a taste aversion in recipient rats and will produce gut-stasis *in vitro* (Garcia, Hankins, & Rusiniak, 1974).

Paradoxically, if the rat is given a free choice of residence between two clearly demarked areas, one exposed to ionizing rays and the other shielded from the rays, it will explore both places repeatedly in a characteristic rat-like fashion, accumulating a fatal dose as it does so, even though it clearly smells the difference between the safe and deadly areas and it becomes increasingly ill as a positive correlative function of time spent in the radiation area. But it does not associate the olfactory stimulus and the gastric malaise in time to save itself (see Garcia y Robertson & Garcia, 1984). The key to the paradox lies in the nature of radiadiation effects and evolutionary history of the rat.

The demarked area exposed to X-ray is a *place* with a particular odor to the macrosmotic rat. Places which produce illness did not exert a selective pressure in the evolutionary history of the rat, so the rat has few habits, instincts, or corporeal structures designed to associate place with gastric malaise. However, odorous predators did exert selective pressure on the rat, and as a result, the rat can quickly associate an odorous place with a peripheral cutaneous insult such as foot-shock. Poisonous plants also imposed strong selective pressures on the omnivorous rat; many plants are poisonous and most plants have germicides, insecticides, and appetite-suppressants to fend off herbivores of various kinds. Therefore, the rat has adaptive mechanisms to quickly associate taste with gastric malaise (Garcia & Hankins, 1975).

The notion of incomplete adaptation can be demonstrated if rats are given special training in avoidance of an X-ray compartment rather than a free-choice between exposed and shielded areas. If rats are trained in a shuttlebox with repeated trials, confined to one distinctive end-box for exposure alternated with confinement to the opposite (safe) end-box for an equal period, they will develop a weak avoidance for the exposed compartment (Garcia, Kimeldorf, & Hunt, 1956). Thus an animal breeder might selectively produce a race of rats with the capacity to form a rapid aversion to places exposed to radiation. Presumably, under appropriate conditions, natural selection might do the same. In both cases, adaptation to radiation might be declared *complete*.

Not everyone accepts the starting point offered by Darwin specifying that all reactions of an animal, be they described as neurological, instinctual, experiential, or anything else, are based on evolutionary outcomes of natural selection pressures operating in a particular ecological niche on the particular organism chosen as the subject for a learning experiment. Some learning theorists prefer to view the animal as an unbiased learning machine with an "equal-acess" capacity to associate any paired stimuli regardless of modality as a function of intensity, frequency, recency, and other features common to all stimuli. The latter view leads to some curious statements at times. For example, in his comprehensive textbook, *The Psychology of Animal Learning,* Mackintosh (1974) writes:

> According to the arguments from adaptation it makes sense for rats to associate flavors with poisons because poisoning is usually a consequence of having eaten a particular type of food. But if *the environment is constrained in this way,* then it is possible that the reason why rats are ready to associate flavors with sickness is not because they came into the world with a particular set of predispositions, but because they are exposed to this natural correlation between gustatory stimuli and internal states, and learn about it (italics added). (p. 56)

In the first sentence, Mackintosh summarizes the adaptive argument describing the rat eating poisonous food in the natural environment. Well enough, but the second sentence obfuscates the issue by implying *the environment* is constrained by the natural correlation between flavors and poisons. Psychologically speaking, the environment is composed of physical and chemical stimuli. Flavors exist in the mouth of the rat, internal toxic states arise out of the rat's gut, and the natural correlation exists in the convergence of nerves from mouth and gut to the rat's brain. Even if we accept the notion of an independent environment out there, the rat is exposed to the regular movement of sun in time and space yet, as far as we know, it does not learn solar navigation like the honey bee. The rat is a social animal, quickly learning the locus of food and perhaps informing its relatives in its own way, but it does not have the honey bee's natural predisposition to relate the locus of the food to the angle of the sun, nor the capacity to convert this photomenotactic information into a geomenotactic code for transmission to its fellows in the dark.

Mackintosh raises one empirical question which was immaterial to Darwin but is very important to psychologists. That is: Does the rat come into the world with the predispositions to associate flavor with poison or does it form that habit after it experiences the natural flavor-poison correlation? The answer to this question hinges on *when* Mackintosh assumes that the rat came "into the world." If he means at birth, then it is obvious that the rat-pup is well-equipped to find the nurturant nipple and to survive in the maternal niche on day one (Blass, Hall, & Teicher, 1979). Selective association between flavor and gastric malaise has been demonstrated in neonate rats (Gemberling & Domjan, 1982; Haroutunian & Campbell, 1979). However, even a newborn rat may have had *prior experience* since flavor-illness learning has been reported in fetal rats (Smotherman, 1982). Living in this *natural* world, enriched odor-taste experience will facilitate flavor-illness aversions promoting even more adaptive feeding habits in young rats (Rusiniak, Garcia, Palmerino, & Cabral, 1983). However, in an *unnatural* world where radiant energy produces toxicosis, the rat will not immediately move away from the deadly source even though it senses the energy gradient with its nose. Instead, it will adjust its diet because its corporeal structures, instincts, and habits are tuned to the natural world where foods, not places, cause nauseous illness.

The quotation from Mackintosh suggests psychological interposition reminiscent of miraculous interposition. The learning rat is a stranger arriving from "out of this world" without evolutionary baggage. This is the antithesis of Darwin's singular view of the origins of animal and plants within a co-evolutionary world. Animals eat plants so plants evolve poisons and animals evolve associative taste-illness mechanisms in turn. Poison has no odor so plants evolve odorous chemicals fending off the gnawing of animals in exactly the same way that caterpillars evolve gaudy colors staving off the pecking of birds (Eisner & Grant, 1981). Then, animals evolve taste-odor potentiation mechanisms which ultimately serve both plants and animals (Palmerino, Rusiniak, & Garcia, 1980). In this give-and-take manner, natural selection produces organisms within an organismic world which are but two aspects of a singular process fitting together like moldings within molds. Darwin (1859) alludes to this earthly harmony in a lyrical passage:

> We see these beautiful co-adaptations most plainly in the woodpecker and the mistletoe; and only a little less plainly in the humblest parasite which clings to the hairs of a guadruped or feathers of a bird; in the structure of the beetle which dives through the water; in the plumed seed which is wafted by the gentlest breeze; in short, we see beautiful adaptations everywhere and in every part of the organic world. (p. 51).

REFERENCES

Barker, L. M., Best, M. R., & Domjan, M. (1977). *Learning mechanisms in food selection.* Waco, TX: Baylor University Press.

Blass, E. M., Hall, W. G., & Teicher, M. (1979). The ontogeny of suckling and ingestive behaviors. In J. M. Sprague & A. N. Epstein (Eds.), *Progress in psychobiology and physiological psychology (Vol. 8).* Orlando, FL: Academic Press.

Cabanac, M. (1979). Sensory pleasure. *The Quarterly Review of Biology, 54*(1), 2–29.

Darwin, C. (1859). *The origin of species by means of natural selection: Or, the preservation of favoured races in the struggle for life.* Reprinted, 1936. New York: The Modern Library.

Darwin, C. (1871). *The descent of man and selection in relation to sex.* Reprinted, 1936. New York: The Modern Library.

Eisner, T., & Grant, R. P. (1981). Toxicity, odor aversion, and "olfactory aposematism." *Science, 213,* 476.

Galef, B. G., Jr. (1977). Social transmission of food preferences: An adaptation for weaning in rats. *Journal of Comparative and Physiological Psychology, 91*(5), 1136–1140.

Galef, B. G., Jr., & Sherry, D. F. (1973). Mother's milk: A medium for the transmission of cues reflecting the flavor the the mother's diet. *Journal of Comparative and Physiological Psychology, 83,* 374–378.

Garcia, J., Ervin, F. R., Yorke, C. H., & Koelling, R. A. (1967). Conditioning with delayed vitamin injections. *Science, 155,* 716–718.

Garcia, J., Forthman Quick, D., & White, B. (1983). Conditioned disgust and fear from mollusk to monkey. In D. L. Alkon & J. Farley (Eds.), *Primary neural substates of learning and behavioral change* (pp. 47–61). New York: Cambridge University Press.

Garcia, J., & Hankins, W. G. (1975). The evolution of bitter and the acquisition of toxiphobia. In D. A. Denton & J. P. Coghlan (Eds.), *Olfaction and taste, Vol. V* (pp. 39–45). New York: Academic Press.

Garcia, J., & Hankins, W. G. (1977). On the origin of food aversion paradigms. In L. Barker, M. Domjan, & M. Best (Eds.), *Learning mechanisms in food selection* (pp. 3–19). Waco, TX: Baylor University Press.

Garcia, J., Hankins, W. G., & Rusiniak, K. W. (1974). Behavioral regulation of the milieu interne in man and rat. *Science, 184,* 581–583.

Garcia, J., Kimeldorf, D. J., & Hunt, E. L. (1956). Spatial avoidance behavior in the rat as a result of exposure to ionizing radiation. *British Journal of Radiology, 5,* 79–87.

Garcia, J., & Koelling, R. A. (1970). The use of ionizing rays as a mammalian olfactory stimulus. In L. M. Beidler (Ed.), *The chemical senses. The handbook of sensory physiology* (pp. 449–464). Basel, Switzerland: Springer-Verlag.

Garcia, J., Lasiter, P. S., Bermudez-Rattoni, F., & Deems, D. A. (1985). A general theory of aversion learning. *Annals of the New York Academy of Sciences, 443,* 8–21.

Garcia, J., Rusiniak, K. W., Kiefer, S. W., & Bermudez-Rattoni F. (1982). The neural integration of feeding and drinking habits. In C. D. Woody (Ed.), *Conditioning: Representation of involved neural functions* (pp. 567–579). New York: Plenum Press.

Garcia y Robertson, R., & Garcia, J. (1984). X-rays and learned taste aversions: Historical and psychological ramifications. In T. G. Burish, S. M. Levy, & B. E. Meyerowitz (Eds.), *Cancer, nutrition and eating behavior: A biobehavioral perspective.* Hillsdale, NJ: Lawrence Erlbaum Associates.

Gemberling, G. A., & Domjan, M. (1982). Selective associations in one-day-old rats: Taste-toxicosis and texture-shock avoidance learning. *Journal of Comparative and Physiological Psychology, 96,* 105–113.

Gould, J. L. (1975). Honey bee recruitment: The dance-language controversy. *Science, 189,* 685–693.

Gould, S. J. (1980). *The panda's thumb.* New York: W. W. Norton.

Green, K. F., & Garcia, J. (1971). Recuperation from illness: Flavor enhancement for rats. *Science, 173,* 749–751.

Haroutunian, V., & Campbell, B. R. (1979). Emergence of interoceptive and exteroceptive control of behavior in rats. *Science, 205*(4409), 927–929.

Lamarck, J. B. (1809). *Philosophie zoologique,* (H. Eliot, Trans.). London: Macmillan.

Lehrman, D. S. (1953). Konrad Lorenz's theory of instinctive behavior. *Quarterly Review of Biology, 7,* 241–286.

Lindauer, M. (1961). *Communication among social bees.* Cambridge, MA: Harvard University Press.

Lorenz, K., & Tinbergen, N. (1939). Der eirollbewegung der graugans. *ZTP, 2,* 1–29.

Mackintosh, N. (1974). *The psychology of animal learning.* London: Academic Press.

Mendel, G. (1865). *Verhandlungen naturforchender verein in brunn. Abhand.* [Experiments in plant hybridization]. In J. A. Peters (Eds.), *Classic papers in genetics* (pp. 2–26). Englewood Cliffs, NJ: Prentice Hall.

Pavlov, I. (1903, April). *Lectures on conditioned reflexes* (S. Belsky, Trans.). Moscow: Foreign Languages Publishing House. Lecture entitled: "Experimental Psychopathology in Animals," read before the International Congress of Medicine, Madrid, Spain.

Palmerino, C. C., Rusiniak, K. W., & Garcia, J. (1980). Flavor-illness aversions: The peculiar roles of odor and taste in memory for poison. *Science, 208,* 753–755.

Poulton, E. B. (1887). The experimental proof of the protective value of color and marking in insects in reference to their vertebrate enemies. *Proceedings of the Zoological Society of London,* pp. 191–274.

Rusiniak, K. W., Garcia, J., Palmerino, C. C., & Cabral, R. J. (1983). Enriched flavor experience facilitates utilization of odor, not taste in toxiphobic conditioning. *Behavioral and Neural Biology, 39,* 160–180.

Sherman, J. E., Hickis, C. F., Rice, A. G., Rusiniak, K. W., & Garcia, J. (1983). Preferences and aversions for stimuli paired with ethanol in hungry rats. *Animal Learning & Behavior, 11,* 101–106.

Smotherman, W. P. (1982). Odor aversion learning by the rat fetus. *Physiology and Behavior, 29,* 769–771.

Spencer, H. (1892).*The principles of psychology,* Vols. I, II, New York: D. Appleton and Company.

Strum, S. C. (1975). Primate predation: Interim report on the development of a tradition in a troop of olive babboons. *Science, 187,* 755–757.

Strum, S. C. (1981). Processes and products of change: Babboon predatory behavior at Gilgil, Kenya. In R. S. O. Harding & G. Teleki (Eds.), *Omnivorous primates: Gathering and hunting in human evolution.* New York: Columbia University Press.

Thorndike, E. L. (1911). *Animal intelligence.* New York: Macmillan.

Tolman, E. C. (1949). There is more than one kind of learning. *Psychological Review, 55,* 189–208.

von Frisch, K. (1967). *The dance language and orientation of bees.* Cambridge, MA: Harvard University Press.

Zahorik, D. M. (1977). Associative and non-associative factors in learned food preferences. In L. M. Barker, M. R. Best, & M. Domjan, *Learning mechanisms in food selection* (pp. 181–199). Waco, TX: Baylor University Press.

3 Evolution and Learning Before Thorndike: A Forgotten Epoch in the History of Behavioral Research

Bennett G. Galef, Jr.
McMaster University

Contemporary accounts of the history of the study of animal learning frequently begin detailed consideration of the field with discussion of the work of E. L. Thorndike (see, for example, Bolles, 1975; Jenkins, 1979). It is not at all a bad place to start. Thorndike's (1898) publication of *Animal Intelligence* marks a turning point in the field of animal behavior generally and the study of animal learning in particular, replacing precedent anecdotalism and informal description with controlled experiment and laying intellectual foundations for decades of subsequent research in animal experimental psychology.

Strangely, one of the most radical departures in Thorndike's approach to the study of animal learning has not, so far as I know, been previously noted. Thorndike (1898) was the first scientist publishing after 1859 to write a major text on any aspect of animal behavior without mentioning Charles Darwin or the theory of evolution. Perhaps in consequence, it has become customary in histories of animal learning largely to ignore the fact that prior to Thorndike's emergence as a dominant figure in the field, study of associative processes in animals was an integral part of the study of evolution. Understanding learning processes was treated as essential to understanding of evolution and understanding evolution was, conversely, considered essential in interpreting learning capacities in animals.

The period from 1855 to 1898, when study of animal learning and study of evolution were integrated, was no golden age. In retrospect, the latter half of the 19th century appears a period of profound error in the study of animal learning, when overcommitment to predictions deduced from evolutionary theory of the day yielded very questionable science. It is, of course, easy to look back from the vantage provided by decades of additional research and discern errors in the

39

contributions of our predecessors. It is more difficult to discern why those working in a period when evolutionary and behavioral sciences were less well developed than they are today reached the conclusions they did.

Following, I discuss a variety of related topics bearing on study of animal learning and evolution during the latter part of the 19th century: The controversy between Darwin and Wallace over the continuity of animal and human mind that motivated much of 19th century study of learning in animals; Darwin's theory of Pangenesis, his ambiguity concerning the possibility of Lamarckian inheritance, and Weismann's rejection of the Darwinian position; the alternative models of phylogeny proposed by Spencer and Darwin; the views of Darwin, Wallace, Romanes, and Morgan concerning both the evolution of instinct and the role of observational learning in the development of instinctive patterns of behavior. Each played a fundamental role in shaping early studies of animal learning and each contributed to Thorndike's eventual rejection of the use of evolutionary models in the study of learning processes. Consequently, each had profound implications for subsequent developments in animal experimental psychology.

DARWIN AND WALLACE: THE CONTROVERSY

Alfred Russell Wallace is widely known as coformulator of the theory of evolution by natural selection. Often, as one reads brief histories of evolutionary thought, one is left with the impression that Wallace's sole contribution to the biological literature was the manuscript he sent to Darwin in June of 1858 that precipitated publication of *The Origin of Species*. Yet Wallace, like many other 19th century scientists, was a prolific author, publishing on a range of topics and espousing his own interpretation of the evolutionary process.

Although both Darwin and Wallace were committed to an evolutionary account of the origin of species, they differed considerably in the theories of evolution they proposed. Most relevant to the present discussion is the disagreement between them concerning the phenotypes that could evolve by the action of natural selection. As a contemporary, George Romanes (1884) stated concerning the major issue that divided Darwin and Wallace:

> We all know that while Mr. Darwin believed the facts of human psychology to admit of being explained by the general laws of evolution, Mr. Wallace does not believe these facts to admit of being thus explained. Therefore, while the followers of Mr. Darwin maintain that all organisms whatsoever are alike products of a natural genesis, the followers of Mr. Wallace maintain that a distinct exception must be made to this general statement in the case of the human organism; or at all events in the case of the human mind. Thus it is that the great school of evolutionists is divided into two sects; according to one the mind of man has been slowly evolved from the lower types of psychical existence, and according to the other the

mind of man, not having been thus evolved, stands apart, *sui generis* from all other types of existence. (p. 9)

Wallace's difficulty in attributing the development of the human mind to the action of natural selection resulted, first, from his commitment to natural selection as the sole mechanism of organic evolution and, second, from his conviction that the process of natural selection could produce only those morphological adaptations and behavioral capacities necessitated by the immediate demands of the environmental niche a species occupied. "No organ, no sensation, no faculty arises before it is needed, or in greater degree than it is needed. This is the essence of Darwinism" (Wallace, 1916, p. 404). In Wallace's view, if members of any species exhibit some capacity that exceeds the needs of that species in its natural habitat, evolution of that capacity could not be attributed to the action of natural selection.

Although Wallace fully accepted Darwin's conclusions as to the descent of man's bodily structure and brain from an ancestor common to ape and man, he rejected the hypothesis that either man's intellectual faculties (such as a musical or mathematical ability) or moral sense could have evolved by natural selection (Wallace, 1870, 1889).

Wallace had traveled widely in South America and the South Pacific as a naturalist and collector of exotic specimens. His observations of native peoples had convinced him that the intellectual and moral faculties required by the aboriginal way of life were not markedly different from those needed by mammals generally to survive in their respective ecological situations. Yet aborigines brought to England and educated there had the capacity to acquire the behavioral sophistication of modern Europeans. Thus, aborigines had moral and intellectual capacities far exceeding the immediate requirements of the environments in which they had evolved. Therefore the intellectual capacities of primitive man, and by implication modern man, could not be the result of natural selection.

This question of the continuity of animal and human mind was the great psychological issue of the last part of the 19th century. It motivated the initiation of the systematic study of comparative animal behavior and led via indirect paths to the form of animal learning theory we know today.

DARWINISM IN 19TH CENTURY PERSPECTIVE

The modern neo-Darwinian theory of evolution is an amalgam of disparate elements. At its center rest Darwin's notions of descent with modification and differential reproductive success. Equally critical to contemporary evolutionary theory are discoveries unknown to Darwin: Mendelian particulate genetics, Weismann's central dogma, Morgan's mutations, etc. Darwin's great genius (and his remarkable good luck) was that in the absence of requisite background information, particularly in the field of genetics, he was able to see, at times clearly, at others less well, the major features of the evolutionary process as we understand them more than 100 years after his death. In retrospect, it is easy to separate the wheat from the chaff in Darwin's published work on evolution. In the 19th century, the distinction was not so clear.

Darwin, in the view of his contemporaries, was the proponent of two competing theories of evolution, one based on natural selection, the other on the mechanism of heredity Darwin called Pangenesis. While Darwin's views on the importance of natural selection in evolution are universally known, his advocacy of the theory of Pangenesis is all but forgotten; unfortunately, it was the latter rather than the former that captured much of the attention of his immediate intellectual heirs. There is no need to go into the details of a disproven hypothesis, but, in brief, the "provisional hypothesis of Pangenesis," as Darwin (1868) termed it, stated that the cells of multicellular organisms throw off minute "gemmules" that collect in the reproductive organs. These gemmules form sperm or ova, packets of gemmules from all the cells of an organism, that, after fusion during reproduction, are capable of developing into somatic cells like those from which they originally derived. Most important to 19th century evolutionary theorists, the production of gemmules was held by Darwin to occur at all stages of life and the characteristics of individual gemmules to depend on the condition of their parent cells at the time they emitted gemmules.

Darwin, through the six editions of the *The Origin* he published from 1859 to 1878, generally held to the position that the random heritable variation observed in natural populations, on which natural selection acts to produce adaptation, is both unoriented with respect to fitness and of unknown origin. Yet the temptation must have been great to attribute naturally occurring heritable variation to effects of experience on the material entering into the reproductive process via the gemmules. Clearly there were profound effects of use or disuse of organs on the morphology of individuals. Also, it was obvious that individual organisms could modify their behavior. Darwin's own Pangenesis theory permitted experientially induced viariation in morphology or behavior to become heritable and thus open to selection. Evidence that such could not be the case was not available, yet Darwin was clearly reluctant to accept the Lamarckian inheritance his Pangenetic hypothesis permitted. Perhaps he realized that if acquired modifications of brain or body structure were heritable, the variation upon which natural selection acts would be directed and not random. Natural selection, the evolutionary process which Darwin studied for most of his adult life, would be relegated the relatively minor role of weeding out the less fit among adaptive variants, rather than creating adaptation out of random variation.

Darwin's contemporaries surely recognized the evolutionary implications of his Pangenetic hypothesis; they saw that, though ostensibly a theory of inheritance, Pangenesis bore the seeds of a theory of evolutionary mechanism that could largely supplant natural selection. "The theory of gemmules can freely entertain the doctrines of Lamarck'' (Romanes, 1893, p. 104) and because the action of Lamarckian inheritance "must always have been *directive* on the one hand and *cumulative* on the other . . . [its] influence in determining the course of organic evolution may have been immense" (Romanes, 1893, p. 107). Wallace, as mentioned above, was clearly committed to a strict selectionist view of the evolution of morphology and behavior in animals, but he was practically unique in his single-minded advocacy. Most of his fellow evolutionists, while accepting a role for natural selection in evolution, were considerably more taken with Darwin's Pangenetic alternative, especially when discussing the evolution of adaptive behavior.

VIEWS OF PHYLOGENY: DARWIN AND SPENCER

In the first edition of *The Origin of Species*, Darwin (1859) provided not only a materialistic explanation of the evolution of adaptation via natural selection, but also an account of the process of speciation as the result of natural selection acting in disparate environments over successive generations to increase divergence in characteristics of isolated populations. Darwin conceived of all organisms as descended from a common ancestor by a continuous process of branching that explained the varying degrees of resemblance among the forms of life on earth both extant and extinct. As Darwin (1859) so eloquently wrote:

> The affinities of all the beings of the same class have sometimes been represented by a great tree. I believe this simile largely speaks the truth. The green and budding twigs may represent existing species; and those produced during each former year may represent the long succession of extinct species. . . . The limbs divided into great branches, and these into lesser and lesser branches, were themselves once, when the tree was small, budding twigs; and this connexion of the former and present buds by ramifying branches may well represent the classification of all extinct and living species in groups subordinanate to groups. Of the many twigs which flourished when the tree was a mere bush, only two or three, now grown into great branches, yet survive and bear all the other branches; so with the species which lived during the long-past geological periods, very few now have living and modified descendants. From the first growth of the tree, many a limb and branch has decayed and dropped off; and these lost branches of various sizes may represent those whole orders, families, and genera which have now no living representatives, and which are known to us only from having been found in a fossil state. . . . As buds give rise by growth to fresh buds, and these, if vigorous, branch out and overtop on all sides many a feebler branch, so by generation I believe it has been with the great Tree of Life, which fills with its dead and broken branches the crust of the earth, and covers the surface with its ever branching and beautiful ramifications. (pp. 120–130)

The important concept emerging from such a view is that extant species, while related to one another as are cousins of varying degree, are not linearly related as grandparents of varying degree are to their grandchildren. The linear forebears of contemporary species, genera, etc., long extinct, are observable only in the geological strata of past ages.

Darwin's view of the historical relationship among the myriad forms of life on earth was not the sole contender for scientific consideration in the latter half of the last century. Four years prior to the first printing of *The Origin of Species,* Herbert Spencer (1855) published a two volume work, *Principles of Psychology,* in which he provided an alternative evolutionary view of the relationships among extant species. It was a view that was to have a more profound impact than Darwin's on the study of the behavior of animals during the succeeding 100 years.

The two central concepts in Spencer's *Principles,* borrowed, perhaps unknowingly, from Aristotle, are, first, that the living world is continuously changing and, second, that the direction of this change is from simple to complex. In Spencer's view, each multicellular organism began life as a simple, relatively undifferentiated embryo and developed during its life into a highly differentiated being composed of specialized, interdependent parts. In an analogous fashion (and here Spencer departed radically from Aristotle), the living world began with a few simple forms of life from which increasingly complex forms evolved. To Spencer, such evolution meant steady linear progress from simple to complex, from lower to higher, from imperfect to more perfect. The history of life was to be viewed as a linear progression from the simplest unicellular organisms to man. Gradually increasing physiological complexity reflected in increasing sophistication of mind and behavioral efficiency was, in Spencer's view, a fundamental law of nature. The main difficulty came in Spencer's insistence that extant species could be linearly ranked using a criterion of increasing complexity in physiological and behavioral elaboration. "From the lowest to the highest forms of life, the increasing adjustment of inner to outer relations is one indivisible progression" (Spencer, 1855, Vol. 1, p. 387).

The notion of a smooth linear increase in the complexity of extant organisms surely did not originate with Spencer, but Spencer provided an evolutionary rather than a theological rationale for the existence of a Great Chain of Being or *scala naturae.* Spencer's linear model of phylogeny was treated as a serious evolutionary alternative to Darwin's branching model by their contemporaries. Spencer's model was consistent with the notion of a continuity of animal and human mind, but required, as Darwin's branching model did not, that this continuity would be directly observable in living species. Darwin realized that even within historical lineages extant species would not form a continuous, graded hierarchy. "A really far greater difficulty is offered by those cases in which the instincts of a species differ greatly from those of related forms. . . . But we should never forget what a small proportion the living must bear to the extinct'' (Darwin, in Romanes 1884, p. 378). His contemporaries failed to heed his admonition.

GEORGE ROMANES: DARWIN'S DISCIPLE?

As discussed above, to Romanes and others of his generation, Darwin and Wallace were advocates of strikingly different positions. Wallace was a strict selectionist, Darwin the proponent of both natural selection and Lamarckian evolution. Wallace denied the continuity of animal and human mind, Darwin affirmed that continuity. Romanes' life work was a defense of the Darwinian orthodoxy against Wallace's apostatic views.

Romanes has been perceived as he presented himself, as an intellectual champion of Darwinism. Consequently, those working in comparative psychology have traced their intellectual heritage to Darwin, using Romanes as the major link between comparative psychology and the theories of the founder of evolutionary biology (see, for example, Gottlieb, 1979). Romanes was both a friend and disciple of Darwin's and an evolutionist yet, as discussed below, he was no Darwinist, at least not as we understand the term today. Romanes was, in fact, unable to make much use of Darwin's lasting contributions to the development of evolutionary theory in formulating his own model of the evolution of mind and behavior.

Romanes' phylogeny. If, as Romanes (1882, 1884, 1889) intended in his three major volumes on mental evolution, one is interested in tracing the historical development of mind, intellectual capacity, and behavioral complexity during the history of life on earth, the relationship among extant taxonomic groups should be a major preoccupation. Yet, Romanes was strangely reticent on the question of the phylogenetic relationship among living species. Perhaps he was discomfited by his break with Darwin on the issue; Perhaps he failed to see the contradiction between the view he presented and the one Darwin spelled out with such clarity in *The Origin*. In any case, Romanes touched upon questions of phylogeny only briefly and only in his introduction to *Mental evolution in animals* (1884):

> For throughout the brute creation, from wholly unintelligent animals to the most highly intelligent, we can trace one continuous gradation; so that if we already believe that all specific forms of life have had a derivative origin, we cannot refuse to believe that all the mental faculties which these various forms present must likewise have had a derivative origin. (p. 8)

If the inference to be drawn from this statement is that at some time in the history of the planet there were forms of intermediate intelligence between any two

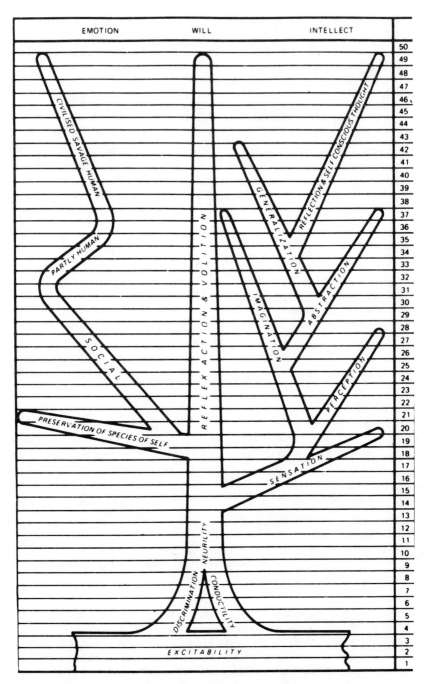

FIGURE 3.1. Romanes' (1884, 1889) tree of mental evolution (left-hand panel) and "psychological scale," (right-hand panel) indicating the relative extent of the mental development of different classes of organism.

PRODUCTS OF EMOTIONAL DEVELOPMENT	THE PSYCHOLOGICAL SCALE	PSYCOGENSIS OF MAN	
			50
			49
			48
			47
			46
			45
			44
			43
			42
			41
			40
			39
			38
			37
			36
			35
			34
			33
			32
			31
			30
			29
Indefinite morality	Anthropoid Apes and Dog	15 months	28
Use of tools	Monkeys and Elephants	12 months	27
Understanding of mechanisms	Carnivora, Rodents and Ruminants	10 months	26
Recognition of Pictures, Understanding of words, Dreaming	Birds	8 months	25
Communication of ideas	Hymenoptera	5 months	24
Recognition of persons	Reptiles, and Cephalopods	4 months	23
Reason	Higher crustacia	14 weeks	22
Association by similarity	Fish and Batrachia	12 weeks	21
Recognition of offspring, Secondary instincts	Insects and Spiders	10 weeks	20
Association by contiguity	Mollusca	7 weeks	19
Primary instincts	Larvae of Insects, Annelida	3 weeks	18
Memory	Echinodermata	1 week	17
Pleasures and pains		Birth	16
	Coelenterata		15
Nervous adjustments			14
			13
	Unknown animals		12
Partly nervous adjustments	probably Coelenterata		11
	perhaps extinct	Embryo	10
			9
			8
Non nervous adjustments	Unicellular organisms		7
			6
			5
			4
Protoplasmic movements	Protoplasmic organisms	Ovum and	3
			2
		Spermtozoa	1

extant species of disparate intelligence in the same historical lineage, then Romanes is simply restating Darwin's position. If to the contrary, the proper interpretation is that we can today trade a continuous gradation of intelligence across extant species, then the proposition remains evolutionary, but is Spencerian rather than Darwinian. The only way to tell what Romanes had in mind is to look at what he did.

The main argument of both *Mental evolution in animals* (1884) and *Mental evolution in man* (1889) is summarized in a single diagram which appears as the frontispiece of both volumes (see Fig. 3.1). Though the diagram incorporates a Darwinian branching tree, the tree bears strange fruit. Its branches are not species, genuses, or families, but an assortment of psychological terms. The relationship among major animal groups is represented not in the tree but in a column to its right labeled "the psychological scale." Here extant groups are linearly ordered from protoplasmic organisms, up through molluscs, insects, fish, reptiles, birds, and rodents to anthropoid apes and dogs. Most revealing, paralleling "the psychological scale" is a list of human ages from embryo to 15 months, the "psycogenesis of man." Each stage in human development is presented as corresponding to a particular level in the taxonomic scale to its left. The diagram is a pictorial representation of Spencer's analogy between ontogenesis and phylogenesis. An historically invalid scale, "the psychological scale," is presented as equivalent to an historically valid one depicting the ontogeny of man. Romanes' view of the relationship among taxonomic groups, while evolutionary, was Spencerian rather than Darwinian.

Romanes on the continuity of animal and human mind.   Romanes sought to resolve the question of the role of evolution in the production of the intellectual faculties of man by demonstrating that all mental and moral faculties exhibited by modern man are observable, at least in rudimentary form, in lower animals. Opponents of a continuity of animal and human capacities had stressed the absence of cumulative knowledge in animals and its presence in humans as a fundamental distinction. Thus, one of the most pressing problems for Romanes was to demonstrate the potential for culture in animals.

The first of the tasks Romanes set himself, the accumulation of evidence of rudimentary human-like intellectual and moral traits in animals, proved relatively easy to accomplish. The majority of information available to 19th century scientists interested in the behavior of animals was a great mass of unsystematic descriptions of behavior collected by amateur naturalists. While there were some exceptions, such as Spalding's (1873) elegant experimental work with domestic chickens, most such descriptions were collected by observers studying the behavior of animals from the perspective provided by the Natural Theologians of the preceding century. Creationist scholars like Paley (1802) had proposed that each species was placed on earth by the Almighty either for man's economic benefit or for his moral instruction (Barber, 1980). Such a perspective encour-

3. EVOLUTION AND LEARNING BEFORE THORNDIKE

aged the incorporation of anthropomorphic, moralistic glosses into descriptions of the behavior of animals. During the years that Romanes was collecting information on animal behavior, these subjective elements had not yet been purged from descriptions of animal behavior, even those published in the most prestigious journals. Romanes (1884, p. 345), for example, cites a publication in *Nature* by Fitch (1883) on the mental faculties of cats. "Grief is shown by the pining, even unto death upon the removal of a favorite companion; Cruelty by a cat's treatment of a mouse and Benevolence [Mr. Fitch's contribution to the catalogue] by the following instances. . . ." The anthropomorphisms of his correspondents played directly to Romanes theoretical predilections.

Convergence of Romanes' desire to provide evidence of intelligence and morality in animals with the predisposition of his correspondents to find moral lessons in the behavior of animals resulted in Romanes publishing, in 1882, *Animal Intelligence*, a "text-book of the facts of Comparative Psychology" (Romanes, 1882, p. iv) that proved to be a compendium of occasional informative description or experiment, frequent wildly implausible anecdote, and consistent overinterpretation of both.

Romanes' anecdotal methods and anthropomorphisms have been disparaged countless times since Thorndike criticized them in 1898. Romanes (1884) himself recognized that experimental evidence rather than "observing mental phenomena and reasoning from these phenomena deductively" (p. 12) was needed to resolve questions concerning the nature of animal mind. However, Romanes argued that experimental evidence wasn't available and that the question of the origin of human intellect was too important to set aside until appropriate experiments had been conducted.

It is important to recognize that the task Romanes set himself was to find evidence of human-like intellectual and moral traits in animals, believing such evidence necessary to demonstrate the evolutionary continuity of animal and human mind. His constant anthropomorphizing was not the result of carelessness or sloppy thinking. Romanes was, in fact, more cautious than many of his contemporaries in accepting the validity of dubious examples. (See the preface to *Animal Intelligence*, 1882, for criteria of selection of data.) Anthropomorphizing and acceptance of what appear today to be absolutely unbelievable examples of intelligent behavior in animals were required, at least as Romanes saw things, by Darwin's evolutionary theory and the deduction from it of a continuity in the intellectual capacities of man and animals.

THE ORIGINS OF INSTINCT

One of the central problems faced both by Darwin and others of his era was to explain the occurrence of similar complex patterns of adaptive behavior in successive generations of a species. Darwin (1859) offered two theories: First, a thoroughly modern proposal, "Under changed conditions of life, it is at least possible that slight modifications of instinct might be profitable to a species; and if it can be shown that instincts do vary ever so little, then I can see no difficulty in natural selection preserving and continually accumulating variations of instinct to any extent that was profitable.'' Second, a hypothesis that captured the imagination of many of his contemporaries: "As modifications of corporeal structures arise from, and are increased by use or habit, and are diminished or lost by disuse, so I do not doubt it has been with instincts.'' Whereas Darwin only reluctantly admitted the nose of the Lamarckian camel under the tent — ''But I believe the effects of habit are in many cases of subordinanate importance to the effects of what might be called spontaneous variations of instinct. . . .'' (p. 209; see also, Darwin, 1871, p. 68), his contemporaries couldn't wait to invite the beast to warm itself by the fire. Eimer (1890) rejected a role for natural selection in the formation of instinct and adopted a purely Lamarckian view. Wundt (1894, p. 389), in discussing theories of instinct, assumed unquestioningly the transmission of acquired characteristics, largely ignored natural selection, and represented that Darwin "explains instinct as inherited habit.'' Romanes (1884), while adopting Darwin's dual view of the origin of instincts, also put the emphasis on Lamarckian processes:

> Instincts owe their origin and development to one or other of two principles [the first is natural selection]. . . . The second mode of origin is as follows: — By the effects of habit in successive generations, actions which were originally intelligent become as it were stereotyped into permanent instincts. . . . The proof that instincts have had a secondary mode of origin requires to show:
> That *intelligent adjustments* when frequently performed by the individual become automatic either to the extent of not requiring conscious thought at all, or as consciously adjustive habits, not requiring the same degree of conscious effort as at first. That automatic actions and conscious habits may be inherited. (p. 180)

In this Romanes is consistent not only with Darwin's but also with Spencer's speculations on the origin of instinct. Spencer had proposed that reflexes and instincts that develop independent of experience in the individual are the consequence of associative learning during the past history of the species.

> Hereditary transmission applies to psychical peculiarities as well as physical peculiarities. While the modified bodily structure produced by new habits of life is bequeathed to future generations, the modified nervous tissues produced by such new habits of life are also bequeathed; and if new habits become permanent, the tendencies become permanent. (Spencer, 1855, p. 422)

> Natural selection, or survival of the fittest, is almost exclusively operative throughout the vegetal world and throughout the lower animal world, characterized by relative passivity. But with the ascent to higher types of animals, its effects are

in increasing degrees involved with those produced by inheritance of acquired characters; until in animals of complex structures, inheritance of acquired characters becomes an important, if not the chief cause of evolution (Spencer; 1893, p. 45).

Romanes goes on to argue (1884,) "that instincts may have, as it were, a double root—the principle of selection combining with that of lapsing intelligence [the notion that habitual acts may become instinctive (Lewes, 1860)] to the formation of a joint result" (p. 201). On such a model the variations in behavior on which natural selection acts are not random with respect to their effects on fitness, but are oriented by the learning capacities of organisms. Such a model, predicting oriented heritable variation, also predicts adaptation in the absence of selection: "intelligent adjustment by going hand in hand with natural selection must greatly assist the latter principle in the work of forming instincts, in as much as it supplies to natural selection variations which are not merely fortuitous, but from the first adaptive" (Romanes, 1884, p. 219). Thus, the capacity of animals to learn and to pass on through their gemmules those acquired behavioral traits that enhance survival was, for Romanes, a major driving force in evolution, providing oriented behavioral variation on which natural selection might work. Darwin's Pangenetic hypothesis and tacit acceptance of the possibility of Lamarckian inheritance provided the basis for an alternative to natural selection in the evolution of instincts, an alternative that made the study of learning processes central to the understanding of evolution.

The dual origin theory of instinct proposed by Romanes also provided a mechanism for the accumulation of knowledge by animals, thus obliterating one proposed fundamental distinction between the mental faculties of animals and man. As mentioned previously, supporters of Wallace's contention that there is a difference in kind between human and animal intellectual capacity had pointed to the importance of culture in the life of man and its absence in animals. Romanes (1889) rejected both premises. "I deny on the one hand that mental progress from generation to generation is a peculiarity of human intelligence; and, on the other hand, I deny that such progress is never found to occur in the case of animal intelligence" (p. 13). Through learning, the lapsing of intelligence, and the inheritance of acquired characteristics animals could gradually accumulate extraordinarily complex patterns of instinctive behavior.

To this point, Romanes had added little to models of the development of instinctive behavior proposed by Darwin, Spencer, and Lewes. In fact, Romanes' sole original contribution was to treat as primary a type of learning to which Darwin had assigned a minor role and Wallace (1870) a more important one. Romanes (1884) argued "With animals, as with men, original ideas are not always forthcoming at the time they are wanted, and therefore it is often easier to imitate than to invent" (p. 210). Imitation, primarily of members of one species by another, was for Romanes the main driving force in the evolution of instinct.

Romanes was quick to confess that he could provide almost no evidence of one species of animal imitating the habits of another, but explained away this lack of examples as due to the fact that imitation among species occurred in the past. Today, all one would expect to see is numbers of disparate species with the same instinctive patterns of behavior, though Romanes also failed to provide examples of interspecific communalities in behavior. Clearly, Romanes was not led to his theoretical positions by the weight of evidence. His goal of demonstrating a continuity in the mental life of animals and man, as Darwin had postulated, required, in Romanes' view, demonstration of "mental progress from generation to generation" in animals. It was this requirement that led Romanes, in the absence of evidence, to emphasize lapsed intelligence acting in concert with observational learning to produce adaptive instinctive behaviors. Incorporation of behavioral novelty into a species' instinctive repertoire, following observation of the adaptive behavior of others and the lapsing of intelligence, provided the crucial links between animal and human mind required by theory.

GEMMULES VS. GERM-PLASM 1: AUGUST WEISMANN

During the years that Romanes was developing his theory of the evolution of instinct, its foundations in Darwin's theory of Pangenesis were already under attack. In 1883, August Weismann, a cytologist and developmental biologist, rejected the notion of inheritance of acquired characteristics. Weismann undertook to demonstrate experimentally that the structure and division of cells is such as to make an inheritance of acquired characteristics impossible. He argued that germ cells segregate early in development and, in consequence, there was no way in which influences acting on the remainder of the organism could be transmitted to the nuclei of germ cells in which heritable information resides. Weismann's attack (1883, in Weismann, 1889) on Romanes' view of the evolution of instinctive behavior was both clear and direct:

It is usually considered that the origin and variation of instincts are also dependent upon the exercise of certain groups of muscles during a single life time; and that the gradual improvement which is thus created by practice is accumulated by hereditary transmission. I believe that this is an erroneous view, and I hold that all instinct is entirely due to the operation of natural selection, and has its foundation, not upon inherited experiences, but upon variation of the germ. (p. 91)

As Romanes (1893) stated in a book he wrote in spirited defense of Darwin's theory of Pangenesis against Weismann's germ-plasm theory, "The theory of germ plasm is not only a theory of heredity, it is also, and more distinctively, a theory of evolution" (p. 103). While Darwin's theory of gemmules allowed

Lamarckian processes, the theory of germ-plasm excluded them as physiologically impossible. If Weismann were correct, learned behavior could not become hereditary, learning played no role in the evolution of instincts, all of Romanes' elaborate demonstrations of ''mental progress from generation to generation'' were false, and much of his evidence of continuity in animal and human faculties was untenable.

To the behaviorist, the critical question became whether the behavioral phenomena Romanes had claimed demonstrated inheritance of acquired characteristics could be explained in other ways (Spencer, 1893).

GEMMULES VS. GERM-PLASM 2: C. L. MORGAN

Morgan's four major texts on animal behavior (1890, 1894, 1896, 1900) are each, in part, concerned with the question of the role of learning in the evolution of instincts, the behavioral version of the gemmule-germ plasm controversy. In *Animal Life and Intelligence,* Morgan (1890) recognized three factors in the origin of instinctive activities: elimination through natural selection, selection through preferential mating [Darwin's (1871) notion of sexual selection] and inheritance of individually acquired modification. These he ranked, as to their respective likelihood, as incontrovertible, highly probable, and ''probable in a less degree'' (p. 447). Yet, following Romanes, Morgan suggests that intelligence may have been a factor in all three paths for the development of instincts. For example, ''Some of the habits which survived elimination under [natural selection] may have been originally intelligent, some of them from the first unintelligent'' (Morgan, 1890, p. 447). At this point in Morgan's thinking he had no doubt that the intelligent adjustments of behavior exhibited by organisms provide at least some of the variability on which both natural and sexual selection act. Like Romanes and Wallace, Morgan also attributed considerable importance to imitative learning and the tuition of young by their parents, though Morgan treated these types of learning as basically conservative, acting to preserve already established behaviors, and only rarely encouraging the spread of novel habits.

In 1896, Morgan began to express serious doubts about the possibility of the lapsing of intelligence and inheritance of acquired characteristics. Observations that in 1890 were fairly compelling evidence of transmission of acquired behavior were, in 1896, treated far more circumspectly. He came to the realization that even the anecdotal evidence of hereditary transmission of learned behaviors was ''surprisingly small in amount'' (Morgan, 1896, p. 294) and open to alternative interpretation. In *Habit and Instinct* (1896) Morgan suggests that experimental rather than observational data are needed to resolve the issue. After some 25 pages of discussion he reaches the conclusion, quite contrary to the one he held in 1890, that ''there is but little satisfactory and convincing evidence in favour of [hereditary] transmission [of acquired traits]'' (1896, p. 305). The previous 45 years of research and theorizing on the role of learning in the evolution of heritable behaviors was finally called into serious question. The growing acceptance by biologists of Weismann's view of the separation of germ cells and somatic cells early in development and the consequent conclusion that the direct transmission of acquired characteristics, whether somatic or behavioral, is impossible, had finally undermined the research program Romanes had undertaken in Darwin's name. However, as Morgan was to make clear, rejection of Lamarckian arguments did not logically preclude an important role of learning in evolutionary process and in the evolution of instinct. Morgan remained convinced that "variation does seem in some cases to have followed the lines of adaptive modification, so as to suggest some sort of connection between them" (1896, p. 305). He proposed a novel theory, integrating learning and natural selection, to explain the proposed connection.

In one of those striking coincidences of intellectual history, three scientists, J. Mark Baldwin (1896), H. F. Osborn (in Dyar, 1896) and C. Lloyd Morgan (1896) each put forward independently, and at nearly the same time, a theory to explain how the learned behavior of organisms might, in the absence of Lamarckian transmission, guide both the course of evolution and the evolution of instinct. C. L. Morgan's (1896) statement of the argument is, to the modern reader at least, the clearest of the three. He asks his reader to imagine a species, capable of learning, whose members face a novel environmental challenge. Morgan proposes, first, that those individuals with greater inherent capacity to modify their behavior to meet the new circumstances would be more likely to survive and reproduce. Further, Morgan suggests, any congenital variation that enhanced the probability of acquisition of the learned modification would be selected for, and any congenital variation which reduced its probability of acquisition would be selected against. Over evolutionary time, the result of such a process would be an increase in the predisposition of members of the species to acquire the adaptive modification of behavior necessary to meet the new challenge. Eventually, a pattern of behavior, originally dependent on individual plasticity for its development, might be expressed in the absence of experiences once necessary for its development. Thus, "plastic modification leads, and germinal variation follows" (Morgan, 1896, p. 320).

Morgan concludes his discussion of his theory with the statement,

. . . we may, in the face of the biological difficulties which render direct transmission more and more hard to accept, adopt some such view as the foregoing, and while still believing that there is some connection between habit and instinct, admit that the connection is indirect and permissive rather than direct and transmissive. (p. 322)

The Morgan-Baldwin-Osborne hypothesis was well received both by contemporaries (e.g., Holmes, 1911) and future biologists (e.g., Mayr, 1976). It might have served as a new focus for the study of the relationship between learning and evolution. For Thorndike, however, it was clearly too little too late. Thorndike's failure to cite Darwin or mention evolution in his 1898 monograph was no simple oversight. He viewed the work of his predecessors, studying learning within an evolutionary framework, as unmitigated failure. Darwin's use of anecdotal evidence provided by correspondents, so effective in unravelling the mysteries of organic evolution, had produced little but confusion in the study of behavior. Thorndike sought to replace such anecdotalism with controlled experiment. Two score years of studying animal learning within an evolutionary perspective had proved futile. Thorndike rejected evolutionary discussion, advocating in its stead careful analyses of learning mechanisms of the sort Morgan had suggested, but seldom employed, in his *Introduction to Comparative Psychology* (1894). Thorndike's research on learning by imitation in animals, a process Spencer, Wallace, Darwin, Romanes, and Morgan had emphasized to varying degree in attempting to exemplify the continuity of mind from animal to man, and his failure to find evidence of such learning in cats, dogs, chickens, and monkeys, broke the major empirical link with the past. The further failure of a series of similar research projects using as subjects birds (Porter, 1910) raccoons (Cole, 1907; Davis, 1907), rats (Berry, 1906; Small, 1899), cats (Berry, 1908), and various primates (Hobhouse, 1901; Kinnaman, 1902; Haggerty, 1909; Watson, 1908) to provide convincing evidence of imitative learning (Holmes, 1911; Washburn, 1908) further discredited the approach of earlier students of animal learning. The study of animal learning was to begin anew with the work of Thorndike on the laws of effect and exercise.

It would have been satisfying to be able to end this chapter where I started, with Thorndike's (1898) rejection of evolutionary theories in the study of learning. The facts are not quite so simple. In an expanded version of the 1898 monograph, published in 1911, Thorndike devoted his final chapter to the question that had motivated Romanes' work on animal intelligence, that of the continuity of animal and human mind. Thorndike's solution is uninteresting. It is largely that proposed more than 60 years earlier by Spencer, "the intellectual evolution of the race consists in an increase in the number, delicacy, complexity, permanence and speed of formation of . . . associations. In man this increase reaches such a point that an apparently new type of mind results, which conceals the real continuity of the process" (Thorndike, 1911, p. 294). It was a view with which Spencer and Romanes, but not Darwin, would have been comfortable, a view that would be incorporated into the work of comparative psychologists of succeeding decades. The notion of a gradual linear increase in complexity of brain, resulting in corresponding increasing complexity of learning, is evolutionary in the broadest sense, but fails to make contact with evolutionary theory as it was understood even at the turn of the century. Thorndike, while embracing the notion of an evolution of associative capacities, abandoned the attempt to employ particular theories of evolutionary process as a tool in the study of the mechanisms of learning. It is only during the past 2 decades that the enterprise initiated by Darwin has again captured the attention of the psychological community.

CONCLUSIONS

The first attempts to integrate the study of animal learning and evolutionary theory failed in large measure because the evolutionary theory adopted by those interested in the evolution of mind and behavior was later shown to be false. It is easy to argue that this failure provides no lesson for those who are today interested in the interaction of learning and evolution. Perhaps our evolutionary models are basically correct and will not lead us into error. However, the lapses apparent in the work of many of the outstanding behaviorists of the nineteenth century do provide a warning that should be heeded regardless of the truth or falsity of our current view of evolution. That warning concerns the relationship between evolutionary theory and the interpretation of behavioral data.

Convincing evidence of both learning by observation and the inheritance of acquired characteristics was reported by almost all 19th-century students of behavior from Darwin to Morgan. By the turn of the century, few saw compelling evidence of either.

Animals have a surprising tendency to behave in accord with the hypotheses of those who observe them. It is difficult to avoid finding those capacities in animals that evolutionary theory suggests they should possess. We should not forget, as 19th-century students of behavior largely did, that natural selection is constrained by limitations imposed by the variations occurring in natural populations. Surely, natural selection would have produced a mechanism for the inheritance of acquired characteristics if the biochemical process for the translation of DNA into protein did not forbid it. Equally surely, natural selection would have produced a robust capacity for observational learning in animals, if as yet poorly understood constraints on the evolution of associative processes did not stand in the way.

Evolutionary theory may prove a useful heuristic in the search for adaptive associative capacities in animals, but the probable adaptive value of a capacity, if it were to evolve, is not evidence of its actual evolution. Overenthusiasm for predictions deduced from logically consistent theory is as rich in potential for error in 1985 as in 1885. There are limitations on the adaptive potential of organisms, phylogenetic or ontogenetic constraints on the directions in which evolution can proceed. Deductions from evolutionary models are not facts, but working hypotheses, requiring rigorous experimental test. The failure to appreciate the distinction between prediction and evidence, so clearly evident in the first attempts to integrate the study of animal learning and evolution, can serve as a caveat for today.

ACKNOWLEDGMENTS

Preparation of this manuscript was greatly facilitated by funds from the Natural Sciences and Engineering Research Concil of Canada and McMaster University Research Board. I thank the faculty and staff of the Department of Psychology of the University of Colorado at Boulder for their hospitality during the writing of the manuscript and Mertice Clark, Jerry Rudy, Michael Wertheimer, David Chiszar, and Steve Maier for their thoughtful comments on earlier drafts.

REFERENCES

Baldwin, J. M. (1896). A new factor in evolution. *American Naturalist, 30,* 441–451, 536–553.

Barber, L. (1980). *The heyday of natural history, 1820–1870.* Garden City, NJ: Doubleday.

Berry, C. S. (1906). The imitative tendency of white rats. *Journal of Comparative Neurology and Psychology, 16,* 333–361.

Berry, C. S. (1908). An experimental study of imitation in cats. *Journal of Comparative Neurology and Psychology, 18,* 1–25.

Bolles, R. C. (1975). *Learning theory.* New York: Holt Rinehart & Winston.

Cole, L. W. (1907). Concerning the intelligence of raccoons. *Journal of Comparative Neurology and Psychology, 17,* 211–261.

Darwin, C. (1859). *On the origin of species by means of natural selection.* London: Watts.

Darwin, C. (1868). *Variation of animals and plants under domestication,* Vols. 1-2. London: Murray.

Darwin, C. (1971). *The descent of man.* London: Murray.

Darwin, C. (1884). Posthumous essay on instinct. In G. J. Romanes (Ed.), *Mental evolution in animals.* New York: Appleton.

Davis, H. B. (1907). The raccoon: A study in animal intelligence. *American Journal of Psychology, 18,* 447–489.

Dyar, H. G. (1896). Untitled. *Transactions of the New York Academy of Sciences,* 1896, *15,* 141–142, 148.

Eimer, G. H. T. (1890). *Organic evolution as the result of the inheritance of acquired characteristics according to the laws of organic growth.* Translated by J. T. Cunningham. London: Macmillan.

Fitch, O. (1883). Benevolence in animals. *Nature, 27,* 580.

Gottlieb, G. (1979). Comparative psychology and ethology. In E. Hearst (Ed.), *The first century of experimental psychology.* Hillsdale, NJ: Lawrence Erlbaum Associates.

Haggerty, M. E. (1909). Imitation in monkeys. *Journal of Comparative Neurology and Psychology, 19,* 337–445.

Hobhouse, L. T. (1901). *Mind in evolution.* London: Macmillan.

Holmes, S. J. (1911). *The evolution of animal intelligence.* New York: Holt.

Jenkins, H. M. (1979). Animal learning and behavior theory. In E. Hearst (Ed.), *The first century of experimental psychology.* Hillsdale, NJ: Lawrence Erlbaum Associates.

Kinnaman, A. J. (1902). Mental life of two macacus rhesus monkeys in captivity. *American Journal of Psychology, 13,* 98–148, 171–218.

Lewes, G. H. (1860). *The physiology of common life.* London: Blackwood.

Mayr, E. (1976). *Evolution and the diversity of life.* Cambridge, MA: Harvard University Press.

Morgan, C. L. (1890). *Animal life and intelligence.* London: Edward Arnold.

Morgan, C. L. (1894). *An introduction to comparative psychology.* London: Scott.

Morgan, C. L. (1896). *Habit and instinct*. London: Edward Arnold.

Morgan, C. L. (1900). *Animal behaviour*. London: Edward Arnold.

Paley, W. (1802). *Natural theology: Or, evidences of the existence and attributes of the Deity, collected from the appearances of nature*. London: R. Fauldner.

Porter, J. P. (1910). Intelligence and imitation in birds: a criterion of imitation. *American Journal of Psychology, 21,* 1–71.

Romanes, G. J. (1882). *Animal intelligence*. London: Kegan, Paul, Trench.

Romanes, G. J. (1884). *Mental evolution in animals*. New York: Appleton.

Romanes, G. J. (1889). *Mental evolution in man*. New York: Appleton.

Romanes, G. J. (1893).*An examination of Weismannism*. Chicago: Open Court Publishing.

Small, W. S. (1899). Notes on the psychic development of young white rats. *American Journal of Psychology, 11,* 133–165.

Spalding, D. A. (1873). Instinct: With original observations on young animals. *Macmillan's Magazine, 27,* 282–293 (Reprinted: *British Journal of Animal Behaviour,* 1954, *2,* 1–11.)

Spencer, H. (1855). *Principles of psychology*. 2 vols. New York: Appleton.

Spencer, H. (1893). *A rejoinder to Weismann*. New York: Appleton. (Reprinted from *The Contemporary Review,* December, 1893.)

Spencer, H. (1893). *The inadequacy of "natural selection."* London: Williams & Norgate. (Reprinted from *The Contemporary Review,* February, March, & May, 1893.)

Thorndike, E. L. (1898). Animal intelligence: An experimental study of the associative processes in animals. *Psychological Review Monographs, 2* (Whole No. 8).

Thorndike, E. L. (1911). *Animal intelligence: Experimental studies*. New York: Macmillan.

Wallace, A. R. (1858). On the tendency of varieties to depart infinitely from the original type. *Journal of the Proceedings of the Linnaean Society (Zoology), 3,* 53–62.

Wallace, A. R. (1870). *Contributions to the theory of natural selection*. New York: AMS Press.

Wallace, A. R. (1889). *Darwinism: An exposition of the theory of natural selection with some of its applications*. London: Macmillan.

Wallace, A. R. (1916). *The world of life*. New York: Moffat, Yard.

Washburn, M. F. (1908). *The animal mind*. New York: Macmillan.

Watson, J. B. (1908). Imitation in monkeys. *Psychological Bulletin, 5,* 169–178.

Weismann, A. (1889). *Essays upon heredity and kindred biological problems*. Oxford: Clarendon Press.

Wundt, W. (1894). *Lectures on human and animal psychology*. (Translated from the 2nd German edition of 1896). New York: Swann Sonnenschein.

4 Learning as Inference

J. E. R. Staddon
Duke University

Psychologist and ethologists usually have different interests and study behavior under different conditions. Ethologists, looking at behavior in rich, natural environments, are impressed by how species-typical it is, and how small and constrained is the role of learning. Psychologists, looking at behavior in impoverished experimental environments, are impressed by the importance and flexibility of learning in this limited domain. The phenomena studied in these two ways and the explanations offered for them seem so divergent that many have abandoned hope for reconciliation. Nevertheless, I believe there is a way of looking at learning that brings all together: Functionally, learning is a process of *Bayesian inference,* and differences between different types of learning reflect differences in what is to be predicted, the predictors available, and the animal's ability to make use of them. In this chapter I show how the inference idea works for some examples of learning.

Historical Background

Years of toil with dog, rat, and pigeon, eyelid, alley, and Skinner box led early experimental psychologists to general learning laws having to do with the order and timing of rewards and punishments and arbitrary stimuli and responses. But about 15 years ago several developments muddied the waters: Rescorla (1967), followed by others, showed that contiguity between conditioned stimulus and unconditioned stimulus is not sufficient for classical conditioning. In addition to being close in time to its unconditioned stimulus (UCS, an electric shock, for example), a conditioned stimulus (CS, a tone, say) must also *predict* the UCS: UCS must follow CS more often than it follows other stimuli if the CS is to "become conditioned." To *contiguity* (pairing) was added *contingency* (relative frequency).

For a while information about these two variables seemed to be sufficient to explain the major forms of learning. But other problems were to follow. Garcia and his colleagues (e.g., Garcia, Clarke, & Hankins, 1973) showed that temporal contiguity is unnecessary for some kinds of learning. Rats, made sick hours after tasting a novel food, avoid the taste thereafter. Novelty also enters into standard classical conditioning: Kamin (1969) showed that if to a tone, established as CS for a shock UCS, is later added a light, the light fails to become conditioned (*blocking*). Evidently, if a new stimulus is not associated with a new consequence, then after a brief initial response, the new stimulus is attended to no more. Tone predicts shock, light is added, tone still predicts shock—light is ignored. But if the shock intensity is increased or decreased coincident with introduction of the light, then the light does gain an effect, as it does also if tone and light are introduced together, rather than one at a time. More recent work (e.g., Rescorla, 1985) has revealed still other complications to "simple" classical conditioning.

Operant conditioning also acquired its share of anomalies. The Brelands (Breland & Breland 1961) showed that raccoons trained with food reward to drop a wooden "coin" into a slot first learned, then became reluctant to give up the coin, "washing" it between their forepaws as wild raccoons do with natural foods. This "instinctive drift" slowed or even prevented delivery of the food reward. Similar effects were found with several other species. Brown and Jenkins (1968) showed that hungry pigeons will peck a key light that is paired with food—classical conditioning of an "operant" response—and Williams and Williams (1969) showed they will continue to do so even if a peck turns off the light and prevents the delivery of food.

These problems were all uncovered by psychologists, but the ethologists were not idle. Thorpe, Marler, and their students studied bird song learning and found that some species, such as chaffinches and white-crowned sparrows, learn their songs, while others, such as song sparrows, need little experience to develop theirs. Moreover, species that learn do so without apparent benefit of reward or punishment ("reinforcement"): The young male white crown hears his species song and remembers it, then learns by practicing to match his remembered "template" 5 months later. Where is the operant or classical conditioning in this? The bird has no reward but hearing himself sing better, and none at all for remembering the standard at which he aims. Noreover, bird song learning is selective. The white crown, although unable to sing its proper song if deprived of experience with song, will not accept any song but can pick out white-crown song from distractors. Marler and Peters (1977) more recently showed that swamp sparrows can also learn selectively, picking out bits of their own song from mixtures adulterated with song-sparrow song fragments.

Imprinting, a long-known phenomenon studied afresh in recent years, poses similar problems. It also occurs only during a limited "critical period"; it is also selective—some imprinting objects are better than others—and usually the best objects are close to the natural one. Recent findings even argue that sexual imprinting of young birds can lead them to preferences that favor an optimal degree of outbreeding—given a choice, quail reared with their sibs prefer to mate with first cousins (Bateson, 1982). Attempts to explain imprinting by reinforcement principles miss the point: chicks will approach their moving parent and even press a lever to bring her closer—she is "reinforcing," but reinforcement theory does not pretend to say when or why.

Evolution of Learning

Behavior has evolved to enable animals to find things they need and avoid things that are harmful. Learning, a particular kind of behavioral plasticity, comes about because most species live in unpredictable environments: Food cannot just be absorbed from the surrounding medium, but must be found and perhaps captured. Predators must be avoided, and mates located.

All environments have some constant features: Even if food is scattered unpredictably, it nevertheless has some temporal and spatial distribution with a certain mean and variance. Perhaps there are reliable signals to tell animals when statistical properties change—signals for patches of food or refuges relatively safe from predators, for example. Across phylogeny, and within ontogeny, these consistencies can impress themselves on species and individuals and enable animals to predict where good things and safe places are to be found—not perfectly, but perhaps as well as can be expected given their own limited intelligence and the stochastic properties of their worlds. The more complex the predictors to which an animal can attend, the more contingent (dependent on circumstance) they are, the more likely we are to call the animal's behavior *learned*. The following examples of learning in laboratory and field show how these phylogenetic and ontogenetic factors combine to build in and update the "priors" of a Bayesian inference system.

LABORATORY LEARNING

Habituation, the waning of a response to repeated harmless stimulation, is the simplest example of learning in the laboratory. For example, Kandel, Carew, and their associates (see review in Quinn, 1984) have studied the mechanisms that underlie habituation of the gill-withdrawal response in the marine snail *Aplysia.* The response, a protective reflex, is elicited by a touch to the siphon, and typically ceases to occur (habituates) after 10 to 15 touches. The response recovers after a day, but if the 10 touches are repeated every day for 4 days, the gill-withdrawal response to touch may be abolished for several weeks.

This simple phenomenon illustrates functional categories that apply to all learning. Why does the withdrawal response occur at first? Preseumably because in the phylogeny of *Aplysia* the probability of danger signaled by a touch is significant in relation to the cost of withdrawal: If the fitness "cost" of an unnecessary response is C, the probability damage will follow a failure to respond is p and the cost of damage is D, then obviously it pays to respond if C < pD. Since C is small, D is likely large and p is not negligible, an initial response makes much sense: The first occurrence of a novel stimulus is (so the animal's phylogeny tells it) a reasonably good predictor of danger. But if danger repeatedly fails to ensue, then the animal has some basis for revising its initial, "default estimate" of p. By the computer term *default* I just mean the initial setting, the value in the absence of any experience—the behavioral equivalent of a Bayesian *prior probability*.

The rate at which p is revised as a function of experience, and the persistence of the change, depend on both phylogenetic and ontogenetic factors. From an epistemological point of view, the process is one of *induction:* How many harmless touches are sufficient to warrant a touch harmless forever? Philosophers tell us that this problem is insoluble by logic. But natural selection acting through phylogeny can provide a serviceable answer, building in the habituation rate (= rate of modification of the animal's estimate of p) that has been the best bet in the past.[1]

The habituation rate will also depend on the properties of the stimulus. For example, the prior probability of ensuing harm may well be higher following a strong stimulus than a weak one, in which case reaction to the strong stimulus will habituate more slowly. If the stimulus is strong enough that its continued occurrence is potentially dangerous in itself, the reaction may even increase—*sensitization.* In most animals, p is also likely to be a function of contextual factors: If these signal *danger,* p will be higher, and habituation slower, than if the context is *safe.*

The temporal pattern of stimulus occurrences provides contextual information: If we hear four explosions in a row, we will not be surprised at a fifth, providing it occurs with much the same spacing as the preceding four. But if it occurs after an hour or a day, we may be surprised again.

The logic of temporal inference is illustrated in Fig. 4.1. Distribution A summarizes the spacing between successive stimuli presented over a single brief period—when *Aplysia* receives 40 touches within a single 2-hour experiment, for example. Distribution B summarizes a different experiment, in which the 40 stimulus presentations are given over a 4-day period. The vertical arrow shows the time between the last experimental presentation and the presentation of a single test stimulus: The test stimulus is quite close to distribution B, but well

---

[1]This is an assertion I cannot prove. But comparative data on habituation rates of different responses of different species with different niches could support or refute it.

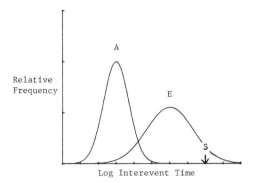

FIGURE 4.1. Distributions of stimuli yielding transient (A) or persistent (B) habituation. S denotes a test stimulus. Time is represented logarithmically, in conformity to Weber's Law.

beyond the confines of distribution A: The animal should—and does—show transient habituation following distribution-A training (i.e., it responds to a test stimulus presented after a delay), but persistent habituation following distribution-B training (it fails to respond).

Formally, the animal's task is to estimate the conditional probability that stimulus S is drawn from *safe* population A (or B): $p(A|t_s)$, where t_s is the interevent time associated with stimulus S. $1 - p(A|t_s)$ is the probability that the stimulus is not from the safe distribution (i.e., the probability that S is not safe); if we denote it by p then, as before, the animal should respond (not habituate) if $C < pD$.

Persistant habituation is sometimes taken as an instance of long-term memory. There are two functional aspects to memory: one relating to the persistence of a change over time, the other to stimulus identification. In the first sense, long- and short-term memory refer to extremes along a continuum of temporal "neighborhoods." For example, one can imagine a niche in which things always change rapidly, so that events now bear little relation to events in 5 or 10 seconds. Under these conditions, habituation should be rapid (short-term memory only). Conversely, if the world changes slowly, so that things now are a good predictor of things in an hour, habituation should be slow (a variety of long-term memory). But unless ecological factors are bimodal—i.e., the world changes either very rapidly or very slowly, but rarely at an intermediate rate—there is no functional reason to suppose two discrete mechanisms responsible for transient vs. persistent habituation. Thus, to distinguish extreme cases by dichotomous terms suggesting different processes is questionable.

The second aspect of memory is the complex matter of stimulus or situation *identification*. The distinctive thing about long-term memory in associative learning is not its persistence but what it tells us about the animal's ability to identify the predictive features of a situation. If an animal classifies the world rather simply, then a given physical stimulus may not be identifiable with precision—which means that the animal connat be sure that a given *percept,* experienced after a long interval, corresponds to the same physical event. But (because the world changes slowly) the same percept experienced in rapid succession *is* likely to represent the same *state of the world* and so may be similarly reacted to.[2] Hence habituation, sensitization, and similar local-memory processes are ubiquitous, but associative learning—true long-term memory—seems restricted to animals with well-developed perceptual apparatus.

Sensitization is a term used in two senses: as the opposite of habituation, that is increasing (rather than decreasing) responsiveness to repeated stimulation; and to refer to the maintenance by the concurrent presentation of a noxious event of a response that would otherwise habituate. For example, when *Aplysia* is presented with a noxious stimulus to the head, the gill-withdrawal to a touch on the siphon is much enhanced. As with habituation, the persistence of the enhanced response depends on the temporal distribution of pairings.

Both kinds of sensitization can be looked at as phylogenetically programmed context effects: In both the animal acts as if p, the probability that a given stimulus will be followed by a damaging consequence, is higher when preceded either by a similar stimulus, or another, noxious, stimulus.

Pseudoconditioning resembles sensitization in that intercalated presentation of a stimulus A, that normally evokes no response, with stimulus B, that does, causes A to evoke the response. The feature that distinguishes pseudoconditioning from classical conditioning is that stimulus A need not predict stimulus B for A to produce the same response. Pseudoconditioning is relatively rare in mammals, and when it occurs is usually attributed to generalization from the effective stimulus (B). It is more common in invertebrates, perhaps because they lack the ability to differentiate clearly among states of the world, as I just suggested. The

---

[2]Another way to look at the same issue is in terms of a sort of regression model. The animal in a habituation experiment is repeatedly presented with a physical stimulus array, S, which is represented by some change in the animal's internal state, S^*. S^* has two properties: S_p^*, which is the representation of the physical properties of S; and t, which is the time since the last presentation of S (strictly: the last time the animal was in state S^*). The animal's phylogeny, and perhaps ontogeny, allows it to use both S_p^* and t as cues to the identity of successive occurrences of S^*. For example, if t is short then the animal may tolerate a larger difference between $S_p^*(0)$ (the internal representation of the first occurrence of S^*) and $S_p^*(t)$ (the representation of the next occurrence, after time t). To an approximation, the animal acts as if it computes a quantity $V = f(S_p, t)$ (e.g., $V = aS_p + bt$, where a and b are positive constants) and acts on the basis of V: if V exceeds some threshold, then the animal reacts as if successive occurrences of S are the same (i.e., it habituates), otherwise, it treats them as different (fails to habituate). An experimental implication of this kind of analysis is that an animal will habituate more rapidly when stimuli are presented in rapid succession than when they are spaced (which will surprise no one), but also that the superiority of massed to spaced presentation will be much greater for a set of variable stimuli (e.g., tones of different frequencies or loudnesses). I don't know if this experiment has been done.

effect is usually adaptive because stimulus changes occuring in the same temporal neighborhood as a hedonic (typically aversive) stimulus are likely (in most niches) to be causally associated with it in fact even if contiguity and contingency relations are imperfect. The predictiveness here is phylogenetic, not ontogenetic.

Habituation, sensitization, and pseudoconditioning share three common elements: (a) Something to be predicted, usually danger; (b) a set of predictors: stimulus intensity and spacing, contextual factors. Each potential predictor seems to have a default (prior) value that is subsequently modified by experience. And (c) a set of constraints that limit the animal's ability to use available information. The traditional hierarchy of learning types, from habituation through sensitization and classical conditioning to operant conditioning, describes the progressive relaxation of constraints that limit the environmental information animals can use. But all learning types share these three features: an object, a set of signals for the object, and means by which signals are detected and processed.

Specific and General Predictors: Classical and Operant Conditioning

Classical conditioning resembles sensitization but is more selective: As we have seen, the hedonic stimulus (UCS) must selectively follow the otherwise-neutral CS if the CS is to have an effect: the conditional probability of UCS given the CS, p(UCS|CS), must be higher than p(UCS|~CS), the probability of the UCS absent the CS. The difference between classical conditioning and sensitization or pseudoconditioning is in the sophistication of the predictors the animal can use to identify a potential CS (i.e., a potential predictor of the UCS). A creature capable only of sensitization is restricted to using the temporal neighborhood of the UCS to identify potential CSs (i.e., contiguity without respect to order). Classical conditioning adds temporal order (a stimulus is more likely to be treated as a CS if it precedes, rather than follows, the UCS), and reliable succession (contingency) as predictive features.

All potential CSs for a given UCS are not equivalent. Some have higher default values (i.e., show more conditioning following the first pairing—and perhaps after subsequent pairings as well) than others. Many animals will sooner learn to take a sound than a light as a signal of danger, for example. Rats and people take taste over appearance as a signal of poison (some birds may do otherwise). These differences in default significances (prior probabilities) and rates of conditioning are peculiar to different species and UCSs and presumably reflect particular selection pressures and, in older and smarter animals, experiences. Presumably taste is preferentially associated with subsequent illness because ancestral animals that jumped to that conclusion were less often wrong than others that attended to sights and sounds.

Predictors can be divided into *specific* and *general*. Specific predictors reflect properties of stimuli that are endowed by an animal's phylogeny with a special significance in relation to particular to-be-predicted (target) events: Taste may have a special significance as a predictor of sickness, sound of danger, certain song elements as identifiers of species-specific song, and so on.

Temporal order and temporal contiguity are the chief general predictors: A cause must always precede its effect; and the time between a candidate cause and its effect is always useful, although the shortest time need not be the best predictor. For example, when an effect is always delayed, as sickness follows poisoning with a lag, intermediate times may carry the greatest weight. Even in standard laboratory classical conditioning, the optimal CS–UCS delay is not zero but half a second or so for many conditioned responses (Landauer, 1969; Staddon, 1973). Even though it has two identifiable components, for simplicity I will lump together temporal order and temporal contiguity under the *contiguity* label.

When learning must take place rapidly, on one or a few trials, the animal has no basis for inference other than order and contiguity, and specific predictors. When repeated opportunities for learning are available, there is in addition the second general predictor, common to all recurrent experiences: reliable succession (contingency), which was Hume's chief attribute of causation.

The two general predictors have a special status, in that they reflect necessary properties of the world (Revusky [e.g., 1985] has argued this point eloquently). Taste need not be the best predictor of sickness, and one can imagine worlds in which any specific predictor becomes invalid. But contingency almost defines the what we mean by predictiveness. Temporal order is an essential aspect of causation: A cause must obviously precede its effect. Contiguity has no such necessary status, but does reflect ineluctable limitations on information gathering, as well as a reliable feature of the real world: A cause remote in time from its effect will be hard to identify because intervening potential causes must first be eliminated (cf. Revusky, 1977), and most identifiable causes closely precede their effects. The only escape from the information-gathering limit is when potential causes for an effect differ in some consistent way from all intervening events—as in taste-aversion learning where a remote taste takes precedence over intervening nontaste stimuli.

Habituation, sensitization, and classical conditioning are all situations in which an animal uses a neutral or low-value stimulus as a signal for something of greater value: as a signal for safety (habituation), of danger (sensitization), or of a good or bad event (classical conditioning). Operant conditioning is a situation where the animal identifies some aspect of its own behavior as a signal for something of value. Operant conditioning adds to the two general factors of contiguity and contingency a third, *control* by the animal, who can produce a potential predictor (response) at will and thus explore the strength of its association (degree of contingency) with a consequence (reward or punishment).

All the kinds of plasticity I have discussed have implications for action. For example, once an animal has habituated it need no longer display protective reflexes and can get on with other necessary activities; once a stimulus has been identified as a signal for food, it can be approached. Action is intrinsic to operant conditioning: To identify an action as a possible signal for (= cause of) something, the action must occur. How should actions be selected? The answer here seems to be much the same as the answer we have already given for classical conditioning. In a given context, there are default *activities*—activities that have high priority—and these occur first. These acts correspond to *hypotheses,* if you like, although no conscious intent is implied by the term. The set of such acts is defined by a combination of phylogenetic and ontogenetic factors. For example, for a raccoon any small object strongly associated with food elicits food-related "washing" behavior, and apparently the stronger the reward contingency, the more constrained the animal to this particular activity. A rat that has learned in one situation to press a bar for food when a tone sounds is likely to press another in a similar situation when it hears the tone. In short, both *transfer,* from other, similar situations, and built-in links between situations with motivational significance and particular activities—food situations indece food-related activities, dangerous situations escape or agonistic activities, and so on—serve to define the set of acts that are likely to occur.

Some restriction on the set of candidate activities is necessary if animals are not to be very inefficient in settling on the appropriate response. Phylogeny can help with a set of initial biases—all animals have a set of activities appropriate in anticipation of feeding, drinking, flight, and so on. Ontogeny helps in two ways: by allowing transfer from other, similar situations, and by the information available from what we have been calling general predictors: contingency and temporal contiguity. Phylogeny is involved here, too, of course, in building in sensitivity to general and specific predictors, and in providing a measure of *similarity* that classifies the world in sensible ways.

Deciding what is, or should be, meant by "similar" is not a trivial problem (here is a rich field indeed for students of animal "cognition"). For example, suppose we train a hungry rat to press a black lever for food reward in a brightly lighted small wire cage. Later on, we place him, still hungry, in a large, dim enclosure with a white lever. What should he do? Since neither environment speaks much to his phylogeny, he comes with few biases, other than caution in the novel environment. Will the second lever be similar enough to the first to elicit pressing? Probably not. There are at least two things that are likely to increase the chance the rat will behave effectively in this new environment: Put him in it soon after a session in the old environment. Give him some free food in the new environment. Temporal proximity between new and old will in and of itself induce some carryover of behavior from one situation to the other, and the presence of food will bring the two even closer. In short, time relations seem built-in as useful predictors; and the presence of food, a predator, or a mate— any event of motivational significance—is perhaps the most important defining property of a situation. Animals classify situations primarily in terms of their motivational significance, and stimulus correlations—classical conditioning—are used for this purpose.

Operant conditioning, can be looked at as an inference process that involves three steps (which may go on concurrently): The situation must be classified in some way—primarily, but not entirely, in terms of its motivational significance. Classical conditioning (CS–UCS relations) and similarity relations are the names we give to this first step. Once classified, the situation defines a set of default activities, each with a different priority and different sensitivity to the general predictors, contiguity, and correlation, that operate in the third step.

For example, a hungry pigeon faces a dark pecking key, that is occasionally briefly illuminated. Lacking prior experience with such objects, the animal may do little. But if each key illumination is followed by food (and food occurs at no other time), soon the light is classified as food-related. Small food-related objects induce pecking as a high-priority activity (*autoshaping*). If the apparatus arranges that pecking produces food, the correlation between light and food is further strengthened, and in addition the general predictors—temporal contiguity and correlation between peck and food—act to favor pecking. In this way, the pigeon *learns* to peck the key.

Food-associated situations elicit food-related activities. Novel situations at first elicit caution, then activities that maximize exposure to new information. For example, rats in a novel multiarm radial maze visit each arm in succession, so that all will usually be visited before any is revisited. Experiments in which entries into specific arms are forced show the animals to be following a "least-recent" rule, always visiting the arm seen least recently (Olton, 1978; Staddon, 1983, 1984). In this situation, the default priorities rank locations in ascending order of recency, an efficient strategy for foraging as well as updating information.

Interesting effects can result when specific and general predictors contradict or interact with one another. For example, general predictors allow a hungry pigeon to detect the significance of a brief colored light that is invariably followed by food. But once identified as a signal for imminent food, specific predictors guide the animal to peck at the light—an adaptive response under natural conditions, where pecking at something associated with food will often reveal more food. What if a perverse experimenter arranges that the peck extinguishes the light and prevents food delivery? Pecking now predicts the absence of food, but even occasional pairings of light and food induce pecking: We know that general predictors should always eventually override specific ones, but, lacking appropriate selection pressures (pecking has probably never *prevented* food in the history of the species), in the pigeon, in this situation, they rarely do so and the animal continues to peck the light enough times to severely reduce its food intake. The Brelands' raccoons (more intelligent, one might have thought) show the same preversity: "washing" a token that can be exchanged for food rather than cashing it in. No doubt there are many human reactions just as *irrational* as these—*vicious circle* patterns of social interaction come to mind.

Learning that must take place rapidly, on one or a few trials, is subject to error because of imperfect information. Nevertheless, it is often necessary to act without certainty. Specific and general predictors may come into opposition in these cases also. For example, in an experiment by Keith-Lucas and Guttman (1975) rats were given a single electric shock while taking a pellet from a small hole in the center of a striped stimulus display. After a brief delay (different for different groups) a spiky toy rubber hedgehog was suddenly introduced into the chamber. The next day the rats were shown hedgehog, striped stimulus, and the location in which the shock had been delivered. By a number of measures, the animals tended to avoid the hedgehog most, even though it came *after* the shock; moreover, the degree of aversion was inversely related to the delay between shock and appearance of the hedgehog—indicating that proximity to the shock was a key factor. This is an example of *backward conditioning,* which violates the Humean general factors.

From another point of view, of course, the animals were acting sensibly. It is impossible to be certain of the validity of a causal inference on the basis of a single instance. Animals make mistakes and predators are often concealed before they attack. The prior probability (from the rat's vantage point) that a striped pattern will be dangerous is small; the prior probability that a lifelike dummy will be dangerous is much higher. Repeated experiences (denied the animal in this experiment) would serve to correct the animal's mistaken inference that hedgehog, rather than striped display, is the object to be feared.

Memory

Memory is the name given to the incompletely understood set of rules describing how an animal's past experiences combine to determine present performance. The *laws* of memory presumably represent both inherent constraints on all information processing systems (the more items stored the harder it is to retrieve any individual item, for example) and ecological regularities in the lives of all or most species. Most information loses validity with time; hence animals should forget older items first, and usually do. Events experienced more frequently are likely more important than events experienced rarely; hence frequency should improve recall. A given number of events experienced at widely (or unpredictably) spaced intervals are more likely to occur again than the same number of events in a cluster, hence should be, and are, better remembered (the superiority of "spaced" to "massed" practice, the "spacing effect"—memory effects that parallel the habituation effect discussed earlier and the extinction effects to be discussed shortly). Experience with things of value is likely to be more useful than experience with neutral events; hence valued events should be better remembered (Staddon, 1974). Storing new information will usually impair somewhat retrieval of information already stored—storing anything incurs some cost. Hence, animals should economize wherever possible—giving preference to changes, for example (as does the visual system, for similar reasons). The familiar serial-position curve, in which items at the beginning and end of a list are better remembered is possibly an example of this process.

Things rarely occur randomly (cf. Taylor, Woiwood, & Perry, 1978). Most people know that the best predictor of tomorrow's weather is today's and this rule holds widely: Events frequently occur in runs, so that the time immediately following an event has special significance (Treisman & Williams, 1984). But as time elapses, an event must lose influence relative to subsequent events, and perhaps also relative to earlier ones. For example, just after dialing a new telephone number, it can be recalled, perhaps better than some poorly remembered event from the previous week. But after 5 minutes, the phone number is lost, whereas older information is little affected. Why this change in relative memorability? Once again, the inference-process model is helpful: The importance of an event for future action (hence its memorability) depends on many factors. Those of general importance include its recency, value, and duration, while more specific factors are *salience* (an ill-defined catchall that includes properties such as stimulus intensity and perceptual distinctness), and semantic relationships with events experienced previously (these are often lumped together under the heading of *stimulus generalization*, but special relationships between food and taste, danger and sound, etc. must also be included). Obviously the recency factor must diminish with time relative to the others. Consequently, old information will generally gain in strength relative to newer information with lapse of time, as Jost's laws assert.

The logic of temporal inference applies also to a classical memory-related problem in learning theory: resistance to extinction. How long should a rat rewarded with food for pressing a lever continue to press when food delivery is abolished? It is well known that animals persist longer if used to getting food on an unpredictable schedule. Extinction is just a period without food. Such periods are fixed in duration under a fixed schedule, variable under a variable schedule. Obviously the animal can be less sure following a variable schedule that a given foodless period represents a change.

Even if the schedule is variable, a rat will sometimes quit sooner if well trained, the so-called overtraining extinction effect (OEE; see Mackintosh, 1974, for a review of this literature). This also makes inferential sense: The more experienced the animal, the surer it can be of the expected distribution of interfood intervals, thus also of deviations from the expected distribution. Rats sometimes fail to show the OEE, but this is also not surprising because the rat necessarily compares[3] the distribution expected on the basis of its experimental history with some prior, default distribution, determined by its phylogeny and history prior to the experiment. The relative weight given to each will depend on variables such as the duration of training, the time between the most recent reward training and earlier, similar experiences, and the time between testing and training. If the experienced period of extinction is probable in terms of the prior

---

[3]By using the word *compare* I do not mean to imply *conscious* comparison, only that whatever processes are involved are likely to incorporate these particular aspects (reward distributions in ontogeny and phylogeny) of the animal's past history.

distribution, but improbable in terms of the training distribution, the animal should quit sooner after longer periods of training, as the more recent experience gains weight. Conversely, if the extinction test is delayed, the animal's earlier experience should regain some of its importance, and extinction will be retarded. Memory principles determine the way that these past experiences combine to affect present performance.

This view implies an interaction between the variability of the training schedule and the onset of the OEE; other things being equal, the more variable the training distribution, the longer it should take the animal to be sure of its properties, hence the more training required to obtain an OEE. Experiments to test this idea do not appear to have been done.

Summary

The study of learning in the laboratory has emphasized learning about food or electric shock, highly valued, species unspecific events. The "general laws of learning" refer to universal factors congenial to a Humean view of causality: contiguity and relative frequency of association. All species rely to some extent on these general factors, using them as part of a Bayesian inference process to predict valued events. But more recent work shows that these factors do not have for animals the exclusive role attributed to them by the philosophers. An animal's phylogeny can tell it that taste, for example, is more likely to be a valid predictor of sickness than a sound or a colored light. Generations of pigeons have flourished by pecking at food-associated objects whether pecking is demanded or not. Laboratory studies have shown that animals learn by using all these factors, specific as well as general, in a relatively automatic and occasionally maladaptive way, as guides to action. Animals oeprate as "inference engines" with biases set by their phylogeny—which necessarily shares features in common with other species (and philosophers), as well as features peculiar to each species' niche and phylogeny. Nevertheless, the process in all cases is the same: to use all available predictors in Bayesian fashion to gain access to valued events or avoid noxious ones.

LEARNING IN NATURAL SITUATIONS

Food and danger are not the only things important in the life of animals. They must also learn something about their species, their parents, how to find and attract a mate.

Imprinting

Imprinting is a much-studied process by which many precocial birds learn about their species and parents. In filial imprinting, for example, key features of the parent—proximity to the young bird, receding movement, the "exodus call," crude visual features—are used by the young birds as clues to the identity of its parent.

In nature these simple predictors work essentially infallibly: any medium-sized moving object in the vicinity of the just-hatched duckling is either a parent—or the bird has no future and will not contribute to the duck gene pool. In the laboratory, the simple cues on which the duckling relies can be used to trick the animal into following boxes and flashing lights. Imprinting has often been considered to be quite different from standard classical and operant conditioning, and in its details and physiological basis it may well be. But functionally it follows the same rules: there is something to be predicted (the parent), and a set of predictors. The difference between imprinting and laboratory learning is that it occurs only once, and must depend entirely on specific predictors, since detection of a cause-effect relation is not involved.

The one-shot property of imprinting may reflect not so much some special property of the learning as its insensitivity to *context*. Numerous studies have shown that pigeons, for example, can remember food-related tasks for many years, so that persistence of imprinting is not unusual. But food can be found in many places and gotten in many ways, so that learning about food is usually very context-specific. A food-related response learned in one place will not reliably generalize to another, therefore, nor will it interfere with learning about food in a new context. Learning about Ma, on the other hand, should not be context-bound, and birds that imprint do not limit their following behavior to the situation in which they first saw their parent, but will follow her wherever they are. The degree of *generalization* shown by any new learning is itself known to be sensibly related to ecological niche. For example, bees learn flower colors slowly and generalize quite widely, but they learn odors readily and with great specificty—corresponding to the great variety of flower colors and their variability in contrast to the more limited and less variable number of flower odors (Gould & Gould, 1981).[4]

Bird Song Learning

In song learning, the thing to be predicted is adult song. Different species go about song development in different ways, depending upon the need for variation

---

[4]The range of generalization for colors and odors in bee flower learning seems to be both innate and unmodifiable. In the associative learning of birds and mammals there is usually a default (innate, a priori) range of generalization that is nevertheless modifiable by subsequent experience. For example, the consensus seems to be that chicks reared in monochromatic light show typical wavelength generalization gradients on first exposure to the full spectrum (e.g., Rudolph & Honig, 1972). But subsequent discrimination training can easily sharpen or flatten this distribution.

and the availability of valid cues. I will consider three cases: song development in the song sparrow (*Melospiza melodia*), the white-crowned sparrow (*Zonotrichia leucophrys*), and the brown-headed cowbird (*Molothrus ater*).

Song sparrows have a complex song, but one that does not differ greatly from place to place, that is, song sparrows appear not to have local *dialects* (see Kroodsma & Miller, 1982, for reviews). Despite its complexity, young male song sparrows do not require exposure to adult song to develop normal songs. While recent studies have shown some dependence on a "supporting" social and acoustic environment, young song sparrows appear to derive little specific song information from their juvenile environment. Their song, despite its complexity, is largely built in.

White crowned sparrows provide one of the most interesting cases. As is now well known, the song-learning of male white-crowned sparrows and some other songbirds proceeds in two phases. For white-crowns the first phase occurs during a critical period from 10 to 50 days after hatching, when the immature males must have the opportunity to hear adult male song. Birds kept in isolation, or deafened, during this critical period never sing normally.

At about 8 months of posthatch age, the birds become sexually mature and begin to sing; this is the second phase. The onset of singing is not immediate, but is preceded by a period of *subsong*, a twittering unorganized pattern quite different from adult song; adult song emerges gradually from subsong over a period of several weeks.

Experiments (see Immelman, 1984; Marler, 1984, for recent reviews) have shown that the first of these phases is essential for the bird to store a model or *template* of adult song. As in imprinting, the animal is selective in what it will store. For example, white-crowns exposed during the critical period only to songs of the song sparrow incorporate none of this into their model. Song development is just as impaired as if the birds had been reared in complete acoustic isolation. On the other hand, in the wild, the birds' early receptivity permits them to learn the local *dialect* of white-crown song (indeed, this may be the evolutionary function of song learning in this species).

Even after the template has formed, song learning is not complete. The period of practice, when the bird is showing subsong and incomplete versions of adult song is also essential. The final song is evidently built up by a circular process in which the bird sings, hears the results of its own singing, and slowly modifies what it sings until its production matches the stored template.

Bird-song learning evidently differs from the standard laboratory procedures in many ways: the long delay between laying down of the *template* and later performance has no obvious parallel. The template itself corresponds to nothing in standard descriptions of operant and classical conditioning. There is no obvious reward—although presumably the maturing male enjoys hearing himself sing and would peck a key for the opportunity if such a contingency could be arranged. But again the inference model works well. The cues to the proper song seem for white crowns to be of two kinds: acoustic, and social. The acoustic cues are of two kinds: intrinsically *salient* song features that are themselves readily accepted as components of the template, and so-called *trigger* features that cause a whole song to be accepted as a model: "A complex song is heard, stored in short-term memory, and then forgotten unless a triggering component from the song or some other source (e.g., visual stimuli from the singer) says 'store.' If triggering stimuli occur, both they and their associated components are likely to be remembered" (Marler, 1984, p. 297).

Social factors are also important. Recent work has shown, for example, that white crowns will more readily accept a species-atypical song (even in the presence of loudspeaker-produced conspecific song) as a model if they hear it from a live bird rather than a loudspeaker. Song learning can also occur after the traditional *critical period* if a live tutor is used (Baptista & Petrinovich, 1984).

The template idea has two aspects: the notion that the bird has a more or less fixed *idea* of what it will accept as a conspecific song; and the notion that once accepted, the stored song acts as a memory model to which the maturing male bird accommodates his initial fumbling efforts at vocal expression. The *mental-model* idea continues to hold water—partly, perhaps, because of the difficulty of sensitive tests. (The only feasible ones are deafening the bird or raising it in a noisy environment, both of which block normal song development. The ideal test—to intervene directly in the loop between the vocal expression and auditory input—has not been attempted.) But the idea that the bird has readily available detailed advance knowledge about the features of an acceptable song seems now invalid. The idea is of course intrinsically paradoxical in the sense that really detailed knowledge would render learning unnecessary. Evidence for the importance of social factors just confirms the utility of the inference view and shows that the immature males use a wide variety of potential predictors for conspecific song. The set of predictors will undoubtedly vary from species to species in ways that reflect niche—and phylogenetic—differences.

Song development in the brown-headed cowbird further emphasizes the importance of social factors. Cowbirds are brood parasites, hence the immature male cowbird, always reared by an alien species, cannot learn his song from adult males in the standard passerine fashion. Isolate-reared males, unsurprisingly, develop normal-sounding song. Less predictably, however, it turns out that the isolate song is *more* effective than normal in performing its function, which is to elicit a *copulatory posture* from a receptive female (King & West, 1977). Cowbird song is not immune to learning however. Adult cowbirds are social creatures. An isolate male, with his highly effective song, introduced into a cowbird flock is attacked by the other males. Only the dominant male is permitted to sing the most effective song, although all are capable of it. The less effective songs of the others reflect active social suppression. Here nothing beyond reward and punishment is needed to explain song modification.

Cowbird song development also follows the predictive model. The brown-headed cowbird comes in two varieties, eastern and western, with slightly different songs. Young males of each subspecies show song components from the other. In a fascinating series of experiments King, West and their associates have shown that rearing eastern males within earshot of western, and vice versa, has little effect, but rearing eastern males with western *females* (and vice versa) has a substantial effect: males of one subspecies will emphasize the song of the sub-species of the females they must court, whether of the same or different sub-species (King & West, 1985). The males are quite flexible in this, whereas the females, in common with the females of many other species, are much more rigid in what they will accept. When the function of song is courtship the bottom line is clearly the behavior of the female. If what she wants to hear is within his capacity, the male cowbird will be guided in operant fashion by this best of all predictors.

CONCLUSION

Learning in both field and laboratory can be looked at in the same functional terms, as a process of inference. In this general scheme species differences show up as different *objectives*—what the animal is programmed to learn about; different *constraints,* of memory, stimulus significance, and information processing, that limit its ability to do so; and different *weightings* given to stimuli (as potential predictors) in particular situations. In psychological jargon, the set of reinforcers, or the preference structure, differs from species to species, as do the weightings given to different stimuli and the information-processing constraints. All three—preference structure, stimulus weightings and constraints—are presumably related to each species' individual niche.

One virtue of this point of view is that like any other functional analysis (optimal foraging theory, for example) it suggests testable hypotheses. Another is that it discourages the tendency (always irritating to ethologists) to ask of some example of natural learning ''is it really classical (or instrumental) conditioning?'' The answer clearly is always ''no'' because classical and instrumental conditioning are not processes, but procedures and effects of procedures. The functional point of view asks instead what is to be predicted and what are the predictors. Sometimes the answer will involve general predictors, contiguity and contingency, which are also involved in conditioning. But sometimes it will involve only specific predictors, such as *trigger* features or social stimuli, which are unique. Most commonly, it will involve both.

ACKNOWLEDGMENT

I thank Meredith West for comments on an earlier draft. Research supported by grants from the National Science Foundation to Duke University.

REFERENCES

Baptista, L. F., & Petrinovich, L. (1984). Social interaction, sensitive phases and the song template hypothesis in the white-crowned sparrow. *Animal Behaviour, 32* 172–181.
Bateson, P. P. G. (1982). Preference for cousins in Japanese quail. *Science, 295,* 236–37.
Breland, K., & Breland, M. (1961). The misbehavior of organisms. *American Psychologist, 16,* 661–664.
Brown, P. L., Jenkins, H. M. (1968). Auto-shaping of the pigeon's key-peck. *Journal of the Experimental Analysis of Behavior, 11,* 1–8.
Garcia, J., Clarke, J., & Hankins, W. G. (1973). Natural responses to scheduled rewards. In P. P. G. Bateson & P. Klopfer (Eds.), *Perspectives in ethology.* New York: Plenum Press.
Gould, J. L.,& Gould C. G. (1981). The insect mind: Physics or metaphysics? In D. R. Griffin (Ed.), *Animal mind—human mind.* Berlin/Heidelberg/New York: Springer-Verlag.
Immelman, K. (1984). The natural history of bird learning. In P. Marler & H. S. Terrace (Eds.), *The biology of learning.* Berlin: Springer-Verlag.
Kamin, L. J. (1969). Selective attention and conditioning. In N. J. Mackintosh & W. K. Honig (Eds.), *Fundamental issues in associative learning.* Halifax: Dalhousie University Press.
Keith-Lucas, T., Guttman, N. (1975). Robust-single-trial delayed backward conditioning. *Journal of Comparative and Physiological Psychology, 88,* 468–476.
King, A. P., & West, M. J. (1977). Species identification in the N. American cowbird (*Molothrus ater*). *Science, 195,* 1002–1004.
King, A. P., & West, M. J. (1985). Social metrics of song learning. *Learning and Motivation, 15,* 441–458.
Kroodsma, D. E., Miller, E. H. (1982). *Acoustic communication in birds.* Orlando, FL: Academic Press.
Landauer, T. K. (1969). Reinforcement as consolidation. *Psychological Review, 76,* 82–96.
Olton, D. S. (1978). Characteristics of spatial memory. In S. H. Hulse, H. Fowler, & W. K. Honig (Eds.), *Cognitive processes in animal behavior.* Hillsdale, NJ: Lawrence Erlbaum Associates.
Mackintosh, N. J. (1974). *The psychology of animal learning.* Orlando, FL: Academic Press.
Marler, P. (1984). Song learning: Innate species differences in the learning process. In P. Marler & H. S. Terrace (Eds.), *The biology of learning.* Berlin: Springer-Verlag.
Marler, P., & Peters, S. (1977). Selective vocal learning in a sparrow. *Science, 198* 519–521.
Quinn, W. G. (1984). Work in invertebrates on the mechanisms underlying learning. In P. Marler & H. S. Terrace (Eds.), *The biology of learning.* Berlin: Springer-Verlag.
Rescorla, R. A. (1967). Pavlovian conditioning and its proper control procedures. *Psychological Review, 74,* 71–80.
Rescorla, R. A. (1985). Associative learning. In N. M. Weinberger, J. L. McGaugh, & G. Lynch (Eds.), *Memory systems of the brain: Animal and cognitive processes.* New York: Guilford.
Revusky, S. H. (1977). Learning as a general process with emphasis on data from feeding experiments. In N. W. Milgram, L. Krames, T. M. Alloway (Eds.), *Food aversion learning.* New York: Plenum.
Revusky, S. H. (1985). The general process approach to animal learning. In T. D. Johnston & A.

T. Pietrewicz (Eds.), *Issues in the ecological study of learning*. Hillsdale, NJ: Lawrence Erlbaum Associates.

Rudolph, R., & Honig, W. K. (1972). Effects of monochromatic rearing on spectral discrimination learning and the peak shift in chicks. *Journal of the Experimental Analysis of Behavior, 17,* 107–111.

Staddon, J. E. R. (1973). On the notion of cause, with applications to behaviorism. *Behaviorism, 1,* 25–63.

Staddon, J. E. R. (1974). Temporal control, attention and memory. *Psychological Review, 81,* 375–391.

Staddon, J. E. R. (1983). *Adaptive behavior and learning*. Cambridge: Cambridge University Press.

Staddon, J. E. R. (1984). Time and memory. *Annals of the New York Academy of Sciences, 423,* 322–334.

Taylor, R. A., Woiwood, I . P., & Perry, J. N. (1978). The density-dependence of spatial behavior and the rarity of randomness. *Journal of Animal Ecology, 47,* 383–406.

Treisman, M., & Williams, T. C. (1984). A theory of criterion setting with application to sequential dependencies. *Psychological Review, 91,* 68–111.

Williams, D. R., & Williams, H. (1969). Auto-maintenance in the pigeon: Sustained pecking despite contingent non-reinforcement. *Journal of the Experimental Analysis of Behavior, 12,* 511–520.

5 Learning and Adaptation in Food-storing Birds

David F. Sherry
University of Toronto

Discussing the evolution of learning has the elements of a confidence trick, because if we are to be honest, nothing is known about the evolution of learning. But many of us who study learning and memory in animals have discovered evolutionary thinking, and have found that it leads us in novel and exciting directions. The evolutionary approach provides us with the opportunity to do something more than complain about the sterility of traditional learning paradigms—"warning people against all the sins of which (we) have grown tired" (Wilde, 1891). It allows us instead to ask new kinds of questions about animal learning.

This chapter discusses evolutionary adaptation and learning. In particular, I examine the difference between the adaptive use of learning to solve certain problems, and adaptive specialization in learning mechanisms (Rozin & Kalat, 1971).

THE ADAPTIVE USE OF LEARNING

Learning is used to solve some problems and not others. It is not employed, so far as we know, to modify the wing patterns of mimetic butterflies in order to avoid predation. But it is used to maintain homeostasis in a variety of physiological systems (Eikelboom & Stewart, 1982; Siegel, 1983) and to solve the familiar problems we usually regard as the domain of learning—detecting change in the environment, predicting environmental events, and assessing the consequences of behavior. Cache recovery in food-storing animals provides an example of the adaptive use of learning. The problem of relocating scattered caches of food

79

could be solved by learning the location of each cache, or by any of several other methods, and for many years the learning solution seemed a rather improbable one (Gibb, 1960; Haftorn, 1974; Källander, 1978; Linneaus, 1748, cited in Swanberg, 1951; Nichols, 1958).

Marsh tits (*Parus palustris*), black-capped chicadees (*P. atricapillus*), Eurasian nutcrackers (*Nucifraga caryocatactes*) and Clark's nutcrackers (*N. columbiana*) establish many widely dispersed caches of food. Chickadees and tits may cache up to a hundred foods items in a single day and recover their stored food within a few days of caching it. Short-term caching allows these birds to counter the effects of changes in food availability that occur within the day, and to prolong the benefits of unpredictable windfalls of food (Sherry, 1985). Each cache contains one food item, such as an insect or a seed, and in the field, no cache site is ever used more than once (Cowie et al., 1981; Sherry et al., 1982). Nutcrackers may establish over 7000 caches during several months in autumn. Each cache contains from 1 to 15 items, usually pine seeds (Tomback, 1978). Nutcrackers recover this food months after storing it, during the winter, spring, and summer (when stored seed is fed to fledglings; Swanberg, 1981; Vander Wall & Hutchins, 1983). Because cache sites are concealed and dispersed over a wide area—about a hectare for chickadees and tits (Cowie et al., 1981; Sherry 1984a; Sherry et al., 1982) and many square kilometres for nutcrackers (Tomback, 1978; Vander Wall & Balda, 1977)—returning to cache sites to retrieve stored food poses a problem for these animals. There are many behavioral adaptations that could be used to solve it however: (1) Birds could rely on encountering their stored food by chance in the course of normal foraging, as suggested by Gibb (1960). (2) They could mark caches in some distinctive way and use these marks to relocate caches. (3) The stored food could provide olfactory, visual or other cues sufficiently strong that caches could be detected from a distance. (4) The birds could use a systematic rule or preference for choosing cache sites and search only places that satisfied this rule when recovering caches (Andersson & Krebs, 1978; Shettleworth & Krebs, 1982). (5) Birds could use the temporal sequence in which caches were established as a mnemonic during recovery. Or (6) they could learn the spatial location of each individual storage site and use this information to retrieve their caches (Löhrl, 1950).

1. Chance encounter.   Cowie et al. (1981) located marsh tit caches in the wild by offering individually color banded birds radioactively labeled seeds to store and then searching the birds' territories with a radiation probe. These cache sites were then used in a test of the chance encounter hypothesis. Near each cache site, control seeds were placed in two other sites identical to the cache site, a "near" control seed 10 cm from the bird's cache, and a "far" control seed 1 m away, in randomly determined directions from the cache site. Although it is difficult to determine if all features of marsh tit cache sites were mimicked perfectly by this procedure, there were no obvious features that could not be duplicated. Seeds were stored by marsh tits in moss, hollow stems, dry leaves, tree bark, and in the ground. They were sometimes plainly visible, sometimes partially or wholly out of sight, and all of these features were duplicated in placing control seeds. Regular inspections were made at 3 h intervals to determine when the seeds disappeared. The logic of the experiment was that if a bird that stored seeds encountered them only by chance, all three seeds would be expected to disappear at the same rate.

Seeds stored by marsh tits had a mean survivorship of 7.7 ± .8 (S.E.M.) daylight hours, significantly shorter than the mean survivorship of far control seeds, 20.4 ± 3.9 daylight hours (Cowie et al., 1981). In winter at the latitude of Oxford, where these data were collected, a mean interval of 7.7 daylight hours corresponds to recovery of stored seeds on the day following caching. A mean survivorship of 20.4 daylight hours for far control seeds is roughly equal to the survivorship of seeds placed a meter apart in the same habitat and subject to normal predation by birds and mammals (Sherry et al., 1982). Although the mean survivorship of near control seeds, 13.5 ± 2.8 daylight hours, did not differ significantly from that of stored seeds, on the 121 occasions when it could be determined from successive inspections whether the stored seed or the near control seed had disappeared first, it was the stored seed 93 times.

Although it was not possible to observe cache recovery directly by this method, it is clear that seeds did not disappear at random. The only animal expected to possess a bias to remove the stored seeds and not others is the marsh tit that stored them. Furthermore, the birds returned quite accurately to cache sites, usually overlooking a seed placed in an identical site 10 cm away. Thus chance encounter could not have produced the observed result.

Marsh tits and chickadees readily store seeds in captivity, where caching and recovery can be observed directly. Marsh tits were provided with beds of moss divided into sectors in which to store seeds (Sherry, 1982; Sherry, Krebs, & Cowie, 1981). Black-capped chickadees were given tree branches with a total of 72 small holes in which to place seeds (Sherry, 1984a). After the birds had stored seeds, and then searched for them 24 h later, rates of encountering caches by chance could be calculated from the number of seeds stored and the number of sites available for storage. All caches were removed by the experimenters before the birds searched for them, to control for the possibility of direct detection of caches (see Section 3 below). When searching in the moss, marsh tits spent over 90% of their time searching sites that had been used for storage, while the proportion expected by chance encounter was 46%. When searching the tree branches, black-capped chickadees spent over 50% of their time at cache sites, while the proportion expected by chance was 6%. Although these results rule out chance encounter as the method of recovery, they do not distinguish among the other methods listed earlier.

2. Marking of caches.   Cache sites found in the field were not marked or covered in any distinctive way, although this has been described for the caches of varied tits (*Parus varius*) and boreal chickadees (*P. hudsonicus*), which are covered with pieces of moss, lichen and other material (Haftorn, 1974; Higuchi, 1977). In the laboratory, the behavior of the birds gave no indication that caches were marked by either marsh tits or black-capped chickadees (Sherry, 1982, 1984a; Sherry et al., 1981).

3. Detecting stored food.   Many species of birds have a well-developed olfactory sense (Wenzel, 1971), despite the widely held view to the contrary. Buitron & Nuechterlein (1985), for example, have recently shown that black-billed magpies (*Pica pica*), a food-caching species, are more likely to find buried food scented with cod liver oil than untreated food. Birds also have keen vision. If stored food could be detected directly from a distance, then it could be recovered simply by orienting and moving to it. This could not, however, account for the results of the marsh tit field study, since hoarded and control seeds should have been detected at the same rate. Similarly, direct detection of caches could not account for the results of the laboratory studies described, because all stored food had been experimentally removed before the birds attempted to find their caches. In the more anecdotal literature on food storage, however, it is rarely clear if observations of ''cache recovery'' are any more than detection by an animal of food not detectable by a human observer.

4. Caching rules and cache site preferences.   In the wild, marsh tits storing food in the same habitat show individual preferences for the kind of storage sites they select. A bird that is distributing its stored food among moss, bark, hollow stems, and leaf sites will, for example, put 60% of its caches in moss. Furthermore, individuals change their preferences from one week to another in the absence of any change in the habitat (Cowie et al., 1981). These changing preferences may have the effect of reducing loss of stored food to animals that pilfer caches, mainly nocturnal rodents, by reducing how effectively they can search for caches (Stevens, 1984; Cowie et al., 1981). But these preferences could also provide a means of recovering stored food.

To determine their importance in cache recovery, Sherry et al. (1981), Sherry (1982), and Sherry (1984a) recorded in the laboratory the initial preferences by birds to search for food in the sites later used for storage. It was then possible to compare the rate of cache recovery expected on the basis of site preferences to the observed rate of cache recovery by the birds. Observed rates of cache recovery were in all seven separate experiments significantly higher than rates expected on the basis of preferences to search particular sites. Shettleworth & Krebs (1982) also investigated the importance of preferences for cache sites by recording the level of preference for individual sites in the laboratory. It was possible to show that for sites of all preference levels the probability of searching a site, given that a seed had been stored in it, exceeded the probability of searching that site when no seed had been stored in it.

Kamil & Balda (1985) have investigated the importance of cache site preferences in the laboratory by experimentally manipulating the cache sites available to Clark's nutcrackers. Birds stored pine seeds in small cups recessed in the floor of an aviary. Ninety cups were available and birds in one group had free choice of where to store. Birds in another group, however, had access to only eight storage sites selected at random by the experimenters. During the subsequent test for accuracy of cache recovery birds of both groups had access to all ninety holes. There was no difference in recovery accuracy between the groups, indicating that the opportunity to exercise cache site preferences when storing is unnecessary for accurate cache recovery.

5. Caching sequences.   The placement of spatially dispersed caches requires a temporal sequence of behavior which could later be used to return to cache sites. Some learning would be necessary because at each cache site birds would have to remember the distance and direction to the next cache site. But this would be quite different from remembering independently the spatial location of every cache site.

The most direct test of this hypothesis is to determine if there exists any correlation between the sequence in which cache sites are created and the sequence in which they are visited during cache recovery. Shettleworth & Krebs (1982) found that when captive marsh tits stored two batches of seeds, separated by a 2–3 h interval, two out of three birds later retrieved more seeds from the second batch than from the first, a result they called "a recency effect" for cache recovery. In the field, however, Cowie et al. (1981) found a significant tendency for seeds stored first to be recovered first.

In other studies no significant relation between storage order and recovery order has been found (Balda, 1980; Kamil & Balda, 1985; Sherry, 1982, 1984a, 1984b; Sherry et al., 1982). To take one example, of 24 Spearman rank correlations calculated between storage and recovery sequences for black-capped chickadees in the laboratory, 13 were positive, the rest negative, and only three were significant (two of which were positive, one negative; Sherry, 1984a). It seems unlikely that food-storing birds use the sequence followed during caching as a mnemonic to return to cache sites.

6. Memory for the location of caches.   The results described to this point have shown that cache recovery was more accurate than could be accounted for by the hypotheses considered. In most cases cache recovery was unimpaired when the mechanism in question could not be used. We are left with one hypothesis that we have been unable to reject by this "strong inference" procedure (Platt, 1964)—that the spatial location of each cache site is retained independently in memory. Although, of course, no one experimental result can prove that this latter hypothesis is correct, I would like to describe two results which show that the visual information about cache sites that is acquired while storing is retained in memory, and must be accessible during recovery for the accurate relocation of caches.

In can be shown in pigeons that there is no interocular transfer of learned discriminations if the stimuli to be discriminated fall on the monocular field of the retina (Goodale & Graves, 1982). This means that if a discrimination is acquired by a pigeon monocularly, the bird may show no evidence of learning when tested with the eye that was covered during training. There is no savings when the task is learned by the *naive* eye, and conflicting discriminations can be trained to the two eyes simultaneously (Goodale & Graves, 1980a, 1980b; Graves & Goodale, 1977, 1979; Levine, 1945). This lack of interocular transfer for monocularly acquired information probably arises because in birds there is complete crossing of the optic pathways at the chiasm, and because information from the monocular area of the retina—the largest part of the retina in birds with laterally placed eyes like pigeons and marsh tits—does not cross the cerebral commissures. Rabbits, which also have laterally placed eyes with small binocular fields, likewise exhibit a failure of interocular transfer (Van Hof & Van der Mark, 1976).

If marsh tits show a failure of interocular transfer for visual information, it would be possible to assess the importance of memory for the visual features of cache sites by requiring the birds to cache and recover food monocularly.

Marsh tits readily cached seeds when one of their eyes was covered with a small opaque plastic cap (Sherry et al., 1981). The cover weighed less than .01 g and did not touch the eye but was attached to the feathers around the eye with cosmetic eyelash adhesive. An analysis of cache sites showed that use of the right or left eye during caching did not lead to significantly different placements of caches. When birds were allowed to search for caches using the same eye they had used while storing, they returned to cache sites with the same high accuracy found in birds that had stored and recovered binocularly. Birds that searched for caches using the eye that had been covered while storing returned to caches at the rate expected by chance. There was no significant effect due to whether the left or right eye had been used initially. What this result shows is that visual information acquired while caching must be retained in memory, and must be accessible during cache recovery, for birds to accurately relocate cache sites.

An experiment with Clark's nutcracker shows what happens if the information retained in memory is no longer a reliable guide to the location of caches (Vander Wall, 1982). Nutcrackers stored seeds in the sand-covered floor of an aviary on which were arrayed a number of rocks and other prominent objects. After the birds had stored seeds, the objects at one end of the aviary were all displaced 20 cm in the same direction, while objects at the other end of the aviary remained in place. When nutcrackers returned to the aviary to search for their caches their probes in the sand were accurate with respect to the objects, not the caches. At the end of the aviary where the objects had not been moved, the birds' probes turned up stored seeds. At the other end of the aviary they missed caches by 20 cm. In the middle, where the birds might be expected to have used as cues some objects which were later moved and others that were not, the birds missed their caches by intermediate distances from 0 to 20 cm.

These two results show the importance for cache recovery of a representation in memory of the spatial location of cache sites—the exact nature of which is unknown.

To return to the question of the adaptive use of learning posed at the beginning of this section, although there are many possible ways of relocating and recovering scattered caches of stored food, the one actually used by chickadees, tits, and nutcrackers appears to be learning the location of each cache. It might be objected that these possible cache recovery methods are not really alternatives to learning, because not all of them would work. It is possible, however, to show that nonlearning solutions to cache recovery problems sometimes are used.

The problem of empty caches.   As food-storing birds return successfully to their caches and collect the food they have stored, they change the nature of the cache recovery problem. Now, instead of remembering the set of spatial locations to be revisited, they must distinguish between the subset that still contains food and the subset that does not, because of their own recovery behavior. Cache recovery would be extremely inefficient if birds returned not only to sites that currently contain food, but also to all sites that had ever contained food.

It can be shown in the laboratory that marsh tits and black-capped chickadees readily solve this problem. They return to cache sites they have previously emptied at the rate expected by chance, but continue to accurately return to cache sites, established at the same time, that they have not yet emptied (Sherry, 1982, 1984a). They do this without marking emptied caches, and when their remaining caches have been experimentally emptied to prevent direct detection of food. The caches which the birds emptied were found not to be significantly clustered in space, nor were they significantly clustered or ordered with respect to the original sequence of caching. Most convincing, however, was the finding that the birds also avoided returning to caches that had been experimentally emptied at random and which the birds had discovered empty during a previous recovery attempt (Sherry, 1984a). These results indicate that marsh tits and black-capped chickadees use a learning solution to the revisiting problem.

But other food-storing animals solve the problem in different ways. Nutcrackers in the laboratory appear unable to remember which caches they have emptied and which they have not (Balda, 1980; Kamil & Balda, 1985). Balda (1980) has suggested a number of reasons why this may be so. Nutcrackers normally disturb the soil and leave seed hulls around caches they have emptied. They may use these marks to avoid emptied sites. Nutcrackers range over a wide area and may exhaust the supply of stored food in one area before moving on to another. They are thus rarely faced with the problem of distinguishing empty from intact caches. Finally, because nutcracker caches usually contain many food items, the birds may return to previously visited caches because many of them still contain some food. Whatever the correct explanation for the cache revisiting behavior of nutcrackers in the laboratory, it is clear that they do not use the learning solution used by chickadees and tits.

Other food-storing animals also use nonlearning solutions to the problem of avoiding previously emptied caches. Red foxes, which appear able to remember the location of caches between caching and retrieval (Macdonald, 1976), urine-mark the caches they have emptied (Henry, 1977), and wolves do the same (Harrington, 1981).

Thus, learning is sometimes, but not always, the adaptation that is favored by natural selection to solve the problem of returning to scattered cache locations and keeping track of which ones are worth visiting and which are not. Adaptation, as Lewontin (1978) puts it, ". . . implies a preexisting world that poses a problem to which an adaptation is the solution" (p. 213). Using learning to solve the cache revisiting problem is an example of what I mean by the adaptive use of learning. Why learning is sometimes used, rather than another solution, I return to in the final section. The adaptive use of learning to solve a problem is very different, however, from the adaptive specialization of learning mechanisms (Rozin & Kalat, 1971).

ADAPTIVE SPECIALIZATION IN LEARNING MECHANISMS

If there exists heritable variation in a learning mechanism, and these variants have different fitness consequences, then there is every reason to expect evolutionary change in learning mechanisms. It was first proposed by Rozin & Kalat (1971) that there exist such variants of learning mechanisms, which they called adaptive specializations in learning. The idea is that some problems posed by the environment, such as forming the association between a novel food and later toxicosis, are so unusual that the conventional learning mechanism could not solve them, and a learning mechanism specialized to solve this problem has evolved. Whether such variants in learning mechanism actually exist is unclear. Shettleworth (1983), in a discussion of specialized learning mechanisms concludes that ". . . most candidates for specialized learning mechanisms that have been closely examined so far have not fared well under the sophisticated scrutiny of learning theorists" (p.10). The properties of learned aversion, for example, which were originally taken as evidence of new, previously undescribed aspects of learning (Garcia, Ervin, & Koelling, 1966), can be embraced by general process learning theory with little modification of the theory, though it does require abandoning the subsidiary idea of equipotentiality (Roper, 1983).

Does the behavior of food-storing birds suggest that they possess an adaptive specialization in the mechanism of learning? Memory in these birds appears to have some unusual features, such as the large numbers of items that can be retained in memory, the long duration of the retention interval, and the rapidity with which new information can be added to memory (Sherry, 1984b). Up to 50 cache locations can be remembered in the laboratory (Vander Wall, 1982), and if the birds use the same methods of cache recovery in the field, hundreds of sites can be remembered by marsh tits and chickadees and thousands by nutcrackers (Tomback, 1980; Vander Wall & Balda, 1981). These locations can be remembered for a minimum of several days by tits and chickadees (Cowie et al., 1981; Sherry, 1984a), and for many months by nutcrackers (Tomback, 1980; Vander Wall & Hutchins, 1983). This is in contrast to maximum retention intervals of 8 hours in the radial-arm maze (Beatty & Shavalia, 1980) and about 1 minute in the delayed matching to sample task (Grant, 1976). As mentioned earlier, cache sites are not reused by chickadees and tits in the wild, so that each cache site is a novel spatial location and all necessary information about it is acquired in a visit that may last only a few seconds.

But these features are not unique in animal memory. Pigeons can remember over 300 different visual shapes and pictures for periods of several years (Vaughan & Greene, 1984). Rats can readily distinguish up to 24 arms of a radial maze, and probably more, and can recall which arms they have previously visited on a particular trial (Olton & Samuelson, 1976; Roberts, 1979). Rats may require only a single pairing with a flavor to form a learned aversion. This is not to say that the behavior of food-storing birds is not remarkable, it is. But the reason it often seems to outstrip the performance of other animals on laboratory memory tasks may not be that these birds possess an adaptive specialization in learning, but that some laboratory tasks do not provide a good estimate of the abilities of other animals (Sherry, 1984b).

Clearly, what is missing is a criterion for distinguishing one kind of learning mechanism from another. Showing that one learning mechanism differs from others would not be proof that it is adaptively specialized to solve the problem at hand (Gould & Lewontin, 1979; Mayr, 1983), but it would be a start. Tulving (1985) has called this the "classification problem" in learning and memory and suggests that the dissociation test might be one criterion. If it is possible to dissociate two putative kinds of learning by finding manipulations that affect the performance of one but not the other, then the two may indeed be different kinds of learning. Caution and suitable controls are necessary for interpreting the results of such studies, but dissociations, based for example on the neural substrates of different learning tasks, seem promising criteria for distinguishing learning mechanisms. Determining whether the learning mechanism thus dissociated is an adaptive specialization of learning is a different problem, but we return to this in the final section.

Anthony Vaccarino and I have recently attempted to dissociate learning the spatial locations of caches from performance of two other laboratory learning problems by studying the effects of hippocampal damage on performance of these tasks. Data was recorded during a 5 day baseline period in which birds cached and recovered food once daily. Bilateral aspirations of the hippocampus were then performed and 2 days following surgery, data were again collected during 5 daily caching and recovery trials. We found that bilateral aspiration of the hippocampus of chickadees had no discernable effect on feeding or caching but reduced the accuracy of cache recovery to chance levels. Hippocampal damage had differential effects on two noncaching problems, however. In a "place" task chickadees learned to go to the same 6 holes on tree branches, out of 72 available, to collect small pieces of food. In a "cue" task all holes were marked with small colored tags. Birds were trained to collect food at 6 holes marked in a color that contrasted with the color on the other 66 holes. In the place task food was always found at the same 6 places, while in the cue task food was always found at the 6 holes marked with cues, which occurred in different places on each trial. Bilateral hippocampal aspiration impaired performance of the place task, as it had cache recovery, but had no effect on performance of the cue task. Following the logic of the dissociation test, this result shows that performance of the cue and place tasks involve different neural mechanisms. An intact hippocampus is necessary for performance of the place task but not the cue task. Following the logic of the dissociation test, this result shows that performance of the cue and place tasks involve different neural mechanisms. An intact hippocampus is necessary for performance of the place task but not the cue task. The data also show that cache recovery is dissociable from performance of the cue task but not from performance of the place task. Further work will clearly be necessary to determine whether the effect of hippocampal damage is restricted to learning and memory mechanisms or also involves other processes. For example, perhaps hippocampal damage has the effect that the birds are unable to recognize the tree branches, but can still recognize the colored cues clearly. This is unlikely, because the birds cached normally, but illustrates the kind of alternative explanation that must be controlled for in the dissociation procedure.

Attempts to dissociate learning mechanisms on the basis of their neural underpinnings may eventually provide criteria for distinguishing one learning mechanism from another. But even if multiple learning mechanisms exist, are they adaptively specialized?

QUESTIONS ABOUT LEARNING AND ADAPTATION

In this section we return to the questions left unanswered at the end of each of the preceeding sections. (1) Can we account for the fact that learning is sometimes the solution to problems posed by the environment and sometimes is not? and (2) Are learning mechanisms adaptively specialized? Two approaches to such evolutionary questions about behavior are the modeling of costs and benefits, and the comparative method. Both approaches could be used with each question, but I discuss modeling in connection with the adaptive use of learning and the comparative method in connection with adaptive specializations in learning mechanisms.

1. Modeling the adaptive use of learning. Solutions to environmental problems may differ in their fitness consequences. By specifying the range of possible solutions to a problem and estimating the fitness consequences of each, we may be able to understand why a learning solution is sometimes favored by natural selection. One way of doing this is by modeling the costs and benefits of the learning and nonlearning solutions available to an animal. A variety of methods are available (Alexander, 1982; Krebs, Stephens, & Sutherland, 1983; Maynard Smith, 1978; Pyke, Pulliam, & Charnov, 1977). Most consist of specifying the range of behaviors (or phenotypes) that could be used to solve a problem—the "strategy set" in Maynard Smith's (1978) terminology—and the features of the environment that can be treated as unchanging. The major assumption concerns what quantity is maximized by behavior. Inclusive fitness is the quantity assumed ultimately to be maximized by natural selection, but this is usually impossible to measure. Other quantities related to fitness, such as the rate of collecting prey (Davies & Houston, 1981) are generally treated as the quantity maximized by behavior.

Once such a model has been constructed, its predictions can be compared to the outcome of controlled observations of behavior. There is no supposition in any of this that behavior is *optimal* in some universal sense, that it is the best solution conceivable for any problem, or that natural selection produces perfection. Modeling is instead an attempt to determine in a formal way whether a purported adaptation serves the function it is hypothesised to serve. It is a test of whether or not the quantity supposed to be maximized has been correctly identified, and whether the strategy set and relevant environmental conditions have been properly understood (Maynard Smith, 1978).

I am not suggesting the incorporation of learning into optimal foraging models, as has been proposed by Houston, Kacelnik, & McNamara (1982) and Krebs et al. (1983). Instead, I am asking if the modeling methods that have been applied to foraging (Pyke et al., 1977), locomotion (Maynard Smith, 1978) and structural morphology (Alexander, 1982) can be applied to the adaptive use of learning.

It would be possible, for example, to compare learning and nonlearning solutions to the problem of recovering scattered caches of food. Specifying strategy sets is not daunting, a number of alternate cache recovery methods were listed earlier. A description of the environment would include such features as daily or annual patterns in food availability, food requirements, and the rate of cache pilfering by other animals. The number of caches successfully recovered seems the appropriate maximization criterion. We might find that some components of the strategy set, for example marking caches, increase the rate of cache pilfering enough to offset any benefit gained through quick recognition of cache sites. Perhaps this is why cache marking in foxes and wolves is restricted to empty caches (Harrington, 1981; Henry, 1977).

The major obstacle to such an approach is that it requires more information than students of learning can presently provide. In particular we are completely in the dark about the neural and developmental costs of learning solutions (Johnston, 1982). The magnitude of these costs, if indeed they are costs at all, remains a major question about the adaptive use of learning.

2. The comparative method and adaptive specialization of learning mechanisms. If a particular behavior or morphological trait consistently occurs in the same environment in a variety of animals, the trait may be an adaptation to that environment. The comparative method was the core of Darwin's argument in support of evolution by natural selection, and it has been used often to analyze adaptations in behavior. Ridley (1983) provides a thorough review. The idea of applying the comparative method to learning is not new (Domjan & Galef, 1983). What is new is a comparative method that is a significant advance over more informal comparative approaches (e.g., Bitterman, 1975) because it provides techniques for dealing with the problem of independence in data on adaptive specialization (Clutton-Brock & Harvey, 1977, 1979, 1984; Harvey & Mace, 1982; Ridley, 1983).

All comparative analyses must confront the problem of independence in some way. If we were attempting to determine whether the ability to tolerate an elevated body temperature is an adaptation to life in a desert environment we could count the incidence of this ability, and the incidence of its absence, in desert-living animals and those that live elsewhere. We could do the same for a human cultural trait, say a method of convective cooling for dwellings. But if evolutionary change or cultural transmission are possible, we need methods for deciding whether many occurrences of a trait in a particular environment are independent innovations, or many derived instances of a single innovation. Clutton-Brock & Harvey (1977) use nested analyses of variance to decide at what taxonomic level incidences of a trait can be treated as independent and Ridley (1983) uses techniques borrowed and modified from cladistics. Harvey & Mace (1982) provide a guide to the methods and pitfalls of the comparative approach. The kind of problems addressed by these methods have included various aspects of primate social organization (Clutton-Brock & Harvey, 1977, 1979, 1984), and precopulatory mate guarding throughout the animal kingdom (Ridley, 1983).

Can comparative methods be used to determine whether specialized learning mechanisms are adaptations to particular environments? In principle, yes. To return to food-storing birds, if we were to perform a comparative analysis of the incidence of large capacity, long-term memory for spatial locations and the incidence of food storing, we would have four cells to fill: memory (with these features) and caching, no memory and caching, memory and no caching, and no memory and no caching. Adequate data on memory of this kind in birds is not available, but it could in principle be collected. But here a problem arises peculiar to the study of learning. It is not sufficient to score the occurrence and nonoccurrence of learning, because learning of some kind is practically universal. Adaptations that are favored by a wide variety of environments, as must be the case for habituation, formation of simple associations, and other learning phenomena, cannot be analyzed by these methods. Nor can traits that are widespread because of their early evolutionary origin. The properties of learning under investigation must be specified in a more restricted way, and this of course requires criteria for distinguishing different kinds of learning. There is no reason that this could not be done, however, and it is an analysis of this kind that could determine whether unusual properties of learning are specializations to solve particular problems.

CONCLUSIONS

The universality of learning suggests that the evolutionary origin and radiation of learning itself may never be understood. Instead, perhaps the contemporary use of learning to solve particular environmental problems can be. The use of learning to solve a problem can be demonstrated and its properties analyzed using the familiar methods of experimental psychology. Understanding why learning, rather than another solution, has been favored by natural selection requires a different approach, and modeling the costs and benefits of learning and its alternatives is one of these. This will require, however, a good deal more information about the costs of implementing learning.

The discovery that learning is used to solve some environmental problem, no matter how *ecological* that problem may seem, does not imply that the learning mechanism used is adaptively specialized. The idea of adaptive specializations in learning mechanism is an important one, and natural selection of such specializations poses no special evolutionary problem. But few unambiguous instances of adaptive specialization in learning mechanism have been described. This is partly because we are unable to distinguish one learning mechanism from another. Dissociating learning mechanisms on the basis of their neural substrate may help. If this were achieved, it would then be possible to apply comparative methods to determine whether different learning mechanisms are adaptations to particular environmental problems or differ for nonadaptive reasons (Gould & Lewontin, 1979; Mayr, 1983).

Perhaps the major conclusion that should be drawn from this discussion of methods of answering evolutionary questions is that a great deal of work remains to be done gathering basic information on the occurrence of learning and devising criteria for distinguishing one kind of learning mechanism from another before we can attempt to answer any of the really interesting questions to which evolutionary thinking has led us.

ACKNOWLEDGMENTS

I would like to thank Gus Craik, Vicki Esses, Janet Greeley, Paul Harvey, and Jerry Hogan for their many helpful comments on the manuscript, and Dan Schacter for valuable discussion.

REFERENCES

Alexander, R. McN. (1982). *Optima for animals*. London: Edward Arnold.

Andersson, M., & Krebs, J. R. (1978). On the evolution of hoarding behaviour. *Animal Behaviour, 26*, 707–711.

Balda, R. P. (1980). Recovery of cached seeds by a captive *Nucifraga caryocatactes*. *Zeitschrift fur Tierpsychologie, 52*, 331–346.

Beatty, W. W., & Shavalia, D. A. (1980). Spatial memory in rats: Time course of working memory and effect of anesthetics. *Behavioral and Neural Biology, 28*, 454–462.

Bitterman, M. E. (1975). The comparative analysis of learning. *Science, 188*, 699–709.

Buitron, D., & Nuechterlein, G. L. (1985). Experiments on olfactory detection of food caches by black-billed magpies. *Condor, 87*, 92–95.

Clutton-Brock, T. H., & Harvey, P. H. (1977). Primate ecology and social organization. *Journal of Zoology, London, 138*, 1–39.

Clutton-Brock, T. H., & Harvey, P. H. (1979). Comparison and adaptation. *Proceedings of the Royal Society of London, 205B*, 547–565.

Clutton-Brock, T. H., & Harvey, P. H. (1984). Comparative approaches to investigating adaptation. In J. R. Krebs & N. B. Davies (Eds.), *Behavioural ecology*, 2nd ed. (pp. 7–29). Sunderland MA: Sinauer Associates.

Cowie, R. J., Krebs, J. R. & Sherry, D. F. (1981). Food storing by marsh tits. *Animal Behaviour, 29*, 1252–1259.

Davies, N. B. & Houston, A. I. (1981). Owners and satellites: The economics of territory defence in the pied wagtail, *Motacilla alba*. *Journal of Animal Ecology, 50*, 157–180.

Domjan, M., & Galef, B. G. Jr. (1983). Biological constraints on instrumental and classical conditioning: Retrospect and prospect. *Animal Learning & Behavior, 11*, 151–161.

Eikelboom, R., & Stewart, J. (1982). Conditioning of drug-induced physiological responses. *Psychological Review, 5*, 507–528.

Garcia, J., Ervin, F. R., & Koelling, R. A. (1966). Learning with prolonged delay of reinforcement. *Psychonomic Science, 5*, 121–122.

Gibb, J. A. (1960). Populations of tits and goldcrests and their food supply in pine plantations. *Ibis, 102*, 163–208.

Goodale, M. A., & Graves, J. A. (1980a). Failure of interocular transfer of learning in pigeons *Columba livia* trained on a jumping stand. *Bird Behaviour, 2*, 13–22.

Goodale, M. A., & Graves, J. A. (1980b). The relationship between scanning patterns and monocular discrimination learning in the pigeon. *Physiology & Behavior, 25*, 39–43.

Goodale, M. A., & Graves, J. A. (1982). Retinal locus as a factor in interocular transfer in the pigeon. In D. J. Ingle, M. A. Goodale & R. J. W. Mansfield (Eds.), *Analysis of visual behavior* (pp. 211–240). Cambridge MA: MIT Press.

Gould, S. J., & Lewontin, R. C. (1979). The spandrels of San Marco and the Panglossian paradigm: A critique of the adaptationist programme. *Proceedings of the Royal Society of London, 205B*, 581–598.

Grant, D. S. (1976). Effect of sample presentation time on long-delay matching in the pigeon. *Learning and Motivation, 7*, 580–590.

Graves, J. A., & Goodale, M. A. (1977). Failure of interocular transfer in the pigeon (*Columba livia*). *Physiology & Behavior, 19*, 425–428.

Graves, J. A., & Goodale, M. A. (1979). Do training conditions affect interocular transfer in the pigeon? In I. Steele Russell, M. W. Van Hof, & G. Berlucchi (Eds.), *Structure and function of the cerebral commissures* (pp. 73–86). London: Macmillan.

Haftorn, S. (1974). Storage of surplus food by the boreal chickadee *Parus hudsonicus* in Alaska, with some records on the mountain chickadee *Parus gambeli* in Colorado. *Ornis Scandanavica, 5*, 145–161.

Harrington, F. H. (1981). Urine-marking and caching behavior in the wolf. *Behaviour, 76*, 280–288.

Harvey, P. H., & Mace, G. M. (1982). Comparisons between taxa and adaptive trends: Problems of methodology. In King's Sociobiology Group (Eds.), *Current problems in sociobiology* (pp. 343–361). Cambridge: Cambridge University Press.

Henry, J. D. (1977). The use of urine marking in the scavenging behavior of the red fox (*Vulpes vulpes*). *Behaviour, 61*, 82–106.

Higuchi, H. (1977). Stored nuts *Castanopsis cuspidata* as a food resource of nestling varied tits *Parus varius*. *Tori, 26*, 9–12.

Houston, A. I., Kacelnik, A., & McNamara, J. (1982). Some learning rules for acquiring information. In D. J. McFarland (Ed.), *Functional ontogeny* (pp. 140–191). London: Pitman.

Johnston, T. D. (1982). The selective costs and benefits of learning: An evolutionary analysis. *Advances in the Study of Behavior, 12*, 65–106.

Källander, H. (1978). Hoarding in the rook *Corvus frugilegus*. *Anser, Supplement, 3*, 124–128.

Kamil, A. C., & Balda, R. C. (1985). Cache recovery and spatial memory in Clark's nutcrackers (*Nucifraga columbiana*). *Journal of Experimental Psychology: Animal Behavior Processes, 11*, 95–111.

Krebs, J. R., Stephens, D. W., & Sutherland, W. J. (1983). Perspectives in optimal foraging. In A. H. Brush & G. A. Clark Jr. (Eds.) *Perspectives in ornithology* (pp. 165–216). New York: Cambridge University Press.

Levine, J. (1945). Studies in the interrelations of central nervous structures in binocular vision: II. The conditions under which interocular transfer of discriminative habits takes place in the pigeon. *Journal of Genetic Psychology, 67*, 131–142.

Lewontin, R. C. (1978). Adaptation. *Scientific American, 239*, 212–230.

Löhrl, H. (1950). Beobachtungen zur Soziologie und Verhaltensweise von Sumpfmeisen (*Parus palustris communis*) im Winter. *Zeitschrift fur Tierpsychologie, 7*, 417–424.

Macdonald, D. W. (1976). Food caching by red foxes and some other carnivores. *Zeitschrift fur Tierpsychologie, 42*, 170–185.

Maynard Smith, J. (1978). Optimization theory in evolution. *Annual Review of Ecology and Systematics, 9*, 31–56.

Mayr, E. (1983). How to carry out the adaptationist program? *American Naturalist, 121*, 324–334.

Nichols, J. T. (1958). Food habits and behavior of the gray squirrel. *Journal of Mammalogy, 39*, 376–380.

Olton, D. S., & Samuelson, R. J. (1976). Remembrance of places passed: Spatial memory in rats. *Journal of Experimental Psychology: Animal Behavior Processes, 2*, 97–116.

Platt, J. R. (1964). Strong inference. *Science, 146*, 347–353.

Pyke, G. H., Pulliam, H. R., & Charnov, E. L. (1977). Optimal foraging: A selective review of theory and tests. *Quarterly Review of Biology, 52*, 137–154.

Ridley, M. (1983). *The explanation of organic diversity.* Oxford: Clarendon Press.

Roberts, W. A. (1979). Spatial memory in the rat on a hierarchical maze. *Learning and Motivation, 10,* 117–140.

Roper, T. (1983). Learning as a biological phenomenon. In T. R. Halliday & P. J. B. Slater (Eds.), *Animal behaviour, Volume 3: Genes, development and learning* (pp. 178–212). Oxford: Blackwell Scientific Publications.

Rozin, P., & Kalat, J. W. (1971). Specific hungers and poison avoidance as adaptive specializations of learning. *Psychological Review, 78,* 459–486.

Sherry, D. F. (1982). Food storage, memory, and marsh tits. *Animal Behaviour, 30,* 631–633.

Sherry, D. F. (1984a). Food storage by black-capped chickadees: Memory for the location and contents of caches. *Animal Behaviour, 32,* 451–464.

Sherry, D. F. (1984b). What food-storing birds remember. *Canadian Journal of Psychology, 38,* 304–321.

Sherry, D. F. (1985). Food storage by birds and mammals. *Advances in the Study of Behavior, 17,* 153–188.

Sherry, D., Avery, M., & Stevens, A. (1982). The spacing of stored food by marsh tits. *Zeitschrift fur Tierpsychologie, 58,* 153–162.

Sherry, D. F., Krebs, J. R., & Cowie, R. J. (1981). Memory for the location of stored food in marsh tits. *Animal Behaviour, 29,* 1260–1266.

Shettleworth, S. J. (1983). Function and mechanism in learning. In M. D. Zeiler & P. Harzem (Eds.), *Advances in the analysis of behaviour, Volume 3* (pp. 1–39). New York: Wiley.

Shettleworth, S. J., & Krebs, J. R. (1982). How marsh tits find their hoards: The roles of site preference and spatial memory. *Journal of Experimental Psychology: Animal Behavior Processes, 8,* 354–375.

Siegel, S. (1983). Classical conditioning, drug tolerance, and drug dependence. In Y. Israel, F. B. Glaser, H. Kalant, R. E. Popham, W. Schmidt, & R. G. Smart (Eds.), *Research advances in alcohol and drug problems, Volume 7,* (pp. 207–246), New York: Plenum.

Stevens, A. (1984). *The food storage behaviour of marsh tits and shrikes.* Unpublished doctoral thesis, Oxford University.

Swanberg, P. O. (1951). Food storage, territory and song in the thick-billed nutcracker. In S. Horstadius (Ed.), *Proceedings of the Xth International Ornithological Congress* (pp. 545–554). Uppsala: Almquist & Wicksells.

Swanberg, P. O. (1981). Kullstorleken hos nötkråka, *Nucifraga caryocatactes* i Skandinavien, relaterad till föregående års hasselnöttillgång. *Vår Fågelvärld, 40,* 399–408.

Tomback, D. F. (1978). Foraging strategies of Clark's nutcracker. *Living Bird, 16,* 123–161.

Tomback, D. F. (1980). How nutcrackers find their seed stores. *Condor, 82,* 10–19.

Tulving, E. (1985). On the classification problem in learning and memory. In L.-G. Nilsson & T. Archer (Eds.), *Perspectives in learning and memory,* (pp. 67–94). Hillsdale NJ: Lawrence Erlbaum Associates.

Vander Wall, S. B. (1982). An experimental analysis of cache recovery in Clark's nutcracker. *Animal Behaviour, 30,* 84–94.

Vander Wall, S. B., & Balda, R. P. (1977). Coadaptations of the Clark's nutcracker and the pinon pine for efficient seed harvest and dispersal. *Ecological Monographs, 47,* 89–111.

Vander Wall, S. B., & Balda, R. P. (1981). Ecology and evolution of food-storage behavior in conifer-seed-caching corvids. *Zeitschrift fur Tierpsychologie, 56,* 217–242.

Vander Wall, S. B., & Hutchins, H. E. (1983). Dependence of Clark's nutcracker, *Nucifraga columbiana,* on conifer seeds during the postfledging period. *Canadian Field-naturalist, 97,* 208–214.

Van Hof, M. W., & Van der Mark, F. (1976). Monocular pattern discrimination in normal and monocularly light-deprived rabbits. *Physiology & Behavior, 16,* 775–781.

Vaughan, W. Jr., & Greene, S. L. (1984). Pigeon visual memory capacity. *Journal of Experimental Psychology: Animal Behavior Processes, 10,* 256–271.

Wenzel, B. M. (1971). Olfaction in birds. In L. M. Beidler (Ed.), *Handbook of sensory physiology, Volume 4,* (pp. 432–448). Heidelberg: Springer Verlag.

Wilde, O. (1891). *The picture of Dorian Gray.* London: Ward Lock.

6

A Comparison of Taste Aversion Learning in Humans and Other Vertebrates: Evolutionary Pressures in Common

A. W. Logue
State University of New York at Stony Brook

Taste aversion learning occurs when an animal eats something, becomes gastrointestinally ill, and then shows a decreased tendency to eat that food again. The name taste aversion learning arises from the fact that frequently the taste of the food becomes aversive. The general presumption is that taste aversion learning assists animals in avoiding poisonous or inadequate food (see, for example, Gustavson, 1977; Logue, 1986; Rozin & Kalat, 1971; Seligman, 1970). Most vertebrates, and possibly also some invertebrates, can acquire taste aversions (Daly, Rauschenberger, & Behrends, 1982; Gustavson, 1977; Terk & Green, 1980).

This chapter uses examples from the taste aversion literature to illustrate how evolution might affect learning, and thereby to demonstrate that there is much to be gained from the study of general principles of learning. To accomplish this, first, the history of the argument concerning taste aversion learning as a different kind of learning is briefly summarized. Second, the acquisition of taste aversions by humans and by other vertebrate species is compared. Attempts are made to assess the adaptiveness of the different species' behavior. Finally, drawing from the evidence presented for these comparisons, some of the ways in which evolution might and might not affect learning are discussed.

Sections that discuss the relationship between taste aversion learning and evolution are of necessity somewhat speculative. Assessment of the adaptiveness of a particular behavior requires extensive experimentation as well as investigation of the subject's ecological niche, work that has yet to be done for taste aversion learning in any substantial way (see Domjan & Galef, 1983, for further discussion). Nevertheless, certain statements about the adaptiveness of taste aversion learning in different species can be made and will be helpful in evaluating the effects of evolution on learning.

THE UNUSUAL PROPERTIES OF TASTE AVERSION
LEARNING

During the 1950s and 1960s a series of publications by John Garcia and others (see, for example, Garcia, Kimeldorf, & Koelling, 1955; Garcia & Koelling, 1967) suggested that taste aversion learning followed laws that differed from the laws followed by more traditional learning tasks. For example, the longest delay between eating food (the conditioned stimulus, the CS) and gastrointestinal illness (the unconditioned stimulus, the US) that would still result in acquisition of a taste aversion was about 24 hours (Etscorn & Stephens, 1973), as compared with a maximum delay of a few seconds between a lever press and food in the acquisition of lever pressing (Kimble, 1961).

The theoretical implications of this research were made explicit in two critical papers published in 1970 and 1971. The first of these, by Seligman, postulated that organisms are biologically prepared to associate certain stimuli with certain reinforcers. For example, most species are prepared to associate tastes with gastrointestinal illness. According to Seligman, the acquisition of prepared associations follows different laws from the acquisition of other associations. Prepared associations might be acquired with longer delays between stimuli and reinforcers, might generalize more easily, and might be harder to extinguish. Thus, while Seligman retained the concept of general laws of learning, he assumed that different sets of general laws applied to prepared and unprepared associations. Within Seligman's theoretical framework, evolution could affect how learning occurred, as well as affecting anatomy.

Rozin and Kalat took this approach a step further with their paper published in 1971. They stated that there are no general laws. Each species' behavior on each task, they argued, is individually shaped by evolution (see also Bolles, 1973).

Over the next decade the number of research articles published on taste aversion learning exploded (see the bibliographies by Riley & Clarke, 1977, and Riley & Tuck, 1985). The properties of taste aversion learning were extensively explored as the key to understanding the effects of evolution on learning. By the end of the 1970s a reaction occurred: The opinion that taste aversion might not be as different from other forms of learning as was once thought became increasingly common (see, for example, Domjan, 1980, 1983; Domjan & Galef, 1983; Logue, 1979; Revusky, 1977; Shettleworth, 1983; Spiker, 1977; Testa & Ternes, 1977). These papers concluded that taste aversion learning followed general laws through comparing taste aversion learning with the learning of more traditional laboratory tasks.

TASTE AVERSION LEARNING IN HUMANS AND OTHER SPECIES

Comparing taste aversion learning with the learning of more traditional laboratory tasks is one of two major strategies that can be employed in examining the generality of taste aversion learning. The other strategy involves comparing taste aversion learning across different species. The following section uses this latter strategy to support the view that there are general laws of learning. Comparisons are made between taste aversion learning in humans and in other vertebrate species.

Such comparisons should provide a strong test of the hypothesis that there are general laws of learning because, while all of the species under comparison are vertebrates, only humans possess language, and language might affect the acquisition of taste aversions. The behavior of human subjects in operant conditioning experiments is apparently strongly affected by the type of instructions given to the subjects, and by the subjects' ability to count and to engage in other language behaviors (see Catania, Matthews, & Shimoff, 1982; Lowe, 1979, 1983). Language might also play a role in taste aversion learning.

Comparisons between taste aversion learning in different species can focus on both how easily aversions are acquired in the different species, as well as on the ways in which aversions are acquired in the different species. Interpretation of the former type of comparisons can be complicated by the fact that different species may react differently when they are exposed to novel foods and when they are made ill (see, for example, Daly et al., 1982). Therefore the focus here is on comparing how taste aversions are acquired in different species.

Another constraint on the comparisons examined here is the fact that findings from experiments on taste aversion learning in humans have so far been limited. Most of these experiments have focused on simply determining whether taste aversions could or could not be obtained. For example, Bernstein (1978; Bernstein & Webster, 1980) has shown that chemotherapy can function as the US in taste aversion learning, and several researchers have shown that taste aversions to alcohol can be acquired by some alcoholics (Baker & Cannon, 1979; Boland, Mellor, & Revusky, 1978; Lemere & Voegtlin, 1940; Logue, Logue, & Strauss, 1983; Mellor & White, 1978; Wiens, Montague, Manaugh, & English, 1976). Because ethical considerations prohibit extensive experimentation on taste aversion learning in humans, it has been necessary with human subjects to rely largely on retrospective questionnaire studies of naturally occurring taste aversions (Garb & Stunkard, 1974; Logue et al., 1983; Logue, Ophir, & Strauss, 1981). A final concern in comparing human taste aversion learning with that of other vertebrate species is the fact that the majority of nonhuman work has been limited to rats. Data collected using other species will be discussed as much as possible.

Long-Delay Learning

One of the properties that most clearly distinguishes taste aversion learning from other types of learning is the 24-hour delays that are possible between the CS and the US when rats are used as the subjects (Etscorn & Stephens, 1973). Humans can also learn taste aversions with long delays. Garb and Stunkard's (1974) subjects reported delays of up to 6 hours between the CS and the US. Logue et al. (1981) studied 123 naturally occurring aversions in which the subjects ate something following illness and then acquired the aversion. Logue et al. obtained delays of up to 3 hours for 91% of the aversions. Another 8% of the aversions were reported as having been acquired with CS–US delays ranging between 3 and 7 hours. One longer CS–US delay, a delay of 72 hours, was reported.

While these delays are generally not as long as those used successfully by Etscorn and Stephens with rats, Garb and Stunkard and Logue et al. were studying reports of naturally occurring taste aversions. Etscorn and Stephens, on the other hand, studied rats in a laboratory situation using unusual tastes (saccharin or HCL solutions) as the CS with no tastes intervening between the CS and the US. This procedure maximizes the acquisition of an aversion (Logue, 1979). Because human subjects occasionally appear to acquire aversions under uncontrolled conditions with as much as 7-hour CS-US delays, using Etscorn and Stephens' procedure with human subjects would probably result in maximum CS-US delays as long as those obtained with rats.

In nature, virtually all species must at least occasionally choose between novel food sources, and frequently some of the alternatives are poisonous (Gustavson, 1977). It is therefore adaptive to avoid eating a food that has preceded illness. Because illness from a poisonous substance sometimes takes several hours to develop, such learning is useless unless aversions can be acquired even with long delays between the CS and the US. Otherwise organisms would fail to avoid many poisonous foods, and would die. Consequently it is not surprising that both rats and humans, two omnivorous species that frequently sample novel foods of all types, show long-delay taste aversion learning.

Stimulus Specificity

Another aspect of taste aversion learning that has attracted a great deal of attention from researchers is the fact that organisms appear to associate some stimuli with illness more easily than other stimuli. Rats are predisposed to associate tastes with illness (Garcia & Koelling, 1966; Larsen & Hyde, 1977; Miller & Domjan, 1981), while a species with a more highly developed visual system, quail, are predisposed to associate visual stimuli with illness (Wilcoxon, Dragoin, & Kral, 1971). Pigeons (Logue, 1980), chicks (Gilette, Martin, & Bellingham, 1980), and blue jays (Brower, 1969) also appear to easily associate visual stimuli with illness. Braveman (1974, 1975) found that guinea pigs, a species whose visual system is no more developed than that of the rat, but which searches visually for food, easily acquire aversions to visual stimuli. Braveman postulated that a species is prepared to associate with illness the types of stimuli that it uses to search for food.

Recent research, however, suggests that for most species taste stimuli are usually involved in the formation of illness-induced aversions to food. If a visual stimulus and a taste are simultaneously paired with illness in either pigeons or quail, the resulting aversion to the visual stimulus is stronger than if the visual stimulus is used alone (Lett, 1980). Similarly, if an odor and a taste are simultaneously paired with illness in rats, the resulting aversion to the odor is stronger than if the odor is used alone (Durlach & Rescorla, 1980; Palmerino, Rusiniak, & Garcia, 1980). Gustavson (1977), summarizing data from 33 species, has found that for most of these species the taste of a food easily becomes aversive.

With humans, taste stimuli also appear to be easily associated with illness. Like rats, humans more easily learn to avoid consuming a beverage with illness as the US than with shock as the US (Lamon, Wilson, & Leaf, 1977). The majority of Garb and Stunkard's (1974) subjects reported acquiring their aversions to the taste of a food. Logue's (Logue et al., 1981; Logue et al., 1983) 410 college student subjects and 48 hospitalized alcoholic subjects reported what aspects of the subsequently aversive food became aversive when they acquired naturally occurring illness-induced food aversions. Both groups of subjects stated that the taste became aversive in approximately 80% of the aversions. The next most frequently reported aspect of the food to become aversive was the food's smell (about 50% of the aversions).

Shettleworth (1983) has argued persuasively that tastes may be easily associated with illness because of certain unique physical characteristics of tastes, such as their rates of onset and termination, and their duration. The fact remains, however, that some characteristic or characteristics intrinsic to tastes are responsible for the ease with which tastes are associated with illness.

Irrespective of the mechanism, the ease of association of taste with illness among most vertebrate species (Gustavson, 1977) is adaptive. Taste is the last modality stimulated before a potentially dangerous food enters the gastrointestinal tract. Taste therefore offers the last opportunity for detection and rejection of a poisonous food (Rozin & Fallon, 1981). An animal's chance of survival is clearly better if it can easily associate taste with illness, even if its sense of taste is not particularly well developed.

Cause of Illness

When shock is paired with a taste, a rat will usually avoid that taste only in the particular environment in which it received the shock. However, if illness is paired with a taste, a rat will avoid that taste wherever it is encountered. Such evidence has been interpreted as demonstrating that a taste paired with shock becomes a signal for shock, while a taste paired with illness actually changes in hedonic value (Garcia, McGowan, & Green, 1972).

In Logue et al.'s (1981) retrospective questionnaire study of naturally occurring taste aversions in college students, the subjects had not eaten the food since the aversion incident for 62% of the aversions. This was despite a mean of over 5 years since the aversions had formed. In Logue et al.'s (1983) similar study with alcoholics, the subjects had not eaten the food since the aversion incident for 58% of the taste aversions. On the average 20 years had elapsed since these aversions had formed. In both studies the subjects reported a mean preference for these foods just after the aversion had formed of approximately 1 on a scale ranging from 1 (lowest) to 5 (highest). These data all suggest that, like rats, when human subjects acquire a taste aversion they avoid that taste wherever it occurs.

Another way of eliciting information from humans relevant to this question is to ask the subjects what caused their illness when they acquired their naturally occurring taste aversions. If the subjects report taste aversions as occurring only due to food-related illness, those findings might suggest that the aversive taste is functioning as a signal for illness in these subjects. However, if nonfood-related causes are reported as well as food-related causes, such findings would suggest that the taste can become aversive simply through its association with illness, independent of its signaling properties for future instances of illness.

Children ranging from 2- to 18-years-of-age in Bernstein's (1978; Bernstein, Webster, & Bernstein, 1982) experiments frequently formed aversions to foods that they consumed prior to chemotherapy even though most of the children knew that their illness had been caused by the chemotherapy. In both of Logue et al.'s previous studies about 60% of the taste-aversion illnesses were attributed by the subjects to the food that became aversive. However, for about 40% of the aversions the subjects either did not know what caused their illness, or they attributed it to another food that did not become aversive or to nonfood-related origins. In many cases, pairing of illness and consumption of a food appears sufficient to result in a taste aversion, independent of the causes of the illness.

When an experimenter injects a rat with the poison lithium chloride after the rat has just drunk saccharin, when a rat acquires an aversion due to tumor anorexia (Bernstein & Sigmundi, 1980), and when a human eats Sauce Bernaise just prior to becoming ill with the stomach flu (Seligman, 1972), the subjects' subsequent aversions are not adaptive. Avoiding future instances of saccharin or Sauce Bernaise in nature will not help the rat or the human to avoid illness. Despite humans' use of language they, like rats, appear susceptible to treating correlations as causations. In this respect both species behave similarly although at times their behavior is maladaptive.

Preference and Familiarity

Rats acquire taste aversions more easily to foods that are less familiar and less preferred (Etscorn, 1973; Kalat, 1974; Kurz & Levitsky, 1982). Similarly, humans report that their naturally occurring taste aversions are more likely to have occurred to foods that were less familiar and less preferred than other foods eaten at the same time or between that time and the onset of illness (Logue et al., 1981, 1983). Likewise, approximately 45% of the aversions reported to Garb and Stunkard (1974) were to foods that the subjects rated as novel, and 53% were to foods that the subjects rated as neutral or nonpreferred.

In many situations, including consumption of food, preference and familiarity tend to be correlated (Birch & Marlin, 1982; Zajonc, 1968). Presumably this is because familiar objects and substances that have not caused harm in the past are unlikely to do so in the future and are therefore preferred. When an organism is faced with two foods, one novel and less preferred, and one familiar and more preferred, it is adaptive to choose the familiar, more preferred food as that food is less likely to be poisonous. Both humans and rats appear to behave similarly, and adaptively, in tending to form taste aversions to less familiar, less preferred foods.

Extinction and Forgetting

It is easier to remove a taste aversion in a rat by exposing the rat to the taste with no accompanying illness (extinction) than by simply allowing time to pass (forgetting, see Balagura & Smith, 1970; Baum, Foidart, & Lapointe, 1974; Domjan, 1975; Garcia, Ervin, & Koelling, 1966; Grote & Brown, 1973; Nowlis, 1974). To obtain sufficient information to examine this question in humans would require inducing illness in many human subjects. This approach is not ethically feasible, but some relevant evidence can be obtained by asking human subjects to report the progression of their past preferences for foods that became aversive under natural conditions. Subjects could be asked what their preferences were for such foods just prior to the aversions forming, just after the aversions formed, just prior to and just after the subjects ate the foods again (if the foods were ever eaten again), as well as what their preferences were for these foods at the time of the study.

When this was done using Logue et al.'s (1981) college-student population, the data were consistent with the hypothesis that for humans, also, taste aversions are more likely to decrease if the food is consumed subsequent to the initial aversion incident than if it is not. Subjects who never ate the food again reported similar, though slightly lower preferences for the aversive foods just prior to and just after the aversions formed than were reported by subjects who did eat the food again. However, at the time of the study, the former subjects reported much lower preferences than did the latter subjects. Further, if a subject reported eating the food again and feeling ill upon doing so, that subject's reported aversion to the food increased, while if a subject reported eating the food again and not feeling ill, that subject's reported aversion decreased.

Given a poisonous food that has become aversive through association with illness, the passage of time by itself is less likely to be correlated with a decrease in the toxicity of that food than is consuming the food without any subsequent illness. The former may or may not indicate that a decrease has occurred, while the latter is proof positive. Therefore it is adaptive that both humans and rats should exhibit a greater decrease in their aversions with an extinction than with a forgetting paradigm.

It is more difficult to explain why there appear to be testosterone-mediated sex differences in the extinction of aversions in rats and some strains of mice (see, for example, Chambers & Sengstake, 1976; Ingram & Corfman, 1981). The adaptive significance of sex, species, or strain differences in the extinction of aversions is not readily apparent. Further investigation is clearly needed on this topic.

The Effects of Age

Taste aversions appear to be easily acquired by children as well as by human adults. Approximately 6% of the aversions reported by the college students in Logue et al.'s (1981) study were reported as having been acquired between the ages of 2 and 5 years. It is possible that these subjects also acquired aversions at even younger ages; infants and toddlers frequently consume new foods and they also frequently become gastrointestinally ill. However, when such events occur prior to the age of 2 years they are unlikely to be remembered (Campbell & Coulter, 1976). Garb and Stunkard's (1974) retrospective questionnaire study also found that many of the reported aversions had been acquired at young ages. Approximately 12% of the aversions reported to them were acquired under the age of 6. Finally, Bernstein (1978; Bernstein et al., 1982) has shown that children as young as 2-years-of-age acquire aversions to a novel ice cream or to familiar foods whose consumption is followed by chemotherapy. These aversions are acquired after only one pairing of the food and the illness resulting from the chemotherapy.

Neonatal rats also acquire aversions easily. Aversions have been formed to tastes by rats as young as 5-days-of-age (Gemberling, Domjan, & Amsel, 1980), and to odors by rats as young as 2-days-of-age (Rudy & Cheatle, 1979). There has been some evidence, however, that young rats do not acquire aversions to tastes as readily as do older rats (Martin & Alberts, 1979; Springer & Fraley, 1981), possibly due to young rats' difficulties in witholding consumption and their relatively low sensitivity to tastes and illness (Martin & Timmins, 1980). Further, similar to humans, aversions acquired by rat pups may not be retained as long as those acquired by adult rats (Steinert, Infurna, & Spear, 1980). Guinea pigs, most of whose behaviors mature at early ages, appear to be able to easily acquire aversions to tastes soon after birth (Kalat, 1975). Chickens are another species whose behaviors are mostly mature at very young ages. Gillette et al. (1980) found that 1.5-day-old chicks easily formed aversions to red food and to red water.

Most young animals, including humans, appear to be able to acquire taste aversions, at least to some extent. The evidence for early taste aversion learning is better for two species, guinea pigs and chickens, that forage for food on their own at young ages, in comparison with two species that do not, humans and rats. Thus, although taste aversion learning appears to occur throughout the lifespan of all of these species, this type of learning appears to be stronger at young ages in species that are more likely to encounter poisonous foods at those ages.

Generalization

In order to increase the likelihood of avoiding foods that cause illness, foods should be avoided in accordance with their qualitative similarity to foods that have previously caused illness. The more qualitatively similar a food is to a food that has previously caused illness, the more that food should be avoided. For example, if one taste causes illness, a qualitatively similar taste may also, and that likelihood increases with the qualitative similarity of the tastes. On the other hand, if a particular stimulus is associated with poison, simply increasing the amount of that same stimulus should indicate more poison, and therefore foods containing large amounts of that stimulus should be avoided more than foods containing small amounts (stimulus intensity dynamism, Hull, 1949).

Humans, rats, hamsters, and quail all seem to follow these adaptive principles. The taste of saccharin appears to change qualitatively as a function of saccharin concentration (Collier & Novell, 1967), and rats poisoned after drinking one concentration of saccharin also show aversions to similar concentrations of saccharin (Logue, 1978).

Both rats and hamsters show aversions to sucrose after being poisoned following consumption of solutions described as sweet by humans, to NaCl following consumption of salty solutions, to quinine hydrochloride following consumption of sour or bitter solutions, and to HCl following consumption of sour solutions (Nowlis, Frank, & Pfaffmann, 1980). Domjan (1975) reported that after saccharin had been made aversive to rats through contingent poison, casein hydrolysate, but not vinegar, was also subsequently avoided. Domjan drew the plausible conclusion that casein hydrolysate tastes more like saccharin than does vinegar. In experiments in which rats actively ingested LiCl (Balagura & Smith, 1970; Nachman, 1963; Smith & Balagura, 1969), the taste of the LiCl became aversive and the aversion generalized to NaCl, a substance that causes responses similar to LiCl in the chorda tympani nerve (Nachman, 1963). Parker and Revusky (1982) examined generalization extensively by testing generalization between all possible pairs of 10 solutions. The subjects, rats, tended to generalize between pairs of solutions that humans would describe as qualitatively similar, for example, sugar and saccharin, and not to generalize between pairs of solutions that humans would not describe as qualitatively similar, for example, sugar and coffee.

On the other hand, quail poisoned after drinking one intensity of blue water show increasing aversions to increasing intensities of blue water (stimulus intensity dynamism, Czaplicki, Borrebach, & Wilcoxon, 1976). In addition, rats poisoned after drinking one concentration of salt show evidence both of aversions to similar concentrations and of stimulus intensity dynamism (Nowlis, 1974).

Finally, human subjects who acquire taste aversions under natural conditions also report aversions to qualitatively similar foods. Logue et al. (1981) found that such generalizations were reported for about one-third of the aversions. For example, an aversion to chili generalized to Sloppy Joes; an aversion to fried chicken generalized to other greasy, fried foods; an aversion to chocolate chip cookies generalized to anything made of chocolate; and an aversion to Southern Comfort generalized to most strong-smelling and strong-tasting liquors.

There are some human subjects, however, who do not report generalization of their naturally occurring aversions. Logue et al. (1983) found that both hospitalized alcoholics and college student heavy consumers of alcohol reported virtually no generalization of their aversions. Only 10% of the aversions reported by the hospitalized alcoholics generalized, while none of the aversions reported by the college student heavy consumers of alcohol generalized. Note that this lack of generalization applied to taste aversions to all foods and drinks, not just to taste aversions to alcoholic beverages.

The maladaptive lack of generalization shown by these subjects may be related to their indulging in another maladaptive behavior: excessive drinking. Excessive drinking frequently causes gastrointestinal illness, and therefore should result in frequent aversions to alcohol. Indeed, approximately one-fourth of the aversions reported in Logue et al.'s (1981) original study with college students were to alcoholic beverages. Perhaps people who drink excessively do so because they do not generalize any acquired alcoholic-beverage aversions to other alcoholic beverages, thus enabling them to continue drinking. This hypothesis is consistent with previous evidence indicating that alcoholics treated using a taste-aversion paradigm will sometimes simply switch to drinking another alcoholic beverage that has not been paired with illness (Mellor & White, 1978; Quinn & Henbest, 1967).

Aversion Formation Without Food Consumption

Aversions to Visual, Textual, and Olfactory Stimuli.   An organism that could avoid a poisonous food without having to actually taste that food would have a survival advantage over an organism that could not. Birds, which can easily form aversions to visual stimuli, clearly have this advantage. For example, after having eaten monarch butterflies, which contain poisonous cardiac glycosides, blue jays form aversions to all butterflies that have the appearance of monarchs (Brower, 1969). Human subjects can use a number of different cues to reject an aversive food prior to its entering the mouth. In Logue et al.'s (1981) original study with college students, 51% of the aversions formed to the smell of the food, 32% to its texture, and 26% to its appearance. One of the 415 aversions reported by Logue's subjects was to an incense that the subject was smelling at the time of illness. Monkeys can also acquire aversions to visual stimuli (Johnson, Beaton, & Hall, 1975), as well as to tactile stimuli (Domjan, Miller, & Gemberling, 1982). Rats' visual systems are not well developed, but this species can still acquire aversions to visual stimuli under controlled conditions (Best, Best, & Henggeler, 1977; Braveman, 1977). Rats can also form aversions to odors (Lorden, Kenfield, & Braun, 1970), and to textual stimuli (Domjan & Hanlon, 1982).

Although taste is frequently the only way to identify a food precisely, various species have apparently evolved so that cues other than taste can be used to identify unsuitable food before it enters the mouth.

Observational Learning.   Another way to learn which foods are posionous without the risk of consuming the food is to watch what happens when someone else eats the food. Observational learning is an established phenomenon among animals (Mackintosh, 1974). Consistent with these findings, there is some evidence that rats can acquire aversions to specific foods by observing other rats which have become ill after eating that food, possibly through the use of olfactory cues (Coombes, Revusky, & Lett, 1980; Lavin, Freise, & Coombes, 1980; Revusky, Coombes, & Pohl, 1982; Stierhoff & Lavin, 1982).

Humans can also acquire knowledge about foods from others. Birch (1980) has shown that nursery school children will increase their preference for specific foods if the children regularly eat those foods with other children who have a high preference for those foods. Further, in Logue et al.'s (1981) college student sample, two subjects appeared to have acquired aversions through observational learning. One subject watched his baby brother dribbling baby food and subsequently developed an aversion to baby food. Another subject ate coconut and became nauseated and consequently developed an aversion to coconut. This subject felt that her nausea was psychological and entirely due to her father having had extreme allergic reactions to coconut every time he had eaten it.

Whatever the mechanisms involved, both rats and humans do appear to demonstrate the adaptive behavior of acquiring aversions to foods that have made other organisms ill. In addition, to the extent that organisms which are related tend to inhabit the same geographical locations, observational learning of taste aversions would increase not only individual organisms' chances of survival, but would increase their relatives' chances of survival as well (their inclusive fitness, Hamilton, 1964a, 1964b).

Order of the CS and the US

It has been easier to obtain taste aversions in rats by presenting the CS prior to the US (forward conditioning) or by presenting the CS and the US simultaneously (simultaneous conditioning), than by presenting the US prior to the CS (backward conditioning, Logue, 1979). Consistent with these findings, Logue et al. (1981, 1983), in their studies of naturally occurring taste aversions in college students, alcoholics, college-student heavy consumers of alcohol, and anorexic/bulimic women, found virtually no reported instances of aversions in which the US had preceded the CS. Only 7 out of 238 aversions examined were reported as involving backward conditioning.

This low frequency of backward conditioning was reported despite the fact that half of the college student subjects (Logue et al. 1981) received instructions that should have biased them to report backward conditioning. While half of the subjects were asked whether they had ever eaten or drunk something and felt nauseated and not wanted to eat or drink that thing afterwards, the other half were asked whether they had ever felt nauseated and eaten or drunk something and not wanted to eat or drink that thing afterwards. There were no significant differences in the patterns of CS–US temporal relationships of the aversions reported by these two groups of subjects.

Apparently, for humans as well as rats, it is easier to associate taste with illness when the taste precedes or accompanies the illness than when the taste follows the illness. Such behavior is adaptive. A food cannot have caused illness if consumption of that food follows illness. Animals' predisposition to associate tastes with illness that accompanies or follows those tastes increases the likelihood that taste aversions will be acquired to foods that actually cause illness.

THE EFFECTS OF EVOLUTION ON LEARNING

The above comparisons of human taste aversion learning with taste aversion learning in other species can be used to examine some of the possible effects of evolution on learning.

Generality

Despite large differences in their physiology and in their abilities, the apparent similarities between taste aversion learning in humans and other species are extensive. To summarize:

1. Aversions can be acquired even with long CS-US delays.
2. The taste of foods is an essential factor in the acquisition of aversions.
3. A food associated with illness will be avoided even in a new environmental context.

4. Aversions are more likely to form to less preferred and less familiar foods.
5. Aversions are removed more easily if the food is eaten without accompanying illness, rather than simply allowing time to pass.
6. Aversions generalize to similar foods.
7. Aversions can form to a food without the food actually being consumed.
8. Aversions can form through observational learning.
9. Aversions are acquired more easily if the CS precedes or accompanies the US.

The only species-specific differences that were found concerned which types of stimuli were most easily associated with illness. Humans and some birds appear to easily associate visual stimuli with illness, while rats do not. However all species appear either to acquire aversions easily to tastes associated with illness, or to acquire greater aversions to visual or olfactory stimuli when they are paired with tastes.

These similarities are not surprising. There are several ways by which they might have arisen through the effects of evolution. For example, different species might acquire taste aversions similarly because of common evolutionary origins. By itself, however, this reason seems insufficient. Birds, rats, and humans have all had sufficient time to evolve into extremely different creatures, not only in terms of their anatomy but in terms of their behavior as well. Humans exhibit complex language behavior, some birds show critical periods during which they may become unusually attached to certain individual organisms (imprinting), and female rats sometimes eat their infant offspring.

The extensive similarities between the taste aversion learning behavior of humans and other animals seem unlikely to have persisted, despite common evolutionary origins, unless at least some of these behaviors were adaptive for all of these species. These species must be subject to common evolutionary pressures in terms of identifying and avoiding poisonous foods. As each of the characteristics of taste aversion learning was described earlier for the different species, the adaptiveness of each characteristic was explored. This adaptiveness did not differ as a function of the species under consideration. All vertebrate species, even those with highly specialized diets, must be prepared to avoid possible poisonous foods (Gustavson, 1977), and these species seem to have all acquired similar, efficient ways of solving this problem. Different species may be exposed to similar situations that result in similar evolutionary pressures and thus in similar behavior across species.

Errors in Adaptiveness

Yet not all of the examples of taste aversion learning examined above for humans and other species were adaptive. Several types of errors can occur, resulting in the formation of aversions to foods that are not poisonous.

One type of error occurs when a taste and illness are both present and an aversion is formed even though the illness was not caused by the food. This type of error is not limited to rats in artificial laboratory situations. As described earlier, someone can acquire an aversion to eating Sauce Bearnaise when the stomach flu, and not the sauce, has caused the illness. Such an aversion is not adaptive. Sauce Bearnaise consists mainly of butter and eggs, and while the butter may not contain significant nutrition, certainly the eggs do.

Because organisms easily associate tastes with illness, an aversion is likely to occur any time that a relatively novel taste and illness occur in close temporal contiguity with the taste preceding or accompanying the illness. The fact that tastes, and not other types of stimuli, most easily associate with illness may decrease the likelihood of this type of error. If all species easily associated visual and olfactory stimuli with illness, they might be more likely to form aversions to one of the many sights and smells that are always present in the environment and that they have experienced prior to an illness, even if no food was actually consumed.

Another type of error that can be made occurs when aversions are formed to foods that are poisonous now, but are unlikely to be poisonous in the future. One of the more commonly reported food classes to which aversions formed in Logue et al.'s studies with normal college students (1981) and with hospitalized alcoholics (1983) was shellfish (20 out of a total of 465 reported aversions). In 11 of these cases the subjects reported that they never again ate the particular kind of shellfish to which their aversion formed. While some of these 11 cases may have involved allergies to shellfish that would indeed persist into the future, others probably involved consumption of temporarily contaminated shellfish or some illness unrelated to consumption of the shellfish. In these latter cases a complete avoidance of eating shellfish in the future would unnecessarily deprive the subjects of the benefits to be derived from consuming them.

A final type of error can occur when a food is poisonous, and an aversion is formed to that food, but aversions are also formed to other foods that are not poisonous but are judged similar. An example of this type of error occurs with blue jays' aversions to monarch butterflies (Brower, 1969). After a blue jay forms an aversion to poisonous monarch butterflies it also shows an aversion to consuming other types of butterflies whose appearance is similar to monarchs, but which do not contain the poisonous cardiac glycosides. The possible benefits of consuming butterflies other than monarchs are obviated by the aversion to monarchs.

The Evolution of Errors

All three of these types of errors result in organisms overavoiding foods. The question then arises why, if evolution affects learning, are the organisms behaving in these nonadaptive ways?

One reason why all of these types of errors may occur is that in the long run these errors may actually themselves be adaptive. Although an animal may lose some benefit from avoiding foods that contain nutrients but do not cause illness, if it were to make a mistake in the other direction, and eat a food that does cause illness, it might die. Therefore it may be safer for animals to overavoid rather than underavoid potentially dangerous foods.

Another possible explanation of these errors that is consistent with the concept of evolution affecting learning, is that animals have not yet had time to evolve to the point at which all situations are handled in an optimal way. Simply because evolution affects learning does not mean that learning must be perfect. In fact, it may be impossible for evolution to proceed to such a point. This would require that learning situations remain constant enough across generations that the genes determining the best behavior for those situations would have the opportunity to become more frequent (Pulliam, 1983). But organisms are frequently faced with new situations. Certainly rats, in all of their past generations, have never experienced some of the taste aversion learning situations to which they are now exposed in the laboratory.

If situations do not remain constant enough for optimal behavior to evolve for every possible situation, the next best solution is the evolution of a series of strategies which deal with most situations optimally. This appears to be what has occurred with taste aversion learning.

CONCLUSION

Because many of the types of problems that different species must face in avoiding poisonous foods are similar, different species appear to have evolved similar poisonous-food avoidance strategies. Although the physiological mechanisms by which each species accomplishes these strategies may differ, their behavior may be similar because each species' behavior evolved to serve similar functions (Shettleworth, 1983). Such findings encourage a focus on the interface between an organism and its environment, in other words, they encourage a focus on the organism's behavior. For taste aversion learning, at least, it is at that level where regularity and predictability appear to occur. Learning experiments performed with one species can be applicable to another, even if the physiology of the two species differs markedly, as long as their behavior has evolved to solve similar problems (see Baum, 1983; Domjan, 1983; Domjan & Galef, 1983). Apparently many of the problems involved in identifying and avoiding poisonous foods are similar across species.

ACKNOWLEDGMENTS

I thank K. R. Logue, I. Ophir, and K. E. Strauss for their contributions to our research reported here, and H. Rachlin, M. Rodriguez, and M. Smith for their comments on a previous version of this chapter. Preparation of this chapter was supported by NSF Grant BNS8416302, A. W. Logue principal investigator.

REFERENCES

Baker, T. B., & Cannon, D. S. (1979). Taste aversion therapy with alcoholics: Techniques and evidence of a conditioned response. *Behaviour Research and Therapy, 17,* 229–242.

Balagura, S., & Smith, D. F. (1970). Role of LiCl and environmental stimuli on generalized learned aversion to NaCl in the rat. *American Journal of Physiology, 219,* 1231–1234.

Baum, M., Foidart, D. S., & Lapointe, A. (1974). Rapid extinction of a conditioned taste aversion following unreinforced intraperitoneal injection of the fluid CS. *Physiology & Behavior, 12,* 871–873.

Baum, W. M. (1983). Studying foraging in the psychological laboratory. In R. L. Mellgren (Ed.), *Animal cognition and behavior* (pp. 253–283). New York: North-Holland.

Bernstein, I. L. (1978). Learned taste aversions in children receiving chemotherapy. *Science, 200,* 1302–1303.

Bernstein, I. L., & Sigmundi, R. A. (1980). Tumor anorexia: A learned food aversion? *Science, 209,* 416–418.

Bernstein, I. L., & Webster, M. M. (1980). Learned taste aversions in humans. *Physiology & Behavior, 25,* 363–366.

Bernstein, I. L., Webster, M. M., & Bernstein, I. D. (1982). Food aversions in children receiving chemotherapy for cancer. *Cancer, 50,* 2961–2963.

Best, P. J., Best, M. R., & Henggeler, S. (1977). The contribution of environmental non-ingestive cues in conditioning with aversive internal consequences. In L. M. Barker, M. R. Best, & M. Domjan (Eds.), *Learning mechanisms in food selection* (pp. 371–393). Waco, TX: Baylor University Press.

Birch, L. L. (1980). Effects of peer models' food choices and eating behaviors on preschoolers' food preferences. *Child Development, 51,* 489–496.

Birch, L. L., & Marlin, D. W. (1982). I don't like it; I never tried it: Effects of exposure on two-year-old children's food preferences. *Appetite: Journal for Intake Research, 3,* 353–360.

Boland, F. J., Mellor, C. S., & Revusky, S. (1978). Chemical aversion treatment of alcoholism: Lithium as the aversive agent. *Behaviour Research and Therapy, 16,* 401–409.

Bolles, R. C. (1973). The comparative psychology of learning: The selective association principle and some problems with "general" laws of learning. In G. Bermant (Ed.), *Perspectives on animal behavior* (pp. 280–306). Glenview, IL: Scott, Foresman.

Braveman, N. S. (1974). Poison-based avoidance learning with flavored or colored water in guinea pigs. *Learning and Motivation, 5,* 182–194.

Braveman, N. S. (1975). Relative salience of gustatory and visual cues in the formation of poison-based food aversions by guinea pigs *(Cavia porcellus). Behavioral Biology, 14,* 189–199.

Braveman, N. S. (1977). Visually guided avoidance of poisonous foods in mammals. In L. M. Barker, M. R. Best, & M. Domjan (Eds.), *Learning mechanisms in food selection* (pp. 455–473). Waco, TX: Baylor University Press.

Brower, L. P. (1969, February). Ecological chemistry. *Scientific American,* 22–29.

Campbell, B. A., & Coulter, X. (1976). Neural and psychological processes underlying the development of learning and memory. In T. J. Tighe & R. N. Leaton (Eds.), *Habituation* (pp. 129–157). Hillsdale, NJ: Lawrence Erlbaum Associates.

Catania, A. C., Matthews, B. A., & Shimoff, E. (1982). Instructed versus shaped human verbal behavior: Interactions with nonverbal responding. *Journal of the Experimental Analysis of Behavior, 38,* 233–248.

Chambers, K. C., & Sengstake, C. B. (1976). Sexually dimorphic extinction of a conditioned taste aversion in rats. *Animal Learning & Behavior, 4,* 181–185.

Collier, G., & Novell, K. (1967). Saccharin as a sugar surrogate. *Journal of Comparative and Physiological Psychology, 64,* 404–408.

Coombes, S., Revusky, S., & Lett, B. T. (1980). Long-delay taste aversion learning in an un-

poisoned rat: Exposure to a poisoned rat as the unconditioned stimulus. *Learning and Motivation,* *11,* 256–266.
Czaplicki, J. A., Borrebach, D. E., & Wilcoxon, H. C. (1976). Stimulus generalization of an illness-induced aversion to different intensities of colored water in Japanese quail. *Animal Learning & Behavior, 4,* 45–48.
Daly, M., Rauschenberger, J., & Behrends, P. (1982). Food aversion learning in kangaroo rats: A specialist-generalist comparison. *Animal Learning & Behavior, 10,* 314–320.
Domjan, M. (1975). Poison-induced neophobia in rats: Role of stimulus generalization of conditioned taste aversions. *Animal Learning & Behavior, 3,* 205–211.
Domjan, M. (1980). Ingestional aversion learning: Unique and general processes. In J. S. Rosenblatt, R. A. Hinde, C. Beer, & M. C. Busnel (Eds.), *Advances in the study of behavior* (Vol. 11, pp. 275–336). New York: Academic Press.
Domjan, M. (1983). Biological constraints and the pursuit of general theories of learning. In R. L. Mellgren (Ed.), *Animal cognition and behavior* (pp. 319–344). New York: North Holland.
Domjan, M., & Galef, B. G. (1983). Biological constraints on instrumental and classical conditioning: Retrospect and prospect. *Animal Learning and Behavior, 11,* 151–161.
Domjan, M., & Hanlon, M. J. (1982). Poison-avoidance learning to food-related tactile stimuli: Avoidance of texture cues by rats. *Animal Learning & Behavior, 10,* 293–300.
Domjan, M., Miller, V., & Gemberling, G. A. (1982). Note on aversion learning to the shape of food by monkeys. *Journal of the Experimental Analysis of Behavior, 38,* 87–91.
Durlach, P. J., & Rescorla, R. A. (1980). Potentiation rather than overshadowing in flavor-aversion learning: An analysis in terms of within-compound associations. *Journal of Experimental Psychology: Animal Behavior Processes, 6,* 175–187.
Etscorn, F. (1973). Effects of a preferred vs a nonpreferred CS in the establishment of a taste aversion. *Physiological Psychology, 1,* 5–6.
Etscorn, F., & Stephens, R. (1973). Establishment of conditioned taste aversions with a 24-hour CS-US interval. *Physiological Psychology, 1,* 251–253.
Garb, J. L., & Stunkard, A. J. (1974). Taste aversions in man. *American Journal of Psychiatry,* *131,* 1204–1207.
Garcia, J., Ervin, F. R., & Koelling, R. A. (1966). Learning with prolonged delay of reinforcement. *Psychonomic Science, 5,* 121–122.
Garcia, J., Kimeldorf, D. J., & Koelling, R. A. (1955). Conditioned aversion to saccharin resulting from exposure to gamma radiation. *Science, 122,* 157–158.
Garcia, J., & Koelling, R. A. (1966). Relation of cue to consequence in avoidance learning. *Psychonomic Science, 4,* 123–124.
Garcia, J., & Koelling, R. A. (1967). A comparison of aversions induced by x-rays, toxins, and drugs in the rat. *Radiation Research Supplement, 7,* 439–450.
Garcia, J., McGowan, B. K., & Green, K. F. (1972). Biological constraints on conditioning. In M. E. P. Seligman & J. L. Hager (Eds.), *Biological boundaries of learning* (pp. 21–43). New York: Appleton-Century-Crofts.
Gemberling, G. A., Domjan, M., & Amsel, A. (1980). Aversion learning in 5-day-old rats: Taste-toxicosis and texture-shock associations. *Journal of Comparative and Physiological Psychology, 94,* 734–745.
Gillette, K., Martin, G. M., & Bellingham, W. P. (1980). Differential use of food and water cues in the formation of conditioned aversions by domestic chicks (*Gallus gallus*). *Journal of Experimental Psychology: Animal Behavior Processes, 6,* 99–111.
Grote, F. W., & Brown, R. T. (1973). Deprivation level affects extinction of a conditioned taste aversion. *Learning and Motivation, 4,* 314–319.
Gustavson, C. R. (1977). Comparative and field aspects of learned food aversions. In L. M. Barker, M. R. Best, & M. Domjan (Eds.), *Learning mechanisms in food selection* (pp. 23–43). Waco, TX: Baylor University Press.

Hamilton, W. D. (1964a). The genetical evolution of social behaviour. I. *Journal of Theoretical Biology, 7,* 1–16.
Hamilton, W. D. (1964b). The genetical evolution of social behaviour. II. *Journal of Theoretical Biology, 7,* 17–52.
Hull, C. L. (1949). Stimulus intensity dynamism (V) and stimulus generalization. *Psychological Review, 56,* 67–76.
Ingram, D. K., & Corfman, T. P. (1981). Strain-dependent sexual dimorphism in the extinction of conditioned taste aversion in mice. *Animal Learning & Behavior, 9,* 101–107.
Johnson, C., Beaton, R., & Hall, K. (1975). Poison-based avoidance learning in nonhuman primates: Use of visual cues. *Physiology and Behavior, 14,* 403–407.
Kalat, J. W. (1974). Taste salience depends on novelty, not concentration, in taste-aversion learning in the rat. *Journal of Comparative and Physiological Psychology, 86,* 47–50.
Kalat, J. W. (1975). Taste-aversion learning in infant guinea pigs. *Developmental Psychobiology, 8,* 383–387.
Kimble, G. A. (1961). *Hilgard and Marquis' conditioning and learning.* New York: Appleton-Century-Crofts.
Kurz, E. M., & Levitsky, D. A. (1982). Novelty of contextual cues in taste aversion learning. *Animal Learning & Behavior, 10,* 229–232.
Lamon, S., Wilson, G. T., & Leaf, R. C. (1977). Human classical aversion conditioning: Nausea versus electric shock in the reduction of target beverage consumption. *Behaviour Research and Therapy, 15,* 313–320.
Larsen, J. D., & Hyde, T. S. (1977). A comparison of learned aversions to gustatory and exteroceptive cues in rats. *Animal Learning & Behavior, 5,* 17–20.
Lavin, M. J., Freise, B., & Coombes, S. (1980). Transferred flavor aversions in adult rats. *Behavioral and Neural Biology, 28,* 15–33.
Lemere, F., & Voegtlin, W. L. (1940). Conditioned reflex therapy of alcoholic addiction: Specificity of conditioning against chronic alcoholism. *California and Western Medicine, 53,* 268–269.
Lett, B. T. (1980). Taste potentiates color-sickness associations in pigeons and quail. *Animal Learning & Behavior, 8,* 193–198.
Logue, A. W. (1978, April). *Generalization of the conditioned stimulus in taste aversion learning.* Paper presented at the meeting of the Eastern Psychological Association, Washington, D.C.
Logue, A. W. (1979). Taste aversion and the generality of the laws of learning. *Psychological Bulletin, 86,* 276–296.
Logue, A. W. (1980). Visual cues for illness-induced aversions in the pigeon. *Behavioral and Neural Biology, 28,* 372–377.
Logue, A. W. (1986). *The psychology of eating and drinking.* New York: Freeman.
Logue, A. W., Logue, K. R., & Strauss, K. E. (1983). The acquisition of taste aversions in humans with eating and drinking disorders. *Behaviour Research and Therapy, 21,* 275–289.
Logue, A. W., Ophir, I., & Strauss, K. E. (1981). The acquisition of taste aversions in humans. *Behaviour Research and Therapy, 19,* 319–333.
Lorden, J. F., Kenfield, M., & Braun, J. J. (1970). Response suppression to odors paired with toxicosis. *Learning and Motivation, 1,* 391–400.
Lowe, C. F. (1979). Determinants of human operant behaviour. In M. D. Zeiler & P. Harzem (Eds.), *Reinforcement and the organization of behaviour* (pp. 159–192). New York: Wiley.
Lowe, C. F. (1983). Radical behaviorism and human psychology. In G. C. L. Davey (Ed.), *Animal models of human behavior* (pp. 71–93). New York: Wiley.
Mackintosh, N. J. (1974). *The psychology of animal learning.* New York: Academic Press.
Martin, L. T., & Alberts, J. R. (1979). Taste aversions to mother's milk: The age-related role of nursing in acquisition and expression of a learned association. *Journal of Comparative and Physiological Psychology, 93,* 430–445.

Martin, G. M., & Timmins, W. K. (1980). Taste-sickness associations in young rats over varying delays, stimulus, and test conditions. *Animal Learning & Behavior, 8,* 529–533.

Mellor, C. S., & White, H. P. (1978). Taste aversions to alcoholic beverages conditioned by motion sickness. *American Journal of Psychiatry, 135,* 125–126.

Miller, V., & Domjan, M. (1981). Specificity of cue to consequence in aversion learning in the rat: Control for US-induced differential orientations. *Animal Learning & Behavior, 9,* 339–345.

Nachman, M. (1963). Learned aversions to the taste of lithium chloride and generalization to other salts. *Journal of Comparative and Physiological Psychology, 56,* 343–349.

Nowlis, G. H. (1974). Conditioned stimulus intensity and acquired alimentary aversions in the rat. *Journal of Comparative and Physiological Psychology, 86,* 1173–1184.

Nowlis, G. H., Frank, M. E., & Pfaffmann, C. (1980). Specificity of acquired aversions to taste qualities in hamsters and rats. *Journal of Comparative and Physiological Psychology, 94,* 932–942.

Palmerino, C. C., Rusiniak, K. W., & Garcia, J. (1980). Flavor-illness aversions: The peculiar roles of odor and taste in memory for poison. *Science, 208,* 753–755.

Parker, L. A., & Revusky, S. (1982). Generalized conditioned flavor aversions: Effects of toxicosis training with one flavor on the preference for different novel flavors. *Animal Learning & Behavior, 10,* 505–510.

Pulliam, H. R. (1983). On the theory of gene-culture co-evolution in a variable environment. In R. L. Mellgren (Ed.), *Animal cognition and behavior* (pp. 427–443). New York: North-Holland.

Quinn, J., & Henbest, R. (1967). Partial failure of generalization in alcoholism following aversion therapy. *Quarterly Journal of Studies on Alcohol, 28,* 70–75.

Revusky, S. H. (1977). Learning as a general process with an emphasis on data from feeding experiments. In N. W. Milgram, L. Krames, & T. M. Alloway (Eds.), *Food aversion learning* (pp. 1–51). New York: Academic Press.

Revusky, S., Coombes, S., & Pohl, R. W. (1982). US preexposure: Effects on flavor aversions produced by pairing a poisoned partner with ingestion. *Animal Learning & Behavior, 10,* 83–90.

Riley, A. L., & Clarke, C. M. (1977). Conditioned taste aversions: A bibliography. In L. M. Barker, M. R. Best, & M. Domjan (Eds.), *Learning mechanisms in food selection* (pp. 593–616). Waco, TX: Baylor University Press.

Riley, A. L., & Tuck, D. L. (1985). Conditoned food aversions: A bibliography. In N. S. Braveman & P. Bronstein (Eds.), *Experimental assessments and clinical applications of conditioned food aversions* (pp. 381–437). New York: The New York Academy of Sciences.

Rozin, P., & Fallon, A. E. (1981). The acquisition of likes and dislikes for foods. In J. Solms & R. L. Hall (Eds.), *Criteria of food acceptance* (pp. 35–48). Switzerland: Forster Verlag AG.

Rozin, P., & Kalat, J. W. (1971). Specific hungers and poison avoidance as adaptive specializations of learning. *Psychological Review, 78,* 459–486.

Rudy, J. W., & Cheatle, M. D. (1979). Ontogeny of associative learning: Acquisition of odor aversions by neonatal rats. In N. E. Spear & B. A. Campbell (Eds.), *Ontogeny of learning and memory* (pp. 157–188). Hillsdale, NJ: Lawrence Erlbaum Associates.

Seligman, M. E. P. (1970). On the generality of the laws of learning. *Psychological Review, 77,* 406–418.

Seligman, M. E. P. (1972). Classical conditioning. In M. E. P. Seligman & J. L. Hager (Eds.), *Biological boundaries of learning* (pp. 8–9). New York: Appleton-Century-Crofts.

Shettleworth, S. J. (1983). Function and mechanism in learning. In M. D. Zeiler & P. Harzem (Eds.), *Advances in analysis of behaviour: Vol. 3. Biological factors in learning* (pp. 1–39). New York: Wiley.

Smith, D. F., & Balagura, S. (1969). Role of oropharyngeal factors in LiCl aversion. *Journal of Comparative and Physiological Psychology, 69,* 308–310.

Spiker, V. A. (1977). Taste aversion: A procedural analysis and an alternative paradigmatic classification. *Psychological Record, 27,* 753–769.

Springer, A. D., & Fraley, S. M. (1981). Extinction of a conditioned taste aversion in young, mid-aged and aged C57/BL6 mice. *Behavioral and Neural Biology, 32,* 282–294.

Steinert, P. A., Infurna, R. N., & Spear, N. E. (1980). Long-term retention of a conditioned taste aversion in preweanling and adult rats. *Animal Learning & Behavior, 8,* 375–381.

Stierhoff, K. A., & Lavin, M. J. (1982). The influence of rendering rats anosmic on the poisoned-partner effect. *Behavioral and Neural Biology, 34,* 180–189.

Terk, M. P., & Green, L. (1980). Taste aversion learning in the bat, *Carollia perspicillata. Behavioral and Neural Biology, 28,* 236–242.

Testa, T. J., & Ternes, J. W. (1977). Specificity of conditioning mechanisms in the modification of food preferences. In L. M. Barker, M. R. Best, & M. Domjan (Eds.), *Learning mechanisms in food selection* (pp. 229–253). Waco, TX: Baylor University Press.

Wiens, A. N., Montague, J. R., Manaugh, T. S., & English, C. J. (1976). Pharmacological aversive counterconditioning to alcohol in a private hospital: One-year follow-up. *Journal of Studies on Alcohol, 37,* 1320–1324.

Wilcoxon, H. C., Dragoin, W. B., & Kral, P. A. (1971). Illness-induced aversions in rat and quail: Relative salience of visual and gustatory cues. *Science, 171,* 826–828.

Zajonc, R. B. (1968). Attitudinal effects of mere exposure. *Journal of Personality and Social Psychology, 9,* 1–27.

7 A Comparative-Ecological Approach to the Study of Learning

Alan C. Kamil
University of Massachesetts, Amherst

John E. Mauldin
State Department of Education, Atlanta, Georgia

The purpose of this chapter is to discuss the effects of a parameter which is present in every learning experiment, but about which we know relatively little—the species being tested. The effects of the species variable have been studied relatively infrequently by animal learning psychologists for at least three reasons. (1) Psychologists have tended to assume that a few general processes will account entirely for most, if not all, of the important phenomena of animal learning in a broad range of species. This assumption has been criticized frequently in recent years (e.g., Seligman, 1970; Seligman & Hager, 1972), but still dominates the field of animal learning. (2) There are serious conceptual problems in attempting to interpret species differences in performance in a learning experiment (Bitterman, 1960, 1965). The basic problem is that if one species performs better than another on a learning task, this does not necessarily represent a species difference in learning ability. It may represent an inadequacy in the design of the experiment for one(or both) species. (3) Psychologists have been without a systematic, biologically sensible method of selecting species for comparative study. As Hodos and Campbell (1969) have pointed out, the psychological view of species has been dominated by the *"scala naturae"* concept.

The scala naturae concept holds that there is a continuous and linear sequence of species, beginning with the most primitive and culminating in the most complex, man. As Mayr (1982) has discussed, this idea became increasingly untenable as biologists became increasingly familiar with the tremendous diversity of life. Mayr (1982) claims that the scala naturae concept was dealt its final death blow in 1812, when Cuvier "asserted emphatically that there are four distinct phyla of animals . . . and that there was absolutely no connection among them" (pp. 201–202). In any event, there can be no doubt that in clinging to the scala naturae, psychologists were adapting a wholly incorrect and untenable view of species, and the nature of the differences between species. The major problems associated with the scala naturae are: (1) its failure to recognize the tremendous diversity of life, and (2) its assumption that differences between species can be thought of as unidimensional.

Hodos and Campbell (1969) suggested a sophisticated strategy for attempting to discern the phylogenetic history of a behavioral trait. This strategy is not based on the scala naturae, but on the judicious choice of species for comparisons based on modern ideas of phylogenetic relationship. But this strategy still faces the problems outlined by Bitterman (1960, 1965). It also is not well suited to the investigation of aspects of species differences other than phylogenetic history.

Another important perspective from which to approach the species variable is provided by the concept of adaptation. From this point of view, animals can learn because the ability to learn confers selective advantage upon those animals which possess it. This implies that the characteristics of learning processes have been shaped by the evolutionary process, and that species differences in learning are to be expected. By definition, each species has a unique evolutionary history. To the extent that this history affects learning, species will differ in their response to a learning experiment. Furthermore, inasmuch as learning is seen as an adaptation, the effects of a learning procedure upon a species will depend on how the learning paradigm makes contact with the adaptations and response repertoire of the animal (Johnston, 1981; Kamil, Peters, & Lindstrom, 1982; Kamil & Yoerg, 1982). In this chapter we offer two examples of research which suggest how this facet of learning can be analyzed: the comparison of closely related species and the analysis of the problems animals are required to learn in nature.

AUTOSHAPING IN THREE PASSERINE SPECIES

In the typical autoshaping experiment with avian subjects, a key light is reliably followed by food reinforcement, regardless of the behavior of the bird. Despite the absence of any contingency, the lit key comes to elicit key pecking responses. It has been suggested that during autoshaping the lit key, or trial stimulus, comes to release the same species-specific fixed action patterns as those released by the reinforcer. This view is supported by several experimental results, particularly those of Jenkins and Moore (1973). They found that the topography of the autoshaped key peck response of a pigeon depended upon the reinforcer used. If food was the reinforcer, a *food-type* open-beak peck was used, while if water was the reinforcer, a *water-type* closed beak peck was used.

Another way to test the hypothesis that autoshaped key peck responses are fixed-action patterns would be to autoshape several different avian species whose species-specific pecking responses differed in topography. If autoshaped responses are species-specific, the response topographies of autoshaped key peck responses of these species would be expected to differ. Mauldin (1981) conducted an extensive autoshaping experiment with three passerine species, blue jays (*Cynanocitta cristata*), starlings (*Sturnus vulgaris*) and robins (*Turdus migratorius*), which provides data to test this hypothesis. These three species were chosen because they vary considerably in the topography of their natural feeding responses (see below), and because each species breeds in the Amherst, MA, area, and was therefore readily available for hand-raising in the laboratory.

Mauldin tested members of each species under two different experimental conditions, positive autoshaping and negative automaintenance. In positive autoshaping, a neutral stimulus is paired with food delivery, as in standard Pavlovian conditioning, but the neutral stimulus is associated with a manipulandum (Brown & Jenkins, 1968). For example, in most autoshaping experiments with birds, the netural stimulus has been a lit pecking key. Even though no response is required for food to be delivered, the birds soon come to peck the key. Even more impressive are the results of negative automaintenance. During negative automaintenance, conditions are exactly the same as those during positive autoshaping, except that if the bird pecks the key, no reinforcement is delivered. The only contingency operating is one that should act against pecking, yet pigeons continue to peck on many trials (Williams & Williams, 1969).

Mauldin also tested each species in three control conditions: trial stimulus only, reinforcement only, and a random control in which both trial stimulus and reinforcement were presented, but the occurrence of each was random with respect to the occurrence of the other. After initial testing under these conditions, each group was transferred to either negative automaintenance (the positive autoshaping group) or to positive autoshaping (all other groups). In general terms, Mauldin found that all three species key pecked during positive autoshaping, that none of the three species showed much key pecking during any of the control conditions, and that all three species showed only low levels of key pecking during negative automaintenance, especially the blue jays. For the purposes of this chapter, we concentrate upon the results of positive autoshaping.

The birds were all taken from the nest at 8–10 days-of-age and hand-raised in the laboratory on a standard diet of Purina turkey starter and myna bird pellets. The birds were 14–26 months-old at the time of the experiment, and had no previous key pecking experience. They were maintained at 80% of their free-feeding weight throughout the experiment.

The apparatus was a modified Lehigh Valley Electronics operant chamber, containing a 33 x 30.5 x 35.5 cm high subject cubicle. All mounting screws in the cubicle were countersunk and puttied, and the cubicle was painted a uniform white. The cubicle was illuminated brightly and evenly by three 120 v. bulbs mounted about a light-diffusing false ceiling. A translucent Lehigh Valley Electronics pecking key was centrally mounted on the intelligence panel, and could be illuminated by a relatively dim 12 v. bulb. The reinforcement magazine was located to the right of the key, and was also illuminated by a 12 v. bulb. A

UF-100 Davis feeder was mounted on top of the chamber, and white noise was provided through a small speaker. A Lehigh Valley Electronics INTERACT computer system controlled all stimulus events and response contingencies, and recorded the data. A Sony video camera and video tape recorder were used to monitor all sessions, and a Beaulieu high speed Super-8 movie camera was used to record selected trials, particularly at asymptote, for each bird.

The birds were habituated to the apparatus, then magazine trained until they met a criterion of retrieving reinforcement (*Tenebrio* larvae) within 4 seconds of delivery on 5 consecutive trials. Once this criterion had been met, each bird received another 30 minutes of testing without reinforcement. Autoshaping began in the next session. Daily autoshaping sessions consisted of 50 trials. Each trial began with illumination of the pecking key with a dim, white light. After 10 seconds, the key went dark and a reinforcement was delivered to the magazine, which was illuminated for 1 second. The intertrial interval averaged 60 seconds, using the schedule values suggested by Fleshler and Hoffman (1962). This training continued until stable levels of responding had been obtained, which required 18–23 sessions.

As shown in Fig. 7.1, all birds acquired the pecking response during autoshaping, but there were species differences in this acquisition. The blue jays began to peck sooner than the other species, but their asymptotic rates were relatively low. The robins pecked at an intermediate level at asymptote. The starlings began pecking relatively late in training, but had the highest asymptotic rates. These differences are interesting, but difficult to interpret. Mauldin (1981) has suggested that they may reflect species differences in foraging behavior and the developmental cycle of the three species. The results correlate with the length of time the young are dependent upon adults for food. Blue jays remain dependent for a month or more, robins for several weeks, and starlings for only 2 to 3 weeks.

The high speed photography revealed that, as expected, there were marked and consistent differences between the species in key peck topography at asymptote (see Fig. 7.2). The blue jays pecked in distinct bouts of several pecks each. Between bouts, the jays moved around the cubicle, maintaining orientation towards the key and magazine area. They pecked the key with two different topographies. Sometimes they pecked upward at the center of the key with a closed beak. At other times, they used a hammering type of peck in which the head and body moved together in a powerful thrust at the key, with the beak wide open and snapped shut at, or just before, contact. This hammering, forceful type of key peck is very similar to that described by Hardy (1961), who observed blue jays using it in the field to open acorns. We have also observed this response when lab-raised blue jays are given items like unhusked sunflower seeds to eat.

In contrast, the robins pecked the key fairly continuously during each trial, with only occasional pauses during which they oriented towards the magazine. Their key peck topography was quite dramatic. Pecks were intiated by a rapid

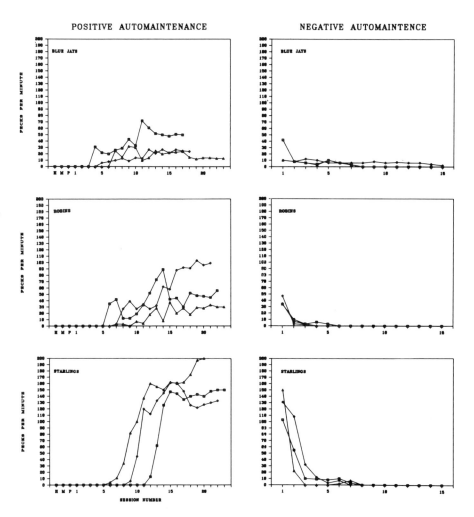

FIGURE 7.1.   Rates of key pecking during habituation (H), magazine training (M), postmagazine training (P), and each session of positive automaintenance (FT+) for each of the blue jays (top), robins (middle), and starlings (bottom) tested.

lunge, often accompanied by a wing flap, beginning from a position 5–8 cm away from the key. During this lunge, one or both feet often left the ground. The head was thrust forward with the beak snapped shut. This behavior strongly resembles the behavior of robins grabbing worms on a lawn.

The key peck topography of the starlings was quite different from those of the other two species. The starlings remained very close to the key when it was illuminated, and pecked constantly with a rhythmic motion of the body. In

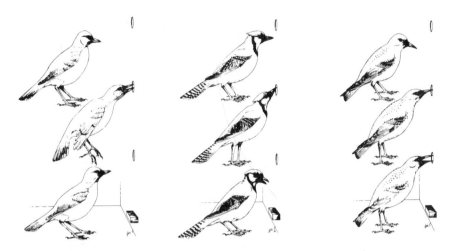

FIGURE 7.2.   Typical response topographies of robins (left), blue jays (center), and starlings (right) observed after positive automaintenance. Prepared from high speed movie frames.

essence, they repeatedly leaned towards the key, with minimal body movement. The starlings contacted the key with a closed beak, opened the beak after contact, paused briefly, then leaned back and closed the beak. This topography is very similar to the "gaping" response pattern which Dunnett (1955) described as typical of this species during virtually all feeding activities in the field.

How should these species differences be interpreted? From one point of view, there is little need to be concerned with them. After all, each species learned to peck the key, and the topographical variations are relatively trivial from a learning theory viewpoint. This argument ignores the differences in the rates of acquisition and of asymptotic pecking. But it still has considerable force, primarily because there is a basic similarity among the species. In spite of these similarities, however, there are differences. How might the topographical differences between species be explained?

A model for the explanation of these differences can be found by looking at how conceptually similar morphological differences are understood by evolutionary biologists. Within many families of birds, particularly insular families that have evolved in geographic isolation, considerable variation in the beak shapes of different species is often observed. One of the most dramatic cases of such variation is found in the family *Drepanididae,* the Hawaiian honey creepers (Berger, 1972). Figure 7.3 shows the beak shapes of three species within this family. This morphological variation is understood in terms of the ecological efficiency of the different beak shapes. As in the case of the Galapagos finches, the beak of each species is well suited to the feeding specializations of each species. The honeycreepers with long, thin, decurved beaks like the Iiwi (*Ves-*

FIGURE 7.3.   The beaks of three Hawaiian honeycreepers, the palila
(left), iiwi (center) and akiapolaau (right).

tiaria coccinea) are nectar feeders, and their beaks are well adapted for probing
flowers. The honeycreepers with large, stout beaks, such as the palila (*Psit-
tirostra bailleui*) are seed eaters. The unusual beak shape of the akiapolaau
(*Hemignathus wilsoni*) is well suited to its woodpecker-like habits. It uses the
short, strong lower beak to pound at bark and rotten wood, the long, thinner
more flexible upper beak to probe and pry holes for insects (see Berger, 1972).
    The variation in beak shapes among the Hawaiian honeycreepers are thus
understood, at least in part, as adaptations which function efficiently for the
animals. The same type of reasoning can be applied to the variation in key peck
topographies observed by Mauldin (1981). In each case, the topography of the
key peck observed in the autoshaping paradigm may have been shaped by natural
selection so that it is particularly efficient for the feeding strategies of the species. The hammering blow of the blue jay for opening acorns, the leap of the
robin for capturing worms, the probing response of the starling for finding
insects in loose earth. It can be argued that the outcome of the autoshaping
acquisition experiment was determined, at least in part, by the adaptations of the
animals being tested.

STAY AND SHIFT LEARNING IN HUMMINGBIRDS

Although the topographical differences observed by Mauldin (1981) are interesting, they may not reflect basic differences in what is learned, and how it is
learned. However, several phenomena in the biological constraints literature
suggest that the adaptations of the organism may affect learning in other ways.
The classic case, of course, is taste-aversion learning (Garcia & Koelling, 1966).
However there is a basic problem with much of this literature. In most cases,
virtually no hard data are available on the natural behavior patterns of the subject
species in nature. This makes the link between laboratory behavior and adaptation highly speculative. In order to study the connections between learning and
adaptation, it is necessary to work with species that have been studied intensively
under natural conditions. One such group of animals is the nectar feeding birds.
In the last 15 years, ecologists have conducted a great deal of field research with

these animals, especially on their foraging behavior (see Pyke, 1981, for review). As a result, the characteristics of the spatiotemporal distribution of their food are well known. If these birds use learning to deal efficiently with these problems, then this information gives us insight into the adaptive function of learning for these animals.

Nectar feeding birds often feed from small flowers which contain very small amounts of nectar, which is quickly depleted and very slowly renewed. Under these conditions, the birds can be most efficient if they avoid revisiting flowers that they have already emptied. Several field studies with individually color marked, territorial birds have found that these birds do, in fact, avoid such revisits not only within foraging bouts, but over longer periods of time (Gass & Montgomerie, 1981; Gill & Wolf, 1977; Kamil, 1978). Some of these data strongly suggest that memory is involved in this avoidance (Kamil, 1978). These findings allow the formulation of several hypotheses about the learning abilities of nectar feeding birds. For example, suppose these birds were given a conditional spatial discrimination problem, in which the conditional cue was a location in which they had recently fed. They would be expected to be able to learn to avoid this location more easily than they could learn to return to it.

This prediction has been tested in a recent experiment by Cole, Hainsworth, Kamil, Mercier, and Wolf (1982). Hummingbirds were placed in a case with two feeding sites at which artificial flowers could be placed. Each trial consisted of two stages, an information stage followed by a choice stage. During the information stage, the hummingbird was presented with a single flower containing a small amount of nectar, and allowed to empty the flower. The position of this single flower varied randomly from trial to trial. The choice stage began 10–12 seconds after the information stage was completed. The bird was presented with two flowers, one at each feeding site. One of these flowers contained nectar, the other did not. If the bird was being trained on stay learning, then the flower containing nectar in the choice stage was in the same position as the single flower presented during the information stage. If the bird was being trained on shift learning, the flower containing nectar was in the other position, and the flower in the same position as that used during the information stage was empty. During the choice stage the bird was allowed to visit (insert its beak into) only one of the flowers. Eight hummingbirds were tested, each receiving both stay and shift training to a criterion of 3 consecutive sessions above 80% correct. Half of the birds received the stay training first, half the shift training first.

The results were very clear (see Table 7.1). In every case, regardless of the order of training, shift learning was much more rapid than stay learning. The slowest shift learning shown by any bird (200 trials, 96 errors) was much quicker than the fastest stay learning (282 trials, 130 errors). Even when shift and stay learning came second, and constituted a reversal, this relationship held. Although the birds in the two conditions began reversal training at almost exactly

TABLE 7.1
Trials and Errors to Criterion of Each Hummingbird during Shift and Stay Learning

		Shift Learning			Stay Learning		
		Trials to Criterion	Errors to Criterion	Percentage Correct Day 1	Trials to Criterion	Errors to Criterion	Percentage Correct Day 1
Stay First	Archilocus 1	160	82	20	640	239	40
	Archilocus 2	180	96	25	620	238	35
	Eugenes 1	96	42	38	282	130	29
	Lampornis 1	144	43	50	624	273	50
	(Mean ± SE)	(145±17.9)	(65.7±13.7)	(33.2±6.8)	(441.5±104.5)	(220±31.0)	(38.5±4.4)
Shift First	Archilocus 3	200	48	60	1240	506	40
	Archilocus 4	80	25	70	360	138	30
	Eugenes 2	24	5	79	360	149	25
	Lampornis 2	96	24	67	790*	341*	35
	(Mean ± SE)	(100±36.7)	(25.5±8.8)	(69.0±3.9)	(687.5±210.2)	(283.5±87.6)	(32.5±3.2)

*Did not reach criterion; this represents a minimum estimate.

125

the same low levels of percentage correct, shift learning took place much more rapidly than stay learning.

There are several possible explanations for these results. The superiority of shift learning may reflect an acquired bias toward shifting, learned before the birds were captured, although it would have to be a bias maintained through the course of extensive stay training. This superiority may also represent some more basic difference in the manner in which the birds solve the two problems, such as an associative predisposition. Either alternative would be consistent with an adaptive approach. Natural selection acts on the phenotype, affecting the gene pool only indirectly. Any phenotype which resulted in rapid shift learning among specific flower locations would be favored by natural selection, whether based on a response bias, associative predisposition, or some other mechanism. Regardless of the mechanism responsible, it is quite clear that the results of the learning experiment are congruent with naturalistic observations describing the problem these animals actually face in nature.

A recent set of experiments by Wunderle & Martinez (personal communication) indicate that the results of Cole et al. (1982) may have been due to learning by the hummingbirds in the field, before they were captured. Wunderle & Martinez worked with bananaquits (*Coereba flaveola*), small nectarivarous birds of the Caribbean. When they tested bananaquits that had been wild-caught as adults, they replicated the findings of Cole et al. However, when Wunderle & Martinez tested birds that were captured quite young and hand-raised in the laboratory, there were no differences between shift and stay learning. It is possible that hand-raised hummingbirds might show superior shift learning, especially since hummingbirds are more specialized for nectar foraging than bananaquits. But these results clearly show that the implications of the Cole et al. (1982) findings must be interpreted cautiously.

There is an interesting paradox here. If the hummingbird results are due to earlier learning in the field, this would imply no specialization for shift over stay learning at birth. On the other hand, the maintenance of shift learning through prolonged laboratory conditions in which stay responses were regularly rewarded, and shift responses were not rewarded, would provide evidence for the importance of learning under field conditions. If learning is important, why isn't it specialized? The shift learning that may have taken place in the field, before the hummingbirds were captured, may have been unusually resistant to extinction. This raises some interesting developmental questions.

Given the dramatic similarities in learning across species demonstrated in many studies (e.g. Couvillon & Bitterman, 1980), the possibility exists that a major evolutionary question is why learning so often appears to have high phylogenetic inertia? That is, although psychologists have often taken the generality of relatively few learning processes for granted, if learning is relatively insensitive to selective pressures, this needs to be understood. Perhaps an answer can be found in a detailed analysis of the advantages learning provides an animal in its natural environment.

RESEARCH TACTICS

An adaptation is any morphological or behavioral characteristic that increases the biological fitness of those animals which possess it. The fact that the ability to learn is so widespread in the animal kingdom implies that it must be adaptive. But we have had relatively little specific evidence that demonstrated how learning could contribute to biological fitness. Recent evidence from behavioral ecology, particularly studies of foraging behavior (see Kamil & Yoerg, 1982, for review) and of social behavior (e.g., Mason, 1982), have shown learning at work in specific natural settings. The results of the two experiments described in this paper indicate that adaptations of the subjects in a learning experiment can affect the outcome of that experiment. The time has come to begin the systematic study of learning as an adaptation.

Unfortunately, psychologists are mostly unaware of the research strategies that have been developed to investigate behavior as adaptation. The fields of animal behavior, behavioral ecology, and ethology offer several useful examples of such strategies. A central theme of these overlapping disciplines, particularly behavioral ecology, is the adaptive significance of behavior. These strategies easily could be applied to research on learning. As several recent articles have discussed this approach (e.g., Johnston, 1981; Kamil & Yoerg, 1982; Shettleworth, 1982) the presentation here is brief.

The essence of the adaptive approach is to examine the relationship between the demands of the natural environment of the animal and the characteristics of the animal. Thus, the first step in analyzing a behavioral trait as an adaptation is to obtain detailed information about the ecology of the species under investigation. In the case of learning, it is necessary to know the types of problems animals may solve through learning in their natural environments (the task descriptions of Johnston, 1981). One relevant type of information would be descriptions of how food is systematically distributed in nature, and how individual animals respond to these distributions. Fortunately, field studies of foraging behavior are beginning to provide this kind of information (see Kamil & Yoerg, 1982, for review; Kamil & Sargent, 1981, for many examples). This literature has provided the basis for some psychological learning experiments (e.g., Baum, 1982; Lea, 1979; Pietrewicz & Kamil, 1977, 1979, 1981), and could be utilized much more extensively.

The importance of the expected fit between the organism and its environment cannot be overemphasized. It is central to any ecological, adaptive approach, but is usually ignored by psychologists. The difference between the ecological and psychological approaches can be seen quite clearly in the different manner in which each field has used the concept of optimization. Within behavioral ecology, optimization theory, such as models of optimal foraging has its roots in the analysis of naturally occurring, well-documented problems. Examples include the patchy distribution of prey (Charnov, 1976), diet selection (MacArthur & Pianka, 1966) or prey crypticity (Hughes, 1979). Mathematical or graphical models of these situations are constructed and solved for their optimum, usually in terms of maximizing net rates of energy intake. These solutions are then used as predictions of behavior. But the models are considered appropriate only for species which actually face these problems in nature.

In contrast, the optimization approach in the operant conditioning literature has viewed the maximization of the rate of reinforcement as a general property of operant behavior (e.g., Shimp, 1969; Rachlin, 1978), which could apply generally across species and situations. For example, consider the recent experiments of Mazur (1981) and Vaughan, Kardish, and Wilson (1981). These two experiments investigated the operant behavior of pigeons on complex schedules in which responses on one alternative increased the probability of reinforcement on the other alternative. Under these conditions, the performance of the pigeons was clearly suboptimal. They obtained many less reinforcements than were available. Most important, perhaps, was the finding that the performance of the pigeons deteriorated with experience on these schedules. As training proceeded, the pigeons obtained fewer and fewer reinforcements.

These experiments are relevant to the operant conditioning version of the optimization theory. Clearly, the maximization of reinforcement rate is not a general principle which governs behavior under all conditions. The fact that the pigeons got worse as training proceeded suggests that even in the face of declining reinforcement rates, the pigeons *could not help themselves*. The rule governing their behavior led to reductions in reinforcement.

But these experiments are irrelevant to ecological optimization theories. The schedules of reinforcement used almost certainly are completely unlike any foraging problem that pigeons, and perhaps any animals, face in nature. To put it baldly, from an ecological perspective, these experiments demonstrate that it is possible for clever human experimenters to fool less clever pigeon subjects. Of course, the cleverness of the experimenters had its origins in knowledge of some of the rules governing choice behavior. The matching law (Herrnstein, 1961) predicted the obtained results.

More substantively, the ecological view of these results might be clearer if they are considered in relation to other learning experiments in which animals performed poorly. Perhaps they are most analogous to observations such as those reported by Breland and Breland (1961) on the "misbehavior of organisms." The Brelands described several operant conditioning situations in which animals achieved very suboptimal rates of reinforcement because of inappropriate behavior patterns. These behavior patterns, which appeared to be species-specific behaviors elicited by various features of the environment, interfered with the behavior patterns which were being reinforced. The experiments of Mazur (1981) and Vaughan et al. (1982) may reflect the same sort of effect. The schedules used elicited inappropriate behaviors which reduced rates of reinforcement, but in a more subtle manner than in the Breland experiments.

Mazur (1981) concludes that his results "suggest that choice behavior is controlled by *a process* that produces a matching of behavioral outputs to reinforcement inputs, not a process of reinforcement maximization" (p. 825; italics added). This is a reasonable conclusion, at least for the conditions tested in these experiments. But it is not very satisfying without some better knowledge of the nature of the underlying process. Our basic point is that in the case of this research, as in the case of the Breland's work, the source of the nonoptimal behavior resides in the structure of the organism. And the structure of biological organisms must be understood, at least in part, in terms of the adaptations and natural response repertoires of the subjects.

As the hummingbird experiment (Cole et al., 1982) demonstrated, it is possible to use the ecological approach to make a priori predictions about within species differences by beginning from a consideration of adaptation. This approach provides a method for alleviating a major problem with concepts such as preparedness (Seligman, 1970). Seligman proposed that different laws of learning might apply to problems for which animals are well prepared by their biological heritage, as opposed to problems for which they are nonprepared or contraprepared. However, Seligman gave no method for determining a priori what problems would be prepared, nonprepared, or contraprepared. The ecological approach provides such a method, based on a careful, empirical analysis of the natural world of the animal.

Within-species experiments will be more valuable when the different tasks which are compared are similar in structure. This was the case with the hummingbird spatial learning experiment. The stay and shift tasks were virtually identical, with the same discriminative stimulus, and very similar response requirements. This similarity in task structure makes it particularly plain that the differences in the rate of acquisition of the two problems tells us something about the structure of the subjects, due to either genetic or learned predispositions. This advantage can be increased considerably by combining this method of predicting within-species effects with an ecologically based method of selecting species for comparative study. From this perspective, the major weakness of the Cole et al. (1982) experiment was the failure to include a second, nonnectar feeding species for comparative purposes (primarily because there are no species closely related to hummingbirds which do not feed on nectar).

The comparative strategy that follows most directly from an ecological perspective is one based on divergence and convergence. Divergence is the evolution of differences among closely related species due to differences in adaptive pressures. The differences in the beak shapes of the Hawaiian honeycreepers provide an excellent example. Convergence is the evolution of similarities among unrelated species due to similar adaptive pressures. For example, nectar feeding birds of several different families have very similar beak shapes, even though the nectar feeding specialization evolved independently in each family. When used in conjunction, divergence and convergence provide a method of species selection which allow repeated, independent tests of hypotheses which relate specific characteristics of learning to particular ecological factors.

For example, consider the ecological view of shift and stay learning. In making predictions about how a particular species will perform on these two tasks, we look to the type of food distribution the species faces in nature. The critical dimensions are the ratio of meals to food patch size, the depletability of the patch, and the rate of renewal of the patch. Animals which feed on small, depletable, slowly renewing patches should show fast shift learning. Those who feed on large, nondepletable or very rapidly renewing patches should show fast stay learning. This hypothesis could be evaluated by selecting closely related species which are divergent along these dimensions, and testing each species on both stay and shift learning. The results of this set of experiments could be extended by identifying distantly related species which are convergent on these dimensions and testing them on stay and shift learning. Thus the hypothesis could be tested several times through careful species selection based upon ecological considerations.

This approach to the comparative study of learning will be a difficult one to carry out. It will require research with a broad range of species and the acquisition of detailed information about the ecology of these species. But it offers an excellent chance to escape many of the difficulties of interpreting comparative learning research pointed out by Bitterman (1960, 1965). Two of the specific advantages to this ecologically based approach are: (1) the use of closely related divergent species will minimize the effects of gross differences in morphology and perceptual abilities. Differences between closely related species could be easier to interpret and attribute to specific causes than differences between unrelated species which differ in many ways. (2) Testing each species under two or more conditions, and focusing upon between species differences in the within species effects can avoid many interpretational problems which center around the suitability of the experimental environment for the species being tested. For example, if we had only tested hummingbirds on stay learning and demonstrated slow stay learning, many interpretations would be possible. It could have been argued that some detail of the experimental procedure—motivational level, intertrial interval, response requirements, etc.—was inappropriate for these animals. But the demonstration of rapid shift learning under identical conditions eliminates these arguments (see Kamil & Yoerg, 1982, for further discussion).

Although an ecological approach has distinct advantages, it also faces problems and challenges. One major challenge will be to learn how to put together different levels of explanation into a single, integrated system. Learning psychologists have been interested primarily in mechanism, while the adaptive approach focuses upon function. Natural selection operates on the phenotype; any mechanism which produces an efficient result can be favored. Thus, knowledge of the function of learning in a given situation does not specify the mechanism (Shettleworth, 1982). But the effort to understand the mechanisms of learning will be more successful if it is carried out in the context of knowledge of the adaptive functions of the ability to modify behavior as a result of experience.

ACKNOWLEDGMENTS

Preparation of this manuscript was supported by NSF Grant BNS-81-02335. Figures 7.1 and 7.3 were drawn by Kathy Sargent.

REFERENCES

Baum, W. M. (1982). Choice, changeover, and travel. *Journal of the Experimental Analysis of Behavior, 38*, 35–49.

Berger, A. J. (1972). *Hawaiian birdlife*. Honolulu: University of Hawaii Press.

Bitterman, M. E. (1960). Toward a comparative psychology of learning. *American Psychologist, 15*, 704–712.

Bitterman, M. E. (1965). Phyletic differences in learning. *American Psychologist, 20*, 396–410.

Breland, K., & Breland, M. (1961). The misbehavior of organisms. *American Psychologist, 16*, 681–684.

Brown, P. L., & Jenkins, H. M. (1968). Auto-shaping of the pigeon's key peck. *Journal of the Experimental Analysis of Behavior, 11*, 1–8.

Charnov, E. L. (1976). Optimal foraging: The marginal value theorem. *Theoretical Population Biology, 9*, 129–136.

Cole, S., Hainsworth, F. R., Kamil, A. C., Mercier, T., & Wolf, L. L. (1982). Spatial learning as an adaptation in hummingbirds. *Science, 217*, 655–657.

Couvillon, P. A., & Bitterman, M. E. (1980). Some phenomena of associative learning in honeybees. *Journal of Comparative and Physiological Psychology, 94*, 878–885.

Dunnet, G. (1955). The breeding of the Starling (*Sturnus vulgaris*) in relation to its food supply. *Ibis, 97*, 619–662.

Fleshler, M., & Hoffman, H. (1962). A progression for generating variable interval schedules. *Journal of the Experimental Analysis of Behavior, 5*, 529–530.

Garcia, J., & Koelling, R. A. (1966). Relation of cue to consequence in avoidance learning. *Psychonomic Science, 4*, 123–124.

Gass, C. L., & Montgomerie, R. D. (1981). Hummingbird foraging behavior: Decision-making and energy regulation. In A. C. Kamil & T. D. Sargent (Eds.), *Foraging behavior: Ecological, ethological, and psychological approaches*. New York: Garland.

Gill, F. B., & Wolf, L. L. (1977). Nonrandom foraging by sunbirds in a patchy environment. *Ecology, 58*, 1284–1296.

Hardy, J. W. (1961). Studies in the behavior and phylogeny of certain New World Jays (*Garrulinae*). *The University of Kansas Science Bulletin, 42*, 13–149.

Herrnstein, R. J. (1961). Relative and absolute strength of response as a function of reinforcement. *Journal of the Experimental Analysis of Behavior, 4,* 267–272.

Hodos, W., & Campbell, C. B. G. (1969). *Scala naturae:* Why there is no theory in comparative psychology. *Psychological Review, 76,* 337–350.

Hughes, R. N. (1979). Optimal diets under the energy optimization premise: The effects of recognition time and learning. *The American Naturalist, 113,* 209–221.

Jenkins, H. M., & Moore, B. R. (1973). The form of the autoshaped response with food and water reinforcers. *Journal of the Experimental Analysis of Behavior, 20,* 163–181.

Johnston, T. D. (1981). Contrasting approaches to the theory of learning. *The Behavioral and Brain Sciences, 4,* 125–139.

Kamil, A. C. (1978). Systematic foraging by a nectar-feeding bird, the Amakihi (*Loxops vikens*). *Journal of Comparative and Physiological Psychology, 92,* 388–396.

Kamil, A. C., Peters, J., & Lindstrom, F. (1982). An ecological perspective on the study of the allocation of behavior. In M. L. Commons, R. J. Herrnstein, & H. Rachlin, (eds.), *Quantitative analysis of behavior II. Matching and maximizing accounts.*

Kamil, A. C., & Sargent, T. D. (Eds.). (1981). Foraging behavior: Ecological, ethological, and psychological approaches. New York: Garland.

Kamil, A. C., & Yoerg, S. I. (1982). Learning and foraging behavior. In P. P. G. Bateson & P. H. Klopfer (Eds.), *Perspectives on ethology, Volume 5.* New York: Plenum.

Lea, S. E. G. (1979). Foraging and reinforcement schedules in the pigeon: Optimal and non-optimal aspects of choice. *Animal Behaviour, 27,* 875–886.

MacArthur, R. H., & Pianka, E. R. (1966). On optimal use of a patchy environment. *American Naturalist, 100,* 603–609.

Mason, W. A. (1982). Primate social intelligence: Evidence from the laboratory. In D. R. Griffin (Ed.), *Animal mind-human mind.* New York: Springer-Verlag.

Mauldin, J. E. (1981). *Autoshaping and negative automaintenance in the blue jay (Cyanocitta cristata), robin (Turdus migratorius), and starling (Sturnus vulgaris).* Unpublished doctoral dissertation, University of Massachusetts.

Mayr, E. (1982). *The growth of biological thought.* Cambridge, MA: Harvard University Press.

Mazur, J. E. (1981). optimalization theory fails to predict performance of pigeons in a two-response situation. *Science, 214,* 823–825.

Pietrewicz, A. T., & Kamil, A. C. (1977). Visual detection of cryptic prey by blue jays (Cyanocitta cristata). *Science, 195,* 580–582.

Pietrewicz, A. T., & Kamil, A. C. (1979). Search image formation in the blue jay (Cyanocitta cristata). *Science, 204,* 1332–1333.

Pietrewicz, A. T., & Kamil, A. C. (1981). Search images and the detection of cryptic prey: An operant approach. In A. C. Kamil & T. D. Sargent (Eds.), Foraging behavior: Ecological, ethological, and psychological approaches.

Pyke, G. (1981). Optimal foraging in nectar-feeding animals and coevolution with their plants. In A. C. Kamil & T. D. Sargent (Eds.), *Foraging behavior: Ecological, ethological, and psychological approaches.* New York: Garland.

Rachlin, H. (1988). A molar theory of reinforcement schedules. *Journal of the Experimental Analysis of Behavior, 30,* 345–360.

Seligman, M. E. P. (1970). On the generality of the laws of learning. *Psychological Review, 77,* 406–418.

Seligman, M. E. P., & Hager, J. L. (1972). *Biological boundaries of learning.* New York: Appleton-Century-Crofts.

Shettleworth, S. J. (1982). Function and mechanism in learning. In M. Zeiler & P. Harzen (Eds.), *Advances in analysis of behavior, Vol 3, Biological factors in learning.* New York: Wiley.

Shimp, C. P. (1969). Optimum behavior in free-operant experiments. *Psychological Review, 76,* 97–112.

Vaughan, W., Jr., Kardish, T. A., & Wilson, M. (1982). Correlation versus contiguity in choice. *Behavior Analysis Letters, 2,* 153–160.
Williams, D. R., & Williams, H. (1969). Auto-maintenance in the pigeon: Sustained pecking despite contingent non-reinforcement. *Journal of the Experimental Analysis of Behavior, 12,* 511–520.

8

The Phylogeny of Information Processing

Roger T. Davis
James D. Dougan
Washington State University

INTRODUCTION

Although there is a vast literature on information processing, and although it spans human beings and a variety of animal species, little or none of it is focused on the biological roots of information processing. Neither biologists nor psychologists seem to have worried much about its evolution. We take an initial step here. Specifically, we approach the problem by trying to develop a general case for the origins of rehearsal in animals.

We may suppose that information from a sensory register decays and disappears within a second or so, if no further processing occurs. The sensory register feeds its message into a short-term storage (STM), which in turn, can hold the information for perhaps 20 seconds, and longer if it is maintained by rehearsal. If rehearsal is prevented, perhaps by engaging the subject in an interpolated task, then the original information is lost. But if rehearsal is allowed to occur for a long enough period of time, then the information is committed to long-term storage (LTM).

Here we focus not on memory as such, but on the process of rehearsal; defining it as: a response of repetition that is caused by an immediate, intense, or unexpected stimulus, and that serves to keep a representation of the stimulus in STM and thus increase the likelihood of its transfer to LTM.

Although concern with memory goes way back to the historical beginnings of psychology, the distinction between the processes of short-term and long-term memory is a comparatively recent development, stemming from the work of Broadbent (1958). The concept of rehearsal as a processes that helps maintain material in short-term memory was then rapidly developed in the human memory literature (e.g., Brown, 1958; Peterson & Peterson, 1959). However, animal psychologists, even those with strong cognitive leanings, appear to have been reluctant to consider rehearsal as a process that contributed to animal learning and memory. Perhaps it was that we were reluctant to attribute the same sort of mechanisms to nonverbal animals that are postulated for human beings. However, it turns out that there is no need for such caution. A recent paper by Watkins, Peynircioğlu, and Burns (1984) presents evidence for pictorial rehearsal in human beings. This finding suggests that rehearsal need not necessarily be carried out in the verbal mode, and thus is compatible with the concept that other animals can rehearse also.

The essence of rehearsal is not that it is oral or verbal in content, we would argue, but that it is repetitive. It brings about a continual or repeated presentation of a stimulus that is only present in the physical world momentarily. Such a mechanism was suggested many years ago by Muller and Pilzecker (1900), who stressed the importance of producing neural perseveration and "consolidation" of memories. A similar concept was apparent in Hebb's (1949) "reverberating circuits," loops of excitation that would keep the stimulus alive, as it were, long enough to become laid down into permanent cell assemblies. The idea was actually anticipated by Sechenov (1889) when he wrote, "The frequent repetition of an actual sensation or of a reflex makes the sensation clearer, and because of this, it is more firmly preserved longer and longer, and the sensation is not so easily forgotten."

Recently, and quite independent of physiological reasoning, Wagner, Rudy, and Whitlow (1973) found it useful to use rehearsal as an explanatory device for the associations between the UCS and CS in classical conditioning in rabbits. They emphasized the importance of a surprising stimulus in bringing about (initiating) rehearsal.

Our thinking about the evolution of rehearsal began when we were reviewing the results of a 29-year project on the behavior of monkeys (Davis, 1985). This longitudinal study led to tentative theorizing concerning cognitive changes accompanying aging of monkeys. Rehearsal mechanisms provided a unifying approach to these data, and led us to contemplate the possibility that the evolution of mechanisms for processing information might have far-reaching consequences for examining cognitive behaviors of animals.

Obviously if rehearsal exists in nonverbal beings, and if it need not be verbal, it is reasonable to ask, what were its evolutionary origins? The purpose of this chapter is to describe rehearsal mechanisms in an evolutionary context. This would be of value in integrating many seemingly unrelated aspects of animal behavior.

If rehearsal mechanisms are not accepted for animals but are for human beings, we might be forced to assume that what occurs in human information processing is discontinuous from biological evolution, and that rehearsal only occurs in human beings. Or might we expect, on the other hand, that there are at least some animal forms, including humans, which manifest rehearsal? Borrowing from Sechenov (1889), we accept the idea that sensations (UCS) are not forgotten easily if they, or reflexes to them (UCRs), are repeated. Our approach also borrowed from Wagner et al. (1973, p. 408) in pointing out that perhaps an unexpected UCS is particularly likely to provide poststimulus rehearsal. We also added Spear's (1978) idea that rehearsal is a part of mnemonic preparation, so that, ". . . it seems quite feasible that animals might employ variation in duration, frequency, or distribution of exposures to certain episodes to promote retention that might be especially adaptive" (p. 436). Finally, considering the above properties of rehearsal, and considering that rehearsal is a repetitive response based on stimulus characteristics, and one which is both species and stimulus specific, we suspect that it would not be far fetched to include rehearsal as a fixed action pattern (FAP), which according to Huntingford (1984), is . . . "a series of regularly repeated stereotyped movements (*responses*) or combination of movements (*responses*) which are characteristic of the species concerned as any of its structural features" (p. 4; Italics are for substituted words inserted by present authors who hold that a response may be an efferent which does not necessarily involve a movement).

EVOLUTIONARY ORIGINS OF REHEARSAL

1. Beginnings of rehearsal.   One of the vague aspects about current theories describing mechanisms of rehearsal is that they do not specify its initiation, speed, frequency, selectivity, or degree of conscious involvement. The present theoretical notions try to be more specific on these characteristics of rehearsal.

In simple organisms, it is highly probable that repetitions of stimuli are necessary for learning and memory, since otherwise there could be no cumulative selectivity between aversive and beneficial stimuli. Thus, we assume that: *a rehearsal mechanism evolved to repeat stimuli internally which are no longer present externally.* Examples of organisms which tend to rely on repeated stimulation or continuous stimulation abound in Fraenkel and Gunn's (1940) classic book, *The Orientation of Animals.* The responses are made to particular as well as to continuous stimulus sources, such as the orthokinetic locomotor response of the woodlouse, *Porcellio scaber,* to a lack of moisture. The stimulus of a moisture gradient is continuously present, and the response of movement, made at the dryer end of the continuum, anticipates mechanisms which in more complex animals make a stimulus continuously available even when one is not present. If this analysis is correct, then it is likely that prototypical orienting responses were evolved to maintain orientation of the organism relative to particular stimuli. Thus, responses of orientation to stimuli may have preceded the evolution of responses to rehearse stimuli.

The mechanisms of rehearsal may have evolved in relatively simple systems in which memory depends on stimulus repetition. If we accept an anagenic position on evolution (See Yarczower, 1984, for a treatment of anagenesis) we might expect processes of information processing to improve with evolutionary history. However, we have no reason to believe that there was a single evolutionary change leading to rehearsal, and furthermore we cannot deny the possibility that the capacity of rehearsal occurred in several parallel lines of evolution. If we assume that relatively long-term memory depends on rehearsal in short-term memory, then we should look first for examples of memory in forms with relatively simple nervous systems.

Kandel and Schwartz (1982), using the marine snail, *Aplysia californica,* postulated memory as a basic aspect of sensitization, habituation, and classical conditioning. These behaviors are related to the amount of neurotransmitter released by the postsynaptic terminals of specific neurons. Also, in accord with our argument, both habituation and sensitization are related to stimulus repetition. Kandel and Schwartz (1982) point out that, ". . . a single noxious stimulus produces a memory that lasts several hours. With four consecutive stimuli, the memory lasts 1 day. Sixteen consecutive stimuli prolong the memory to several days and with 16 spaced stimuli (four per day for 4 days) it lasts several weeks" (p. 439). This suggests that a mechanism for storage evolved before one of rehearsal. In other words, the repetition of a stimulus may suffice to store information in aplysia and some other species, but for many animals, it must have been necessary to intrinsically repeat stimuli (rehearsal) in order to escape dependence on stimuli being immediately present. If basic intrinsic rehearsal first evolved as a synaptic effect, there is no reason to suppose that rehearsal ultimately resulted in molecular change in the nervous system of more evolved forms. Kandel and Schwartz (1982) recognize molecular change as an alternative mechanism for storing information. Possibly this is a mechanism of long-term storage.

The propensity of many animals to exhibit rhythmic patterns of responding is well documented. Fraenkel and Gunn (1940) describe orientations to unidimensional light by head wagging in worms, and Kristan (1980) discusses the nearly universal phenomenon of rhythmic motor patterns in invertebrate organisms. The latter patterns are generally centrally generated rather than being dependent on sensory feedback. Why could a unique (*surprising* in the terminology used by Wagner et al., 1973) stimulus not initiate a centrally generated efferent pattern— in this case rehearsals?

2. Frequency and speed of rehearsal.   Another aspect of rehearsal is that as a neural mechanism it must be limited by its frequency and its speed. Salthouse (1982), commenting on the universal slowing down of people with age, suggested that deficits in memory in older people might be a result of slower information processing including rehearsal. We suppose that faster and more frequent rehearsal evolved in many species and is related to speed of neural transmission.

We point out later that Bitterman (1965) found that some species were unable to learn reversal problems. Also, old monkeys (and old people) have more difficulty in reversing the solution to a problem than do younger individuals (Davis, 1978; 1985). This would seem to be the effect of slower rehearsal, once rehearsal was initiated, and we would expect slower rehearsal in nonmammals than mammals, as well as in older rather than younger mammals.

3. Components of rehearsal.   The basic mechanism of rehearsal that we have described is covert in that it occurs without intent; whereas, much research on rehearsal with human beings has been with overt or deliberate rehearsal. We submit that covert, stimulus initiated, rehearsal evolved independently of overt rehearsal, and evolved in conjunction with direct orienting responses. An incidental advantage of covert rehearsal to a species is that, as opposed to dependence on stimulus repetition, it prohibits transmission of intent to conspecifics. Subject controlled (overt) rehearsal has been described extensively in human beings, and is probably present in monkeys (Flagg, 1975; Ruggiero, 1974), evolving independently of covert rehearsal and probably only occurring in relatively complex animals. Overt rehearsal involves perception of meaning in a situation and the selection of particular material to rehearse, and is probably accompanied by motor manifestations such as orienting, reaching, and subvocal movements.

If the foregoing description is correct, we would expect to have species differences, the first between organisms which require repeated stimulation to remember and those which can perform the repetitions internally, i.e., rehearse. In basic covert rehearsal, one might expect that sensory inputs are rehearsed indiscriminately. However, selective rehearsal would have much more advantage than indiscriminant because, if particular stimuli were favored for rehearsal, the animal could better fit into a particular niche.

Not necessarily next in order, going from primitive to complex, is the need to evolve mechanisms for initiating rehearsal. Quite probably there are initiating mechanisms for implicit rehearsal in simple organisms, and additional mechanisms tied to explicit rehearsal. Either one of these could be accompanied by species differences. Obviously speed of rehearsal depends on the physiological state of the neurons with large differences in possible speed of neural conduction separating poikilothermic and homeothermic animals. Other evolutionary changes undoubtedly occurred in the frequency of rehearsal although it is difficult to imagine how one could differentiate the effects of speed from number of rehearsals.

4. Rehearsal and reinforcement.   Basically, rehearsal of every stimulus would be inefficient. Therefore, some mechanisms must have evolved to provide an advantage to particularly relevant stimuli. One possibility might be differential access to the permanent store such that an organism would only access some special stimuli. Another possibility is that only some, and not other, stimuli are rehearsed. Finally, some stimuli (may be novel or surprising) are more likely to initiate the rhythmic response of rehearsal. The examples of differences between species in response to different relevant stimuli could be explained by such an evolutionary change.

If rehearsal is a response, the simplest mechanism for acquiring information would be that of triggering the rehearsal response. We suggest that there is selective rehearsal. What then, would be the most important stimulus to be rehearsed? Obviously, rehearsal of those stimuli which lead to individual survival and to reproduction by individuals of a species would lend that individual the greatest Darwinian fitness. If these stimuli and correlated stimuli were rehearsed together, the resulting compound would be stored. *We submit that this initiating of rehearsal of stimulus compounds is what many psychologists call reinforcement.*

In R–S (instrumental) conditioning, the animal emits a series of responses, each one of which has sensory consequences, and each one of which has the potential of bringing about memory of this stimulus and its correlated reward. Quite possibly command responses occurring within the nervous system set the rate of responding. The sensory consequences, memories, and commands are providing input at the time a reinforcement is delivered. This stimulus compound is rehearsed as a result of reward and the resulting memory is robust.

How does defining reinforcement as the initiation of rehearsal add to an account of reinforcement dependent on temporal contiguity? It is better, in part, because lapse of time, per se, is seldom a good explanation. Moreover, there are good examples, such as the Garcia Effect (described later), which fit better into our explanation than one of contiguity.

If rehearsal is a mechanism responsible for learning and memory in animals, it might have evolved in relatively simple animals, and, if we accept an anagenic position on evolution (See Yarczower, 1984) we might expect the process to improve during an evolutionary history. Thus, we begin by looking at apparently large differences in behavior to see if these differences might be related to an evolving and improving process of rehearsal.

SPECIES DIFFERENCES

First let us look at Nissen's (1951) largely psychological treatment of large species differences in behavior relying on what he said about possible evolutionary mechanisms to explain these differences. Nissen points out that, ". . . whether we are impressed more by similarities or by differences of behavior within the animal kingdom depends on the scale of observation used. The broader the category, the more the similarities stand out, and vice versa." He believed that behavior is continuously evolving so that once a form has evolved, new forms will evolve out of the original one so that each phyla has a range of behavioral capacities distinct from the range of capacities of other phyla. The behavioral differences result from the particular aggregate of morphological and behavioral characteristics acting as an integrated organism.

The following is a list of five broad categories of behavior in which there appear to be large differences across species: (1) learning, (2) perception, (3) memory, (4) species specific repertoires, and (5) responses to specific situations. These differences are more familiar in the psychological than in the ethological literature, partly because the former is laboratory based. This bias seems appropriate since theories about information processing are also based on laboratory studies.

Some of the proposed differences may merely represent wide departures from the way in which psychologists had previously described behavior. All of the differences are within the broad classification of being cognitive, although obviously not all are subsumed under *learning*. In some instances the categories overlap with those suggested by Nissen (1951), but other categories are based on more recent experimentation or explanation.

These differences, we submit, may be related to the existence of different systems in information processing, and we are going to develop a case for this by first describing: (a) large differences which occur within these five categories of behavior, then (b) introduce some ideas about information processing in animals, and finally (c) suggest how the evolution of information processing could account for the large differences in the behavior of different species.

1. Differences of learning.   Clearly, learning is a type of behavior that has evolved out of responses to repeated stimulation in protista. Nissen (1951) points out that some of these one-celled organisms have evolved response variability which he regards as a prerequisite for learning; for example, they are capable of acclamation, adaptation, and sensitization without having nerve cells.

In classical conditioning, the CS is neutral by definition. Thus, it has a low probability of initiating rehearsal. On the other hand, the UCS, by our definition of a reinforcer, initiates rehearsal of the immediate stimulus milieu. If the CS is still present when the UCS is presented, rehearsal will be quite frequent. With less overlap between the CS and UCS, the CS will be rehearsed less frequently, and certainly if the CS occurs after the cessation of the UCS (backward conditioning), the CS will not be rehearsed.

Other specially rehearsed stimuli probably are surprising events in which something previously reinforced is no longer reinforced, as well as the converse. If surprising events in the occurrence of rewards initiate rehearsal, the rewarding of a previously nonrewarded stimulus and the nonreinforcement of a previously reinforced stimulus would be expected to initiate rehearsal of the newly rewarded stimulus, and lead to subsequent storage in a permanent store. This, of course meets the criterion of being learned because subsequent presentation of the CS will elicit a CR.

Based on the work of Wagner et al. (1973), we accept the idea that a surprising stimulus is probably rehearsed more intensively or more often than a nonsurprising stimulus. Wagner and Rescorla (1972) and Wagner et al. (1973), were studying classical conditioning and the reinforcing effects of unexpected aspects of the UCS. They found that the reinforcing effects of the UCS depends on the degree to which it is surprising. They postulated that when the UCS was unexpected, it would initiate *scanning backwards*.

One psychologist who has been grouped with Nissen in holding a discontinuous and anagenic position (unidimensional and having progressive improvement—see Demarest, 1983) is Bitterman. Bitterman's (1965) approach is primarily empirical and consists of attempts to give similar problems to different species. He and his coworkers assign problem solving to two categories, rat-like and fish-like. In giving tests of reversal learning and probability matching, either spatially or visually, to animals of different species, Bitterman (1965) is able to assign his categories in a manner that agrees with intuitive progression from *lower* to *higher* forms without reversals. This assumes that there is a sequence of different species which goes from earthworm through cockroach, fish (one reference animal), decorticated rat, turtle, pigeon, and rat (another reference animal) to monkey. One weakness of Bitterman's scheme is that it appears to assume a hierarchy of evolution which is an exception to the prevailing idea of evolution as a branching tree rather than a direct line between one-celled organisms and the deity (Hodos & Campbell, 1969).

Bitterman's results clearly show fish do not seem to be able to reverse a discrimination and tend to probability match, whereas a rat seems to be capable of reversal and tends to maximize rather than probability match. Obviously, it is more interesting if there are two different kinds of learning rather than either learning or no learning because in the latter case there is always the danger, which Bitterman recognizes, that the differences in learning or not learning could be motivational or otherwise artifactual.

Suppose the differences in kinds of learning, described by Bitterman, depended on differences in the capacity or propensity for information processing. Take reversal learning: An animal must first learn to choose one stimulus instead of another. To do this it must be able to encode information about different stimulus properties of the stimuli, so that it remembers which of the stimuli has occurred with a reward. Reversal adds the element of surprise as the previously rewarded stimulus no longer predicts food, whereas the previously incorrect stimulus does predict reward. To be surprised the animal must have remembered and retrieved from memory the previous stimulus-reward relationships. Surprise, as we mentioned earlier, has the effect of selectively initiating rehearsal of the stimulus-reward relationships, so we would expect more rapid learning of the reversal than the original discrimination. There are several possible reasons, using the ideas of information processing, that the gap might occur. Maybe *rat-like* animals do not retrieve prior memories of changed stimulus-reward relationships. Another possibility would be that a surprising stimulus may only initiate rehearsal when an animal can compare the memory of the retrieved stimulus-response relationships with the reversed relationship. Finally, the difficulties which are experienced by Bitterman's *lesser* animals in discrimination reversals maybe due to slower or nonexistent rehearsal.

One of the more promising techniques for demonstrating cross-species differences in learning, according to Hinde (1970), is Harlow's (1949) learning set procedure. In its simplest form, this paradigm involves presenting many successive and distinct two-object simultaneous discrimination problems. Each problem consists of a unique pair of stimuli and is presented a limited number of times. There is intraproblem improvement early in practice, but as practice proceeds there is also an interproblem practice effect. This is determined by comparing the amount learned between Trial-1 (which is chance) and Trial-2 in successive blocks of problems. Performance on Trial-2 improves relatively rapidly in children and rhesus monkeys, but, as Miles (1965) and Miles and Meyer (1956) point out, squirrel monkeys and marmosets are much slower than rhesus monkeys in forming discrimination learning sets. Similarly, Davis, Leary, Stevens, and Thompson (1967) found considerable cross-species differences among nonhuman primates in comparing learning set performance on 120 different 24-trial oddity problems. A given oddity problem consists of presenting three of four objects selected from two identical pairs, and the object which is different is correct and rewarded—obviously chance performance on oddity problems is 33.3% correct. The animals were representatives of four different species of old world monkeys (*Macaca mulatta, M. neministrina, M. arctoides* and *Cercopithecus nictitans;*) three species of new world monkeys (*Cebus apella, Lagothrix lagothrix,* and *Saimiri sciurea*); and one prosimian species (*Lemur catta*). By the end of training, the average performance of these species groups ranged from approximately 50% correct for lemurs and spotnosed monkeys to slightly better than 90% correct for woolly monkeys.

Learning sets, although more developed theoretically, have much in common with nonspecific transfer in verbal learning and perceptual learning (Gibson, 1969). These different theoretical treatments have one feature in common: Subjects must respond to rules concerning relationships between stimuli and correctness (reward) rather than to particular stimuli and their consequences. Thus, the subjects must perceive this relationship and remember it for use in a subsequent problem or stimulus situation. This could be done by rehearsing and storing information about the relationship between a stimulus and its context rather than information about a particular stimulus. (See Medin, 1977, pp. 37–54 for a treatment of learning sets as information processing.) Learning sets also are confused with transfer experiments employing similar stimuli, and several investigators have provided aids, such as a limited number of problems, to supposedly demonstrate learning sets in rodents.

2. Differences in perception.   Nissen (1951) made a good case for evolutionary differences in perception before the time that many psychologists were applying the term *perception* to animals. He clearly tied developmental changes to phylogenetic differences, pointing out that . . . "the difference between initial and ultimate perceptual ability increases as we go from earlier to more recent stages of phylogeny." As an example of this he cites Riesen's (1947) work which showed the necessity for chimpanzees to have early perceptual experience in order to see. We now know that rearing in darkness not only impedes perception in chimpanzees but it also causes retinal degeneration (Reisen, 1961). Rats, unlike apes, do not show sensory or perceptual impairment after prolonged rearing in the dark (Riesen, 1961).

Nissen (1951), in the paper cited earlier, contrasts behavior in mammals and nonmammals, suggesting that the former, unlike the latter, use distance rather than contact receptors, and can respond to still objects as well as to movement. From there, he discusses phylogenetic differences in the perception of relations and the formation of concepts.

One of the most dramatic perceptual differences between species, not mentioned by Nissen, is that described in experiments on *sensory recombination,* a phrase first used by Weiss (1941). Sensory recombination involves reversing, inverting, or distorting the perceptual field either surgically or optically. This literature was put into a comparative perspective by Taub (1968) who pointed out that the effects of recombination differs for various species. This is exemplified by the fact that whereas appropriate responses can be learned by human beings after reversed insertions of muscles or optical reversal of the visual field, these changes supposedly cannot be compensated well by many other species.

Taub (1968) also makes clear that although early work by Weiss (1941) and Sperry (1951) employed surgical procedures with nonmammals, adaptation to optical recombination was studied using human beings and monkeys (Foley, 1940; Stratton, 1897). The differences in ability to recombine stimulus discordance at first appeared to be procedural, but later were shown to differ between species, with larger brained animals able to compensate for recombination and neither smaller brained mammals, amphibians, nor reptiles able to compensate. A football player who has surgical reversal of tendons in his leg following an injury can learn to walk and play again, whereas a rat with a similar operation on its rear limbs continues to make inappropriate responses. Taub (1968) points out that differences in compensation are found between the front but not the hind end of the rat and in both ends of mammals with large brains and neither end of birds, reptiles, or amphibia.

Welch (1978) argues that the evidence for differences is not as clear as Taub suggested since Rossi (1968) apparently found evidence for some adaptation for slight visual displacement in chickens. Rossi (1972) also apparently found that adaptation in the chicken was dependent on development, and that extended periods of feeding enabled adjustment to the distorted visual field. However, even granting that there were no artifacts in Rossi's data, there are existing species which cannot compensate for recombination and species which can compensate.

The change in ability to compensate for sensory recombination must represent a difference in the way animals of different species perceive sensory signals and use the information to make new responses. This is illustrated by the work combining sensory rearrangement with forelimb deafferentiation of rhesus monkeys by Taub and Berman (1968) which shows, at least for this species, that feedback from proprioceptors of the forelimbs are not combined with visual information in adaptation. Rather, compensation must require a change in the manner in which stimuli are perceived and remembered. There must be some mechanism which allows storage or visual information and selection of an alternative, but previously available, motor response. Thus, differences in the ability to compensate for sensory recombination would be related to the more recently evolved explicit rehearsal overriding implicit rehearsal.

Anyone who has worn Iwo Kohler's special spectacles which separately invert the visual field, transpose it from left to right, or displace the image a given number of degrees, can testify to the fact that these optical recombinations are difficult for a person to master and require a great deal of effort and overt rehearsal of movements in a new perceptual arrangement. (See Kohler, 1962, for a popular account.)

An effect that is probably closely related to sensory recombination is the ability of animals to perform motor acts which are discordant to visual information. This occurs in barrier and detour problems—to get to an incentive an animal must circumvent a barrier and take a detour which often requires an animal to go away from the incentive or move the incentive away from rather than toward itself. Davis (1974, Ch.5) reviewed experiments on the solution of bent wire detour problems by a number of species and age groups. In these problems, barriers, which are also detours, were constructed of welding rods in segments separated by 90° bends. Lures of hard candy with holes in the middle (Life Savers) or center punched paper poker chips were slid along the detour until free.

Ordinarily when an animal sees food, it reaches out to grab the food and bring it to its mouth. The main impediment to detour problems is the difficulty experienced by animals in first pushing the candy away so as to ultimately pull it toward their mouths. This was accomplished immediately by 3–5 year-old children and adult chimpanzees, but was more difficult for 2 year-old children and younger chimpanzees. Old world monkeys learned to solve these problems with much practice but lemurs had great difficulty and raccoons could not learn the problem of pushing the food away except by being shaped by a series of approximations. The differences in performance of monkeys and apes were not due to manual dexterity, as Passingham (1982) suggests, since the chimpanzee, which was superior in performance among nonhuman primates, was the most disadvantaged manually.

The difference in performance on problems with food being pulled toward the animal as compared to being pushed away is lessened if an animal is prohibited from seeing what it is doing when moving the candy (Davis, 1974, Experiment

28). While most monkeys learn to solve detour problems under normal conditions, it is a difficult task requiring many repetitions of the situation. In order for an animal to compensate recombination or to solve detour problems, it must be able to perceive that the proprioceptive consequences of approach and retrieval responses are contradicted by other sensory information (usually visual). We might accept the possibility that a person could compensate through deliberate practice to the point of making recompensation responses automatically, so why is it unreasonable to suggest that if a nonhuman animal can perceive discordance of sensory input, it also can process information by a rehearsal mechanism. If overt rehearsal can override covert rehearsal, one would expect that the consequences of sensory recombination would be very different in animals with the capacity for both explicit and implicit rehearsal, as opposed to those only capable of implicit rehearsal.

3. Species differences in memory.   The third notable example of behavioral differences between species in cognitive functioning is the *specificity and persistence of memory* to particular kinds of stimulation. There are at least five examples of this:

a. The Garcia effect is a phenomenon in which there is adequate learning about S–R relationships with considerable time elapsing between the stimulus and response. Thus, if the taste of saccharin is sufficiently distinctive (surprising) and appropriate, it should cause rehearsal and memory of the taste and its context. Considerably later when the rat gets sick (from irradiation), the memory of saccharin is retrieved from long-term memory because of contextual cues, and this memory is rehearsed again along with the stimulus associated with sickness, and is associated with the taste as a cue for aversion (Garcia, Kimeldorf, & Hunt, 1961; Garcia & Koelling, 1966). Note, as we have already indicated, some stimuli are more appropriate for rehearsal by a particular species than other stimuli, so, in this case it is the surprising taste which is rehearsed.

b. Similarly, quail associate sight but not taste of food with long delayed illness (Wilcoxon, Dragoin, & Kral, 1971).

c. Salmon learn the chemical properties of their home stream and remember it years later as a place to go when it is time to spawn (Hasler, 1966).

d. Imprinting is reported in chicks or ducklings which remember the first moving objects they see after hatching as the appropriate thing to follow and ultimately as a model for mating (Lorenz, 1937). This behavior is dissimilar to that seen in other species since it appears to be restricted to certain birds. Conspicuous and round stimuli are particularly effective as stimuli for imprinting (Smith, 1962), and time of viewing the stimulus seems to be of paramount importance.

e. The last example of differences in memory between various species is infantile amnesia which really provides two subexamples. First, there is the inability of human beings and adults of several other species to remember pertinent early experiences, whereas later events can be remembered after time spans which are as long as the interval of time between infancy and adulthood. Second, although the effect of infantile amnesia is seen in atrical animals, it is not seen in animals which are born with a relatively mature nervous system (Campbell, Misanin, White, & Lytle, 1974). An interesting aspect of this phenomenon is that amnesia occurs with the passage of time but does not occur if reminders (a part of the original stimulus) are provided during the intervening period of maturation (Campbell & Jaynes, 1966).

An up-to-date review of the infantile amnesia literature is found in Spear and Campbell's (1979) collection of papers on *Ontogeny of Learning and Memory*. These contributions make it clear that there are various explanations for infantile amnesia and some indirect support for the idea. As Coulter (1979) points out, some of these attempts at explanation are behavioral, such as retroactive inhibition (RI), and some are developmental and neurological, such as in immaturity of the nervous system. The basis for evoking RI is that individuals have more experiences as they age and thus have greater opportunity for subsequently learned ideas to interfere retroactively, an explanation that is not compatible with the fact that infantile amnesia does not occur in species having a mature brain at birth (Campbell et al., 1974).

There are two kinds of neurological theories of developmental differences in memory; one, that immature structures may not yet be functioning, the other that because of maturational changes previously acquired memories may not be available. Another explanation, which is both behavioral and neurological, such as overshadowing mentioned by Gordon (1979), reminds us that when stimulus compounds are conditioned the more intense or more salient one may be remembered and the other one forgotten. Thus, the immaturity of the nervous system causes one part of a stimulus compound to overshadow another component of the compound. Generally, there are logical and empirical contradictions to each of the theories which have been proposed. Therefore, a more inclusive theory is needed.

Coulter (1979) entertains the idea that animals of different ages have various strategies of learning, attend to different stimuli, develop different response patterns, or acquire different associations. It would be tidier to suppose that developmental differences in learning involve the maturation or senescence of one mechanism such as rehearsal, or, following an ethological bias, multiple levels of the mechanism.

Although the five examples of species differences in memory, as well as examples of apparent species differences in memory for locations of stored food, are typically treated as distinct phenomena, each could be related to differences in the persistence of memory in different species. The first four examples pertain to particularly robust memories which are characteristic of some species but not others, and the persistence of memory in the last three examples is related to the time at which the memory is encoded. We feel that it is reasonable to suggest that processing of information by selective rehearsal, or by selectively initiating rehearsal might be an acceptable explanation of each of these examples.

4. Species differences in behavioral repertoire.   Another large area of species differences is that of particular behavioral repertoires. Many of the examples provided by ethologists of fixed action patterns fit into this category. Differences in repertoire probably overlaps with examples given above as examples of differences between species in learning and perception, but particular repertoires are included separately because they have been treated independently in the literature of comparative psychology. Psychologists talk about such phenomena as preparedness (Breland & Breland, 1961; Dobrzecka, Szwejkowska, & Konorski, 1966) in which particular stimuli are relevant for a particular response; that is, animals of a particular species learn some responses to some stimuli more readily than responses to other stimuli.

Related to this is the phenomenon described by Bolles (1970) of species specific defense reactions in escape and avoidance. He reports that each species is predetermined to use a particular form of avoidance and that it is quite difficult to get a species to employ any other method of avoiding noxious stimuli. Species specific responses probably include the attentiveness of human infants to the sound of the human voice and the production of speech sounds.

Logically, it would be disastrous if all stimuli were rehearsed and remembered equally well. Ethologists have noted that not all stimuli are equal in eliciting responses, and the stimuli which bring about responses are identified as releasers. Releasers produce responses having to do with survival of the species—eating of regurgitated food by the young, escaping predation, care of young and eggs, and consuming food and water.

If some stimuli can be selected to produce some specific responses, it is reasonable to make an assumption that *a mechanism could evolve which selected stimuli for the response of rehearsal* leading, of course, to memorization. Stimuli selected to be rehearsed undoubtedly are involved with the persistence of a species. Imprinting in birds and recognition of streams by fish might be related to orientation and repetition of the stimulus, although one might expect habituation to occur. However, if each organism has a tendency to rehearse particular kinds of stimuli, permanent memory of those stimuli is possible. After all, we are not surprised by memory in an adult lifetime in human beings, and we should not be surprised if there were long-term memory of selectively rehearsed stimuli by chickens and salmon.

Assuming selective rehearsal, and if the speed and number of rehearsals is subject to phylogenetic change, we would expect that more and more aspects of a given stimulus could be rehearsed in more highly developed than simpler species. Rehearsal then would be more and more specific. Suppose that a rat is given several hundred repetitions of a black-white discrimination in a Y-maze (Grice box) or a jumping stand. Ultimately the attribute of lightness (black or white) is rehearsed in the presence of reward which initiates rehearsal of the compound. The presentation of a particular reflected light intensity will initiate rehearsal of the reward so that the particular lightness will be stored and later chosen. This is a slow and inefficient process unless there is high selectivity of stimuli or a high rate of rehearsal of particular visual stimuli.

Repetition of part of a previous stimulus may also function in the retrieval of memory. Spear (1973), in discussing warm-up and facilitation of retention in animals, makes the point from Postman's (1969) work that even in verbal memory, human beings benefit more from warm-up if they receive stimuli containing some attributes of that original memory. We suggest that stimuli repeating something that is already in secondary memory, calls forth, to working memory (presumably STM), the stimulus compound of which the segment is a part. This may then cause re-rehearsal of the compound in working memory. As Wagner (1981) points out, neither he (Wagner, 1978) nor Konorski (1967) accept the idea that the retrieved memories are rehearsed in the manner of new stimulation. Wagner (1981) employs the idea of *spread of activation* to account for the disposition of retrieved memories. This notion was developed by Collins and Loftus (1975). Since this spread of activation is in terms of initiating nodes and associative links, we prefer to stick to the simpler idea that a component of a stimulus compound is sufficient to initiate the previously stored compound, and that since responses only result from working memory, the compound must be rehearsed again. This is not necessarily contradictory to the idea that long-term storage has nodes which represent special retrievability.

5. Responses to specific situations.   A fifth general area of considerable differences in the behavior of different species or strains can be identified as situation or paradigm specificity. Are all species equally capable of performing on a given kind of problem? Do their response proclivities depend on species specificity? These questions are usually posed by psychologists in terms of traditional classifications of learning such as a contrast in the ability of different species to master classical and instrumental conditioning. Describing these studies under the classification of paradigm specificity rather than differences in learning is arbitrary, but is done because of the fact that many of the examples are relatively recent and frequently within a rather narrow theoretical structure. Sometimes, the differences in these studies are not between different species of subjects but in the experimenter's inability to employ homologous situations for testing analogous kinds of learning in animals with different behavioral repertoires.

There is a tendency to regard preference for specific situations as being a species specific phenomenon. However, Wecker (1963), trapping different races of deermice, one race living in forests and the other in grasslands, showed that offspring of grassland living mice preferred a field over a forest habitat, but after 12 generations of laboratory rearing, the young animals preferred the field only if they had been subjected to field rearing. This indicated to Wecker that the genotype has an initial but not ultimate influence on preference.

This example may appear only remotely related and difficult to describe in terms of information processing. However, it is obvious in human beings that many if not most preferences are learned, including appropriate habitat. However, preferences in the form of likes and dislikes for tastes, body comfort, and textures are seen in human infants and in newborn rhesus monkeys (Harlow & Zimmerman, 1959). Obviously, some animals can learn new preferences. In the present context, something may be learned if it is rehearsed sufficiently often to be remembered and subsequently retrieved. One would expect in the above example, that the deermice reared in the laboratory would experience a different set of stimuli than those reared in the field and that they would rehearse the stimuli in the particular environment, thereby, through retrieval of memories, acquiring a preference for the particular habitat.

This explanation does not deal with the difference in preference between offspring of field living mice and offspring from mice after twelve generations in the laboratory. It creates a difficult problem for our scheme unless we ask whether Wecker's (1963) experiment controlled for the social behaviors of the dams reared in the wild and laboratory, and how these social behaviors affected preferences of the offspring. Obviously, cross-fostering would be a good control.

In recent years many examples of species differences can be found in the literature on operant conditioning, generally under the rubric of the generality of a particular model. Among the many possible examples are autoshaping and behavioral contrast (Boakes, 1977; Dougan, McSweeney, & Farmer, 1985), and postfast anorexia (Rowland, 1982). In each case animals of particular species do not behave in the same manner as predicted by models devised from the behavior of animals in other species or strains within a species. There are many other strain differences, particularly in rodents, which we have not noted, such as differential preference for alcohol and degree of aggressiveness. Obviously one reason these examples lack generality is because the predictions are very specific.

The above list of species differences in cognition is certainly not exhaustive since within each of the broad areas we identified there are numerous other examples, particularly in the ethological literature. However, by outlining differences familiar to comparative psychologists, we have provided a context which might have greater appeal to the reader not particularly familiar with the ethological literature.

COMPONENTS OF REHEARSAL

Realizing that monkeys not only rehearse but do so both overtly and covertly, and being stimulated by Salthouse's (1982) idea that the progression of aging slows down information processing, we wondered if factors of initiation, speed, frequency, duration, number of rehearsals, and selection of stimuli to be rehearsed might not provide the basis for a more parsimonious explanation of memory phenomena than what Underwood (1972) referred to as a presently overloaded theoretical structure.

The structure we offered is based on the evolution and development of the information processing mechanism of rehearsal. First we described this mechanism, then reviewed examples of species differences to determine if our suggestions have generality. It is the authors' opinion that every one of the seeming discontinuities we described can be related to the evolution of rehearsal mechanisms.

Domjan and Galef (1983) wrote a provocative paper in which they pointed out that so called biological constraints on learning need not be incompatible with general principles of associative learning. Rather than regarding these as biological constraints, they suggest a theory be built that first looks at biological adaptations, then examines existing theories of learning to explain the phenomena in closely related species. We have taken a somewhat different tack in this paper. Rather than looking at the behavior of closely related species we have looked at apparent gaps between the cognitive behaviors in different species and asked if these differences might be explained by an evolutionary model of information processing. Upon these apparent discrepancies we have superimposed our ideas that the evolution of information processing rehearsal mechanisms manage to explain many of the apparent differences in cognitive functioning.

There probably are phylogenetic differences between species occurring as: (1) biochemical synaptic changes based on stimulus repetition, (2) internal automatic mechanisms of repetition (rehearsal), (3) mechanisms of initiating rehearsal as well as to increasing its speed and frequency, (4) selection of which stimuli should be rehearsed, and, finally, (5) overt mechanisms of rehearsal.

SUMMARY

This paper describes mechanisms of rehearsal basic to cognitive function by all animals, including human beings, then illustrates apparent species differences in the behaviors of animals that appear to be related to the evolution of these mechanisms. It entertains the idea that factors of rehearsal, including initiation, speed, frequency, duration, method of storage, and stimulus specificity of rehearsal, are critical to learning and memory of various species. Various examples of apparent discontinuities of behavior suggest that these mechanisms of rehearsal were evolved. We review the reasons for this position.

1. *Initiation of rehearsal.* As various species evolved, certain stimuli which are related to survival, such as food and water, took on the property of causing rehearsal to begin. Correlated stimuli are rehearsed at the same time and stored. These stimulus situations have become known as reinforcers.

2. *Speed of information processing.* We borrowed the idea from the gerontological literature that speed of information processing including rehearsal is related to speed of neural conduction. Speed of conduction differentiates warm and cold blooded animals, as well as to a lesser extent, younger and older mammals. Thus, the evolution or development of faster or slower neural conduction would affect speed of rehearsal and ultimate storage and retrieval of information.

3. *Duration and number of rehearsals.* It is difficult to separate the duration of rehearsal and the frequency of rehearsal, either one of which may facilitate long-term memory for weak stimuli. This more extensive long-term memory also may have been accomplished by mechanisms which evolved to store information through molecular changes in neurons as well as changes in the chemistry of presynaptic terminals. The evolution of long-term memory apparently decreased the number or duration of rehearsals required for permanent store.

4. *Control of rehearsal.* It is our position that stimulus repetition was the first method of rehearsing. It became particularly advantageous for survival for animals to be able to rehearse stimuli intrinsically. Subsequently, in the history of evolution, there was a particular advantage for some species to rehearse stimuli which were particularly relevant for survival in a given niche. Then, with increasing encephalization, there was an advantage to select particular stimuli which were rehearsed. This demanded the ability of an animal to perceive episodes having significance and to be able to override motor commands with available sensory information.

ACKNOWLEDGMENTS

This chapter was written during a time the first author was at the University of Missouri, Columbia, on professional leave from Washington State University, Pullman. He is especially grateful to the collegiality of members of the Psychology Department at Missouri. Particular thanks are due to Drs. Dennis Wright, Charles Brown, and Donald H. Kausler for their suggestions when the first author was in the early stages of preparing this ms; to an anonymous reviewer who critically read the first draft, and to John Hinson at Pullman who read and made comments on later drafts. Finally, the first author is very grateful to his wife, Margaret L. Davis, for applying her excellent editorial and word processing skills.

REFERENCES

Bitterman, M. E. (1965). Phyletic differences in learning. *American Psychologist, 20,* 396–410.
Boakes, R. A. (1977). Performance on learning to associate a stimulus with positive reinforcement. In H. Davis & H. M. B. Hurwitz (Eds.), *Operant-Pavlovian Interactions.* Hillsdale, NJ: Lawrence Erlbaum Associates.
Bolles, R. C. (1970). Species-specific defense reactions and avoidance learning. *Psychological Review, 77,* 32–48.
Broadbent, D. E. (1958). *Perception and communication.* New York: Pergamon.
Breland, K., & Breland, M. (1961). The misbehavior of organisms. *American Psychologist, 16,* 681–684.
Brown, J. (1958). Some tests of the decay theory of immediate memory. *Quarterly Journal of Experimental Psychology, 10,* 12–21.
Campbell, B. A., & Jaynes, J. (1966). Reinstatement. *Psychological Review, 73,* 478–480.
Campbell, B. A., Misanin, J. R., White, B. C., & Lytle, L. D. (1974). Species differences in ontogeny of memory: Support for neural maturation as a determinant of forgetting. *Journal of Comparative and Physiological Psychology, 87,* 193–202.
Collins, A. M., & Loftus, E. F. (1975). A spreading effect theory of semantic processing. *Psychological Review, 82,* 407–428.
Coulter, X. (1979). The determinants of infantile amnesia. In N. E. Spear & B. A. Campbell (Eds.), *Ontogeny of learning and memory.* Hillsdale, NJ: Lawrence Erlbaum Associates.
Davis, R. T. (1974). Monkeys as perceivers. In L. A. Rosenblum (Ed.), *Primate behavior: Developments in field and laboratory research,* Vol. 3 (whole volume). New York: Academic Press.
Davis, R. T. (1978). Old monkey behavior. *Experimental Gerontology, 13,* 237–250.
Davis, R. T. (1985). The effects of aging on the behavior of rhesus monkeys. In R. T. Davis & C. W. Leathers (Eds.), *Pathology and behavior of old rhesus monkeys.* New York: Alan R. Liss.
Davis, R. T., Leary, R. W., Stevens, D. A., & Thompson, R. F. (1967). Learning and perception of oddity problems by lemurs and seven species of monkey. *Primates, 8,* 311–322.
Demarest, J. (1983). The ideas of change, progress, and continuity in the comparative psychology of learning. In D. W. Rajecki (Ed.), *Comparing behavior: Studying man studying animals.* Hillsdale, NJ: Lawrence Erlbaum Associates.
Dobrzecka, C., Szwejkowska, G., & Konorski, J. (1966). Qualitative versus directional cues in two forms of differentiation. *Science,* 87–89.
Domjan, M., & Galef, B. G. (1983). Biological constraints on instrumental and classical conditioning: Retrospect and prospect. *Animal Learning and Behavior, 11,* 115–161.
Dougan, J. D., McSweeney, F. K., & Farmer, V. A. (1985). Some parameters of behavioral contrast and allocation of interim behaviors in rats. *Journal of the Experimental Analysis of Behavior, 44,* 325–335.
Flagg, S. F. (1975). *Transformation of position and short-term memory in rhesus monkeys.* Unpublished doctoral dissertation, Washington State University, Pullman.
Foley, J. P. (1940). An experimental investigation of the effect of prolonged inversion of the visual field of the rhesus monkey (*Macaca mulatta*). *Journal of Genetic Psychology, 56,* 21–51.
Fraenkel, G., & Gunn, D. L. (1940). *The orientation of animals, kineses, taxes and compass reactions.* New York: Oxford University Press.
Garcia, J., & Koelling, R. A. (1966). The relation of cue to consequence in avoidance learning. *Psychonomic Science, 4,* 123–124.

Garcia, J., Kimeldorf, D. J., & Hunt, E. L. (1961). The use of ionizing radiation as a motivating stimulus. *Psychological Review, 68,* 363–385.

Gibson, E. J. (1969). *Principles of perceptual learning and development.* New York: Appleton-Century-Crofts.

Gordon, W. C. (1979). Age: Is it a constraint on memory content? In N. E. Spear & B. A. Campbell (Eds.), *Ontogeny of learning and memory.* Hillsdale, NJ: Lawrence Erlbaum Associates.

Harlow, H. F. (1949). The formation of learning sets. *Psychological Review, 56,* 51–65.

Harlow, H. F., & Zimmerman, R. R. (1959). Affectional responses in the infant monkey. *Science, 130,* 421–432.

Hasler, A. D. (1966). *Underwater guideposts.* Madison: University of Wisconsin Press.

Hebb, D. O. (1949). *The organization of behavior.* New York: Wiley.

Hinde, R. A. (1970). *Animal Behaviour: A synthesis of Ethology and Comparative Psychology* (2nd Ed.). New York: McGraw-Hill.

Hodos, W., & Campbell, C. B. G. (1969). Scala naturae: Why is there no theory in comparative psychology? *Psychological Review, 76,* 337–350.

Huntingford, F. A. (1984). *The study of animal behaviour.* London: Chapman and Hall.

Kandel, E. R., & Schwartz, J. H. (1982). Molecular biology of learning: Modulation of transmitter release. *Science, 218,* 433–443.

Kohler, I. (1962). Experiments with goggles. *Scientific American, 206,* 62–86.

Konorski, J. (1967). *Integrative activity of the brain.* Chicago: University of Chicago Press.

Kristan, W. B. (1980). Generation of rhythmic motor patterns. In H. M. Pinsker & W. D. Willis, Jr. (Eds.), *Information processing in the nervous system.* New York: Raven Press.

Lorenz, K. (1937). Uber die bildung des instinktbegriffs. *Naturwissenschaften,* 25.

Medin, D. L. (1977). Learning sets. In A. M. Schrier (Ed.), *Behavioral primatology: Advances in research and theory.* Hillsdale, NJ: Lawrence Erlbaum Associates.

Miles, R. C. (1965). Discrimination learning sets. In A. M. Schrier, H. F. Harlow, & F. Stollnitz (Eds.), *Behavior of nonhuman primates: Modern research trends* (Vol. 1). New York: Academic Press.

Miles, R. C., & Meyer, D. R. (1956). Learning sets in marmosets. *Journal of Comparative and Physiological Psychology, 49,* 219–222.

Muller, G. E., & Pilzecker, A. (1900). Experimentelle Beitrage zur Untersuchung des Gedachtnes. *Zeitschrift fur Psychologie, Erganzungsband, 1.*

Nissen, H. W. (1951). Phyletic comparison. In S. S. Stevens (Ed.), *Handbook of experimental psychology.* New York: Wiley.

Passingham, R. E. (1982). *The human primate.* San Francisco: W. H. Freeman.

Peterson, L. R., & Peterson, M. J. (1959). Short-term retention of individual verbal items. *Journal of Experimental Psychology, 58,* 193–198.

Postman, L. (1969). Experimental analysis of learning to learn. In G. R. Bower & J. T. Spence (Eds.), *Psychology of learning and motivation* (Vol. 3). New York: Academic Press.

Riesen, A. H. (1947). The development of visual perception in man and chimpanzee. *Science, 106,* 107–108.

Riesen, A. H. (1961). Stimulation as a requirement for growth and function of behavioral development. In D. W. Fiske & S. R. Maddi (Eds.), *Functions of varied experience.* Homewood, IL: Dorsey Press.

Rossi, P. J. (1968). Adaptation and negative aftereffect to lateral optical displacement in newly hatched chicks. *Science, 160,* 430–432.

Rossi, P. J. (1972). Population density and food dispersion on the development of prism-induced aftereffects in newly hatched chicks. *Developmental Psychobiology, 5,* 239–248.

Rowland, N. (1982). Failure by deprived hamsters to increase food intake: Some behavioral and physiological determinants. *Journal of Comparative and Physiological Psychology, 96,* 591–603.

Ruggiero, F. T. (1974). Coding processes and contextual cues in monkey short term memory. (Doctoral dissertation, Washington State University, 1974). *Dissertation Abstracts International,* 35B, No. 1, 555–556 (University Microfilms No. 74-16, 392).

Salthouse, T. A. (1982). *Adult cognition: An experimental psychology of aging.* New York: Springer-Verlag.

Sechenov, I. M. (1889). *Reflexes of the brain.*

Smith, F. V. (1962). Perceptual aspects of imprinting. *Symposia of the Zoological Society of London, 8,* 171–191.

Spear, N. E. (1973). Retrieval of memory in animals. *Psychological Review, 80,* 163–194.

Spear, N. E. (1978). *The processing of memories: Forgetting and retention.* Hillsdale, NJ: Lawrence Erlbaum Associates.

Spear, N. E., & Campbell, B. A. (1979). *Ontogeny of learning and memory.* Hillsdale, NJ: Lawrence Erlbaum Associates.

Sperry, R. W. (1951). Mechanisms of neural maturation. In S. S. Stevens (Ed.), *Handbook of experimental psychology.* New York: Wiley.

Stratton, G. M. (1897). Vision without inversion of the retinal image. *Psychological Review, 4,* 341–360, 463–481.

Taub, E. (1968). Prism compensation as a learning phenomenon: A phylogenetic perspective. In S. J. Freeman (Ed.), *The psychology of spatially oriented behavior.* Homewood, IL: Dorsey Press.

Taub, E., & Berman, A. J. (1968). Movement and learning in the absence of sensory feedback. In S. J. Freeman (Ed.), *The neuropsychology of spatially oriented behavior.* Homewood, IL: Dorsey Press.

Underwood, B. J. (1972). Are we overloading memory? In A. W. Melton & E. Martin (Eds.), *Coding processes in human memory.* New York: Wiley.

Wagner, A. R. (1978). Expectancies and the priming of STM. In S. H. Hulse, H. Fowler, & W. K. Honig (Eds.), *Cognitive processes in animal behavior.* Hillsdale, NJ: Lawrence Erlbaum Associates.

Wagner, A. R. (1981). SOP: A model of automatic memory processing in animal behavior. In N. E. Spear & R. E. Miller (Eds.), *Information processing in Animals.* Hillsdale, NJ: Lawrence Erlbaum Associates.

Wagner, A. R., & Rescorla, R. A. (1972). Inhibition in Pavlovian conditioning: Application of a theory. In R. A. Boakes & M. S. Halliday (Eds.), *Inhibition and learning.* Orlando, FL: Academic Press.

Wagner, A. R., Rudy, J. W., & Whitlow, J. W. (1973). Rehearsal in animal conditioning. *Journal of Experimental Psychology, 97,* 407–426. (Monograph)

Watkins, M. J., Peynircioğlu, Z. F., & Burns, D. J. (1984). Pictorial Rehearsal. *Memory and Cognition, 12,* 553–557.

Wecker, S. C. (1963). The role of early experience in habitat selection by the prairie deermouse (*Peromyscus maniculatus bairdi*). *Ecology Monographs, 33,* 307–325.

Weiss, P. A. (1941). Self-differentiation of the basic patterns of coordination. *Comparative Psychology Monographs, 17,* 1–96.

Welch, R. B. (1978). *Perceptual modification: Adapting to altered sensory environments.* Orlando, FL: Academic Press.

Wilcoxon, H. C., Dragoin, W. B., & Kral, P. A. (1971). Illness-induced aversions in rat and quail: Relative salience of visual and gustatory cues. *Science, 171,* 826–828.

Yarczower, M. (1984). Behavior and evolutionary progress: anagenesis, grades and evolutionary scales. In G. Greenberg & E. Tobach (Eds.), *Behavioral evolution and integrative levels: The T. C. Schneirla Conference series.* Hillsdale, NJ: Lawrence Erlbaum Associates.

9

Contrasting Styles of Song Development and Their Consequences Among Passerine Birds

Donald E. Kroodsma
University of Massachusetts, Amherst

INTRODUCTION

Diversity, complexity, beauty, and myriad superlatives are the stuff of which bird song is made. Poets, philosophers, and naturalists have been busy and entertained for centuries with these sounds. Yet, the fuss, observes an objective but not necessarily dispassionate modern-day "avian bioacoustician," is not distributed equally among all bird groups.

The interest in bird sounds has focused disproportionately on a group of birds that we call songbirds, or, to brandish the latin, the oscines. Larks, nightingales (and other thrushes), wrens, blackbirds, warblers, and sparrows are but a few of the different forms, and altogether these "dickey birds" of the birdwatcher constitute about 46% of the approximately 9000 species of birds in the world (Bock & Farrand, 1980). This group of birds has been overwhelmingly successful by all measures, and is believed to be the pinnacle of avian evolution.

Together with these songbirds in the same taxonomic order (Passeriformes) is a second group of birds, the "suboscines," or "sub-songbirds." This is largely a New World group, and includes species such as flycatchers, ovenbirds, woodcreepers, and antbirds. These suboscines evolved primarily on the continent of South America before the Panamanian land-bridge joined the two Americas (Feduccia, 1980). The name of this suboscine group is intriguing, for these birds are known more by what they are not and by what they have not achieved than by what they are in themselves! They are *beneath* the songbirds, and are considered to be the more evolutionarily *primitive* of the two groups.

According to several taxonomic studies, the oscines and suboscines had a common ancestor (Raikow, 1982) and they are clearly two distinct groups that have since had separate evolutionary histories (Sibley & Ahlquist, 1985; Feduccia, 1980). Several characters have been used to distinguish these two groups, including the shapes of several bones and the complexity of the sperm. More important here is that the syrinx, or vocal organ, of the songbirds is considerably more complex (Feduccia, 1980), for it is controlled by a larger number of muscles than is the syrinx of the sub-songbirds.

This syringeal complexity may be only the tip of the "vocal iceberg," for these two groups seem to differ in another fundamental way. Vocal learning, or the ability to imitate sounds of other birds, has been exploited to the fullest by the songbirds, and evidence now exists for this learning in hundreds of songbird species (Kroodsma & Baylis, 1982). The result of this form of learning has been some of the finest melodies in the animal world. All songbirds seem to learn their songs to some degree, but there is no solid evidence of vocal learning in the suboscine suborder of the Passeriformes (Kroodsma, 1984, 1985a).

There are perhaps two dozen other orders of birds, including such forms as the chicken-like birds (Galliformes), the parrots (Psittaciformes), and the hummingbirds (Apodiformes). The vast majority of orders are nonpasserine orders, yet all combined these orders contain only about 42% of all the bird species in the world. Parrots, of course, are excellent vocal imitators (e.g., Pepperberg, 1981; Todt, 1975), and some limited evidence also implicates vocal learning by quails (Bailey & Baker, 1982, unpublished data) and hummingbirds (Snow, 1968; Wiley, 1971).

In order to understand the evolutionary consequences of vocal learning in birds, I wish to compare here in detail the vocal behavior of selected species from the two passerine subgroups. I address two major issues, geographic variation and song repertoires, and attempt to understand the developmental process that must be tailored to achieve different ends. Selective pressure on the adult song, the functional stage of the behavior, leads to both geographic variation and song repertoire sizes, but these selective pressures must be reflected in and or be constrained by the developmental process. In short, insights on the process can be gleaned by a study of the product.

I begin with a discussion of the behaviors in the more *primitive* suborder, the suboscines. This discussion provides an excellent baseline against which to compare the complex vocal behaviors of the more advanced oscines.

VOCAL BEHAVIOR AND ITS DEVELOPMENT AMONG SUBOSCINES

The suboscines are primarily a Central and South American group, and only the flycatchers (family Tyrannidae) have successfully invaded North America. Because these species are "inconvenient" for the north temperate-zone bioacoustician to study, little is known about their biology relative to that of the oscines.

However, several studies of suboscines have provided some striking contrasts with what is now known for the oscines.

Geographic Variation

Among the approximately 375 tyrannid flycatchers, the genus with the most species is *Myiarchus*. In North America the two most common representatives are the Great Crested Flycatcher (*M. crinitus;* eastern N.A.) and the Ash-throated Flycatcher (*M. cinerascens;* southwestern U.S.). The geographic ranges of 20 other species are concentrated south of the Mexico–U.S. border.

In his taxonomic studies of the 11 South American species in this genus, Lanyon (1978) extensively recorded the songs as one character for study. He conclusively documented for most species that "there is no evidence . . . to suggest that there is geographical veriation in any of the vocal characters . . ." (p. 493). The dawn song of *M. tuberculifer* nicely demonstrates this stereotypy over space (see Fig. 9.1); from Argentina to Panama, spanning five subspecies, the form of the song is remarkably constant. In addition, songs of this same species from Arizona consist of the very same three elements (dawn song available on Kellogg, 1962, a 33 ⅓rpm record).

The only geographic variation that Lanyon found in these *Myiarchus* species involved (a) a negative correlation between body size (as measured by mean wing length) and the mean frequency of vocalizations in two species, (b) the

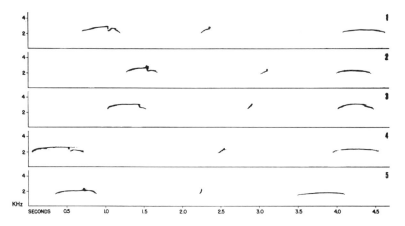

FIGURE 9.1.   Examples of dawn songs of the suboscine *Myiarchus tuberculifer,* the Dusky-capped Flycatcher, illustrating a remarkable uniformity in song characteristics from Argentina to Panama. These sonagrams were made with a 45 Hz. filter and are from recordings of the following populations: *M. t. brunneiceps* (Panama, 3); *M. t. pallidus* (Venezuela, 2); *M. t. nigriceps* (Colombia, 4); *M. t. atriceps* (Argentina, 5); *M. t. tuberculifer* (Bolivia, 1). From Lanyon (1978).

apparent absence of a "hiccup" vocalization in one subspecies of *M. cephalotes,* and (c) in one subspecies of *M. swainsoni* a modification of one call and the elimination of the "hiccup" call from the daytime repertoire but not the dawn song. Contrary to what is routinely discovered among oscines (see below), the geographic differences are not found among neighboring populations of the same subspecies. On the contrary, geographic variation seems to occur (a) only between subspecies where sufficiently large genetic differences have occurred to render the groups morphologically distinct, or (b) only as a result of corresponding differences in body size.

Work with other tyrannid flycatchers has also demonstrated a relative lack of geographic variation. Payne and Budde (1979) found no microgeographic variation in songs of the Acadian Flycatcher (*Empidonax virescens*) along a 26 km section of the Potomac River in Maryland, and Stein (1963) recognized no geographic variation in songs of the Alder Flycatcher (*Empidonax alnorum*) and Willow Flycatcher (*Empidonax traillii*). However, Johnson's (1980) thorough analyses of the vocalizations of the Western Flycatcher (*Empidonax difficilis*) and the Yellowish Flycatcher (*Empidonax flavescens*) have demonstrated very clear examples of geographic trends in both songs and calls: "Broad regions of uniformity in note structure are separated by relatively narrow belts where the character changes abruptly or where a mixture of note types is seen" (p. 70). Examples of these broad regions include the Channel Islands off the coast of California, the coast of northwestern North America, the interior of the United States and Mexico, and the Central American highlands. Given the style of vocal development in this genus (see next section), it is quite likely that the geographic differences in vocalizations actually reflect genetically different populations, subspecies, or perhaps even undescribed species.

There has been little work with other suboscine groups. Snow (1977) believes that the individual variation in calls of male Three-wattled Bellbirds (*Procnias tricarunculata*), the regional variation in calls, and the extended period of practice for juvenile males all implicate vocal learning in this cotinga (family Cotingidae of the suboscines). While the *practice* could be a form of maturation without learning, the individual and population variation certainly suggest behaviors different from the flycatchers. Further data on this species and perhaps other cotingids would be very interesting.

Vocal Development

To my knowledge, the vocal development of only three suboscine species has been studied spectrographically (Kroodsma, 1984, 1985a). Those three species are the Alder Flycatcher, Willow Flycatcher, and the Eastern Phoebe (*Sayornis phoebe*), all members of the family Tyrannidae. Both females (when given testosterone) and males of all three species developed remarkably normal wild-type songs, even if they had not heard those songs since removed from the nest as early as 7-days-of-age.

The Alder Flycatcher male typically sings just one song form, the *fee-bee-o* (Fig. 9.2), and juveniles utter a vocalization similar to this adult song immediately after leaving the nest. The Willow Flycatcher sings three different vocalizations during a typical session: the *creet, fizz-bew*, and *fitz-bew* (Fig. 9.2). All three adult songs are recognizably different to the (discriminating) human ear, and the first vocalizations that the fledgling Willow Flycatcher utters are very similar to the "creet." A few days later, other two-noted calls develop that vaguely resemble either the *fizz-bew* or *fitz-bew*. The third tyrannid, the Eastern Phoebe, has a repertoire of two song forms (Smith, 1977). I did not hear any of the juveniles utter vocalizations similar to either of the adult song forms; in this regard the phoebe seems to differ from the two *Empidonax* species.

Both the geographic variation and vocal development in these tyrannid flycatchers indicate that vocal imitation is not required to produce the normal wild-type song form. Juveniles taken from the nest at 7-days-of-age and then either isolated or tutored with hetero-specific vocalizations develop good wild-type songs. Geographic variation is limited, with subspecies or extensive regions of semi-isolated populations singing slightly different songs that may even reflect genetic differences among the groups. The conclusion that the adult songs of these flycatchers are genetically programmed, and can develop without imitation

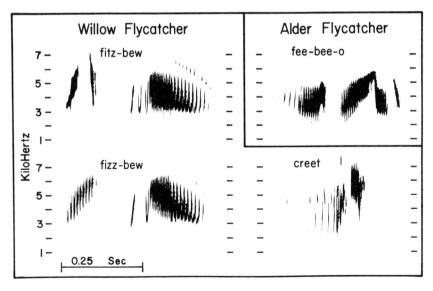

FIGURE 9.2. The highly stereotyped songs of two suboscines, the Alder Flycatcher and the Willow flycatcher. The analyzing filter used for these sonagrams and those in subsequent figures was 300 Hz.

of conspecifics, is based on data from several different tyrannid species, and it is the only reasonable conclusion consistent with all of the data.

While these flycatchers may not *require* vocal imitation in order to develop normal songs, they may be able to modify some of the finer details of their vocalizations to match those of social partners or rivals. Bailey and Baker (1982, unpublished data) have demonstrated this process with Bobwhites (*Colinus virginianus*), and I am currently testing whether interacting phoebes converge in subtle song characteristics. If these flycatchers can modify minor aspects of their songs it would suggest that vocal development in oscines (and other obvious vocal learners) may not differ qualitatively, but only quantitatively, from birds in other orders (or suborders). This distinction is an important one to make before we can properly understand the evolution of vocal learning among birds.

The process of vocal learning itself can be dissected still further. Songbirds actually have two "critical periods" during which song must be *learned* (Nottebohm, 1969; Marler & Peters, 1982). During the first phase, songs of adults are memorized; during the second phase, the young bird attempts to match its motor output with this model stored in the brain. In some species these two phases overlap, but in others they may not. The three flycatcher species that I have studied clearly do not require the first learning phase, for young birds do not have to imitate songs of other adults in order to produce normal songs. Thus, the song *template* (Marler, 1976) does not *need* to be refined by vocal learning.

It is unclear whether these flycatchers have a developmental phase analogous to the second learning phase of songbirds. Fledgling flycatchers use calls that are rudimentary forms of the adult songs, and it is possible that the motor output is gradually perfected by comparing the vocal output with an innate song template. Determining whether or not these flycatchers are *learning* to match the motor output of the syrinx with an inherited song template will require experimental work with deafened subjects (Konishi & Nottebohm, 1969; Nottebohm, 1975).

The Interplay of Geographic Variation, Song Repertoires, and Ontogeny

The "dawn song" of these (north temperate zone) suboscine flycatchers is typically sustained, given from exposed perches, and usually uttered only by the adult breeding male. It is very likely homologous with what is so readily identified as the "song" in most oscines. When so defined, then, the *song* repertoire of these flycatchers is quite limited. The Alder Flycatcher, Eastern Phoebe, and Willow Flycatcher sing one, two, and three song types, respectively, all of which develop normally in hand-reared birds that are isolated from conspecific songs. Male Western, Yellowish, and Acadian Flycatchers, all *Empidonax* species, have a single very simple song type [see Fig. 27 of Johnson (1980), Fig. 2 of Payne & Budde (1979)], and *Myiarchus* species studied by Lanyon (1978) uttered very simple songs consisting of one to a few different notes (e.g., Fig. 9.1). Thus, the song repertoire of these tyrannid flycatchers consists of, at most, three different song types, as in the Willow Flycatcher and the Eastern Wood Pewee (*Contopus virens*—Craig, 1943).

These flycatchers have a fail-safe approach to song development. A full set of instructions for the proper development of each song type seems to be encoded in the genes, and no imitation of adults is necessary. On the other hand, if a young songbird is not tutored with any songs, it develops a song that is much simpler than the songs of wild males. It is as if the songbird hatchling were endowed only with a set of instructions that specified the proper models for vocal imitation. If these model songs are absent from the social environment, young songbirds may then learn songs from the wrong species (examples listed in Kroodsma & Baylis, 1982).

It is unknown how much genetic coding is required to insure the proper development of one song type. Perhaps it is beyond the capability of birds to encode genetically extremely large repertoires of both highly stereotyped yet reasonably complex songs (Nottebohm, 1972). Song repertoires among oscines can number in the hundreds (e.g., Dowsett-Lemaire, 1979) or even thousands (Boughey & Thompson, 1981). Vocal learning appears to allow the development of very large song repertoires within individuals and this results in some song variation both among individuals and especially populations. The fail-safe approach to song development characteristic of flycatchers is correlated with small repertoires of relatively simple songs shared by all individuals over broad geographic areas. It would be interesting to examine the vocal development and geographic variation in other flycatchers or members of other suboscine groups that have larger repertoires, if such species exist. Selective pressures for larger repertoires, as might be found in very dense populations or perhaps non-monogamous mating systems (see Catchpole, 1980; Kroodsma, 1977), could lead to increased variability, both among individuals of a population and among populations. An examination of several well-selected suboscine species may well hold the key to understanding the interplay between the selective forces for song repertoires, individual and population variability, and the developmental process required to accomplish such tasks.

VOCAL BEHAVIOR AND ITS DEVELOPMENT AMONG OSCINES

The inflexibility of the developmental program and the vocal stereotypy over broad geographic regions in tyrannid flycatchers provides a phenomenal contrast to the elaborations and flexibility that vocal imitation has permitted among the oscines. No longer are adult songs limited to those relatively simple, conservative, inherited vocalizations encoded in the genes; rather, vocal learning has provided great potential for a rapid evolutionary change in vocal signals, encouraging endless variations, leading to some of the most complex and diverse sounds in the animal world.

This diversity among the oscines can be best appreciated by examining the contrasting degrees of geographic variation, sizes of song repertoires, and underlying styles of vocal development at a variety of taxonomic levels. Using largely the comparative method, I examine the interplay of these three facets of vocal behavior among the oscines by discussing differences among species, between populations within a single species, among individuals of a population, and between different song types of the same individual. Finally, I conclude with a discussion that attempts to interpret correlations of vocal behavior and its development with function and ecology.

Geographic Variation

As a result of highly canalized (*sensu* Waddington, 1957; see also Marler, Zoloth, & Dooling, 1981) vocal development, tyrannid flycatchers minimize geographic variation in songs. Among oscines, however, the ability to imitate songs seems to have enabled the choice of a variety of evolutionary options. At one extreme, illustrated by the White-crowned Sparrow (*Zonotrichia leucophrys*) of the coastal chapparal in California, songs of males often change more over a kilometer than do songs of flycatchers change over an entire continent. Not all songbirds have exploited this "dialect phenomenon," though, and other species by other styles of development maintain relative uniformity of vocal patterns throughout extensive geographic ranges.

I here consider some of this perplexing variety. I begin by examining several examples in which a species shows limited geographic variety in its songs, and conclude by taking a close look at what we know about the biology of song dialects in the White-crowned Sparrow, the "white rat" of song dialect research.

Geographic uniformity via song improvisation (and dispersal?). One intriguing example in which vocal development and geographic variation seem to mesh with other life history parameters involves two closely related species in the New World family Troglodytidae. The Marsh Wren (*Cistothorus palustris*) and the Sedge Wren (*Cistothorus platensis*) are placed in the same genus, indicating that taxonomists believe they had a common ancestor during recent evolutionary history. Today, the Marsh Wren lives primarily in cattail and bullrush marshes throughout North America, while the Sedge Wren in North America specializes in wet, sometimes ephemeral meadows primarily in the Great Plains region. In both species males have a polygynous tendency (Crawford, 1977; Verner, 1965) and sing their large repertoires of up to 200 song types, sometimes during the day and the night, throughout the breeding season.

These birds appear very similar in their vocal behaviors, but the mode of vocal development and extent of geographic variation in song are strikingly different in the two species (Table 9.1; Kroodsma & Verner, 1978). The Marsh Wren develops its sizeable repertoire through precise imitation of other Marsh Wrens. This learning is easily demonstrated in the laboratory, where males imitate the details of song types from loudspeakers or from other males (Kroodsma, 1978). As a consequence, neighboring males in nature sing nearly identical song repertoires and countersing (i.e., answer each other) with identical song types (e.g., Verner, 1975). Breeding habitat is relatively stable, and males faithfully return to the same territories year after year. Songs vary microgeographically and J. Verner has obtained pilot data suggesting that, as in other species with song dialects, Marsh Wren males tend to respond more weakly to songs of increasingly distant dialects (see review in Becker, 1982).

The Sedge Wren, on the other hand, apparently does not imitate songs. Males appear programmed to improvise large repertoires of species-typical songs that, like snowflakes, are all variations on a basic theme but, nevertheless, are not exactly like others in the population. Neighboring males do not share identical song type repertoires, and geographic variation is virtually unrecognizable: Songs of neighbors appear no more like one another than do the songs of males separated by hundreds of kilometers. Playback experiments with local and distant songs should be done to test whether the birds agree with this interpretation of the sonagrams, but I would predict no difference in responsiveness to songs of different localities. This singing behavior and its development appear well adapted to the seminomadic life style of the Sedge Wren (Kroodsma & Verner, 1978), which is characterized by "high mobility during the breeding season and low site tenacity between seasons" (Burns 1982, p. 346). Singing males will routinely encounter individuals originating from distant localities, and the generalized song appears well adapted as a common "language" for such an opportunistic breeding style.

TABLE 9.1
A Comparison of the Breeding Biology and Vocal Behavior of the
Marsh Wren and Sedge Wren

	Species	
Biological Character	Sedge Wren	Marsh Wren
Mating system	Polygynous	Polygynous
Relative stability of breeding habitat	Low	High
Population movements	Seminomadic	Site-faithful
Repertoire sizes	Large, 90-150	Large, 30-200
Vocal development via	Improvisation	Imitation
Individual variation	High	Low
Microgeographic variation (i.e., dialects)	No	Yes

This apparent match between vocal development, geographic variation in song, and site-fidelity (faithfulness to the same breeding site year after year) is highly satisfying, for it provides an organizing framework for studying the co-evolution of vocal behavior and other life history parameters. If this relationship is a general one, there should be other examples among the oscines.

I am now studying eastern and western populations of the Red-winged Black-bird (*Agelaius phoeniceus*) and the Rufous-sided Towhee (*Pipilo erythrophthalamus*) to see if I can find similar correlations among these param-eters. In western populations of both the towhee and the red-wing, neighboring males have nearly identical songs, and the songs differ among populations, producing local dialects (Brenowitz, 1983; Kroodsma, 1971). These data indicate that extensive vocal imitation of neighboring males must occur in the western populations.

Something quite different is occurring in the eastern birds. While eastern towhees are *capable* of imitating songs (Anonymous, 1900; Borror, 1977; Rich-ards 1979; Kroodsma, unpublished data), no evidence of local dialects has been found in the field despite some intensive studies (Borror, 1959, 1975; Ewert, 1978; Richards, 1978). Red-wings can also imitate in the laboratory, but Marler, Mundinger, Waser, and Lutjen (1972) discovered that extensive improvisation or invention overshadowed the small amount of imitation that had occurred. As with the towhees, the eastern red-wings do not have dialects like their western counterparts.

There are several possible explanations for these east-west differences.

1. If the degree of song learning is the same in all populations, then indi-viduals in eastern populations must simply be dispersing further from the site of learning.

2. Alternatively, population movements and site fidelity may be identical in eastern and western populations, but eastern males may place less em-phasis on precise imitation and more on improvisation.

3. A third possibility, one most consistent with the wren example, would involve a reduction in both site-fidelity and precision in song imitation among eastern birds.

The more *generalized* rather than locale-specific songs would help in commu-nicating with individuals of more distant geographic origins. Site fidelity in a population may be related to environmental patchiness, or the rate of environ-mental change over distance. With greater patchiness, as in western populations, there may be advantages for locally adapted gene complexes that encourage site fidelity (e.g., see discussion in Baker & Cunningham, 1985). The apparent relationship between vocal dialects and nonmigratory status (Ewert, 1978) could then be only secondary.

With these towhees and red-wings I am now testing in the laboratory whether there is a relationship between the extent of microgeographic song variation and the mode of song development. The absence of local song traditions and absence of extensive song sharing with neighbors in eastern populations may have led to a relaxation of selection for precise imitation and/or stronger selection for improvisation. Both the extent of microgeographic song variation and the mode of song development may in turn be related to levels of selection for site fidelity.

Geographic uniformity and mate selection.   Among most bird (and many other animal) species, the female chooses her mate, rather than vice versa, and her caution relative to the indiscriminate tastes of males has been discussed in terms of gamete sizes and investments in future progeny (e.g., Orians, 1969; Trivers, 1972). If the female identifies an appropriate male based, at least in part, on his singing behavior, she imposes a strong force on the evolution of male singing behaviors. While Catchpole (1980, 1982, 1984) has emphasized that intersexual selection may lead to very large song repertoires, it is also possible that females, in order to ensure proper species identification during mate selection, would be more conservative in their tastes. Two examples now suggest that females may be attuned to some of the more stereotyped or even innate portions of male songs, and that intersexual communication could actually be an impediment to the elaborations that can result from vocal learning.

In the Brown-headed Cowhead (*Molothrus ater*), for example, the simple songs of isolated males are more stimulating to females than are songs that males develop via imitative elaboration (King & West, 1977). Furthermore, the female prefers songs of her own subspecies (*M. a. ater* vs. *M.a. obscurus;* King, West, & Eastzer, 1980), and this preference expressed by both hand-reared naive and wild-caught adult female cowbirds of both subspecies cannot be modified by experience (King & West, 1983). While the male is capable of learning a wide variety of song types, including those of the other subspecies, the female enforces uniformity in some song parameters by preferring males that court with songs characteristic of her own subspecies. Behavioral but not necessarily vocal feedback from the female to the male is sufficient to stimulate development of the proper song and ensure some uniformity over geographic space (West, King, & Harrocks, 1983).

When they first described their findings in this brood parasite, King and West (1977) added that, while it might be ''tempting to label the cowbird's response to isolate song as idiosyncratic or unrepresentative of other songbirds, this cannot be done, as little comparative information exists regarding the responses of other species to isolate songs'' (p. 1004). There still exist no other data comparable to those obtained by King and West, but data from several North American warblers suggest that this phenomenon could be more pervasive among the songbirds.

In some species of the Parulinae (family Emberizidae), different learned song types are used in different situations (see Ficken & Ficken, 1965; Gill & Murray,

1972; Kroodsma, 1981; Kroodsma, Meservey, & Pickert, 1983; Lein, 1978; P. Marler, unpublished data; Morse, 1970; Nolan, 1978; Payne, Payne, & Doehlart 1984). One song form (here labeled Type II) is used primarily in male-male interactions on the edge of the territory, while the other (Type I) is used more towards the center of the territory, and perhaps more in male to female communication (see Fig. 9.3). The Type I form is relatively stereotyped throughout the range of the Blue-winged Warbler (*Vermivora pinus*) and the Chestnut-sided Warbler (*Dendroica pensylvanica*), and male Blue-winged Warblers do not discriminate between songs from a local population and from those of a population about 150 km distant. On the other hand, the Type II songs of these same two warbler species vary microgeographically, and males respond more strongly to local songs than to songs recorded from a population about 150 km distant (Kroodsma, Meservey, Whitlock, & VanderHaegen, 1984).

Field data suggest that the more stereotyped song form is involved in male-female communication (summarized in Kroodsma, 1981; Nolan, 1978). Further-

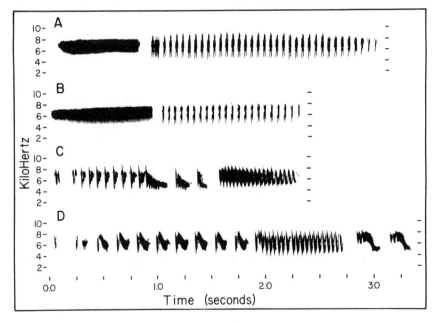

FIGURE 9.3. Sonagrams of the stereotyped Type I and geographically variable Type II Blue-winged Warbler songs. A and C, Type I and Type II songs, respectively, from the Rockefeller University Field Research Center, Millbrook, New York. B and D, Type I and Type II songs, respectively, from Amherst, Massachusetts. These two locations are approximately 150 km apart. These songs were used in playback experiments demonstrating that males respond differentially to Type II songs but not Type I songs from the two localities (from Kroodsma, Meservey, Whitlock, & VanderHaegen, 1983).

more, a wild-caught adult female Blue-winged Warbler responded selectively to the Type I song in the laboratory (I used the estradiol implant technique of Searcy & Marler, 1981, and the song playback technique of King & West, 1983). I am now testing additional blue-wings and other warbler species to evaluate further the intersexual messages in these warbler songs.

The cowbird and warbler examples suggest that vocal signals used in intersexual communication in these species may be genetically encoded and/or highly stereotyped relative to those more elaborate or variable signals used in intrasexual communication. The imprinting literature provides further evidence of a related phenomenon. In sexually dimorphic ducks, Schutz (1965) has demonstrated that the female has an inborn capacity to recognize a potential mate, and she becomes sexually responsive to conspecific males at maturity regardless of her earlier experience. Males, on the other hand, readily imprint on the females of other species. Likewise, in the oscine Zebra Finch (*Poephila guttata*), the female appears less imprintable on another species, the Bengalese Finch (*Lonchura striata*), than is the male (Sonnemann & Sjolander, 1977).

Geographic uniformity via limited species-typical repertoires of learned song components. Shiovitz and Thompson (1970), Thompson (1970), and Emlen (1971) described a perplexing lack of geographic variation in the learned song syllables of the Indigo Bunting (*Passerina cyanea*). Neighboring males often share peculiar arrangements of these syllables, but the syllables themselves are for the most part species-typical and not confined to particular localities. Males clearly learn their songs (Payne, 1981; Payne, Thompson, Fiala, & Sweany, 1981; Rice & Thompson, 1968). The most plausible explanation here is that learning of a restricted set of syllables in the Indigo Bunting is somehow genetically programmed.

Similar mechanisms undoubtedly occur in other oscines. One such example is the Swamp Sparrow (*Melospiza georgiana*). Each Swamp Sparrow song typically consists of a single syllable that is repeated 5 to 12 times per sec in a 1 to 2 sec song, and each syllable consists of from 2 to 5 distinct sounds or notes recognizable on sonagrams. Of 234 total song types that I studied from Dutchess Co., New York, 24, 161, 39 and 10 songs consisted of 2, 3, 4, and 5 notes, respectively. I recorded eight or more song bouts from 26 males at Thompson Pond in northern Dutchess Co.; three birds sang two song types, 10 sang three, 10 sang four, and three birds sang five song types.

To study the vocal development of this sparrow, during June, 1973, I collected eight 5- to 6-day-old nestling males (see Figs. 9.4 and 9.5). Four tutor tapes, each with three different song types, were prepared. Birds 1–4 were isolated in sound attenuation chambers and exposed to training tapes 1, 2, and 3 when 19–30, 40–51, and 61–71 days old, respectively. Birds 3–6 were tutored with tape 4 in the spring of 1974, when approximately 250 days old, and Birds 7 and 8 never heard Swamp Sparrow songs in the laboratory.

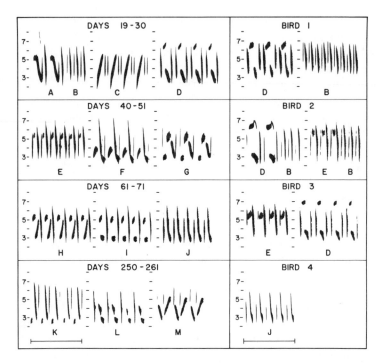

FIGURE 9.4. Four laboratory-reared Swamp Sparrows (Birds 1–4) were tutored with four tapes during days 19–30, 40–51, 61–71, and 250–261, respectively. Song types are indicated by the letters A–M. Males learned at least one (Bird 4) and as many as three (Bird 2) songs from the training tapes. The abscissa is time (0.5 sec indicated), and the ordinate kiloHertz.

The four birds (1–4, Fig. 9.4) tutored during their first summer copied one to three songs from the tutor tapes, with an apparent peak of learning between the ages of 19 to 30 days: five songs were copied from the 19–30 day tape, two from the 40–51 day tape, and one from the 61–71 day tape. Birds 3–6 showed no evidence of learning songs from the fourth tutor tape the following spring. The eight songs of birds 5–8 and the three songs improvised by Birds 2 and 4 (Fig. 9.5) were similar to wild-type songs in frequency measures, but the syllables were less complex and were delivered at highly abnormal rates.

At Thompson Pond I classified a total of 195 song types from 70 males into 37 song patterns. Six song patterns were shared by 10 or more recorded birds at the pond, and 13 were shared by five or more birds; 16 were recorded from only one male. Neighboring males frequently sang the same patterns, and tended to share more song patterns with each other than with more distant birds ($p = 0.14$, two-tailed Mann-Whitney U test).

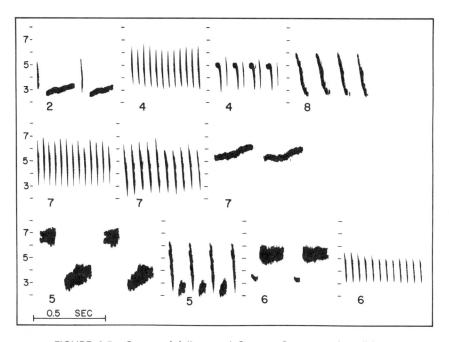

FIGURE 9.5. Songs of fall-tutored Swamp Sparrows that did not match the training tapes (Birds 2 & 4; see also Fig. 4), songs of birds tutored in the spring only (Birds 5 & 6), and songs of acoustically isolated birds (Birds 7 & 8) were abnormal in both rate of syllable delivery and syllable complexity. Axes as in Fig. 9.4.

Several of the song patterns were found at other locations in Dutchess Co., and many even as distant as Minnesota (Fig. 9.6). By my classification, 34 of 45 (0.76) songs from other Dutchess Co. populations and 12 of 24 (0.50) Minnesota songs were of the same pattern as songs found at Thompson Pond (difference not statistically significant, chi-square test). [Swamp Sparrow research reported here was originally presented in Kroodsma (1975); for additional data on vocal development in Swamp Sparrows see Marler and Peters (e.g., 1977, 1982).]

Marler and Pickert (1984) have taken a closer look at this lack of geographic variation in the Swamp Sparrow. They discovered that all song syllables in their sample of 452 "were assembled from the same species-universal set of note types, consisting of six basic categories . . . While some degree of selection of within-type note variants is possible, the structure of the major categories of Swamp Sparrow note types is in large degree preordained, and presumably under genetic control."

Thus, while most studies of geographic variation in oscine song have focused on the differences among populations, underlying this variability may be considerable stereotypy. Whether or not the variability and stereotypy can be attributed

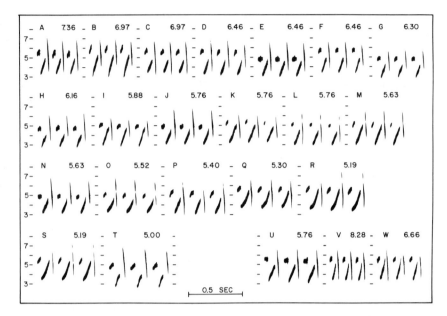

FIGURE 9.6.   Examples of a song pattern that is found throughout the population at Thompson Pond in northern Dutchess Co., New York (Birds A through T), at other locations in Dutchess Co. (U, Rockefeller University Field Research Center, and V, Poughkeepsie, approximately 24 and 35 km SSW of Thompson Pond, respectively), and as far away as Lake Itasca, Minnesota, 1700 km to the west (W, courtesy of Dr. James Mulligan). Numbers above each sonagram indicate the number of syllable repetitions/sec. Axes as in Fig. 9.4.

to intra- and inter-sexual selection, respectively, as may be the case among Brown-headed Cowbirds and some warblers, must await further study.

Song dialects.   One of the most obvious consequences of vocal learning in songbirds is the formation of song dialects. Among dialect species, young birds learn the songs of adults and then remain in that local area to breed. In some species a sharp boundary between dialect ''areas'' can be identified, but in other species local males simply share similar, learned song patterns more with one another than with more distant birds.

It is possible that the evolutionary success of songbirds is due in part to their mastery of vocal learning. Baker (1982) points out that population or subspecific differentiation has been greater in songbirds than in the nonlearning ''sub-song-birds.'' However, the comparison may be slightly biased: Songbirds have simply been studied more because of their north temperate zone geographic distribution, and as a result their geographic variation and differentiation have been evaluated in greater detail. Nevertheless, this is an exciting *hypothesis*. If vocal learning does increase the genetic isolation between local populations, more rapid evolutionary divergence and speciation would result, and there would be an exciting link established between cultural and biological evolution in songbirds (Cavalli-Sforza & Feldman, 1981; Lumsden & Wilson, 1981).

The central issues of this hypothesis are whether or not (a) young males and (b) young females in nature learn preferentially (and irreversibly) the natal song dialect, (c) females pair assortatively with males according to song type, (d) males are excluded from adjacent dialect areas because they sing the wrong song, and (e) as a consequence of these behaviors, dispersal between dialects is lower than expected. Data gathered in the field have been largely for the White-crowned Sparrow (especially the subspecies *Z.l. nuttalli*), and whether or not the data support the hypothesis remain highly controversial (see, for example, Baker & Mewaldt, 1978; Petrinovich, Patterson, & Baptista, 1981; Kroodsma, Baker, Baptista, & Petrinovich, 1984; Baker & Cunningham, 1985, with associated commentaries).

Baker, Thompson, Sherman, Cunningham, and Tomback (1982) have demonstrated, at least to their satisfaction, that there exists some concordance between song dialects and genetic populations. They believe that reduced dispersal between the dialects as a consequence of items a–d) listed above, has led to this concordance. Reanalyses of their data have either supported (e.g., Hafner & Petersen, unpublished manuscript; E. Balaban, personal communication) or seriously questioned (Zink & Barrowclough, 1984) both their techniques and results. Yet, I believe that these arguments don't really get to the heart of the matter. Genetic differences between dialect areas might actually be *expected* if these dialect groups represent descendents from small founder populations. After secondary contact genetic differentiation would be *maintained* over time in direct proportion to the degree that dispersal and gene flow across the secondary contact zone (i.e., the dialect boundary) are inhibited. We still need, then, a direct assessment of dispersal.

Several studies have demonstrated that some dispersal does occur across these *Z.l. nuttalli* dialect boundaries (e.g., Baptista & Morton, 1982; Petrinovich & Patterson, 1982), but only Baker and Mewaldt (1978) have had sufficient data to attempt a test of whether or not fewer individuals disperse across a dialect boundary than would be expected by chance alone. Unfortunately, several problems with that study have made their results unsuitable as *the* test of the dispersal hypothesis (see Kroodsma, Baker, Baptista, & Petrinovich, 1984, for details). Attempts to determine the extent of dispersal from laboratory studies of song learning in males and females, from field studies of song matching by mated pairs, or from responses of males to song playback are all indirect, and these approaches often require assumptions that are simply untenable. I am convinced that the only possible conclusive approach to testing the effects of vocal learning on reduced dispersal and increased population differentiation can come from a carefully designed assessment of dispersal and its consequence in the field (Kroodsma, 1985b). Until then, this hypothesis remains, in my mind at least, an untested but nevertheless a very exciting and plausible hypothesis.

Song Repertoires

Song repertoires are the rule rather than the exception among the oscines (e.g., Dobson & Lemon, 1975). They may number in the thousands in some species, as in the Brown Thrasher (*Toxostoma rufum*—Boughey & Thompson, 1981), which may continuously improvise new songs as it sings, or be much more modest, as in many finches or warblers, which usually sing from 2 to 10 different songs apiece. In some species there is undoubtedly strong selection for larger repertoires, while in others it is possible there may be equally strong selection for smaller repertoires; a "phylogenetic inertia" argument need not be invoked to explain why individual White-crowned Sparrows, for example, have only a single song type. Here I review an apparent relationship between repertoires and population density, discuss genetic and environmental determinants of repertoires, and conclude with a comment on selection for small repertoires.

Repertoires and population density. Within two groups of species, the North American wrens and the European *Acrocephalus* warblers, there appears to be a positive relationship between population density and the size of the learned song repertoire (Catchpole, 1980; Kroodsma, 1977).

Styles of male interactions, especially among the wrens, may have led to these escalations in song repertoire size. Increased density leads to more frequent contacts and countersinging bouts with neighbors, producing faster singing rates (Kroodsma & Verner, 1978). More rapid repetition of a single song type would quickly lead to habituation (e.g., Krebs, 1976). To decrease these dangers of habituation (Hartshorne, 1973), species that typically sang with eventual variety (where one song type is repeated over and over before another is introduced) would change to immediate variety, delivering a sequence of highly contrasting, different song types. With further increases in the intensity of interactions, repertoire sizes would enlarge to increase the recurrence interval between successive renditions of a song type. [See Fig. 9.7 and additional supporting evidence in Kroodsma (1983)].

Environmental and genetic determinants of repertoire sizes. Variation in repertoire sizes within a population may be explained to some extent by environmental differences that juveniles encounter during the developmental period. For example, adult males in a population typically sing only during the breeding season, and the amount of singing wanes late in the season. Young hatching at

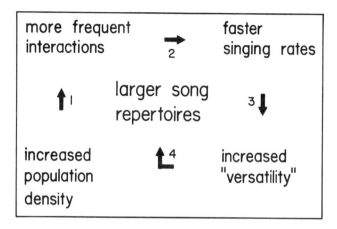

FIGURE 9.7.   Several proposed steps by which large song repertoires may evolve in dense populations. Steps 3 and 4 reduce habituation that can result from rapid repetition of a limited repertoire, which in turn is a natural consequence of increased encounter rates in dense populations (after Kroodsma, 1983).

different times during the season will be exposed to differing amounts of adult tutoring and different daylengths that could, in turn, affect hormonal levels and the ability to learn songs (see Fig. 9.8).

In migratory populations, some birds may even hatch after adults have stopped singing for the year. In New York populations of the Marsh Wren, juveniles that are placed on daylengths simulating a late-season hatching *and* that are deprived of adult songs during their first summer learn more songs the next spring than do males raised on longer days and hearing adult songs (Kroodsma & Pickert, 1980). These late-season hatchers may still develop a sizeable repertoire the next spring, but breeding for them may be delayed. The environmental differences encountered by juvenile Marsh Wrens may account for much of the individual variability in repertoire size, which ranges from approximately 40 to 70 song types in this New York population (Canady, Kroodsma, & Nottebohm, 1984).

In nonmigratory populations, such as the Bewick's Wren in the Willamette Valley of Oregon, males may have to develop their full repertoire by the first autumn in order to defend a territory effectively. Young birds hatching later in the season may then have a disadvantage in developing large repertoires. In this wren the repertoire size is strongly correlated with the date of hatching; early-hatching individuals may develop up to 20 song types, those hatching later as few as 13 (Kroodsma, 1974).

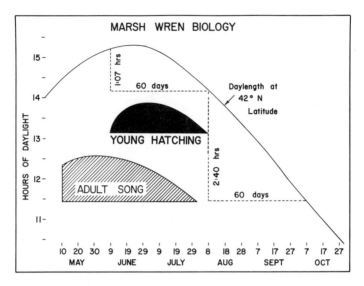

FIGURE 9.8.   Relevant features of Marsh Wren breeding biology that
may influence vocal development. Marsh Wrens that hatch in early
June experience long days (at least 14 hours of light) and hear many
adult songs from breeding males. Those young hatching at the end of
the breeding season hear fewer or no adult songs and encounter much
shorter daylengths. In the laboratory most song learning occurs during
the first 60 days of life, but the daylength and acoustic environment
can influence whether some song learning is delayed until the next
spring.

Environmental differences between populations can, over evolutionary time,
lead to genetic differences in the ability to learn and produce large song type
repertoires. In populations of the Marsh Wren, for example, song repertoire size
averages about 150 songs/male in some San Francisco populations but only 55 in
New York populations on the Hudson River. Collecting nestlings from these two
populations and rearing them under identical conditions in the laboratory has
demonstrated that the western individuals are capable of learning larger repertoires
than are their eastern counterparts (Kroodsma & Canady, 1985). The western
wrens are resident, live on smaller territories in denser populations, and are more
polygynous than the eastern populations; all these factors could lead to enhanced
repertoire sizes, and partitioning the influence of each would require studying
populations of the Marsh Wren, or other species, that varied in mating systems,
density, and degree of residency. Other geographic differences in repertoire sizes,
such as occur in the Winter Wren (*Troglodytes troglodytes;* Kroodsma, 1980),
Northern Mockingbird (*Mimus polyglottos*; Wildenthal, 1965), Rufous-sided
Towhee (Ewert, 1978; Kroodsma, 1971), and other species may also involve

genetic differences in the ability to learn rather than merely environmental differences that influence developing individuals within their respective populations.

Selection for small repertoires.   The evolution of larger repertoires has been the focus of several recent literature reviews (e.g., Catchpole, 1982; Krebs & Kroodsma, 1980; Slater, 1983), and here I will not belabor those issues further. Of equal interest, though, is the opposing question: Why are repertoires so limited in some species?

As Searcy, McArthur, Peters, and Marler (1981) and Falls and d'Agincourt (1981) have demonstrated, neighbor recognition appears more difficult as repertoire sizes increase. Recognition of other individuals, such as potential mates, may also be more difficult. Nottebohm (1972) proposed that both male and female Zebra Finches may learn the song of the father in order to avoid close inbreeding; the male sings a song identifiable to his lineage, while the female then chooses nonkin based on song. Bateson's (e.g. 1978) work on imprinting suggests a similar strategy in pairing with individuals that are (slightly) different from the parental form, and research on mate selection in Great Tits (*Parus major*) appears consistent with this hypothesis (McGregor & Krebs, 1982). Jenkins also (1977) proposed that his male Saddlebacks (*Creadion carunculatus*) dispersed to nonnatal dialect areas to prevent inbreeding, though his data were limited and not significantly different from random dispersal. More recently, Grant (1984) has demonstrated that females in one species of Darwin's finch may choose a male based on the song type he sings; the female can avoid pairing with males that sing the same form as her father ($0.1 > p > 0.05$). Grant further speculates that natural selection has limited repertoires to two major song types and several subtypes in order to ensure the ability of females to recognize nonkin in a small island population.

Neighboring males may share nearly identical song types regardless of repertoire size (from one song in the White-crowned Sparrow to 100 or more in western Marsh Wrens; Baptista, 1975; Verner, 1975). Even though dialect boundaries might be definable by a prepondernace of coinciding isogloss lines (Mundinger, 1982), species with smaller repertoires can undoubtedly achieve and maintain much sharper dialect boundaries than would be possible with larger repertoires. The functions of dialect boundaries remain unclear (see above section, *Song Dialects*), and therefore the role of limited repertoire sizes in accomplishing such boundaries also remains in question.

Another possible reason for limiting variability in a singing performance might be to insure species recognition. In complex avifaunal communities, both repertoire size and variability (as measured by coefficients of variation) might be reduced to ensure species recognition. Miller (1982) found no evidence among the oscines to support this speculation. While in theory there must be a limit to the variety of sounds that a species can produce and still be recognizable, it is unclear whether these theoretical limits to complexity or diversity are ever reached in nature (Kroodsma, 1985c).

DISCUSSION

Evolution of Vocal Learning: Suboscines vs. Oscines?

There are two notable consequences of vocal learning: (1) microgeographic vocal variation, with local populations of the same species often singing different "dialects," and (2) elaboration of the vocal repertoire, with imitation, invention, and improvisation (see Marler & Peters, 1982, for definitions) leading to sizeable repertoires of song types among many oscines. Vocal development that is not as rigidly canalized as it is in the suboscine flycatchers allows considerable flexibility in the developmental process. This flexibility may lead to striking differences in microgeographic vocal variation for songs of closely related species (e.g., *Cistothorus* wrens) or even for different song types of the same species (paruline warblers). This flexibility also permits (or promotes) the development of differing sizes of vocal repertoires among different populations of the same species (Marsh Wren, Winter Wren) or even among individuals of the same population (Marsh Wren, Bewick's Wren).

Studies of song development, geographic variation, and repertoire sizes among suboscines may be crucial to understanding the interplay of these three factors. If there are suboscines that develop songs through vocal imitation, then rich comparative material would exist to understand the consequences of different developmental styles and adult behaviors. If, on the other hand, the flycatcher mode of song development ("innately preordained") is a primitive characteristic shared by all members of the suborder, the data would indicate that vocal learning evolved among the songbirds after the oscine-suboscine divergence about 85 to 90 million years ago (Sibley & Ahlquist, 1985). Only additional data from other suboscines will clarify this issue.

Vocal learning, to varying degrees, is so ubiquitous among oscines that it is tempting to conclude that the three tyrannid flycatchers are also typical of the entire family Tyrannidae, if not all suboscines. E. S. Morton (unpublished data) has hand-reared a Barred Antshrike (*Thamnophilus doliatus*); as with the tyrannid flycatchers, its fledgling calls were similar to the adult song, and by ear the adult song of this experimental bird was identical to those of males in nature. This species is a suboscine but is from a different Infraorder (Cracraft, 1981) or Parvorder (Sibley & Ahlquist, 1985) than are the flycatchers, and this suggests that the conservative mode of song development may be more pervasive among the suboscines.

In a sibling species complex such as in the *Empidonax* group, abandoning the heritable, conservative, and fail-safe mechanism of vocal development might prove catastrophic, for identifying conspecifics could prove very difficult. Among two sympatric, sibling oscine meadowlarks (*Sturnella neglecta* and *S. magna*), where heterospecific songs are frequently learned, potential mates are probably identified on the basis of the nonlearned calls (Lanyon, 1957). The use of identical song forms by both males and (testosterone-treated) females in the *Empidonax* and *Sayornis* flycatchers might prove indispensable in mate choice and species recognition. Perhaps the degree of vocal variation, both within individuals and within and among populations, could also be inversely related to the extent of morphological distinctiveness in a given species (see Nottebohm, 1972); if visual species-recognition markers are available, there could be a relaxation on the distinctiveness necessary in vocal parameters. Monotypic suboscine genera from Central and South America would certainly be worth investigating.

Are there Strategies of Vocal Development?

A behavioral strategy is one that has coevolved with other life history parameters, and the evolutionary biologist assumes that vocal communication systems, like other aspects of biological systems, are adapted to particular life styles. Among oscines the diversity is perplexing, though, and for each *story* there is often a *counter-story*. Sedge Wrens, for example, are nomadic, and improvise their large song repertoires; compared to the more site-faithful and congeneric Marsh Wren, this style of vocal development makes good sense. However, the Dickcissel (*Spiza americana*) is seminomadic like the Sedge Wren, yet W. L. Thompson (unpublished data) has recorded identical songs from neighboring birds, indicating that the birds must learn their songs from one another. Perhaps Dickcissels travel in cohesive groups, or perhaps repertoires are smaller so they can change their songs from one season to the next depending on the breeding location (e.g., Payne, 1981). Data on other species are needed before any clear picture will emerge.

The conservative, fail-safe development of songs in flycatchers might be viewed as a strategy. Yet, if no alternative such as vocal learning has ever arisen in flycatcher evolutionary history, it may be less of a strategy than a primitive but stable plateau from which no adaptive peaks have arisen. Or, in other words, this absence of learning may simply be a good example of phylogenetic inertia.

In some studies of oscine vocal behavior there is considerable intermale variability. Payne (1982, 1983), for example, found that Indigo Buntings that matched the songs of other adults in the neighborhood were more successful in breeding than were the non-matchers. A considerable number of birds did not match, though. Is it possible there are alternative strategies being expressed by the first-year birds here? Or perhaps the matching and non-matching are merely inescapable consequences of chance events during the first year of life.

Clearly further information is needed on these systems before *strategies* of vocal development can be assessed meaningfully. Particular attention must be paid to functions and consequences of individual variation, in the field setting, in order to understand alternatives in the developmental program. Populations of the same species that differ in vocal behavior but in a minimum of other life history parameters should provide some critical insights into the coevolution of vocal development, the resulting adult behaviors, and other life history strategies.

ACKNOWLEDGMENTS

I thank the National Science Foundation for research support (e.g., BNS 85-06996) and Joyce Britt for her help in preparing the manuscript. W. E. Lanyon kindly provided Figure 1, and J. A. Mulligan generously made available his Swamp Sparrow recordings from Minnesota.

REFERENCES

Anonymous. (1900). Untitled. *Abstracts of the Linnaean Society, New York, 1899–1900, 12*,5.
Bailey, E. D., & Baker, J. A. (1982). Recognition characteristics in covey dialects of Bobwhite Quail. *Condor, 84*, 317–320.
Baker, M. C. (1982). Genetic population structure and vocal dialects in *Zonotrichia* (Emberizidae). In D. E. Kroodsma & E. H. Miller (Eds.), *Acoustic communication in birds*, (Vol. 2, pp. 209–235). New York: Academic Press.
Baker, M. C., & Cunningham, M. A. (1985). The biology of bird song dialects. *Behavioral and Brain Sciences, 8*, 85–133.
Baker, M. C., & Mewaldt, L. R. (1978). Song dialects as barriers to dispersal in White-crowned Sparrows, *Zonotrichia leucophrys nuttalli. Evolution, 32*, 712–722.
Baker, M. C., Thompson, D. B., Sherman, G. L., Cunningham, M. A., & Tomback, D. F. (1982). Allozyme frequencies in a linear series of song dialect populations. *Evolution, 36*, 1020–1029.
Baptista, L. F. (1975). Song dialects and demes in sedentary populations of the White-crowned Sparrow (*Zonotrichia leucophrys nuttalli*). *University of California Publications in Zoology, 105*, 1–52.
Baptista, L. F., & Morton, M. L. (1982). Geographical variation in song and mate selection in montane White-crowned Sparrows. *Auk, 99*, 537–547.
Bateson, P. P. G. (1978). Sexual imprinting and optimal outbreeding. *Nature, 273*, 659–668.
Becker, P. H. (1982). The coding of species-specific characteristics in bird sounds: In D. E. Kroodsma & E. H. Miller (Eds.), *Acoustic communication in birds*, (Vol. 2, pp. 213–252). New York: Academic Press.
Bock, W. J., & Farrand, J., Jr. (1980). The number of species and genera of recent birds: A contribution to comparative systematics. *American Museum Novitates, No. 2703*, 1–29.
Borror, D. J. (1959). Variation in the songs of the Rufous-sided Towhee. *Wilson Bulletin, 71*, 54–72.
Borror, D. J. (1975). Songs of the Rufous-sided Towhee. *Condor, 77*, 183–195.
Borror, D. J. (1977). Rufous-sided Towhee mimicking Carolina Wren and Field Sparrow. *Wilson Bulletin, 89*, 447–480.
Boughey, M. J., & Thompson, N. S. (1981). Song variety in the Brown Thrasher (*Toxostoma rufum*). *Zeitschrift für Tierpsychologie, 56*, 47–58.
Brenowitz, E. A. (1983). The contribution of temporal song cues to species recognition in the Red-winged Blackbird. *Animal Behaviour, 31*, 1116–1127.
Burns, J. T. (1982). Nests, territories, and reproduction of Sedge Wrens (*Cistothorus platensis*). *Wilson Bulletin, 94*, 338–349.

Canady, R. A., Kroodsma, D. E., & Nottebohm, F. (1984). Population differences in the complexity of a learned skill are correlated with the brain space involved. *Proceedings of the National Academy of Science, 81,* 6232–6234.

Catchpole, C. K. (1980). Sexual selection and the evolution of complex songs among European warblers of the genus *Acrocephalus. Behaviour, 74,* 149–166.

Catchpole, C. K. (1982). The evolution of bird sounds in relation to mating and spacing behavior: In D. E. Kroodsma & E. H. Miller (Eds.), *Acoustic communication in birds* (Vol. 1, pp. 297–319). New York: Academic Press.

Catchpole, C. K. (1984). Differential responses to male song repertoires in female songbirds implanted with oestradiol. *Nature, 312,* 563–564.

Cavalli-Sforza, L. L., & Feldman, M. W. (1981). *Cultural transmission and evolution: A quantitative approach.* New Jersey: Princeton University Press.

Cracraft, J. (1981). Toward a phylogenetic classification of the recent birds of the world (Class Aves). *Auk, 98,* 681–714.

Craig, W. (1943). The song of the Wood Pewee *Myiochanes virens* Linnaeus: A study of bird music. *New York State Museum Bulletin, 334,* 1–186.

Crawford, R. (1977). Polygynous breeding of short-billed marsh wrens. *Auk, 94,* 359–362.

Dobson, D. W., & Lemon, R. E. (1975). Reexamination of monotony threshold hypothesis in bird song. *Nature, 257,* 126–128.

Dowsett-Lemaire, F. (1979). The imitation range of the song of the Marsh Warbler, *Acrocephalus palustris,* with special reference to imitations of African birds. *Ibis, 121,* 453–468.

Emlen, S. T. (1971). Geographic variation in Indigo Bunting song (*Passerina cyanea*). *Animal Behaviour, 19,* 407–408.

Ewert, D. N. (1978). *Song of the Rufous-sided Towhee (Pipilo erythophthalmus) on Long Island, New York.* Unpublished doctoral dissertation, City University of New York.

Falls, J. B., & d'Agincourt, L. G. (1981). A comparison of neighbor-stranger discrimination in Eastern and Western Meadowlarks. *Canadian Journal of Zoology, 49,* 2380–2385.

Feduccia, A. (1980). *The age of birds.* Cambridge, MA: Harvard University Press.

Ficken, M. S., & Ficken, R. W. (1965). Comparative ethology of the Chestnut-sided Warbler, Yellow Warbler, and American Redstart. *Wilson Bulletin, 77,* 363–375.

Gill, F. B., & Murray, B. G., Jr. (1972). Song variation in sympatric Blue-winged and Golden-winged warblers. *Auk, 89,* 625–643.

Grant, B. R. (1984). The significance of song variation in a population of Darwin's finches. *Behaviour, 89,* 90–116.

Hafner, D. J., & Petersen, K. E. (1985). Song dialects and gene flow in the White-crowned Sparrow, *Zonotrichia leucophrys. Evolution, 39,* 687–694.

Hartshorne, C. (1973). *Born to sing. An interpretation and world survey of bird song.* Bloomington: Indiana University Press.

Jenkins, P. F. (1977). Cultural transmission of song patterns and dialect development in a free-living bird population. *Animal Behaviour, 25,* 50–78.

Johnson, N. K. (1980). Character variation and evolution of sibling species in the *Empidonax difficilis-flavescens* complex (Aves: Tyrannidae). *University of California Publications in Zoology), 112,* 1–153.

Kellogg, P. P. (1962). *A field guide to western bird songs.* Boston: Houghton Mifflin Company.

King, A. P., & West, M. J. (1977). Species identification in the North American cowbird: Appropriate responses to abnormal song. *Science, 195,* 1002–1004.

King, A. P., & West, M. J. (1983). Female perception of cowbird song: A closed developmental program. *Developmental Psychobiology, 16,* 335–342.

King, A. P., West, M. J., & Eastzer, D. H. (1980). Song structure and song development as potential contributors to reproductive isolation in cowbirds (*Molothrus ater*). *Journal of Comparative Physiological Psychology, 94,* 1028–1036.

Konishi, M., & Nottebohm, F. (1969). Experimental studies in the ontogeny of avian vocalizations. In R. A. Hinde (Ed.), *Bird vocalizations* (pp. 29–48). London and New York: Cambridge University Press.

Krebs, J. R. (1976). Habituation and song repertoires in the Great Tit. *Behavioral Ecology and Sociobiology, 1,* 215–227.

Krebs, J. R., & Kroodsma, D. E. (1980). Repertoires and geographical variation in bird song. In J. S. Rosenblatt, R. A. Hinde, C. Beer, & M. C. Busnel (Eds.), *Advances in the study of behavior* (pp. 143–177). New York: Academic Press.

Kroodsma, D. E. (1971). Song variations and singing behavior in the Rufous-sided Towhee, *Pipilo erythrophthalmus oregonus. Condor, 73,* 303–308.

Kroodsma, D. E. (1974). Song learning, dialects, and dispersal in the Bewick's Wren. *Zeitschrift für Tierpsychologie, 35,* 352–380.

Kroodsma, D. E. (1975). Dialect occurrence and possible functions in versatile songsters. *Proceedings on Symposium on Dialects in Bird Song.* St. Louis University: Media Services.

Kroodsma, D. E. (1977). Correlates of song organization among North America wrens. *American Naturalist, 111,* 995–1008.

Kroodsma, D. E. (1978). Aspects of learning in the ontogeny of bird song: Where, from whom, when, how many, which, and how accurately? In G. Burghardt & M. Bekoff (Eds.), *Ontogeny of Behavior* (pp. 215–230). New York: Garland.

Kroodsma, D. E. (1980). Winter Wren singing behavior: a pinnacle of song complexity. *Condor, 82,* 356–365.

Kroodsma, D. E. (1981). Geographical variation and functions of song types in warblers (*Parulidae*). *Auk, 98,* 743–751.

Kroodsma, D. E. (1983). The ecology of avian vocal learning. *BioScience, 33,* 165–171.

Kroodsma, D. E. (1984). Songs of the Alder Flycatcher (*Empidonax alnorum*) and Willow Flycatcher (*Empidonax traillii*) are innate. *Auk, 101,* 13–24.

Kroodsma, D. E. (1985a). Song development and use of two song forms by the Eastern Phoebe (*Sayornis phoebe*). *Wilson Bulletin, 97,* 21–29.

Kroodsma, D. E. (1985b). Limited dispersal between dialects?: hypotheses testable in the field. *Behavioral and Brain Sciences, 8,* 108–109.

Kroodsma, D. E. (1985c). Geographic variation in songs of the Bewick's Wren: a search for correlations with avifaunal complexity. *Behavioral Ecology and Sociobiology, 16,* 143–150.

Kroodsma, D. E., Baker, M. C., Baptista, L. F., & Petrinovich, L. (1984). Vocal "dialects" in Nuttall's White-crowned Sparrow. *Current Ornithology, 2,* 103–133.

Kroodsma, D. E., & Baylis, J. R. (1982). Appendix: A world survey of evidence for vocal learning in birds. In D. E. Kroodsma & E. H. Miller (Eds.), *Acoustic communication in birds* (Vol. 2, pp. 311–337). New York: Academic Press.

Kroodsma, D. E., & Canady, R. (1985). Differences in repertoire size, singing behavior, and associated neuroanatomy among Marsh Wren populations have a genetic basis. *Auk, 102,* 439–446.

Kroodsma, D. E., Meservey, W. R., Whitlock, A. L., & VanderHaegen, W. M. (1984). Blue-winged Warblers (*Vermivora pinus*) "recognize" dialects in Type II but not Type I songs. *Behavioral Ecology and Sociobiology, 15,* 127–132.

Kroodsma, D. E., Meservey, W. R., & Pickert, R. (1983). Vocal learning in the Parulinae. *Wilson Bulletin, 95,* 138–140.

Kroodsma, D. E., & Pickert, R. (1980). Environmentally dependent sensitive periods for avian vocal learning. *Nature, 288,* 477–479.

Kroodsma, D. E., & Verner, J. (1978). Complex singing behaviors among *Cistothorus* wrens. *Auk, 95,* 703–716.

Lanyon, W. E. (1957). The comparative biology of the meadowlarks (*Sturnella*) in Wisconsin. *Publ. Nuttall Ornithol. Club,* No. 1.

Lanyon, W. E. (1978). Revision of the *Myiarchus* flycatchers of South America. *Bulletin of the American Museum of Natural History, 161,* 429–627.

Lein, M. R. (1978). Song variation in a population of Chestnut-sided Warblers (*Dendroica pensylvanica*): Its nature and suggested significance. *Canadian Journal of Zoology, 56,* 1266–1283.

Lumsden, C. J., & Wilson, E. O. (1981). *Genes, mind, and culture.* Cambridge, MA: Harvard University Press.

Marler, P. (1976). Sensory templates in species-specific behavior. In J. Fentress (Ed.), *Simpler networks and behavior* (pp. 314–329). Sunderland, MA: Sinauer.

Marler, P., & Mundinger, P., Waser, M. S., & Lutjen, A. (1972). Effects of acoustical stimulation and deprivation on song development in Red-winged Blackbirds (*Agelaius phoeniceus*). *Animal Behaviour, 20,* 586–606.

Marler, P., & Peters, S. (1977). Selective vocal learning in a sparrow. *Science, 198,* 519–521.

Marler, P., & Peters, S. (1982). Subsong and plastic song: Their role in the vocal learning process. In D. E. Kroodsma & E. H. Miller (Eds.), *Acoustic communication in birds* (Vol. 2, pp. 25–50). New York: Academic Press.

Marler, P., & Pickert, R. (1984). Species-universal microstructure in the learned song of the Swamp Sparrow (*Melospiza georgiana*). *Animal Behaviour, 32,* 673–689.

Marler, P., Zoloth, S., & Dooling, R. (1981). Innate programs for perceptual development: an ethological view. In E. S. Hollin (Ed.), *Developmental plasticity: Behavioral and biological aspects of variations in development* (pp. 135–172). New York: Academic Press.

McGregor, P. K., & Krebs, J. R. (1982). Mating and song types in the Great Tit. *Nature, 297,* 60–61.

Miller, E. H. (1982). Character and variance shift in acoustic signals of birds. In D. E. Kroodsma & E. H. Miller (Eds.), *Acoustic communication in birds* (Vol. 1, pp. 253–295). New York: Academic Press.

Morse, D. H. (1970). Territorial and courtship songs of birds. *Nature (London), 226,* 659–661.

Mundinger, P. C. (1982). Microgeographic and macrogeographic variation in acquired vocalizations of birds. In D. E. Kroodsma & E. H. Miller (Eds.), *Acoustic communication in birds* (Vol. 2, pp. 147–208). New York: Academic Press.

Nolan, V., Jr. (1978). The ecology and behavior of the Prairie Warbler (*Dendroica discolor*). *Ornithological Monographs,* No. 26.

Nottebohm, F. (1969). The song of the Chingolo, *Zonotrichia capensis*, in Argentina: Description and evaluation of a system of dialects. *Condor, 71,* 299–315.

Nottebohm, F. (1972). The origins of vocal learning. *American Naturalist, 106,* 116–140.

Nottebohm, F., (1975). Vocal behavior in birds. In D. S. Farner & J. R. King (Eds.), *Avian biology* (Vol. 5, pp. 287–332). New York: Academic Press.

Orians, G. H. (1969). On the evolution of mating systems in birds and mammals. *American Naturalist, 102,* 589–603.

Payne, R. B. (1981). Song learning and social interaction in Indigo Buntings. *Animal Behaviour, 29,* 688–697.

Payne, R. B. (1982). Ecological consequences of song matching: Breeding success and intra-specific song mimicry by Indigo Buntings. *Ecology, 63,* 401–411.

Payne, R. B. (1983). The social context of song mimicry: song-matching dialects in Indigo Buntings (*Passerina cyanea*). *Animal Behaviour, 31,* 788–805.

Payne, R. B., & Budde, P. (1979). Song differences and map distances in a population of Acadian Flycatchers. *Wilson Bulletin, 91,* 29–41.

Payne, R. B., Payne, L. L., & Doehlert, S. M. (1984). Interspecific song learning in a wild Chestnut-sided Warbler. *Wilson Bulletin, 96,* 292–294.

Payne, R. B., Thompson, W. L., Fiala, K. L., & Sweany, L. L. (1981). Local song traditions in Indigo Buntings: Cultural transmission of behaviour patterns across generations. *Behaviour, 77,* 199–221.

Pepperberg, I. M. (1981). Functional vocalizations by an African Grey Parrot (*Psittacus erithacus*). *Zeitschrift für Tierpsychologie, 55,* 139–160.

Petrinovich, L., & Patterson, T. L. (1982). The White-crowned Sparrow: Stability, recruitment, and population structure in the Nuttall subspecies. *Auk, 99,* 1–14.

Petrinovich, L., Patterson, T. L., & Baptista, L. F. (1981). Song dialects as barriers to dispersal: A re-evaluation. *Evolution, 35,* 180–188.

Raikow, R. J. (1982). Monophyly of the Passeriformes: Test of a phylogenetic hypothesis. *Auk, 99,* 431–445.

Rice, J. & Thompson, W. L. (1968). Song development in the Indigo Bunting. *Animal Behaviour, 16,* 462–469.

Richards, D. G. (1979). *Environmental acoustics and song communication in passerine birds.* Unpublished doctoral diss., University of North Carolina at Chapel Hill.

Richards, D. G. (1978). Recognition of neighbors by associative learning in Rufous-sided Towhees. *Auk, 96,* 688–693.

Schutz, F. (1965). Sexuelle Pragung der Anatiden. *Zeitschrift für Tierpsychologie, 22,* 50–103.

Searcy, W. A., & Marler, P. (1981). A test for responsiveness to song structure and programming in female sparrows. *Science, 213,* 926–928.

Searcy, W. A., McArthur, P. D., Peters, S. S., & Marler, P. (1981). Response of male Song and Swamp Sparrows to neighbor, stranger, and self songs. *Behaviour, 77,* 152–163.

Shiovitz, K. A., & Thompson, W. L. (1970). Geographic variation in song composition of the Indigo Bunting (*Passerina cyanea*). *Animal Behaviour, 18,* 151–158.

Sibley, C. G., & Ahlquist, J. E. (1985). The phylogeny and classification of the passerine birds, based on comparisons of the genetic material, DNA. *Proceedings of the 18th International Ornithological Congress,* Moscow, pp. 83–121.

Slater, P. J. B. (1983). Bird song learning: Theme and variation. In G. A. Clark, Jr., & A. R. Brush (Eds.), *Perspectives in ornithology* (pp. 475–499). New York and London: Cambridge University Press.

Smith, W. J. (1977). *The behavior of communicating.* Cambridge, MA: Harvard University Press.

Snow, B. K. (1977). Territorial behavior and courtship of the male Three-wattled Bellbird. *Auk, 94,* 623–645.

Snow, D. W. (1968). The singing assemblies of Little Hermits. *Living Bird, 7,* 47–55.

Sonnemann, P., & Sjolander, S. (1977). Effects of cross-fostering on the sexual imprinting of the female Zebra Finch (*Taeniopygia guttata*). *Zeitschrift für Tierpsychologie, 45,* 337–348.

Stein, R. C. (1963). Isolating mechanisms between populations of Traill's Flycatchers. *Proceedings of the American Philosophical Society, 107,* 21–50.

Thompson, W. L. (1970). Song variation in a population of Indigo Buntings. *Auk, 87,* 58–71.

Todt, D. (1975). Social learning of vocal patterns and models of their application in the Grey Parrot. *Zeitschrift für Tierpsychologie, 39,* 178–188.

Trivers, R. L. (1972). Parental investment and sexual selection. In B. Campbell (Ed.), *Sexual selection and the descent of man* (pp. 139–179). Chicago: Aldine.

Verner, J. (1965). Breeding biology of the Long-billed Marsh Wren. *Condor, 67,* 6–30.

Verner, J. (1975). Complex song repertoire of male Long-billed Marsh Wrens in eastern Washington. *Living Bird, 14,* 263–300.

Waddington, D. H. (1957). *The strategy of the genes.* London: Allen and Unwin.

West, M. J., King, A. P., & Harrocks, T. J. (1983). Cultural transmission of cowbird song: measuring its development and outcome. *Journal of Comparative Psychology, 97,* 327–337.

Wildenthal, J. L. (1965). Structure in primary song of the Mockingbird (*Mimus polyglottos*). *Auk, 82,* 161–189.

Wiley, R. H. (1971). Song groups in a singing assembly of Little Hermits. *Condor, 73,* 28–35.

Zink, R. M., & Barrowclough, G. F. (1984). Allozymes and song dialects: A reassessment. *Evolution, 38,* 444–448.

10 A Functional Behavioristic Approach to Aversively Motivated Behavior: Predatory Imminence as a Determinant of the Topography of Defensive Behavior

Michael S. Fanselow
Laurie S. Lester
Dartmouth College

Since the 1960s (Breland & Breland, 1961; Garcia & Koelling, 1966) learning theorists have found that the so called general learning processes are bounded by biologically determined constraints. These data indicate that psychologists cannot ignore evolutionary biology when studying behavior. But what approach do we take to integrate biology with psychology? One approach is to search for situations in which the general laws of learning fail (Seligman, 1970). Unfortunately, this approach has not advanced significantly, our thinking about learning or behavior (Domjan & Galef, 1983). Another approach, which we call the functional behavioristic approach, is to view the organism as confronted with a series of environmental problems that must be solved to insure future reproductive success. Such an approach focuses on behavior rather than general processes and suggests that we examine behavior in terms of the problems it has evolved to solve.

The historical pattern just described is manifested in the literature on aversively motivated behavior. Prior to the publication of Bolles' (1970) paper on species-specific defensive reactions and avoidance behavior, the study of aversive motivation was primarily concerned with fear reduction reinforcement. The general reaction to Bolles' paper was to force psychologists to consider evolutionary constraints on reinforcement processes (Domjam & Galef, 1983; cf. Shettleworth, 1983). An alternative reaction has been that aversive motivation will be best understood in terms of an analysis of defensive behaviors, that is, in terms of the behaviors' evolutionary function as antipredator strategies (e.g.,

Bolles & Fanselow, 1980; Masterson & Crawford, 1982).[1] This paper attempts
to develop a conceptualization of defensive behavior from this functional behavioristic perspective.

In undertaking a functional analysis it is often profitable to characterize the
problem to be solved into a series of subproblems defined by the organism's
proximity to the goal object[2] (e.g., Collier, 1981; Timberlake, 1983). For feeding, Collier (1981) has discussed times when food is not in hand but must be
found (search), present but not immediately available (procurement), available
(handling and consumption), or ready to be utilized (metabolism). Thus, the
problem of energy intake is broken down into a series of tasks defined by the
subjects geographic/temporal relationship to food. This compartmentalization is
useful in that manipulations of task relevant environmental variables have different effects on behavior that depend on the subproblem (e.g., Collier, 1983).

An analysis of defensive behavior may also be facilitated by a similar compartmentalization into subproblems (Edmunds, 1974). The prey's task is to avoid
being killed by the predator, and the immediate geographic/temporal relationship
of the predator to the prey may be a determinant of the form of the defensive
behavior. This relationship can be described as a continuum, the endpoints being
the situation in which the prey is safest from predation, its nest site for example,
and the point at which the prey is killed by the predator. It is our hypothesis that
both qualitative and quantitative changes in defensive behavior occur as a function of the prey's perception of where it is on this continuum. This perception is
in part determined by the physical distance between predator and prey (Ratner,
1967, 1975). According to Ratner (1967), predators at a moderate distance elicit
freezing, at shorter distances elicit flight and at zero distance (contact) elicit tonic
immobility. However, factors other than absolute physical distance contribute to
the prey's perception of where it is on the continuum. The animal in a safe nest
does not know whether or not a predator is close to its foraging area when it
decides to forage but its decision when, where, and how to forage should reflect
the potential of predation. Likewise, a predator at a fixed distance may or may
not release flight in the prey depending upon its behavior (Walther, 1969). The
prey reacts as if an approaching predator is closer than one at the same distance
moving along a tangent. The approaching predator has a shorter *psychological*
distance. Therefore, we refer to this continuum as one of *predatory imminence*
because it reflects both physical and psychological distance.

---

[1]When we use the term strategy we are referring only to a particular organism's solution to a
particular environmental problem. There is no intention to imply either the presence or absence of
awareness or cognition. Nor do we wish to imply that the particular strategy is or is not the optimal
solution to the problem. Once the strategy is identified it can be tested for those characteristics
(awareness, cognition or optimality) but the first task is to identify the strategy.

[2]When described in this way the functional approach has a strong resemblance to Tolman's
(1932) view of purposive behavior.

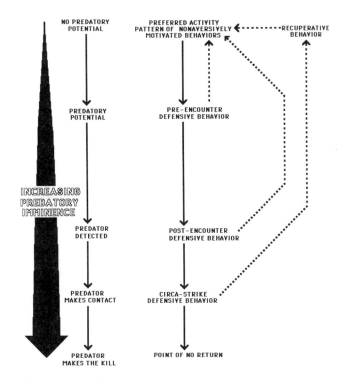

FIGURE 10.1.   The predatory imminence continuum.

THE PREDATORY IMMINENCE CONTINUUM

The predatory imminence continuum is diagrammed in Fig. 10.1. It is hypothesized that behavioral changes will occur as a function of changes in the prey's perception of its location on the continuum. If predatory imminence is at a zero level we can assume that the prey's activity patterns reflect an optimal balance between nonaversively motivated behaviors such as foraging, feeding, exploration, mating, nursing, and nest maintaining. We call this point the preferred activity pattern for it is assumed that in the absence of predatory pressures animals will always revert back to this pattern.[3] As predatory imminence increases the animal's activity patterns must deviate from this preferred pattern to

---

[3]Of course there is no time in a prey animal's life when the probability of predation is truly zero. When we refer to a zero level of predatory imminence or the absence of predatory pressures we are really referring to situations in which the probability of predation is at, or very near, the lowest level that that particular prey animal experiences. It is at such a point that the preferred activity pattern emerges.

allow for defense. Evolution would select for defensive behaviors that produce minimal time away from this preferred point. We propose that the strategy employed by an animal to accomplish this is to behave in a way that reduces the probability of further movement down the continuum. Different defensive behavior patterns would be necessary at different points along the continuum to prevent further increases in imminence. Thus it is predicted that defensive behaviors will be qualitatively different at different sections on the continuum and that the environmental stimuli that control defensive behavior will also change as well. The remainder of this paper focuses on laboratory studies of rats that exemplify defensive behaviors at different sections along the continuum. These sections are described in order of increasing imminence.

PRE-ENCOUNTER DEFENSIVE BEHAVIOR

If an animal is never at risk of predation (e.g., when a rodent is in its burrow) its behaviors will be organized into the preferred activity pattern. However, certain nonaversively motivated behaviors (e.g., foraging for food or seeking a mate) may be associated with an increase in the probability of encountering a predator. For example, the risk of encountering a predator is likely to be higher when the animal is foraging than when it is in the nest. The animal may modify its foraging behavior to reduce the probability of an encounter with a predator. Such a modification is a pre-encounter defensive behavior and the degree of this modification should reflect the likelihood of encountering a predator. Thus pre-encounter defense reflects a reorganization of activities that serve functions other than defense because the situation in which these activities occur has the potential for predation. It is important to note that pre-encounter defense is not a response to a specific predatory individual; no particular predator is present when the prey decides to forage. Rather, the prey alters its activity patterns according to the likelihood of an encounter while engaged in a particular activity.

We have been examining pre-encounter defense in terms of changes in meal frequency and meal size when a risk of predation is associated with foraging. Collier (1983) has suggested that a given species has a typical range of daily meal frequencies. Meal frequency is always inversely related to meal size. Therefore, there is also a range of meal sizes. When the cost of foraging and meal procurement is low (as it is for a rat with *ad libitum* access to food) meal frequency is at the high end of the range and meal size is small. Collier suggests that these values are determined by digestive efficiency, as frequent small meals are processed more efficiently than infrequent large meals. However, as the costs associated with meal procurement increase meal frequency decreases and meal size increases. The rat uses this strategy and successfully defends body weight until procurement cost is so great that meal frequency drops below a single meal per day (the low end of its species-typical range). Collier and his colleagues (see

Collier, 1981, 1983, for reviews) have manipulated cost by manipulating the work required to procure a meal. We have manipulated a different sort of cost by manipulating the potential of predation associated with foraging and feeding. Frequency of electric shock is used as a model of predation because of the ease with which shock can be controlled. The use of shock appears to be a valid way of modelling predation as stimuli that predict a high imminence of shock elicit species-specific antipredatory behaviors such as freezing (Bouton & Bolles, 1980; Fanselow, 1980a; Fanselow & Bolles, 1979a).

If the potential of predation is absent the rat will be at the high frequency (small meal size) end of its range of meal patterns, where digestion is most efficient. As foraging becomes associated with an increase in the potential of predation meal patterns should shift toward the low frequency (large meal size) portion of the range. That is, if the rat is at risk while searching for a patch of food, when it encounters a patch it should exploit that patch to a greater extent (eat a larger meal) than when it is not at risk. This would reduce the number of times the animal would have to search for a patch and thus the total amount of time the animal is at risk would be reduced. This strategy would allow the rat to reduce time at risk without sacrificing total daily food intake. Such shifts in meal patterning in response to the potential of predation would be an example of pre-encounter defensive behavior.

The design of our experiment is quite similar to that developed by Collier and his colleagues (e.g., Collier, 1983). A rat lives in the apparatus depicted in Fig. 10.2. The animal is never food-deprived in the usual sense. It has unlimited access to water from the tube protruding through the rear of the intelligence panel. Forty-five mg food pellets (Bio-Serv) are delivered, to the food magazine on the front of the left hand wall, contingent upon pressing of the adjacent bar. Food is made available on chained FR:CRF reinforcement schedules (Gunn, 1983). Once the FR component is executed, the overhead cue light turns on and each bar press results in a single pellet. This CRF schedule remains in effect as long as the rat makes at least one bar press every 4 minutes. If the animal forgoes pressing for 4 min the cue light is extinguished and the rat must once again execute the FR component to gain access to food. Thus we have a convenient operationalization of the period of foraging (the FR component), number of meals taken (the number of individual CRF components entered), and meal size (mean number of responses in each individual CRF component). A rat started at FR-1 and was slowly progressed to FR-32. Like Collier, Hirsch, & Hamlin (1972), we found that as the foraging cost increased, meal frequency decreased but there was a compensatory increase in meal size.

On FR-32 the rat was taking almost 4 daily meals of 76 pellets each. At this point electric shock (1mA, 1 sec) was introduced. As shock was delivered through the grid floor the animal was only at risk when it was out of the nesting area. First, 6 shocks per day were delivered but the number of shocks was slowly increased to 20 per day. The effects of shock frequency on meal size and meal

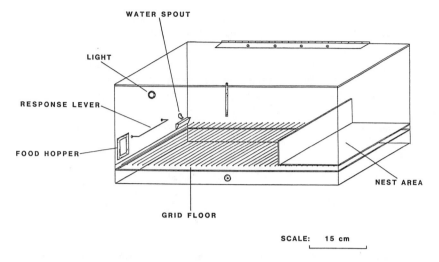

FIGURE 10.2. The entire chamber was 58 × 26.5 × 20.5 cm. The flat platform and barrier at the right contained wood shavings and constituted the nest area. The nest area was about the size of a standard single laboratory home cage.

frequency are presented in Fig. 10.3. As shock frequency increased, meal frequency decreased; at 20 shocks per day the animal was taking less than 2 1/2 meals per day. However, these decreases in meal frequency were always accompanied by increases in meal size—at 20 shocks per day meal size increased to 112 pellets. The programmed number of shocks per day and the number of FR bar presses made by the rat showed a correlation of −.92, indicating that as risk increased the behavior became more efficient.

At this point, the FR requirement was gradually decreased to FR-4 with the 20 shocks per day schedule in effect. Decreases in meal frequency, with compensatory increases in meal size, relative to the shock-free schedules were observed at all FR requirements. On the average, 20 shocks per day decreased meal frequency by 43%, and increased meal size by 55% of what it was on the shock-free FR requirement. While on FR-4, shock was discontinued and meal frequency gradually rose while meal size gradually fell (i.e., shock-induced meal pattern changes tended to extinguish). However, the meal pattern did not completely return to preshock FR-4 levels indicating carryover effects of the past shock experience.

Notice that the risk of predation did not simply suppress appetitively motivated behavior. Rather, it produced orderly changes in the organization of that behavior. Throughout the experiment the rat held daily intake constant despite dramatic alterations in meal patterning. Body weight showed the normal level of increase throughout the experiment going from a pre-experiment weight of 242g to 311g at the experiment's conclusion.

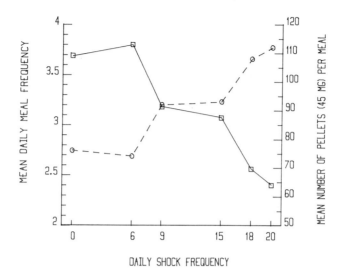

FIGURE 10.3.   This figure represents the data from a single female rat. Each data point represents the mean of about 13 days. The □———□ line represents the mean number of meals a day with its axis to the left. The ○- - -○ line represents the meal size of each daily meal with its axis to the right.

In summary, it was found that when a rat was placed at risk during its time of foraging and consumption the animal's meal pattern varied with that risk. Essentially, as risk increased, meal frequency decreased but there was a compensatory increase in meal size such that total daily intake and body weight were defended. Such a reorganization of nonaversively motivated behavior as a function of predatory imminence, is an example of pre-encounter defensive behavior.

POST-ENCOUNTER DEFENSIVE BEHAVIOR

The subtle pre-encounter reorganization of activity can be contrasted with the dramatic changes in the animal's behavior when a predator is actually present in the vicinity and the prey has detected it. When such an encounter takes place the prey's ongoing behavior is immediately suppressed and its behavioral repertoire is limited to what Bolles (1970) has referred to as species-specific defense reactions. For example, Mollenauer, Plotnik, and Snyder (1974) found that when a cat was present in a situation where a hungry rat usually drank a sucrose solution the rat gave up drinking and engaged in freezing. Similar results are found when a rat is confronted by laboratory stimuli that have been previously paired with aversive electric shock (Bouton & Bolles, 1980). These active defensive behaviors, in response to detection of a particular predator, are post-encounter defensive behaviors. They reflect activities whose entire function is directed toward avoiding contact with the predator. Post-encounter defensive behaviors are responses to the immediate presence of a predatory individual. Such a predatory presence, of course, reflects an increase in imminence over the level that results in pre-encounter defense.

It is generally thought that the rat has several such defensive behavior patterns available and that certain features of the environment (Blanchard, Fukunaga, & Blanchard, 1976a, 1976b; Bolles & Fanselow, 1980; Fanselow, 1982; Fanselow & Baackes, 1982) or certain response contingencies (Bolles, 1970; Masterson & Crawford, 1982) select between them. However, at this point on the imminence continuum behavior may be much simpler and far less flexible than these models suggest. In the Norway Rat, it appears that the freezing response is the dominant post-encounter defensive behavior. During this stage of defense flight is rare and may only appear if there is an easily and safely available, highly practiced, escape route. Therefore, our discussion of post-encounter defense concentrates on the freezing response.

Although cessation of motor activity is the most salient feature of freezing, this response should not be thought of as a simple inhibition of movement. Rather, it is an integrated, functional behavioral pattern. Inactivity is to freezing as locomotion is to flight.[4] Freezing does not occur arbitrarily, the rat freezes next to walls, usually in corners (thigmotaxis—see Grossen & Kelly, 1972). If a lighting differential is present in the immediate vicinity the rat will tend to freeze in the darker area (Allison, Larson, & Jensen, 1967). If certain aspects of the environment are less strongly associated with aversive stimulation the animal will gravitate to those areas and freeze there. Thus, the animal will approach and freeze near contextual stimuli that are less predictive of the occurrence of electric shock (Fanselow, 1980b, 1980c; LeClerc & Reberg, 1980) and they will freeze on *operant* levers that are associated with the termination of shock (Bolles & McGillis, 1968; Davis & Burton, 1974). Freezing is accompanied by specific physiological changes such as shallow but rapid respiration (Hofer, 1970). When we say that freezing is functional we mean that it is of adaptive value—in the animal's phylogenetic history freezing presumably has been successful at preventing further increases in predatory imminence. Thus, rats that froze during an encounter with a predator were more likely to reproduce than those that did not.

---

[4]The relationship of the analogy is one of dependent measure to the response of interest. Freezing is measured by scoring the time spent immobile. Flight is measured by scoring locomotion (e.g., lines crossed). It is no different than measuring bar pressing by counting microswitch closures. Thus the dependent measure of freezing is highly objective and interobserver agreement is extremely high. The reason we are emphasizing freezing as a functional unit is that historically the defensive responses of flight and fighting have been defined functionally whereas freezing has been defined topographically. This has led to the inappropriate inference that freezing is therefore of less functional value than flight (e.g., Blanchard et al., 1976a).

We do not mean that freezing is, or need be, functional in the proximal sense of reducing the current amount of aversive stimulation (cf. Miller, Greco, & Vigorito, 1981; Miller, Greco, Vigorito, & Marlin, 1983).

There are several demonstrations of rats innately freezing to predators such as cats (e.g., Blanchard & Blanchard, 1971; Blanchard, Fukunaga, & Blanchard, 1976a; Blanchard, Mast, & Blanchard, 1975; Bronstein & Hirsch, 1976; Mollenauer et al., 1974; Satinder, 1976), snakes (Hofer, 1970), canines (Blanchard et al., 1975; Fox, 1969) and humans (Suarez & Gallup, 1981a). A powerful demonstration that freezing is innately elicited by predators was conducted by Hirsch and Bolles (1980) using deermice as subjects. The mice were laboratory reared, F^1 generation offspring of two substrains trapped in ecologically distinct environments. These animals differentially froze to predators as opposed to nonpredators of their native ecology but could not distinguish between predators and nonpredators from another region. Freezing was functional in that survival time was greater when the prey was pitted against a predator of its natural environment.

While freezing is elicited unconditionally by innately recognized predators, it also occurs in situations in which rats receive aversive electric shock. It is in shock-related situations that freezing has been most thoroughly analyzed. Freezing will follow a single, brief, mild electric shock (Fanselow & Bolles, 1979b). It is not reinforced by shock avoidance, nor is it suppressed by punishment (Bolles & Riley, 1973; Brener & Goesling, 1970). When freezing is programmed to act as an avoidance response all other forms of activity would be punished (Bolles, 1970). Because an avoidance contingency does not enhance freezing, freezing does not emerge because of punishment of other behaviors (and that includes other defensive responses—see Bolles, 1975, pp. 360–364). Clearly, freezing is under respondent, not operant control.

This failure of reinforcement contingencies to influence freezing is illustrated by an experiment, conducted in our laboratory by John Isaacson. Animals were trained with either a discrete trial-signaled punishment response contingency or a discrete trial-signaled avoidance response contingency. Freezing continuously for 5 sec was the criterion response. Each rat in these conditions served as a master for a yoked control animal. The yoked controls received the same pattern of the white noise signal and shock as their masters but there was no response contingency. Mr. Isaacson found substantial amounts of freezing in all conditions but the masters never differed from the yoked controls. Additionally, the animals that were punished for freezing froze reliably *more* than the animals that could avoid shock by freezing. This occurred because the high level of conditioned freezing interacted with the programmed response contingency so that punishment animals received more tone-shock pairings (Pavlovian acquisition trials) and fewer tone-alone pairings (Pavlovian extinction trials) than the avoidance animals.

While freezing occurs in situations where rats are given electric shock, the shock does not unconditionally elicit freezing. Rather, freezing is a conditional response to stimuli associated with shock (Fanselow, 1980a). If some explicit stimulus, such as a tone or a light, precedes shock then the tone or light acquires the capacity to elicit freezing (Bouton & Bolles, 1980; Fanselow & Bolles, 1979a; Sigmundi, Bouton, & Bolles, 1980). If no explicit conditional stimulus (CS) is paired with the shock then the apparatus stimuli present just before shock onset will acquire the ability to elicit freezing (Blanchard & Blanchard, 1969a; Bolles & Collier, 1976; Fanselow, 1980a, 1981; 1984a; Fanselow & Baackes, 1982). Rats never freeze during shock, nor do they freeze immediately after shock, rather the unconditional reaction to shock is a burst of activity (Fanselow, 1982—see circa-strike behavior below). Thus, the conditional response to shock associated stimuli—freezing—and the unconditional reaction to shock—activity bursting—are different in form (Fanselow & Bolles, 1982). Freezing is an unconditional reaction to an encounter with an innately recognized predator, and stimuli that predict a high imminence of a sudden nociceptive event like electric shock also acquire the capacity to elicit this post-encounter defensive behavior.

We say that freezing is the dominant post-encounter defensive behavior because given the opportunity to engage in another defensive response, freezing is still the rat's response of first choice (e.g., Moser & Tait, 1983). We have conducted several experiments that have pitted freezing against alternative defenses and found that freezing predominates over those alternatives. In one experiment we used a two-compartment test chamber. The chamber was lighted by a 7.5-W overhead light (see Fanselow, 1984a, 1984b for a description of the chamber). The two compartments were separated by a metal wall that had an 8 × 8 cm passageway at floor level, in the center of the wall. One compartment had a grid floor the other compartment had a solid masonite floor. The solid-floored side had an opaque ceiling which kept the compartment darkened. Four groups of rats were preexposed to this chamber for 15 min a day for 3 days. During this time they were free to move between compartments. Another four groups received no preexposure but were handled. On the 4th through 6th days all the rats received Pavlovian fear conditioning in a different chamber that had the same overhead light (see Fanselow 1984a, 1984b for a description of the chamber). The CS was 3-min of flashing of the overhead light (.4-sec on, .4-sec off), the unconditional stimulus (US) was a .75-sec, .8-mA scrambled grid shock. Four trials a day were given at an 18-min intertrial interval. Two groups in each preexposure condition received forward pairings of CS and US and the four other groups received backward pairings. Following conditioning the preexposed animals received 3 more days of exposure to the test chamber while the others were handled. The 10th through 12th days consisted of test sessions. Half the animals had the passageway in the test chamber barricaded by a solid plate made of the same steel as the dividing wall. The other half had it barricaded with 3 (1mm diameter) rods spaced 1.8cm apart. The design is summarized in Table 10.1.

Each test session was 12 min long. A rat was placed in the grid-floor section of the test apparatus and 6 min later the CS was presented for 3 min. The animals remained in the chamber for an additional 3 min (see, e.g., Fanselow, 1984a). Freezing behavior was recorded according to a time-sampling procedure. In addition, the time the rat was in contact with the barricade was recorded.

We predicted that the forward-paired CS would elicit freezing in the animals that had the exit obscurred by the steel plate. However, this experiment was conducted before we were convinced that freezing was the dominant post-encounter defense so we also expected freezing to be replaced by escape attempts directed at the exit in the animals that had the exit obstructed by only a few thin rods. We also thought that familiarization with traveling through the exit would facilitate escape attempts and decrease freezing. We thought the blocked compartment would be attractive to the rats because it was dark (Allison et al., 1976) and it had a solid floor as opposed to a grid floor (the rats had been shocked on a grid floor). We chose to use a light CS because Sigmundi and Bolles (1983) reported that lights elicit freezing less strongly than tones. In short, we stacked the odds in favor of getting reduced freezing and increased flight.

Analyses of variance on the data revealed that we were wrong in most of our predictions. Figure 10.4 presents the data in terms of the mean of the three test trials. The freezing data are presented in the left panel in the form of a freezing ratio. This ratio is the probability of freezing during the 3-min CS divided by the sum of that quantity and the probability of freezing during a 3-min period prior to the CS presentation. A value of 1.0 indicates that freezing is confined to the CS as opposed to the preCS period; .5 indicates that the CS does not change the probability of freezing from that during the preCS period and a value of 0 indicates that the CS disrupts freezing that is occurring during the preCS period. It can be seen that the CS elicited freezing in all the forward-conditioned groups. (The forward-conditioned animals froze on average, 87% of the time during the CS.) The CS had little effect on freezing in the backward-conditioned animals;

TABLE 10.1
Experimental Design

Group	Preconditioning Exposure to Test Chamber	Off-baseline Pavlovian Conditioning	Postconditioning Exposure to Test Chamber	Type of Barricade
1	Yes	Forward	Yes	Rods
2	Yes	Forward	Yes	Steelplate
3	Yes	Backward	Yes	Rods
4	Yes	Backward	Yes	Steelplate
5	No	Forward	No	Rods
6	No	Forward	No	Steelplate
7	No	Backward	No	Rods
8	No	Backward	No	Steelplate

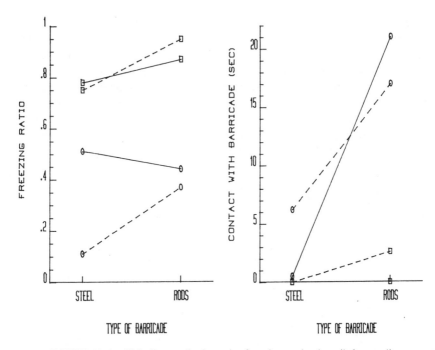

FIGURE 10.4.   This figure displays the freezing ratio data (left panel) and the barricade contact data (right panel) when either the steel or rod barricade was used during testing of rats that had been preexposed (———) or nonexposed (- - -) and had received forward (☐) or backward (○) CS-US pairings.

three of those four groups had mean ratios near .5. The backwards CS disrupted freezing in the backwards-paired nonexposed animals that had a steel plate barrier. The data presented in the right panel of Fig. 10.4 are the mean number of seconds of contact with the barricade during the three CS test presentations. It can be seen that the backwards-conditioned animals spent more time in contact with the rods than the steel plate but this behavior was suppressed by the forward-trained CS. In all cases behavior directed at the barricade appeared to be exploratory, mostly sniffing. What is apparent from this study is that the behavior elicited by a Pavlovian conditioned fear stimulus is freezing even when there is an obvious escape route. If anything, the CS suppressed activity directed at this portal.

Bolles and Collier (1976) suggested that the geometry of the test situation determined whether or not freezing was the dominant defensive response. Following their suggestion, we tested the effects of presenting the flashing light CS to the subjects of the above experiment in one of three geometrically different contexts. One context was a 32 × 32 × 32 cm box with hardware cloth floor and ceiling. The front wall of this box was clear acrylic plastic. The back wall and one side wall were of wood painted black. The other side wall was opaque white acrylic plastic. This white wall had two 5 × 5 cm holes each just off the midline of the wall. The bottoms of these holes were 8 cm above the floor. One hole was covered from the outside with brown Masonite; one was an open exit. The second context was a clear plastic tubcage, the floor of which was covered with 4 cm of clean wood shavings. The third context was a rather small, confining, saltbox-shaped wheel turn apparatus (Weiss, 1972); it had a 13 cm high front, a 4 cm high back and the floor length was 15 cm.

The subjects were assigned to a context in groups balanced for their experience in the previous experiment. The test procedure was identical to that of the previous experiment except that only a single test was given. The data are presented in Fig. 10.5. The left panel gives the probability of freezing during the CS. PreCS freezing curves, closely resembled the backward conditioning groups' CS curves for both forward-and-backward conditioned subjects. Freezing ratios are presented in the right panel.

Notice that the forward-conditioned CS increased the probability of freezing

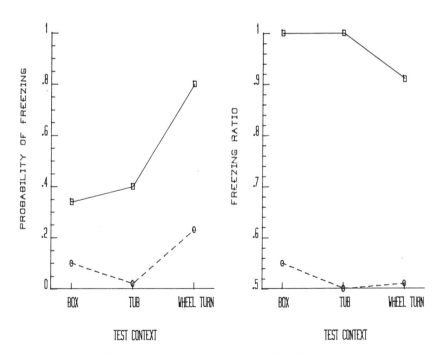

FIGURE 10.5. This figure displays the freezing data in terms of its probability during the CS (left panel) and in the form of freezing ratios (right panel). The data are shown for each test context for rats that received forward (□———□) or backward (○- - -○) CS-US pairings.

relative to backward-conditioned animals in all contexts (see the left panel of Fig. 10.5). There was more freezing, regardless of conditioning history, in the wheel-turn apparatus than in the other contexts and this was true of preCS as well as CS scores. Thus, we have a replication of Bolles & Collier's (1976) effect of contextual geometry determining the overall level of freezing. However, we have a rather unexciting alternative explanation of our results—they may have been due to greater generalization between the original conditioning context and the wheel-turn apparatus as both had grid floors, a feature lacking in the other two contexts. There is, obviously, a high degree of spatial contiguity between the shock US and the grid floor and thus the floor might be expected to have a high level of associative strength. If we turn our attention to the freezing ratios (right panel of Fig. 10.5, we see that the behavior strongly controlled by the CS was freezing regardless of context.

Other behaviors were examined in the different contexts. In the box we looked for head-poking or escape attempts directed at the holes (during preCS exploration some rats climbed halfway out of the open hole!) and locomotion. In the tubcage we looked for locomotion and manipulation of sawdust (Pinel & Treit, 1978). In the wheel-turn box we looked for struggling and directly measured wheel turning. *All of these behaviors were suppressed by the forward-conditioned CS.* One advantage of our observation technique, over the indirect appetitive bar press suppression measure typically used in Pavlovian fear conditioning, is that if the animals were making any specific response other than freezing we were there to observe it. Yet we have never observed such a response.

In the previous two studies we manipulated associatively neutral features of the environment thought to have the potential to support defensive behaviors other than freezing. Possibly in order for a stimulus to control defensive behavioral topography that stimulus must have some associative strength. Holland (1977) has made such an argument for the topography of conditioned appetitive responses. Using the two-compartment box described earlier we ran a differential conditioning experiment in which the barriers served as discriminative stimuli. Naive rats were placed in the grid-floored section twice daily. These placements were 3.5-min long and spaced 15-min apart. For one of these placements the rods were in place and for the other the steel plate was in place. Order of presentation was counterbalanced between subjects within a day and within subjects over days. There were 2 days of adaptation followed by 20 days of conditioning. Adaptation days were shock-free. On conditioning days Group R+/S− received a shock (.8mA, .75sec) 3 min after confinement in the chamber when the rods were in place. This group received no shock when the steel plate was in place. Group R−/S+ received similar shock if the steel plate was in place and no shock when the rods were in place. Group R-50/S-50 received one shock trial and one shock-free trial a day but which barrier had shock associated with it was varied over days in a randomized block fashion.

Two dependent variables were scored during the first 3 min of each exposure, the probability of freezing and the time (in sec) spent in contact with the barrier. The data for both of these dependent measures for the three groups are presented in Fig. 10.6, in terms of 2-day blocks. Animals tended to explore the rods, but not the solid plate, during the two adaptation days. Analyses of variance on the conditioning days showed that for both measures the Group × Barrier Type × Blocks interaction was reliable. Group R+/S− showed rapid acquisition of freezing over blocks with little differentiation occuring. While these animals spent some time in contact with the rods prior to the first two trials, this behavior was rapidly suppressed.

Group R−/S+ acquired the freezing response as rapidly as Group R+/S−. These rats showed some differentiation of freezing on blocks 5-7 but this was not maintained over continued training. Exploration of the rods was suppressed after the first shock. Contact with the rods began to increase after trial Block 5 and reliable differentiation of contact behaviors between the rods and steel plate emerged. However, the form of this contact was that the animals froze next to the rods; no exploratory behavior or escape attempts were ever directed at the rods.

Group R-50/S-50 showed as rapid acquisition of freezing as the other groups but freezing was equivalent whether or not the rods were present. Time in contact with the rods was immediately and permanently suppressed.

This experiment shows that making a potential escape route a stimulus predictive of either the presence or absence of shock does not result in escape attempts. In both cases freezing predominates; we never observed escape attempts directed at the rods. The relationship of the potential exit with shock influenced where the animal froze but did not alter the level of freezing.

Blanchard et al. (1976b) suggested that freezing dominates over escape only in situations where the animal has learned that no escape routes exist. They based this suggestion on their finding that freezing occurred in a novel chamber if a 2-min period preceded shock, but no freezing was found if shock was given immediately upon placement in the chamber. They suggested that the 2-min preshock period allowed rats to learn that the chamber was inescapable. The immediate shock animals did not have the benefit of this experience and, therefore, Blanchard et al. suggested that these animals engaged in escape related behavior. Unfortunately, Blanchard et al. did not directly record freezing or escape attempts, rather they measured suppression of movement. In replications of their study, we (Fanselow, 1986c) have found that the animals in the immediate shock condition failed to form an association between the chamber and shock. The immediate shock animals were not freezing because they were not afraid! These rats showed no freezing, no escape related behavior, and no elevation in defecation.

In our laboratory, like the others cited above, we have found that rats react to cats by freezing. We have tested rats with bedding in the test cage to see if they would direct spraying at this predator (Modaresi, 1982; Pinel & Treit, 1978). What we found is that the presence of a cat caused a statistically reliable 35%

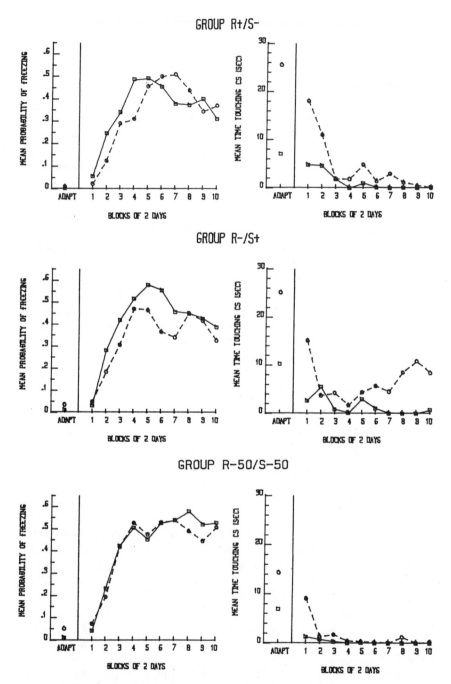

FIGURE 10.6. These six graphs illustrate the probability of freezing (left three) and the time touching the CS (right three) for the free groups when the rod (- - -○) or steel (□———□) barrier was in place.

reduction in the time spent manipulating sawdust relative to controls that had no cat present. The groups did not differ in terms of the height of bedding piles created nor in the directedness of bedding movement. Moser and Tait (1983) have suggested that even in the shock-prod situation, where some directed spraying occurs, freezing is the dominant defensive response. These researchers question whether burying is a post-encounter defensive response at all. Rather, they suggest that burying might be a pre-encounter defense of burrow maintenance, an attempt to better hide the nesting area.

We are forced to conclude that in most situations freezing is by far the dominant post-encounter defensive behavior. This runs counter to the opinion expressed by many writers in the field of aversive motivation that freezing is a response of last resort that occurs only when *coping* fails. For example, it has been suggested that freezing will occur only if a number of strong shock trials are given and there is no means of escape (e.g., Dickinson, 1980, p.4), when animals are "paralyzed in fear" (Davis & Astrachan, 1978, p.102). Rather, freezing occurs after only a single brief (.75 sec) shock (Fanselow & Bolles, 1979b; Experiments 3 & 4). The response emerges with intensities as low as .25mA and reaches asymptote at 1mA (Fanselow & Bolles, 1979b; Experiments 2 & 4). If anything, very strong shocks tend to disrupt organized defensive behavior and *reduce* freezing (Leaton & Borszcz 1985; Fanselow, 1984a, Experiment 3). Finally, in the experiments described we saw that freezing occurs even in the face of a potential escape route. Rodents continue to freeze even when a predator such as a snake has moved extremely close (Hirsch & Bolles, 1980; Hofer, 1970). Blanchard and Blanchard (1969b) have reported a similar result for a prod associated with electric shock. Animals that had previous experience being shocked by the prod froze and let the prod come closer than animals that had never been shocked by it.

While Blanchard et al. (1976a) have suggested that "if a means of escape is available, then flight is usually the more beneficial response, while freezing is advantageous when escape is impossible" (p. 179), we suggest that freezing is the response of greater adaptive value. Suarez and Gallup (1981a) have indicated that there is both experimental and field research support for the hypothesis that freezing can serve as an effective defensive strategy in four different ways:

1. If the prey spots the predator first, freezing may reduce the liklihood of the predator detecting the prey.
2. "If a predator detects a prey in motion freezing can cause the predator to loose sight of the prey, since many predators rely almost exclusively on moving visual cues for prey identification and prey capture" (p. 343).
3. Freezing may cause the predator to shift its attention away from the prey (toward some other moving or noisy stimulus) and this may prevent further pursuit.

4. Movement cues are important releasing stimuli for predatory behavior, and freezing eliminates these cues.

While much of the analysis of the effectiveness of freezing has emphasized reduced visual input to the predator, reduced auditory information (noise incidental to locomotion) may also play a role. The fact that prey movement is a (maybe *the*) critical releasing stimulus for predatory attacks (Fox, 1969; Herzog & Burghardt, 1974; Kaufman, 1974; Leyhausen, 1979; Thompson et al., 1981) may explain why freezing is such a prepotent response; even if the prey is detected by the predator, and the predator moves extremely close, freezing may still be a highly successful strategy.

CIRCA-STRIKE DEFENSIVE BEHAVIOR

When the predator is about to strike the prey we may again see dramatic changes in the prey's behavior. We refer to these contact related behaviors as *circa-strike defensive behaviors* because they occur just prior to, during, and just after physical contact. These behaviors function to allow the prey to escape from contact with the predator. For example, Hirsch and Bolles (1980) reported that while a certain subspecies of deermouse would freeze to the presence of a gopher snake it would engage in a characteristic "last second vertical leap *as the snake was striking*" (p. 81, emphasis added). Apparently, the same behavior is observed in Kangaroo Rats (Lockard, described by Hirsch & Bolles, 1980). It is as if the freezing animal is tensed up and ready to explode into action if the freezing response fails it. This explosive response probably has been studied in the laboratory for over 30 years under the rubric of potentiated startle (Brown, Kalish, & Farber, 1951). In this paradigm one typically examines the magnitude of the startle response to a loud noise in the presence of a conditioned fear stimulus such as a light, that has been previously paired with electric shock. Under certain conditions the CS will potentiate the startle response (Davis & Astrachan, 1978). As we have seen before, the CS would elicit freezing. In the potentiated startle paradigm the loud noise acts as a striking snake releasing the explosive motor burst on the part of the prey. If potentiated startle occurs because the freezing animal is ready to burst into action, then we would expect potentiation to vary positively with freezing. A recent experiment by Leaton and Borszcz (1985) confirms this; the amplitude of the acoustic startle reflex is directly related to the probability of freezing just prior to presentation of the startle eliciting stimulus. It seems that the releasing stimulus for this explosive motor burst is a sudden change in the stimulus context of an already freezing rat. If a freezing rat is presented with an electric shock or a sudden light/noise/vibration compound an activity burst is unconditionally elicited (Fanselow, 1982, 1984b).

Bolles, Riley, and Meissner (1975) have described the circa-strike behaviors of hooded rats to a ferret (*Mustela putorius*). The first time a ferret contacted a naive rat, the rat reacted with the vertical leap described above. Following this leap the prey locomoted away from the predator but subsequent contact elicited an on-the-back-fighting response, a stereotyped behavior in which the rat turns toward the ferret, flips onto its back, presses its neck to the ground and fends the ferret off with its paws. The time at which this response occurs illustrates why we call these strike related responses, circa-strike defensive behaviors: 88% occur when the ferret physically touches the prey, but 12% are like *peromyscus'* vertical leap in that they occur immediately prior to contact. Thus, very close and rapidly approaching dangerous stimuli may elicit circa-strike responses before actual physical contact (see Blanchard & Blanchard, 1969b, for an example with a shock prod).

Struggling, fighting, and biting, usually in the on-the-back or upright posture, also characterize this stage of defense. If these responses do not eliminate contact some species react with tonic immobility (Ratner, 1967, 1975; Suarez & Gallup, 1981b; Thompson et al., 1981). Tonic immobility appears to decrease the liklihood of continued attack (Thompson et al., 1981) allowing for an opportunity to escape (Sargeant & Eberhardt, 1975).

Endogenous Analgesia as a Circa-Strike Defensive Response

When the predator contacts the prey that contact is likely to result in injury. Nociceptive stimulation arising from the injury might result in a tendency to direct behavior toward the injury (see section on recuperative behavior) and such tendencies would compromise the effectiveness of circa-strike defensive behaviors. Prey have evolved a remarkable strategy for dealing with these competing tendencies for in such situations endogenous analgesic systems are activated (Bolles & Fanselow, 1980; Fanselow & Sigmundi, 1982). Endogenous analgesia has adaptive value because, by reducing nociception, it attenuates pain-elicited disruption of defensive behavior. These analgesic systems rely on a group of opioid-like peptides that are referred to as endorphins (see Bolles & Fanselow, 1982, for a review).

Analgesia is of value to defense only if the defending animal is also experiencing nociceptive stimulation (Fanselow, 1984b). Obviously, such stimulation is most likely to be present following contact with a predator. Thus, endogenous analgesia offers its primary advantage during the circa-strike stage of defense. Therefore, we have classified it as a circa-strike defensive response: it reduces probability of further movement down the imminence continuum from this point. It is interesting to note, however, that many of the stimuli that activate endogenous analgesic systems are the same stimuli that activate post-encounter defensive behaviors (Fanselow, 1984a, 1984b). Such an activation of a defensive response *in advance* of when it is needed is an example of what Hollis (1982) has called prefiguring. Cats (Lester & Fanselow, 1985), shock associated stumuli (Fanselow, 1984a; Fanselow & Baackes, 1982; Fanselow & Bolles, 1979a), and the odors of stressed conspecifics (Fanselow, 1985) are some of the stimuli that control defensive behavior and elicit analgesia in the rat. Opioid peptides are apparently involved in mediating the analgesic effects of these danger stimuli because the stimuli's ability to inhibit recuperative behavior (but not their ability to elicit freezing) can be reduced by treating the animal with an opioid antagonist such as naloxone or naltrexone.

Prefiguring in the Circa-Strike Stage of Defense

Some defensive responses, like freezing, are elicited exactly at the time they offer an advantage. However, other defensive responses, analgesia for example, are elicited prior to the stage in which they offer an advantage. We shall refer to this *activation-advantage asynchrony* as prefiguring.

Stimuli that activate post-encounter defensive behaviors elicit other responses that tend to give the prey a better chance of survival if it enters the circa-strike stage. Such responses would be examples of prefiguring. Hollis (1982) has defined prefiguring as responding in such a way as to "optimize interaction with a *forthcoming* biologically important event" (p. 3, emphasis added). We have already described endogenous analgesia as a prefigured response, it is activated during the post-encounter stage but is of value after contact-related injury has been received. There are additional examples. The freezing rat's readying itself for an explosive motor burst (potentiated startle) may be one (see above). Another is Gallup and his colleagues' (e.g., Gallup, 1973; Maser, Gallup, & Barnhill, 1973; Suarez & Gallup, 1981b) finding that stimuli activating post-encounter defenses (freezing) enhance the tonic immobility that is produced by contact with a predator.

It is important to note that the prefiguring occurring here is most often not at the level of overt behavior. The prefiguring responses that occur do not interfere with freezing. Rather, they tend to be physiological adjustments that the animal may make that will be of benefit if the animal enters the circa-strike phase but do not compromise post-encounter defense. Selection pressure on the prey is such that the greatest benefit to the prey is to be successful at post-encounter defense which serves to prevent entrance into the circa-strike stage. The rule is that prefigured circa-strike behaviors must not reduce the efficacy of post-encounter defenses. Prefiguring of circa-strike defenses during the post-encounter stage is therefore limited to responses that would facilitate circa-strike defense if it did occur but would not increase the probability of entering the circa-strike stage. Such responses would often be physiological adjustments, but are not restricted to those responses. Evolution would also select for overt behaviors that fulfill the above requirements.

RECUPERATION AND THE RETURN
TO THE PREFERRED ACTIVITY PATTERN

The prey enters the circa-strike stage of defense because its defenses at earlier points in the sequence failed. If the prey's circa-strike defense is also unsuccessful the prey is killed and perhaps consumed, with obvious consequences to both prey and predator's reproductive fitness. During the course of a predatory episode the prey may move between points on the continuum (escaping from the grasp of a predator might be followed by freezing until the predator leaves the vicinity) but if the prey successfully avoids being killed it will eventually return to the preferred activity pattern. The dashed lines in Fig. 10.1 indicate the prey's return to the preferred activity pattern as imminence decreases. The purpose of defense is to prevent and minimize deviations from the preferred activity pattern.[5] The evolutionary costs and benefits of predation and defense, respectively, can be scaled with regard to the appetitive costs of deviation from this preferred activity pattern.

As can be seen in Fig. 10.1, animals that have entered the circa-strike stage have a more circuitous route back to the preferred activity pattern than animals that have not. This is because an animal that has entered into the circa-strike stage of defense is likely to have received injuries. When predatory imminence has returned to near zero (the prey has escaped the predator and is in a place safe from further predatory attempts) the presence of injury will determine whether or not the animal can return to the preferred activity pattern. If there are no injuries the animal will return to that preferred pattern. However, if it has received some injuries in the confrontation the activity pattern may be constrained by recuperative behavior. Recuperative behaviors are behaviors directed at the injury and resting responses that serve to promote healing (Fanselow & Sigmundi, 1982). Note that at this point the function of the behavior has changed; the object of functional significance is no longer the predator but the injury. Thus, recuperative behavior is not defensive behavior but is still aversively motivated. Bolles & Fanselow, (1980), refer to pain motivation when speaking of recuperation and to fear motivation when addressing defense. This explains why recuperative behavior is located where it is in Fig. 10.1. Recuperation occurs when predatory imminence is close to zero; it is not defensive, but it still represents a deviation from the preferred activity pattern.

---

[5]One might argue that the function of defense is to maximize survival rather than minimize the costs of deviation from the preferred activity pattern. Since these are the endpoints of the predatory imminence continuum it is really a question of which endpoint to emphasize. The cost of failing to survive may be thought of as a permanent and total deviation from the preferred activity pattern. However, even if the prey survives, there are costs of encountering a predator (e.g., injuries) that are better conceptualized as relating to an appetitive cost. In addition, by emphasizing appetitive costs one has the potential to use the same scaling models as those used in the analysis of appetitive behavior.

Since the prey does not return completely to the preferred activity pattern until it has recuperated, there is often an additional evolutionary cost in allowing imminence to increase to the circa-strike stage where injury is likely. Such a cost would place additional selection pressure on the evolution of effective pre- and post-encounter defenses. It may be costly to rely on circa-strike defenses even if those defenses are successful.

The recuperative stage is, in part, a response to nociceptive stimulation arising from injury and tissue damage (Bolles & Fanselow, 1980; Fanselow & Sigmundi, 1982). However, nociceptive stimulation does not lead to recuperative behavior while the animal is engaged in defense because the defending animal is also analgesic (Bolles & Fanselow, 1980; Fanselow, 1984a; Fanselow & Sigmundi, 1982; see above). Once predatory imminence is reduced to near zero the analgesic system becomes quiescent and the animal reacts to the injury. Therefore, the model implies that nociception itself does not lead to analgesia (Bolles & Fanselow, 1980). Rather, it is that the stimuli that lead to antipredator defenses also lead to analgesia.

There is considerable experimental support for the argument that nociception is neither necessary, nor sufficient, for activation of endogenous analgesic systems (Fanselow, 1984a). From a functional point of view it is illogical for nociception to lead to analgesia. If analgesia is adaptive and nociception invariably leads to analgesia then why should the organism have evolved the ability to appreciate nociceptive stimuli in the first place? Likewise, if the appreciation of nociceptive stimuli is adaptive then why evolve an analgesic system that is unconditionally activated by nociceptive stimuli since that analgesic system would always depress the organism's appreciation of nociception? It could be argued that the immediate reaction to nociception of withdrawal and arousal is adaptive and long term nociception is dysfunctional. However, such withdrawal and arousing functions are well handled by spinal and lower central nervous system structures; why also evolve an ability to appreciate higher order dimensions of pain (Melzack, 1973)? The answer we propose is that nociceptive stimulation does not lead to analgesia. Rather, it leads to adaptive recuperative behavior. Danger signals lead to analgesia. When recuperation would be maladaptive, such as when an animal must defend itself, endogenous analgesic systems are activated so that defense can go on uncompromised.

TEMPORAL AND SPATIAL ASPECTS OF PREDATORY IMMINENCE

We have described predatory imminence predominantly in spatial terms, as the distance between prey and predator. However, there must also be a temporal dimension to imminence. For example, the number of times a prey animal has previously encountered a predator in a particular location should influence the prey's perception of imminence and therefore its defensive behavior. Thus the location on the predatory imminence continuum is a joint function of spatial and temporal factors.

We have described defensive behavior at three points along the predatory imminence continuum. When imminence is low, but greater than zero (e.g., when a prey engages in an activity that has some potential for it to be preyed upon but no predator is detected in the vicinity) pre-encounter defense emerges. If the prey detects a predator in the vicinity, predation is of greater imminence and post-encounter defense (i.e., freezing in the rat) emerges. Certainly, the imminence of predation is even greater when the predator is making, or is just about to make, a strike at the prey than it is if a predator is merely in the vicinity. At this point of confrontation circa-strike defense emerges.

It is interesting to note that we were able to move the prey along the entire predatory imminence continuum using the same aversive stimulus, electric shock. Shock resulted in very different defensive behaviors depending on what point on the continuum we were modeling. Some procedural aspect must have varied to produce these topographical differences. One possibility is shock density, that is the number of shocks per unit of time spent in the procedure. In our studies of pre-encounter defense the most dense shock schedule used was 20 shocks per day or .83 an hour. In studies of freezing we typically exposed rats to some stimulus or context for about 3 min before a shock was given. Bolles (1975) suggests that even this is too dense a shock schedule to see maximal freezing; he suggested that one shock every 15 min might be better. So post encounter defense is found in the range of 4–20 shocks per hour. The post-shock activity burst, which is an example of circa-strike defense, lasts for about 15 sec (Fanselow, 1982). Indeed, very dense shock schedules result in so much circa-strike behavior that freezing is virtually eliminated (Bolles & Riley, 1973). It is with such dense schedules that the upright posture and defensive boxing emerge (e.g., Blanchard, Blanchard, & Takahashi, 1977; Fanselow, Sigmundi, & Bolles, 1980; O'Kelly & Steckle, 1939; Ulrich & Azrin, 1962). Thus, circa-strike defense occurs with schedules of about 240 shocks per hour. What we are suggesting is that momentary shock density may determine what stage of defense or what level of predatory imminence, the subject perceives itself to be at. In addition, density may provide a useful metric for scaling predatory imminence.

The animal's appreciation of density is likely to be an associative process. It is density during a particular configuration of environmental stimuli that determines defensive topography. The rat in the pre-encounter defensive study received a maximum of 20 shocks a day associated with a stimulus configuration that was presented 24 hours a day. Thus, density in that stimulus context was low and that stimulus context controlled pre-encounter defensive behavior. If each of those shocks had been preceded by a 3-min tone, that 3-min tone would have had a higher density of shock associated with it and most likely the tone would have elicited post-encounter defensive responses (freezing). It would be interesting to determine if post-encounter defenses to a brief tone would compete with pre-encounter defenses to a continuously present context in the same way that briefly presented contexts and tones compete with each other for post-encounter defenses (Fanselow, 1980b, 1980c; Fanselow & Bolles, 1979a; cf. Rescorla & Wagner, 1972).

With manipulations of shock density we may find the transition points between various defensive behavioral topographies. Indeed, these transition points can be seen even with a single shock, as if the animal is performing a running integration over time. Circa-strike defenses occur immediately with shock-onset and persist for a very brief period beyond shock termination. However, as the brief period passes freezing begins to emerge (Fanselow, 1982). The duration of the activity burst may indicate the transition point between circa-strike and post-encounter defense.

In addition to determining topography, changing levels of imminence are supposed to control the level of defense within a topography as well. Such results can be obtained when shock density is manipulated. For pre-encounter defense, meal pattern alterations were first encountered at 0.38 shocks per hour and increased through .82 shocks per hour (see Fig. 10.3). Freezing also increases with the number of shocks given in a brief session (Fanselow & Bolles, 1979b, Experiment 3). Both of these responses are controlled by contextual stimuli associated with shock, and not the shock itself, so it is the associative mechanism performing the integration of shock frequency over time.

In the field predatory imminence has most often been defined spatially in terms of predator-prey distance but in the aversive conditioning laboratory imminence has most often been defined temporally in terms of shock density. In reality, the prey must integrate both of these sources of information to determine where it is on the predatory imminence continuum. Undoubtably, additional factors will influence the prey's perception of predatory imminence. Speed of the predator's approach and intensity of electric shock are examples. But it is the prey's perception of the imminence of predation that will determine both the particular defensive behavioral topography and the strength of that topography. This perception is a function of the prey's phylogenetic and ontogenetic experiential history with regards to the environmental stimuli present at the time of imminence determination.

ACKNOWLEDGMENTS

We are indebted to R. A. Sigmundi for many critical discussions during the preparation of this manuscript. We thank M. E. Bouton and R. A. Sigmundi for their insightful comments on an earlier draft. This research was supported by awards from the Faculty Research Committee of Dartmouth College and NIMH

(Grant #MH39786), as well as a Dartmouth Faculty Fellowship to the first author.

REFERENCES

Allison, J., Larson, D., & Jensen, D. D. (1967). Acquired fear, brightness preference, and one-way shuttlebox performance. *Psychonomic Science, 8,* 269–270.
Blanchard, R. J., & Blanchard, D. C. (1969a). Crouching as an index of fear. *Journal of Comparative and Physiological Psychology, 67,* 370–375.
Blanchard, R. J., & Blanchard, D. C. (1969b). Passive and active avoidance reactions to fear-eliciting stimuli. *Journal of Comparative and Physiolgoical Psychology, 68,* 129–135.
Blanchard, R. J., & Blanchard, D. C. (1971). Defensive reactions in the albino rat. *Learning & Motivation, 2,* 351–362.
Blanchard, R. J., Blanchard, D. C., & Takahashi, L. K. (1977). Reflexive fighting in the rat: Aggressive or defensive behavior? *Aggressive Behavior, 3,* 145–155.
Blanchard, R. J., Fukunaga, K. K., & Blanchard, D. C. (1976a). Environmental control of defensive reactions to a cat. *Bulletin of the Psychonomic Society, 8,* 179–181.
Blanchard, R. J., Fukunaga, K. K., & Blanchard, D. C. (1976b). Environmental control of defensive reactions to footshock. *Bulletin of the Psychonomic Society, 8,* 129–130.
Blanchard, R. J., Mast, M., & Blanchard, D. C. (1975). Stimulus control of defensive reactions in the albino rat. *Journal of Comparative and Physiological Psychology, 88,* 81–88.
Bolles, R. C. (1970). Species-specific defensive reactions and avoidance learning. *Psychological Review, 71,* 32–48.
Bolles, R. C. (1975). *Theory of motivation* (2nd Ed.). New York: Harper & Row.
Bolles, R. C., & Collier, A. C. (1976). Effect of predictive cues on freezing in rats. *Animal Learning and Behavior, 4,* 6–8.
Bolles, R. C., & Fanselow, M. S. (1980). A perceptual-defensive-recuperative model of fear and pain. *Behavioral and Brain Science, 3,* 291–323.
Bolles, R. C., & Fanselow, M. S. (1982). Endorphins and Behavior. *Annual Review of Psychology, 33,* 87–101.
Bolles, R. C., & McGillis, D. B. (1968). The non-operant nature of the barpress escape response. *Psychonomic Science, 11,* 261–262.
Bolles, R. C., & Riley, A. L. (1973). Freezing as an avoidance response: Another look at the operant-respondent distinction. *Learning and Motivation, 4,* 268–275.
Bolles, R. C., Riley, A., & Meissner, D. J. (1975). *Defensive behavior of the rat encountering Mustela putorius.* Unpublished manuscript, University of Washington and American University.
Bouton, M. E., & Bolles, R. C. (1980). Conditioned fear assessed by freezing and by the suppression of three different baselines. *Animal Learning and Behavior, 8,* 429–434.
Breland, K., & Breland, M. (1961). The misbehavior of organisms. *American Psychologist, 16,* 681–684.
Brener, J., & Goesling, W. J. (1970). Avoidance conditioning of activity and immobility in rats. *Journal of Comparative and Physiological Psychology, 70,* 276–280.
Bronstein, P. M., & Hirsch, S. M. (1976). The ontogeny of defensive reactions in Norway rats. *Journal of Comparative and Physiological Psychology, 90,* 620–628.
Brown, J. S., Kalish, H. I., & Farber, I. E. (1951). Conditioned fear as revealed by magnitude of startle response to auditory stimulus. *Journal of Experimental Psychology, 41,* 317–328.
Collier, G. H. (1981). *Determinants of choice.* Nebraska Symposium on Motivation, 29, 69–127.
Collier, G. H. (1983). Life in a closed economy: The ecology of learning and motivation. In M. D.

Zeiler & P. Harzem (Eds.), *Advances in analysis of behavior: Biological factors in learning, 4,* 223–274.

Collier, G. H., Hirsch, E., & Hamlin, P. (1972). The ecological determinants of reinforcement in the rat. *Physiology and Behavior, 9,* 705–716.

Davis, M., & Astrachan, D. J. (1978). Conditioned fear and startle magnitude: Effects of different footshock or backshock intensities used in training. *Journal of Experimental Psychology: Animal Behavior Processes, 4,* 95–103.

Davis, H. & Burton, J. (1974). The measurement of response force a lever-press shock-escape procedure in rats. *Journal of the Experimental Analysis of Behavior, 22,* 433–440.

Dickinson, A. (1980). *Contemporary animal learning theory.* Cambridge, England: Cambridge University Press.

Domjan, M., & Galef, B. G. (1983). Biological constraints on instrumental and classical conditioning: Retrospect and prospect. *Animal Learning and Behavior, 11,* 151–161.

Edmunds, M. (1974). *Defense in animals.* Essex: Longmans.

Fanselow, M. S. (1980a). Conditional and unconditional components of postshock freezing. *Pavlovian Journal of Biological Science, 15,* 177–182.

Fanselow, M. S. (1980b). Signaled shock-free periods and preference for signaled shock. *Journal of Experimental Psychology: Animal Behavior Processes, 6,* 65–80.

Fanselow, M. S. (1980c). Extinction of contextual fear and preference for signaled-shock. *Bulletin of the Psychonomic Society, 16,* 458–460.

Fanselow, M. S. (1981). Naloxone and Pavlovian fear conditioning. *Learning and Motivation, 12,* 398–419.

Fanselow, M. S. (1982). The postshock activity burst. *Animal Learning & Behavior, 10,* 448–454.

Fanselow, M. S. (1984a). Shock-induced analgesia on the formalin test: Effects of shock severity, naloxone, hypophysectomy, and associative variables. *Behavioral Neuroscience, 98,* 79–95.

Fanselow, M. S. (1984b). Opiate modulation of the active and inactive components of the postshock reaction: Parallels between naloxone pretreatment and shock intensity. *Behavioral Neuroscience, 98,* 169–277.

Fanselow, M. S. (1985). Odors released by stressed rats produce opioid analgesia in unstressed rats. *Behavioral Neuroscience, 99,* 589–592.

Fanselow, M. S. (1986). Associative vs topographical accounts of the immediate shock-freezing deficit in rats: Implications for the response selection rules governing species-specific defensive reactions. *Learning and Motivation, 17,* 16–39.

Fanselow, M. S., & Baackes, M. P. (1982). Conditioned fear-induced opiate analgesia on the formalin test: Evidence for two aversive motivational systems. *Learning and Motivation, 13,* 200–221.

Fanselow, M. S., & Bolles, R. C. (1979a). Triggering of the endorphin analgesia reaction by a cue previously associated with shock: Reversal by naloxone. *Bulletin of the Psychonomic Society, 14,* 88–90.

Fanselow, M. S., & Bolles, R. C. (1979b). Naloxone and shock-elicited freezing in the rat. *Journal of Comparative and Physiological Psychology, 94,* 736–744.

Fanselow, M. S., & Bolles, R. C. (1982). Independence and competition in aversive motivation. *Behavioral and Brain Sciences, 5,* 320–322.

Fanselow, M. S., & Sigmundi, R. A. (1982). The enhancement and reduction of defensive fighting by naloxone pretreatment. *Physiological Psychology, 10,* 313–316.

Fanselow, M. S., Sigmundi, R. A., & Bolles, R. C. (1980). Naloxone pretreatment enhances shock-elicited aggression. *Physiological Psychology, 8,* 369–371.

Fox, M. W. (1969). Ontogeny of pre-killing behavior in *canidae. Behaviour, 35,* 259–272.

Gallup, G. G. (1973). Tonic immobility in chickens: Is a stimulus that signals shock more aversive than the receipt of shock? *Animal Learning & Behavior, 1,* 228–232.

Garcia, J., & Koelling, R. A. (1966). Relation of cue to consequence in avoidance learning. *Psychonomic Science, 4,* 123–124.

Grossen, N. W., & Kelley, M. J. (1972). Species-specific behavior and acquisition of avoidance behavior in rats. *Journal of Comparative and Physiological Psychology, 81,* 307–310.

Gunn, K. P. (1983). Qualification of rat's behavior during reinforcement periods. *Journal of the Experimental Analysis of Behavior, 39,* 457–464.

Herzog, H. A., & Burghardt, G. M. (1974). Prey movement and predatory behavior of juvenile western yellow-bellied racers, *Coluber constrictor mormon. Herpetologica, 33,* 285–289.

Hirsch, S. M., & Bolles, R. C. (1980). On the ability of prey to recognize predators. *Zietschrift fur Tierpsycholiogie, 54,* 71–84.

Hofer, M. A. (1970). Cardiac and respiratory function during sudden prolonged immobility in wild rodents. *Psychosomatic Medicine, 32,* 633–647.

Holland, P. C. (1977). Conditioned stimulus as a determinant of the form of the Pavlovian conditioned response. *Journal of Experimental Psychology: Animal Behavior Processes, 3,* 77–104.

Hollis, K. L. (1982). Pavlovian conditioning of signal-centered action patterns and autonomic behavior: A biological analysis of function. *Advances in the study of behavior, 12,* 1–64.

Kaufman, D. W. (1974). Differential owl predation on white and agouti *Mus musculus. The Auk, 91,* 145–150.

Leaton, R. N., & Borszcz, G. S. (1985). Potentiated Startle: Its relation to freezing and shock intensity in rats. *Journal of Experimental Psychology: Animal Behavior Processes, 11,* 421–428.

LeClerc, R., & Reberg, D. (1980). Sign-tracking in aversive conditioning. *Learning and Motivation, 11,* 302–317.

Leyhausen, P. (1979). *Cat behavior: The predatory and social behavior of domestic and wild cats.* New York: Garland.

Lester, L. S., & Fanselow, M. S. (1985). Exposure to a cat produces opioid analgesia in rats. *Behavioral Neuroscience, 99,* 756–759.

Maser, J. D., Gallup, G. G., & Barnhill, R. (1973). Conditioned inhibition and tonic immobility: Stimulus control of an innate fear response in the children. *Journal of Comparative and Physiological Psychology, 83,* 128–133.

Masterson, F. A., & Crawford, M. (1982). The defense motivational system: A theory of avoidance behavior. *Behavioral and Brain Sciences, 5,* 661–696.

Melzack, R. (1973). *The puzzle of pain.* New York: Basic.

Miller, R. R., Greco, C., & Vigorito, M. (1981). Classically conditioned tail flexion in rats: CR-contingent modification of US intensity as a test of the preparatory response hypothesis. *Animal Learning and Behavior, 9,* 80–88.

Miller, R. R., Greco, C., Vigorito, M., & Marlin, N. A. (1983). Signaled tailshock is perceived as similar to a stronger unsignaled tailshock: Implications for a functional analysis of classical conditioning. *Journal of Experimental Psychology: Animal Behavior Processes, 9,* 105–131.

Modaresi, H. A. (1982). Defensive behavior of the rat in a shock-prod situation: Effects of the subject's location preference. *Animal Learning and Behavior, 10,* 97–102.

Mollenauer, S., Plotnik, R., & Snyder, E. (1974). Effects of olfactory bulb removal on fear responses and passive avoidance in the rat. *Physiology and Behavior, 12,* 141–144.

Moser, C. G., & Tait, R. W. (1983). Environmental control of multiple defensive responses in a conditioned burying paradigm. *Journal of Comparative Psychology, 97,* 338–352.

O'Kelly, L. E., & Steckle, L. D. (1939). A note on long-enduring emotional responses in the rat. *Journal of Psychology, 8,* 125–131.

Pinel, J. P. J., & Treit, D. (1978). Burying as a defensive response in rats. *Journal of Comparative and Physiological Psychology, 92,* 708–712.

Ratner, S. C. (1967). Comparative aspects of hypnosis. In J. E. Gordon (Ed.), *Handbook of clinical and experimental hypnosis. New York: Macmillan.*

Ratner, S. C. (1975). Animal's defenses: Fighting in predator-prey relations. In P. Pliner, L. Krames, & T. Alloway (Eds.), Nonverbal communication of aggression. New York: Plenum.

Rescorla, R. A., & Wagner, A. R. (1972). A theory of Pavlovian conditioning: Variations in the effectiveness of reinforcement and nonreinforcement. In A. H. Black & W. F. Prokasy (Eds.), Classical conditioning: II. Current research and theory. New York: Appleton-Century-Crofts.

Sargeant, A. B., & Eberhardt, L. E. (1975). Death feigning by ducks in response to predation by red foxes (Vulpes fulva). American Midland Naturalist, 93, 108–119.

Satinder, K. P. (1976). Reactions of selectively bred strains of rats to a cat. Animal Learning and Behavior, 4, 172–176.

Seligman, M. E. P. (1970). On the generality of the laws of learning. Psychological Review, 77, 406–418.

Shettleworth, S. J. (1983). Function and mechanism in learning. In M. D. Zeiler & P. Harzem (Eds.), Advances in analysis of behavior: Biological factors in learning, 3, 1–39.

Sigmundi, R. A., & Bolles, R. C. (1983). CS modality, context conditioning, and conditioned freezing. Animal Learning & Behavior, 11, 205–212.

Sigmundi, R. A., Bouton, M. E., & Bolles, R. C. (1980). Conditioned freezing in the rat as a function of shock intensity and CS modality. Bulletin of the Psychonomic Society, 15, 254–256.

Suarez, S. D., & Gallup, G. G. (1981a). An ethological analysis of open-field behavior in rats and mice. Learning & Motivation, 12, 342–363.

Suarez, S. D., & Gallup, G. G. (1981b). Predatory overtones of open-field testing in chickens. Animal Learning & Behavior, 9, 153–163.

Thompson, R. K. R., Folton, R. W., Boylan, R. J., Sweet, A., Graves, C. A., & Lowitz, C. E. (1981). Animal Learning and Behavior, 9, 145–149.

Timberlake, W. (1983). The functional organization of appetitive behavior: Behavior systems and learning. In M. D. Zeiler & P. Harzem (Eds.), Advances in analysis of behavior: Biological factors in learning, 3, 177–221.

Tolman, E. C. (1932). Purposive behavior in animals and men. New York: Appleton.

Ulrich, R. E., & Azrin, N. H. (1962). Reflexive fighting in response to aversive stimulation. Journal of the Experimental Analysis of Behavior, 5, 511–520.

Walther, F. R. (1969). Flight behaviour and avoidance of predators in Thomson's Gazelle. Behavior, 34, 184–221.

Weiss, J. M. (1972). Psychological factors in stress and disease. Scientific American, 226, 106–112.

11

Reproductive Behavior: A Potential Model System for Adaptive Specializations in Learning

Michael Domjan
University of Texas at Austin

Karen L. Hollis
Mount Holyoke College

Psychological research on animal learning has been dominated by the assumption that learning has general characteristics that can be effectively discovered by studying learning in biologically arbitrary situations. However, this pursuit of general mechanisms of learning through intensive investigation of a few arbitrary laboratory preparations was strongly attacked in the early 1970s in discussions about biological constraints on learning. Numerous investigators argued that specialized skills and mechanisms have evolved to mediate learning in biologically significant situations (e.g., Bolles, 1970; Hinde, 1973; Seligman, 1970; Shettleworth, 1972; Rozin & Kalat, 1971). Given these adaptive specializations, writers advocated a retreat from the search for general learning processes and cautioned that the study of biologically arbitrary laboratory paradigms may not provide information relevant to understanding learning outside the laboratory.

The issue of adaptive specializations and biological constraints on learning was widely discussed in the field of animal learning in the 1970s. Several books devoted to the topic were published (e.g., Hinde & Stevenson-Hinde, 1973; Seligman & Hager, 1972), and the issue was treated prominently not only in advanced textbooks on animal learning but also in introductory psychology books. Given the challenge and prominence of claims of adaptive specializations and biological constraints on learning, a revolution in the study of animal learning seemed imminent. Some commentators encouraged abandoning altogether the pursuit of general mechanisms of learning through intensive investigation of arbitrary laboratory preparations and advocated investigations that would be more sensitive to the natural history of organisms and the adaptive significance of the form of learning under scrutiny.

Discussions about adaptive specializations and biological constraints on learning have stimulated extensive and productive research (see Domjan, 1983, for a recent review). However, the new knowledge provided by this research has not resulted in retreat from the pursuit of general theories of learning. Rather, deeper understanding of biological constraints on learning has led to significant revisions of general process theory to accommodate the new findings (see, for example, Domjan, 1983). Interest in adaptive specializations and biological constraints on learning has waned in recent years because many of the original phenomena have been incorporated into revisions of general process learning theory and very few new instances of adaptive specializations have been discovered (see Domjan & Galef, 1983). Early theoretical discussions about biological constraints did not provide a sufficiently detailed strategy for the discovery of new instances of specialized learning, and investigators concentrated on finding ways to incorporate known instances of biological constraints into general conceptions of learning rather than on discovering new phenomena.

New Directions in the Study of Learning Specializations

The decline in interest in adaptive specializations and biological constraints on learning is an unfortunate development because consideration of these issues involved a valuable attempt to integrate traditional research on the mechanisms of animal learning with more comprehensive biological approaches to the study of animal behavior. Such integration remains a laudable goal. Instances of biological constraints also provided a rich source of learning phenomena for empirical and theoretical analysis. Thus, biological constraints enriched the study of animal learning by extending its scope and furthering the understanding of its mechanisms.

The study of animal learning would no doubt continue to profit from discovery and analysis of new instances of learning unpredicted by general process theory and from attempts to integrate research on learning mechanisms with broader concerns about animal behavior. Several proposals for the integration of studies of animal learning with biological approaches to the study of animal behavior have been made recently. Johnston (1981), for example, suggested that investigations of animal learning should start anew with observations of learning in nonlaboratory situations. Hollis (1982, 1984b) and Shettleworth (1983) have discussed how considerations of adaptive function can contribute to the understanding of learning phenomena, and Domjan and Galef (1983) described how comparative investigations of animal learning can provide further knowledge about relationships between learning and ecological variables. These proposals have helped clarify conceptual issues involved in integrating animal learning with biological approaches to the study of animal behavior.

Continuation of the progress that has resulted from studies of adaptive specializations and biological constraints on learning requires discovering new phenomena that challenge general process learning theory and reflect natural selection. Although no method of search for such phenomena can guarantee success a priori, such phenomena may be discovered in response systems with the following two features. First, the response system should be one that is either shaped directly by natural selection or is closely related to a directly selected system. If a response system is shaped directly by natural selection, learning mechanisms involved in that response system may also be subject to natural selection. The second feature the response system should have is species specificity and diversity. Species specificity and diversity in response systems shaped by natural selection are apt to reflect adaptive specializations related to particular ecological circumstances. Therefore, learning in such response systems may also reflect adaptive specializations related to ecological factors.

One response system that has both of these features is reproductive behavior. Thus, reproductive behavior is directly involved in the transmission of genetic material to future generations and is therefore directly shaped by natural selection. In addition, reproductive behavior is characterized by considerable species specificity and diversity, and this diversity is related to ecological variables and other aspects of each species. Therefore, reproductive behavior may provide a model system in which to investigate adaptive specializations in learning.

EVIDENCE OF LEARNING IN ANIMAL REPRODUCTIVE BEHAVIOR

Although learning in reproductive behavior systems has not been investigated extensively by students of animal learning, several types of experiential effects have been documented in studies of animal sexual behavior.

Sexual Imprinting

Although results vary across species and test procedures, much evidence exists that mate choice can be influenced by early social experience (see Bateson, 1978; Immelman, 1972; Marler & Terrace, 1984; Shapiro, 1980). Cooke and his colleagues, for example, have obtained evidence of sexual imprinting in both field and laboratory studies with lesser snow geese (Cooke, Finney, & Rockwell, 1976; Cooke & McNally, 1975; Cooke, Mirsky, & Seiger, 1972). These birds exist in a white and a blue phase and mate with individuals whose coloration is like their own despite the fact that mate selection takes place in colonies where birds of the two phases are intermixed. In the laboratory, incubator-hatched goslings were placed with foster parents of the same or different color. Birds from pure-color "families" later showed greater preference for mates whose color matched their own than birds from mixed-color families. Strong evidence of sexual imprinting has been also obtained in other laboratory experiments, including studies with brown and white leghorns (Lill & Wood-Gush, 1965), white and black king pigeons (Warriner, Lemmon & Ray, 1957), and normal and white zebra finches (Walter, 1973).

Protection from Castration Induced Decline in Sexual Behavior

Much of sexual behavior in vertebrates is mediated by gonadal hormones. Nevertheless, copulatory behavior in males does not always decline with declining testosterone levels following castration (Hart, 1974; McGill, 1978). Of particular interest in the present context is the finding that persistence in copulatory behavior after castration is greater in males that had sexual experience prior to castration than in sexually naive males. This effect was first noted in cats (Rosenblatt, 1965; Rosenblatt & Aronson 1958) and has been also reported in rats (Larsson, 1978; but see Bloch & Davidson, 1968). Further research is required to discover what aspects of prior sexual experience are critical for protection from castration-induced decline in sexual behavior and what mechanisms of learning mediate this phenomenon.

Female-Specific Satiation of Male Sexual Behavior

When a male is placed with a receptive female following a period without sexual opportunity, initially high levels of sexual behavior decline until the male shows little interest in the female (e.g., Beach & Jordan, 1956). Introduction of a novel receptive female after sexual satiation sometimes results in recovery of the sexual behavior (see Dewsbury, 1981, for a review). Novelty-induced invigoration of sexual behavior has been observed in a variety of species including rats (Fisher, 1962; Fowler & Whalen, 1961; Wilson, Kuehn & Beach, 1963), domestic bulls (Hale & Almquist, 1960; Schein & Hale, 1965), cats (Whalen, 1963), deermice (Clemens, 1969), guinea pigs (Grunt & Young, 1952), and rhesus monkeys (Michael & Zumpe, 1978). A recently mated novel female is sometimes as effective in producing recovery from satiation as an unmated novel female (e.g., Hsiao, 1965), but reintroduction of the original female does not lead to recovery (e.g., Grunt & Young, 1952).

Findings similar to female-specific satiation of male sexual behavior have been obtained in measures of neuroendocrine response to a female. Exposure to a female results in a surge in plasma concentrations of luteinizing hormone in mice. This neuroendocrine response habituates with repeated exposures to the same female but can be reinstituted by presentation of a novel female (Coquelin & Bronson, 1979).

Although female-specific satiation of sexual behavior has been observed in a variety of species, behavioral mechanisms responsible for the effect have not always been identified. For example, in many studies males only had access to one female at a time. Increased sexual behavior may have reflected increased motivation induced by female novelty. Alternatively, the novel female may have been a more attractive target for male reproductive behavior.

A recent study with Japanese quail indicates that novelty can increase sexual motivation without increasing the attractiveness of the female (Domjan & Kurth, 1986). Sexually mature males were first permitted to become familiar with two adult females. One of those females was then replaced with a novel female. Female novelty increased the sexual behavior of the male Japanese quail, but their behavior was directed indiscriminantly to the novel and familiar females.

Improvement in Reproductive Performance with Experience

Numerous field studies of bird species have investigated the effects of age and experience on reproductive performance. The general finding has been that compared to females mating for the first time, older more sexually experienced females return to the breeding area earlier in the year, lay eggs sooner, lay more eggs, hatch a greater proportion of eggs, and have more surviving offspring. Improved reproductive success with age and experience has been reported for the Kittiwake gull (Coulson & White, 1958; Wooler & Coulson, 1977), Great tit (Perrins, 1965; Perrins & Moss, 1974), Brown pelican (Blus & Keahey, 1978), Razor-billed gull (Lloyd, 1979; Mills, 1973), California gull (Pugesek, 1981), Gannet (Nelson, 1966), Yellow-eyed penguin (Richdale, 1955, 1957), and Blackbird (Snow, 1958). Analogous results have been observed in elephant seals (Reiter, Panken, & LeBoeuf, 1981).

Although improvements in reproductive behavior with experience may have contributed to the results obtained in the field studies cited above, other plausible interpretations must be also considered. Because most of the data were obtained in cross-sectional studies, the superior performance of older more experienced animals may have reflected a shorter life span of reproductively incompetent individuals. Consideration of this possibility is especially important in species like the Great tit in which only 50% of the birds survive from one annual breeding season to the next (Perrins & Moss, 1974). The greater reproductive success of older, sexually more experienced animals also may have reflected their greater physiological maturity, higher social status, access to better nest sites, improved foraging skills, or better territorial defense (e.g., Reiter et al., 1981; Snow, 1958; Pugesek, 1981).

Evidence of improved reproductive performance with sexual experience is also available from laboratory studies with ring doves (Lehrman & Wortis, 1960, 1967; Michel, 1977), domestic chickens (Fisher & Hale, 1957), mice (McGill, 1962), domestic cats (Michael, 1961; Whalen, 1963), and guinea pigs (Valenstein & Goy, 1957). These studies did not involve confounding due to factors such as differential attrition, age, social status, and foraging skill, but many questions remain about what aspects of sexual encounters are necessary for later improved reproductive performance and what mechanisms of learning mediate these effects.

Instrumental Conditioning with Sexual Reinforcement

The examples of learning in reproductive behavior described earlier were discovered during general investigations of sexual behavior and involved procedures not often studied in traditional experiments on animal learning. The role of learning in reproductive behavior has been also investigated using the conventional paradigms of instrumental and classical conditioning. In instrumental conditioning, subjects are required to perform a response specified by the experimenter to gain access to a reinforcer. Application of this paradigm to the study of reproductive behavior has involved requiring animals to perform a particular response to obtain access to a sexually receptive mate. Male rats, for example, have been conditioned to run down an alley and climb over a hurdle to gain access to a receptive female (e.g., Sheffield, Wulff, & Backer, 1951), and female rats have been conditioned to go to one side of a T-maze or press a response lever to gain access to a male (e.g., Bermant & Westbrook, 1966; Elliason & Meyerson, 1975). This kind of procedure has been used often to study questions about sexual preference and motivation rather than questions about learning mechanism (e.g., Bermant, 1961; French, Fitzpatrick, & Law, 1972).

Studies directed at issues in animal learning have been concerned with determining what kinds of responses can be conditioned with sexual opportunity as reinforcement. Sevenster (1973), for example, observed that biting the tip of a rod in stickleback fish did not increase when occurrences of this response were followed by presentation of a sexually receptive female. However, other combinations of instrumental responses and reinforcers led to successful learning. Biting was readily increased by presentation of a male stickleback (that elicited aggression), and courtship opportunity was an effective reinforcer when swimming through a loop was the instrumental response. Biting may not have been increased by contingent courtship opportunity because courtship opportunity appeared to elicit responses incompatible with biting.

In a related study with pigeons, Gilbertson (1975) found that courtship was less effective than food in reinforcing pecking of an illuminated response key in males. As was observed by Sevenster (1973), courtship reinforcement appeared to inhibit the instrumental pecking response. The pigeons made weak "nibbling" responses toward the response key and remained very close to it for 5–6 sec, hesitating to peck. These types of responses were not observed with food reinforcement. Gilbertson suggested that the hesitation and weak nibbling reflected incompatibility between pecking (which often occurs in aggressive but not courtship encounters) and anticipation of courtship opportunity.

The responses Sevenster (1973) and Gilbertson (1975) attempted to condition with sexual reinforcement were unrelated to sexual behavior. In contrast, Silberberg and Adler (1974) explored the possibility of altering a component of sexual behavior itself with sexual reinforcement. Adult male rats received access to a receptive female during 20 mating trials. For the experimental group, each trial lasted long enough for 7 intromissions or an ejaculation response, whichever occurred first. Thus, to experience ejaculation, these rats had to ejaculate within the first 7 intromissions. One control group was permitted to reach ejaculation on every trial regardless of how many intromissions that required. A second control group was yoked to the experimental group for number of intromissions permitted but no contingency between intromissions and ejaculation was imposed. The instrumental contingency in the experimental group resulted in a greater percentage of subjects ejaculating within 7 intromissions than was observed in either of the control groups. These findings indicate that ejaculation can modify through instrumental conditioning earlier components of sexual behavior in male rats.

Classical Conditioning and Sexual Behavior

A second experimental paradigm that has been extensively used in studies of animal learning is classical or Pavlovian conditioning. In this paradigm, the effectiveness of an initially *neutral* stimulus (the conditioned stimulus or CS) in eliciting behavior is altered through its association with a biologically significant event (the unconditioned stimulus or US). Classical conditioning can be investigated in reproductive behavior systems by presenting a conditioned stimulus in conjunction with opportunity for reproductive behavior, and seeing if the CS comes to elicit some form of sexual arousal, courtship, or anticipation. Several lines of evidence suggest that cues that accompany sexual opportunity or copulation can become conditioned.

Sexual classical conditioning in instrumental conditioning studies. Indirect evidence of classical conditioning of sexual behavior was noted by Sevenster (1973) and Gilbertson (1975) in their instrumental conditioning experiments. As was described earlier, Sevenster required male sticklebacks to bite a rod to obtain exposure to a receptive female, and Gilbertson required male pigeons to peck a key to obtain access to a female. As a result of these procedures, courtship-like responses came to be directed toward the rod by the sticklebacks and toward the response key by the pigeons. Such responses may have reflected the association of the rod and response key with exposure to female subjects.

Increased responsiveness to sexual odors and visual cues. Other suggestive evidence of classical conditioning is provided by studies demonstrating increased responsiveness to sexual odors and visual cues following sexual experience. A number of experiments have demonstrated that sexually experienced rats prefer the odor of estrous as compared to diestrous females whereas sexually inexperienced rats do not show such a preference (e.g., Carr, Loeb, & Dissinger,

1965; Lydell & Doty, 1972; Stern, 1970). Sexual experience also increases discrimination between estrous and diestrous female odor in male hamsters (Lisk, Ziess, & Ciacco, 1972), and sexually experienced female mice show a greater preference than naive females for the odor of preputial gland extract (Caroum & Bronson, 1971). Analogous results have been recently found involving visual cues in an avian species: Sexual experience has been observed to increase the preference of male Japanese quail for visual cues provided by a female conspecific (Domjan & Hall, 1986). Such phenomena may be mediated by classical conditioning involving the association of sexual odors (in small mammals) and visual cues (in Japanese quail) with reproductive experience.

More convincing evidence of the involvement of classical conditioning is provided by studies of ultrasound courtship vocalizations in response to olfactory cues in mice. Social experience with female conspecifics induces male mice to emit ultrasound vocalizations in response to the odor of female urine (Dizinno, Whitney, & Nyby, 1978). Such vocalizations are not observed in sexually inexperienced males and do not occur in response to the odor of male urine or distilled water in socially experienced mice. Male mice appear to learn an association between the odor of female urine and some aspect of social interaction with females. Furthermore, there is some flexibility in this conditioning. In a comparison of the effects of social experience with normal and hypophysectomized females, males were found to vocalize more in response to odors from the particular type of female (normal or hypophysectomized) they previously encountered (Maggio, Maggio, & Whitney, 1983). Males can also learn to perform ultrasound vocalizations in response to a musk odor sprayed on females. However, the odor of ethanol sprayed on females does not come to elicit courtship vocalizations (Nyby, Whitney, Schmitz, & Dizinno, 1978; see also Nyby, Bigelow, Kerchner, & Barbehenn, 1983).

Classical conditioning of courtship and approach behavior in Japanese quail.   Clear evidence of classical conditioning of reproductive behavior has been also obtained in studies with Japanese quail. Farris (1964, 1967) studied the reponse of male Japanese quail to a soft buzzer that signaled the presentation of a receptive female. Within less than 30 conditioning trials, the buzzer came to elicit responses previously observed only during courtship with a female. Such results were not obtained in subjects that had experienced the buzzer unpaired with presentations of female quail. Additional evidence that conditioning had taken place was provided by the fact that conditioned courtship responses declined when presentations of the buzzer were no longer followed by presentations of female quail (extinction).

Domjan, Lyons, North, and Bruell (1986) recently completed a study similar to that of Farris using a localized red light instead of a buzzer as the conditioned stimulus. Male Japanese quail were continuously housed in a large (12 sq. ft.) arena. The subjects received access to a female once a day for 5 min. For the experimental group, the CS light was turned on 30 sec before each of these mating opportunities. For the control group, the CS was presented several hours after the mating trial each day. Twenty-five conditioning trials were conducted. Contrary to the observations of Farris (1967), the conditioned stimulus did not come to elicit courtship responses in the experimental subjects. However, sexual conditioning was evident in approach to the red light CS. After about 10 conditioning trials, experimental subjects approached the red light when it was turned on and spent significantly more time near it than control birds did. Domjan, Lyons, North, and Bruell (1986) also obtained evidence of the acquisiton and extinction of sexual conditioned approach behavior using a procedure that involved brief daily mating trials in an experimental chamber different from the home cages in which the birds were otherwise housed.

Classical conditioning of courtship and Appeasement in Fish. Sexual classical conditioning has been also demonstrated in a fish species (blue gouramies, *Trichogaster trichopterus*) (Hollis, 1985). Male-female pairs of gouramies were housed in individual aquaria, visually separated from one another by a partition. Four of the subject pairs served in the experimental group and received Pavlovian conditioning training in which a red light CS was presented to the male and female simultaneously for 10 sec, followed by an opportunity to view one another for 15 sec (the US). Ten such conditioning trials were conducted daily. The remaining four pairs of fish received an *explicitly unpaired* control treatment in which ten CS presentations were followed, 6 hours later, by 10 US presentations. After 12 days of training, all subjects received the same test treatment: The CS was presented to each male-female pair simultaneously and was followed immediately by an opportunity to mate. In the experimental group, both male and female subjects acquired a conditional response to the CS consisting of the frontal display posture in which the fish erect their fins. Such frontal displays did not occur during the CS in the control group. The behavior of the two groups differed significantly in the test as well. Control males responded aggressively to female pairmates, biting and chasing them and causing them to flee and hide. Conditioned males, in contrast, exhibited significantly less of this aggressive behavior and showed significantly more courtship appeasement.

The above results demonstrate that sexual classical conditioning occurred in the gouramies as a result of signaled exposure to a conspecific of the opposite sex. The study also provides evidence of the functional significance of sexual classical conditioning in this species. Males for which the red light signaled presentation of a sexual partner were much more likely to engage in courtship appeasement behavior rather than aggression when they received access to the female.

Classical conditioning of sexual arousal in rats. Sexual classical conditioning has also been investigated in rats. Zamble, Hadad, Mitchell, and Cutmore

(1985) used placement of male rats in a holding cage for 10 min as a conditioned stimulus signaling access to a receptive female. Independent experimental groups received three different types of social experience. One group was permitted to interact with the female across a wire-mesh partition. Other groups were allowed physical contact with the female until three intromissions or an ejaculation occurred. Three corresponding control groups received the same types of social experience but separated at least 1 hr from CS presentations. After 8 conditioning trials, all groups were tested with a female immediately after exposure to the CS. Experimental subjects that were permitted to interact with the female across a wire screen and those that were allowed intromissions without ejaculation during training had significantly shorter latencies to ejaculate during the test trial than corresponding control subjects. A significant difference between experimental and control subjects was not observed for animals allowed to ejaculate during training trials. However, in this case both the experimental and control groups had very short ejaculation latencies. The mating trials for these subjects may have reduced ejaculation latencies so much that the added benefit of signaling the mating opportunity could not be detected. In a subsequent experiment, Zamble et al. (1985) also demonstrated second-order conditioning of sexual arousal in rats (see also Zamble, Mitchell, & Findlay, 1986).

Conclusive evidence of classical conditioning of reproductive processes was also obtained in a recent study by Graham and Desjardins (1980) who found that an arbitrary odor paired with access to a female rat came to elicit secretions of luteinizing hormone and testosterone in males. These hormonal secretions reflected the conditioned anticipation of sexual opportunity because they did not occur in groups of animals that received access to a receptive female without the odor CS or access to the odor CS without exposure to females. Such conditioned sexual arousal and gonadal hormone release may have significant impact on reproductive outcome. Testosterone has been shown to potentiate penile reflexes, and penile reflexes are important in the deposition of seminal plugs and in dislodging plugs from previous copulations (Hart, 1983). Through this mechanism, conditioned sexual arousal and accompanying release of gonadal hormones may influence sperm competition during multimale mating sessions (Hart, 1983).

METHODOLOGICAL PROBLEMS AND OPPORTUNITIES

Heterosexual reproductive behavior involves a complex interaction between male and female and is controlled by a variety of neurophysiological, neuroendocrine, and environmental factors. In many species of vertebrates, the occurrence of sexual behavior is closely related to gonadal hormones. Castration eliminates sexual behavior and hormone replacement produces a recovery in the response (e.g., Kelly & Pfaff, 1978). In other species, climatic and nutritional factors are more important. Male red-sided garter snakes, for example, engage in courtship and mating behavior upon emerging from winter dormancy regardless of gonadal or pituitary hormonal status (Garstka, Camazine, & Crews, 1982). In desert birds, mating occurs in response to rainfall, which increases the food supply (Immelman, 1973). The complexity of male-female sexual interactions and their diverse controlling mechanisms present both methodological problems and opportunities for investigations of learning processes.

Methodological Problems

The complexity of reproductive behavior creates difficulties in the identification of particular sexual behavior phenomena as involving learning. A universally accepted definition of learning is difficult to formulate. However, any definition is likely to make reference to three critical features. First, learning is expected to lead to a change in behavior. The behavior change may not always be evident, but it must be observable under certain circumstances. Second, the behavior change is expected to be an enduring one, and third it is expected to result from some form of environmental experience. Many investigators of learning employ a relatively small number of behavioral situations. This has facilitated agreement on what behavioral changes reflect learning. The diversity of experiential effects in sexual behavior and differences between these and more conventional situations in which learning is investigated makes interpretation more difficult.

Reproductive behavior typically involves a dynamic interaction of two participants whose actions critically depend on one another's reactions. This can create difficulties in figuring out which of the participants in the interaction is responsible for observed changes in behavior. In many studies of female-specific satiation of male sexual behavior (see above), for example, males are first repeatedly tested with the same female until a decline in mating behavior is observed. A new female is then introduced, and recovery in sexual behavior occurs. The decline and subsequent recovery of mating behavior may reflect changes in the behavior of the male. However, subtle changes in the female may also be critical. Recently mated females may provide altered olfactory, visual, auditory, and/or behavioral cues to the male (Carter & Schein, 1971; Goldfoot & Goy, 1970). Investigators have been sensitive to this possibility. For example, in a study of female-specific satiation in male rhesus monkeys, Michael and Zumpe (1978) noted that the new females were comparable to the familiar females in the number of invitations and refusals they presented to the males and in the quality of their vaginal secretions. Other investigators have attempted to rule out the contribution of female behavior to male satiation and recovery by using as new females animals that had recently mated with other males (e.g., Hsiao, 1965).

Once the critical participant in a behavior change has been identified, one must decide whether the behavior change represents sexual or some other form of learning. This question is particularly prominent in considering improvements in sexual performance with practice. Such performance changes result from experience and are enduring; they also involve sexual behavior. Hence, they seem to be instances of sexual learning. However, as we noted earlier, in nonlaboratory situations, improvements in sexual behavior and reproductive performance with practice may reflect improved social status, choice of nest site, territorial behavior, or foraging. In laboratory experiments that exclude such factors, improvement in sexual behavior with practice may reflect habituation of nonspecific arousal to the test situation rather than learning specific to sexual behavior. Domjan et al (1986), for example, observed a more than three-fold decrease in the latency to copulate among male Japanese quail given a mating trial on each of 5 successive days. This effect may have reflected habituation to the procedures involved in placing a female in the male's cage or habituation to having a conspecific in the cage, rather than learning something particular about sexual behavior.

Other interpretive problems arise from the nature of the unconditioned stimulus in many experiential effects on sexual behavior. In most of the phenomena we have already reviewed, exposure or interaction with conspecific females served as the unconditioned stimulus. Exposure to a member of the opposite sex can have enduring unconditioned effects that may be mistakenly interpreted as instances of learning. The neuroendocrine consequences of courtship and copulatory behavior have been well documented in ring doves (e.g., Cheng, 1978; Lehrman, 1965). Copulation or mere exposure to a female or her odor have been observed to increase serum testosterone levels in rabbit, guinea pig, rat, hamster, mouse, pig, sheep, cow, rhesus moneky, and man (see Harding, 1981, for a review). Increases in plasma luteinizing hormone following copulation also have been observed in rabbit, rat, mouse, mole, pig, sheep, and cow. Many of the endocrine effects of copulation are short-lasting and dissipate within minutes, or at most hours (e.g., Bronson & Desjardins, 1982; Kamel & Frankel, 1978). However, copulation also can result in enduring increases in gonadal and other androgen-dependent body tissues (e.g., Hunt, 1969). These profound and sometimes enduring endocrine, neuroendocrine, and physiological consequences of courtship and copulatory behavior may influence later sexual behavior (e.g., Cheng, 1978; Lehrman, 1965). New sexual responses (nest building, for example) that appear because of the recruitment of the neuroendocrine system by earlier courtship and copulation would be considered unconditioned rather than learned responses according to accepted conceptions of learning. Although the chain of events leading to such responses is initiated by earlier experience (courtship and copulation), the new responses presumably do not have to be practiced once the requisite hormonal state is achieved. Given the profound endocrine and physiological changes that can occur as a result of exposure and copulation with a conspecific, investigations of sexual learning have to consider carefully whether observed changes in behavior are attributable merely to repeated exposures to a sexual partner or to associations learned as a result of the social contact.

Methodological Opportunities

Reproductive behavior systems also provide some methodological opportunities for the study of learning. As we noted earlier, occurrence of courtship and copulatory behavior often depends on particular hormonal, climatic, and other ecological conditions. These conditions are not sufficient for the occurrence of sexual behavior but serve to enable social cues to stimulate courtship and copulation. In the absence of the necessary enabling conditions, particular social cues may be without effect or cause aggression instead of courtship (Payne & Swanson, 1970). Experimental manipulation of these conditions in relation to training and test procedures for learning can provide important insights into reproductive behavior and learning mechanisms.

One possibility is to conduct training procedures at a time when the enabling conditions are absent, and test for learning later when the necessary hormonal and ecological supports for sexual behavior are available. Studies of this sort would provide information about occurrence of latent learning in reproductive behavior systems. Research on sexual imprinting (see above) provides one well documented instance of sexual latent learning. In sexual imprinting, the training experience (exposure to conspecifics of particular coloration, for example) is provided early in life, prior to ontogenetic emergence of courtship and copulatory behavior. The effects of this training are not evident until sexual maturity, when the earlier stimulus exposure is observed to influence mate choice.

Another possibility is to conduct training procedures in the presence of hormonal and other supports necessary for sexual behavior and then test for learning effects when these enabling conditions are absent or degraded. Findings of protection from castration-induced decline in sexual behavior (see above) illustrate this case. In cats, for example, sexual experience in the presence of the required hormonal enabling conditions increases sexual persistence when the hormonal enabling conditions are subsequently degraded by castration.

Alteration of the enabling conditions for unconditioned behavior has become a powerful experimental technique for the investigation of learning mechanisms in a variety of response systems (e.g., see Mackintosh, 1983). Such manipulations may also provide important insights into mechanisms of sexual learning. In addition, manipulations of the hormonal and other preconditions for sexual behavior can provide important insights into the nature of reproductive behavior generally. The extent to which courtship and copulatory behavior is restricted to certain hormonal and other conditions is a critical issue in understanding reproductive behavior. One interesting possibility is that sexual learning serves to liberate reproductive behavior from its hormonal and other controls to some extent. Through learning, animals may become able to engage in reproductive behavior under less than optimal hormonal and environmental conditions. The phenomenon of protection from castration-induced decline in sexual behavior provides perhaps the best documented evidence that learning can reduce hormonal constraints on reproductive behavior. This kind of mechanism may also explain why, compared to naive animals, sexually experienced seasonal breeders are able to initiate reproductive behavior earlier in the breeding season, when the climate presumably is not yet optimal and when their gonads have not yet fully recovered from winter dormancy.

CRITICAL VARIABLES IN ADAPTIVE SPECIALIZATIONS IN SEXUAL LEARNING

Investigation of learning mechanisms in reproductive behavior will require detailed analysis of particular instances of learning, such as the examples described above. Available knowledge about sexual behavior (see Daly & Wilson, 1983, and Krebs & Davies, 1981, for reviews) suggests that two variables will be critical not only in detecting adaptive specializations but in systematizing information about learning in reproductive behavior systems. One of these is the sex of the subject and the other is the mating system of the species. Although we recognize that these variables do not represent mutually exclusive categories in terms of their influence on behavior, we have attempted to separate them for purposes of discussion.

Sex Differences

Numerous sex differences exist between males and females, two of which appear to be fundamental. First, in all multicellular sexually reproducing species, there is a size difference between the gametes of the two sexes (Parker, Baker, & Smith, 1972). Gametes of one sex (sperm) contain little more than the genetic material itself, whereas the gametes of the other sex (eggs) contain not only genetic material but also nutritional stores for the developing zygote. Because of this size difference, eggs are more costly to produce than sperm. The eggs of many birds provide a familiar example. Bird eggs often represent as much as 15–20% of the female's body weight, and a few species produce eggs that are nearly a third of the female's body weight (Lack, 1968). The second major sex difference is that in most species, females—which by definition are the producers of the developmentally advantaged gametes—are more likely to offer parental care than are males (Maynard Smith, 1978; Wilson, 1975).

According to Trivers (1972), the above differences between males and females in parental investment give rise to different optimal reproductive strategies. In general, the sex that makes the greater investment per offspring becomes the limiting resource for the other. Because "investors" are a resource to be exploited, there is compeition to gain access to them (Wilson, 1975). Thus, in the typical case, males compete with one another for access to females; and, differences between males in reproductive success are largely dependent upon the number of matings a male can secure. Females, on the other hand, make a costly investment in each offspring and have more to lose by selecting mates indiscriminately: The best strategy for a heavy investor is to choose from amongst available mates very carefully.

Implications for sexual learning. Trivers' (1972) theory of parental investment has been highly successful in explaining both the typical differences in male and female reproductive tactics as well as exceptions to the rule where the sex roles are reversed (Emlen & Oring, 1977; Jenni, 1974; Oring & Lank, 1982). Although the theory has not been extended to learning capacities of the sexes, there is no reason why this category of behavior should not be included. Many adaptations have evolved that increase a male's chances of successfully inseminating a female or of competing with other males (Wilson, 1975). Learning capacities (for example the ability to predict the appearance of mates and rivals) certainly would seem to be subject to the same selection pressures.

One adaptation in particular—males' lower threshold for sexual arousal (Orians, 1969)—is an especially likely source of adaptive specializations in sexual conditioning. Because a male's reproductive success depends more on the quantity rather than quality of matings secured, males should be ready to take advantage of every available sexual opportunity. This readiness is accomplished through the male's lower threshold for sexual arousal, an adaptation which insures that the male rarely misses a sexual opportunity—at the cost of perhaps frequent false alarms. Males are far more likely than females to attempt matings with inappropriate objects (Orians, 1969) and to engage in forced copulations (Siniff, Stirling, Bengston, & Reichle, 1979). One would expect to see these differences reflected in conditioning as well. Sexual arousal may be conditionable to a wider range of cues in males than in females. Indeed, differences in sexual arousal might be reflected in a range of learning phenomena: Because there is less cost to males of becoming sexually aroused by inappropriate stimuli, they might be expected to become more easily sensitized, to habituate less readily, to form associations more quickly, and perhaps to extinguish more slowly.

In addition to a lowered threshold for sexual arousal, intrasexual selection has resulted in numerous other adaptations that play a role in competition between males (see Alcock, 1984, for a review). Dominance behavior, territoriality, sneak copulations and rape increase a male's chances of obtaining copulations. Other adaptations, such as guarding and the insertion of mating plugs, help a male to ensure that his sperm, and not that of another male, will fertilize the eggs of the female he has inseminated. Lastly, behavior such as interference and assault lower the reproductive success of competitors (Alcock, 1984).

Pavlovian conditioning of intraspecific aggression is well documented (see Hollis, 1982, for a review). Moreover, performance of a conditional aggressive response has been shown in recent experiments with blue gouramies (*Trichogaster trichopterus*) (Hollis, 1984a) to increase a male's ability to defend successfully his territory. Whether the success of such behavior as interference, guarding and sneak copulations also is altered by learning remains to be investigated.

As differences between the sexes in parental investment become less—and even reverse in direction, with males investing more than females (e.g., Oring & Lank, 1982)—selection pressures on mechanisms of intrasexual competition should also decrease (Trivers, 1972). Because learning capacities would seem to be subject to these same selection pressures, differences in learning capacities should parallel differences in parental investment. Not much disparity in sexual learning between males and females should be evident in species in which both parents care for the young, or in which male parenting tends to offset differential gametic contribution of the sexes. A few species of teleosts (bony fish), in which the male tends the nest of eggs, would be good candidates for this case. Finally, sex role reversals in sexual learning would be expected, for example, in polyandrous species, like the jacana (Jenni, 1974) and the spotted sandpiper (Oring & Lank, 1982).

An experiment with blue gouramies (Hollis, 1985) provides some evidence for the above view. In this species the male builds a floating foam bubble nest which he must tend regularly. In addition, once the eggs have been deposited by the female, the male assumes sole responsibility for their care. Thus, the greater gametic investment by the female is, in in a sense, compensated by the male's parenting. Of special interest to a parental investment approach to sexual learning is that not only do males and females both learn to associate a cue with the appearance of a mate, but they do so at an equal rate.

Mating Strategies

To a large extent, the mating system of a species is inextricably linked with its ecology. Mating strategies of males and females are strongly affected by ecological variables, such as the distribution of food or of nest sites, the duration of the breeding season, and the strength of predation (Emlen & Oring, 1977). For example, differences in food scarcity or in predation upon unattended offspring may cause differences in male parental investment, which in turn determines how many partners a male may have.

In general, two mating strategies are possible. Individuals can mate with one partner per breeding period (monogamy) or with several different partners (male polygyny and female polyandry). Polygynous and polyandrous systems have been further subdivided into several different functional types each reflecting the influence of various ecological constraints (Emlen & Oring, 1977).

Monogamy, though frequent in birds where reproductive success can be limited by the amount of food brought to the nest, is rare among mammals where the female provides the greater parental investment (Krebs & Davies, 1981). Although monogamy is more often associated with biparental care, it also occurs in a few species where female receptivity is restricted and female density is low. Here, the males remain with a single female and guard her until the time of mating (Wickler & Seibt, 1981).

The most common mating system is polygyny, of which four subtypes have been described (Alcock, 1984; Emlen & Oring, 1977). In two of these, males defend possession of a valuable resource, either a group of females themselves (harem, or female defense, polygyny) or some other resource such as food or nesting sites (resource defense polygyny). The mating system of gorillas and lions is an example of the former, whereas the highly territorial behavior of red-winged blackbirds exemplifies the latter. In the two remaining polygynous systems, males cannot monopolize a resource economically. This might occur because the resource is too widespread, for example, or because its distribution is scattered and unpredictable. In such cases, males either compete with one another at a traditional display arena, termed the ''lek'' (lek polygyny), or they race to contact clusters of receptive females (scramble competition polygyny). Leks are found in many species of grouse; the familiar picture of the prairie chicken, displaying to females in a posture of extended wings and bloated yellow air sacs, is one example. Anyone familiar with the behavior of male wood frogs on warm spring evenings will immediately recognize the meaning of the term ''scramble competition.''

Implications for sexual learning. In biparental pair-bonded species, intra-sexual selection is low, and therefore learning is not likely to play a critical role in male competition. However, one might predict that in pair-bonded species learning would be important in individual recognition of one's mate and off-spring (e.g., Tinbergen, 1960).

Intrasexual selection of male competition is high in polygynous species, and a variety of traits for male competition have evolved. We might expect the diversity of male competition traits to be accompanied by a corresponding diversity in learning phenomena supporting those traits. In systems where fitness depends on a male's ability to defend aggressively some resource (female defense and resource defense polygyny), learning capacities should act to increase effective male aggression. For example, males might react with an innate aggressive response to all intruders, lest they be rivals. Learning processes of habituation and sensitization could then be utilized to suppress reactivity to inappropriate stimuli and enhance reactivity to stimuli that present a serious threat. These predictions closely decribe the behavior of the convict cichlid (*Cichlasoma nigrofasciatum*) (Peeke & Peeke, 1973) as well as the white-crowned sparrow (Petrinovich & Patterson, 1981; see Hollis, 1984b, for a further discussion of these examples). One might predict, too, that Pavlovian conditioning of aggressive behavior to cues predicting the appearance of a rival would be more common in polygynous males that monopolize a resource than in males that do not. Not surprisingly, male aggression is especially intense when males attempt to monopolize females directly (Clutton-Brock, Guinness, & Albon, 1982) and, thus, learned expression of aggression would be expected to play an especially important role here.

In species that practice resource defense polygyny, often males must compete not only with conspecifics but with members of other species that find the resource valuable (Losey, 1982a). Therefore, in such cases, aggressive behavior should be modulated by both intra- and interspecific learning capacities. This prediction finds support in the literature on the habituation of interspecific aggression in fish. Several experiments by Losey (1982b) suggest that individuals learn which species to attack and are capable of making fine discriminations between different species within the same genera.

In contrast with males that attempt to monopolize a resource, the males of species that practice lek polygyny and, especially, scramble competition, depend far less on aggressive competition with one another. Instead, mechanisms that directly enhance a male's ability to inseminate females are favored here. Thus, in these species, learning capacities will be more likely to support such tactics as lowered threshold for sexual arousal and the prediction of sexual opportunity than they would support aggressive behavior.

Mirroring two types of polygynous sytems, two forms of polyandry involve a sex role reversal. Both in resource defense polyandry—practiced by the spotted sandpiper (Oring & Lank, 1982) and the jacana (Jenni, 1974)—and in lek polyandry (Emlen & Oring, 1977), the behavior of the female is like her polygynous male counterpart. Here the males assume all or most of the parental duties while the larger females compete for territories or aggregate at a prime breeding area where they attempt to attract males. These examples provide an important opportunity to test predictions involving adaptive specialization in sexual learning, just as they have been important in testing theories of parental investment and sexual selection.

IMPLICATIONS FOR GENERAL PROCESS LEARNING THEORY

The diversity of reproductive behaviors in the animal kingdom no doubt reflects adaptive specializations. Instances of sexual learning that contribute to fitness also may be considered adaptive specializations. Whether or not such adaptive specializations constitute a challenge for general process learning theory depends on what aspect of the learning is specialized.

The domain of general process learning theory is learning processes, the underlying mechanisms mediating learning. General process theory assumes that these mechanism are universal. However, it does not claim that all animals will learn the same things. Universality of learning processes does not imply universality of the contents of learning. Many instances of adaptive specializations in sexual learning will no doubt turn out to reflect specializations in the contents rather than the processes of learning. Given an effective conditioned stimulus and an effective unconditioned stimulus, how these become associated is assumed to follow generally applicable mechanisms. However, conditioned and unconditioned stimuli that are effective for one species may not be effective for another species.

The diversity of reproductive strategies in the animal kingdom and the diversity of neuroendocrine and ecological factors influencing reproductive behavior have resulted in great diversity in the potential stimuli and responses that can be involved in instances of sexual learning. This diversity contributes to diversity in sexual learning, but does so in part without challenging general process learning theory. For example, as we noted earlier, males of many species have a lower threshold for sexual arousal than females, and this may lead to important differences in sexual learning between males and females. In males, sexual arousal may become conditioned to a wider range of cues, may become conditioned more rapidly, and may extinguish more slowly. Such results may reflect general learning processes if they are due to differences in the intensity or effectiveness of the relevant unconditioned stimuli for males as compared to females.

Sexual learning presents a challenge to general process theory only to the extent that it involves unique or specialized learning processes. We are not familiar with any clear demonstrations of this to date. One might consider as representing biological constraints or adaptive specializations in learning the failure of Sevenster (1973) and Gilbertson (1975) to reinforce instrumentally biting in sticklebacks and pecking in pigeons, respectively, with access to a female. However, as has been pointed out elsewhere (e.g., Domjan, 1983; Timberlake, Wahl, & King, 1982), such results may be explained by the intrusion of incompatible classically conditioned responses. Thus, the contents of learning rather than its mechanisms may be responsible for the findings. A more interesting possibility is presented by the results of Nyby et al. (1973), who found that the odor of musk but not of ethanol can become conditioned to elicit courtship ultrasound vocalizations in mice. However, additional research evaluating the importance of stimulus intensity, novelty, duration, and unconditioned effects of the odors is required to ascertain the basis of this constraint on conditionability.

Even if adaptive specializations in sexual learning are not found, investigations of learning in reproductive behavior systems are bound to have an important impact on the understanding of learning generally. Because reproductive behavior involves a response system that has not been the subject of systematic learning research to date, investigations of sexual learning will increase the range of learning phenomena that any comprehensive theory of learning has to address. Because the diversity of reproductive behavior focuses attention on differences in sex, mating systems, and ecological conditions, investigations of sexual learning may provide increased insights into comparative aspects of learning (Domjan & Galef, 1983). Finally, because reproductive behavior is intimately related to the transmission of genetic information, studies of sexual learning can increase knowledge about the biological functions of learning processes (Hollis, 1982).

REFERENCES

Alcock, J. (1984). *Animal behavior: An evolutionary approach* (3rd edition). Sunderland, MA: Sinauer.

Bateson, P. P. G. (1978). Early experience and sexual preferences. In J. B. Hutchison (Ed.), *Biological determinants of sexual behavior* (pp. 29–53). New York: Wiley.

Beach, F. A., & Jordan, L. (1956). Sexual exhaustion and recovery in the male rat. *Quarterly Journal of Experimental Psychology, 8,* 121–133.

Bermant, G. (1961). Response latencies of female rats during sexual intercourse. *Science, 133,* 1771–1773.

Bermant, G., & Westbrook, W. H. (1966). Peripheral factors in the regulation of sexual contact by female rats. *Journal of Comparative and Physiological Psychology, 61,* 244–250.

Bloch, G. J., & Davidson, J. M. (1968). Effects of adrenalectomy and experience on postcastration sex behavior in the rat. *Physiology & Behavior, 3,* 461–465.

Blus, L. J., & Keahey, J. A. (1978). Variation in reproductivity with age in the brown pelican. *Auk, 95,* 128–134.

Bolles, R. C. (1970). Species-specific defense reactions and avoidance learning. *Psychological Review, 77,* 32–48.

Bronson, F. H., & Desjardins, C. (1982). Endocrine responses to sexual arousal in male mice. *Endocrinology, 111,* 1286–1291.

Caroum, D., & Bronson, F. H. (1971). Rsponsiveness of female mice to preputial attractant: Effects of sexual experience and ovarian hormones. *Physiology & Behavior, 7,* 659–662.

Carr, W. J., Loeb, L. S., & Dissinger, M. L. (1965). Response of rats to sex odours. *Journal of Comparative and Physiological Psychology, 95,* 370–377.

Carter, C. S., & Schein, M. W. (1971). Sexual receptivity and exhaustion in the female golden hamster. *Hormones and Behavior, 2,* 191–200.

Cheng, M. F. (1978). Progress and prospects in ring dove research: A personal view. *Advances in the study of behavior, 9,* 97–129.

Clemens, L. G. (1969). Experimental analysis of sexual behaviour of the deermouse, *Peromyscus maniculatus gambeli. Behaviour, 34,* 267–285.

Clutton-Brock, T. M., Guinness, F. E., & Albon, S. D. (1982). *Red deer: Behavior and ecology of two sexes.* Chicago: University of Chicago Press.

Cooke, F., Finney, G. H., & Rockwell, R. F. (1976). Assortative mating in lesser snow geese *(Anser caerulescens). Behavior Genetics, 6,* 127–139.

Cooke, F., & McNally, C. M. (1975). Mate selection and colour preferences in lesser snow geese. *Behaviour, 53,* 151–170.

Cooke, F., Mirsky, P. J., & Seiger, M. B. (1972). Colour preferences in the lesser snow geese and their possible role in mate selection. *Canadian Journal of Zoology, 50,* 529–536.

Coquelin, A., & Bronson, F. H. (1979). Release of luteinizing hormone in male mice during exposure to females: Habituation of the response. *Science, 206,* 1099–1101.

Coulson, J. C., & White, E. (1958). The effect of age on the breeding biology of the Kittiwake *Rissa tridactyla. Ibis, 100,* 40–51.

Daly, M., & Wilson, M. (1983). *Sex, evolution, and behavior* (2nd edition). Boston: Willard Grant.

Dewsbury, D. A. (1981). Effects of novelty on copulatory behavior: The Coolidge effect and related phenomena. *Psychological Bulletin, 89,* 464–482.

Dizinno, G., Whitney, G., & Nyby, J. (1978). Ultrasonic vocalizations by male mice (*Mus musculus*) to female sex pheromone: Experiential determinants. *Behavioral Biology, 22,* 104–113.

Domjan, M. (1983). Biological constraints on instrumental and classical conditioning: Implications for general process theory. In G. H. Bower (ed.), *The psychology of learning and motivation* (Vol. 17, pp. 215–277). New York: Academic Press.

Domjan, M., & Galef, B. G., Jr. (1983). Biological constraints on instrumental and classical conditioning: Retrospect and prospect. *Animal Learning & Behavior, 11,* 151–161.

Domjan, M., & Hall, S. (1986). Determinants of social proximity in Japanese quail (*Coturnix coturnix japonica*): Male behavior. *Journal of Comparative Psychology, 100,* 59–67.

Domjan, M., & Kurth, S. (1986). Effects of novelty on the reproductive behavior of male Japanese quail (*Coturnix coturnix japonica*). *Journal of Comparative Psychology, 100,* 203–207.

Domjan, M., Lyons, R., North, C., & Bruell, J. (1986). Sexual Pavlovian conditioned approach behavior in male Japanese quail (*Coturnix coturnix japonica*). *Journal of Comparative Psychology, 100,* 413–421.

Elliason, M., & Meyerson, B. J. (1975). Sexual preference in female rats during estrous cycle, pregnancy, and lactation. *Physiology & Behavior, 14,* 705–710.

Emlen, S. T., & Oring, L. W. (1977). Ecology, sexual selection and the evolution of mating systems. *Science, 198,* 215–223.

Farris, H. E. (1964). Behavioral development, social organization and conditioning of courting behavior in the Japanese quail, *Coturnix coturnix japonica.* Doctoral Dissertation, Michigan State University, University Microfilms No. 65-1738.

Farris, H. E. (1967). Classical conditioning of courting behavior in the Japanese quail, *Coturnix coturnix japonica. Journal of the Experimental Analysis of Behavior, 10,* 213–217.

Fisher, A. E. (1962). Effects of stimulus variations on sexual satiation in the male rat. *Journal of Comparative and Physiological Psychology, 55,* 614–620.

Fisher, A. E., & Hale, E. B. (1957). Stimulus determinants of sexual and aggressive behaviour in male domestic fowl. *Behaviour, 10,* 309–323.

Fowler, H., & Whalen, R. E. (1961). Variation in incentive stimulus and sexual behavior in the male rat. *Journal of Comparative and Physiological Psychology, 54,* 68–71.

French, D., Fitzpatrick, D., & Law, O. T. (1972). Operant investigation of mating preference in female rats. *Journal of Comparative and Physiological Psychology, 81,* 226–232.

Garstka, W. R., Camazine, B., & Crews, D. (1982). Interactions of behavior and physiology during the annual reproductive cycle of the red-sided garter snake (*Thamnop his sirtalis parietalis*). *Herptologica, 38,* 104–123.

Gilbertson, D. W. (1975). Courtship as a reinforcement for key pecking in the pigeon, *Columba livia. Animal Behaviour, 23,* 735–744.

Goldfoot, D. A., & Goy, R. W. (1970). Abbreviation of behavioral estrus in guinea pigs by coital and vagino-cervical stimulation. *Journal of Comparative and Physiological Psychology, 72,* 426–434.

Graham, J. M., & Desjardins, C. (1980). Classical conditioning: Induction of luteinizing hormone and testosterone secretion in anticipation of sexual activity. *Science, 210,* 1039–1041.

Grunt, J. A., & Young, W. C. (1952). Psychological modification of fatigue orgasm (ejaculation) in the male guinea pig. *Journal of Comparative and Physiological Psychology, 45,* 508–510.

Hale, E. B., & Almquist, J. O. (1960). Relation of sexual behavior to germ cell output in farm animals. *Journal of Dairy Science Supplement, 43,* 145–169.

Harding, C. F. (1981). Social modulation of circulating hormone levels in the male. *American Zoologist, 21,* 223–231.

Hart, B. L. (1974). Gonadal androgen and sociosexual behavior of male mammals: A comparative analysis. *Psychological Bulletin, 81,* 383–400.

Hart, B. L. (1983). Role of testosterone secretion and penile reflexes in sexual behavior and sperm competition in male rats: A theoretical contribution. *Physiology & Behavior, 31,* 823–827.

Hinde, R. A. (1973). Constraints on learning: An introduction to the problem. In R. A. Hinde & J. Stevenson-Hinde (Eds.), *Constraints on learning* (pp. 1–19). London: Academic Press.

Hinde, R. A., & Stevenson-Hinde, J. (eds.). (1973). *Constraints on learning.* London: Academic Press.

Hollis, K. L. (1982). Pavlovian conditioning of signal-centered action patterns and autonomic behavior: A biological analysis of function. *Advances in the study of behavior, 12,* 1–64.

Hollis, K. L. (1984a). The biological function of Pavlovian conditioning: The best defense is a good offense. *Journal of Experimental Psychology: Animal Behavior Processes, 10,* 413–425.

Hollis, K. L (1984b). Cause and function of animal learning processes. In P. Marler & H. S. Terrace (Eds.), *The biology of learning* (pp. 357–371). Berlin: Springer-Verlag.

Hollis, K. L. (1985). *Pavlovian conditioning: Mechanisms for mating success.* Unpublished manuscript.

Hsiao, S. (1965). Effects of female variation on sexual satiation in the male rat. *Journal of Comparative and Physiological Psychology, 60,* 467–469.

Hunt, W. L. (1969). Responses of rat testes and accessory glands to testosterone, pilocarpine, and copulation. *Nature, 221,* 669–670.

Immelman, K. (1972). Sexual and other long-term aspects of imprinting in birds and other species. In D. S. Lehrman, R. A. Hinde, & E. Shaw (Eds.), *Advances in the study of behavior* (Vol. 4, pp. 147–174). New York: Academic Press.

Immelmann, K. (1973). Role of environment in reproduction as source of "predictive" information. In D. S. Farner (Ed.), *Breeding biology of birds.* Washington, D.C.: National Academy of Sciences.

Jenni, D. A. (1974). Evolution of polyandry in birds. *American Zoologist, 14,* 129–144.

Johnston, T. D. (1981). Contrasting approaches to a theory of learning. *The behavioral and brain sciences, 4,* 125–173.

Kamel, F., & Frenkel, A. (1978). Hormone release during mating in the male rat: Time course, relation to sexual behavior and interaction with handling procedures. *Endocrinology, 103,* 2172–2179.

Kelly, D. B., & Pfaff, D. W. (1973). Generalizations from comparative studies on neuroanatomical and endocrine mechanisms of sexual behavior. In J. B. Hutchison (ed.), *Biological determinants of sexual behavior* (pp. 225–254). New York: Wiley.

Krebs, J. R., & Davies, N. B. (1981). *An introduction to behavioural ecology.* Sunderland, MA: Sinauer.

Lack, D. (1968). Ecological adaptations for breeding in birds. London: Methuen.

Larsson, K. (1978). Experiential factors in the development of sexual behavior. In J. B. Hutchison (Ed.), *Biological determinants of sexual behavior* (pp. 55–86). New York: Wiley.

Lehrman, D. S. (1965). Interaction between internal and external environments in the regulation of the reproductive cycle of the ring dove. In F. A. Beach (Ed.), *Sex and behavior* (pp. 355–380). New York: Wiley.

Lehrman, D. S., & Wortis, R. (1960). Previous breeding experience and hormone-induced incubation behavior in the ring dove. *Science, 132,* 1667–1668.

Lehrman, D. S., & Wortis, R. P. (1967). Breeding experience and breeding efficiency in the ring dove. *Animal Behaviour, 15,* 223–228.

Lill, A., & Wood-Gush, D. G. M. (1965). Potential ethological isolating mechanisms of assortative mating in the domestic fowl. *Behaviour, 25,* 16–44.

Lisk, R. D., Ziess, J., & Ciacco, L. A. (1972). The influence of olfaction on sexual behavior in the male golden hamster (*Mesocricetus auratus*). *Journal of Experimental Zoology, 181,* 69–78.

Lloyd, C. S. (1979). Factors affecting breeding of Razorbills *Alca torda* on Stokholm. *Ibis, 121,* 165–176.

Losey, G. S. (1982a). Intra- and interspecific aggression by the Central American Midas cichlid fish, *Cichlasoma citrinellum*. *Behaviour, 79*, 39–80.

Losey, G. S. (1982b). Ecological cues and experience modify interspecific aggression by the damselfish, *Stegastes fasciolatus*. *Behaviour, 81*, 14–37.

Lydell, K., & Doty, R. L. (1972). Male rat odor preferences for female urine as a function of sexual experience, urine age, and urine source. *Hormones and Behavior, 3*, 205–212.

Mackintosh, N. J. (1983). *Conditioning and associative learning*. New York: Oxford University Press.

Maggio, J. C., Maggio, J. H., & Whitney, G. (1983). Experience-based vocalizations of male mice to female chemosignals. *Physiology & Behavior, 31*, 269–272.

Marler, P., & Terrace, H. S. (Eds.). (1984). *The biology of learning*. New York: Springer-Verlag.

Maynard Smith, J. (1978). The ecology of sex. In J. R. Krebs & N. B. Davies (Eds.), *Behavioural ecology: An evolutionary approach* (pp. 159–179). Oxford: Blackwell.

McGill, T. E. (1962). Reduction in "head mounts" in the sexual behavior of the mouse as a function of experience. *Psychological Reports, 10*, 284.

McGill, T. E. (1978). Genotype-hormone interactions. In T. E. McGill, D. A. Dewsbury, & B. D. Sachs (eds.), *Sex and Behavior* (pp. 161–187). New York: Plenum.

Michael, R. P. (1961). Observations upon the sexual behavior of the domestic cat (*Felis catus L.*) under laboratory conditions. *Behaviour, 18*, 1–24.

Michael, R. P., & Zumpe D. (1978). Potency in male rhesus monkeys: Effects of continuously receptive females. *Science, 200*, 451–453.

Michel, G. F. (1977). Experience and progesterone in ring dove incubation. *Animal Behaviour, 25*, 281–285.

Mills, J. A. (1973). The influence of age and pair-bond on the breeding biology of the red-billed gull (*Larus novaehollandiae scopulinus*). *Journal of Animal Ecology, 42*, 147–162.

Nelson, B. (1966). The breeding biology of the Gannet *Sula bassana* on the Bass Rock, Scotland. *Ibis, 108*, 584–626.

Nyby, J., Bigelow, J., Kerchner, M., & Barbehenn, F. (1983). Male mouse (*Mus musculus*) ultrasonic vocalizations to female urine: Why is heterosexual experience necessary? *Behavioral and Neural Biology, 38*, 32–46.

Nyby, J., Whitney, G., Schmitz, S., & Dizinno, G. (1978). Post-pubertal experience establishes signal value of mammalian sex odor. *Behavioral Biology, 22*, 545–552.

Oring, L. W., & Lank, D. B. (1982). Sexual selection, arrival times, philopatry, and site fidelity in the polyandrous spotted sandpiper. *Behavioral Ecology and Sociobiology, 10*, 185–192.

Orians, G. H. (1969). On the evolution of mating systems in birds and mammals. *American Naturalist, 103*, 589–603.

Parker, G. A., Baker, R. R., & Smith, V. G. F. (1972). The origin and evolution of gamete dimorphism and the male-female phenomenon. *Journal of Theoretical Biology, 36*, 529–553.

Payne, A. P., & Swanson, H. H. (1970). Agonistic behaviour between pairs of hamsters of the same and opposite sex in a neutral observation area. *Behaviour, 36*, 359–269.

Peeke, H. V. S., & Peeke, S. C. (1973). Habituation in fish with special reference to intraspecific aggressive behavior. In H. V. S. Peeke & M. J. Herz (Eds.), *Habituation: Vol. 1. Behavioral Studies*. Orlando, FL: Academic Press.

Perrins, C. M. (1965). Population fluctuations and clutch size in the Great Tit, *Parus major*. *Journal of Animal Ecology, 34* 601–647.

Perrins, C. M., & Moss, D. (1974). Survial of young Great Tits in relation to the age of the female parent. *Ibis, 116*, 220–224.

Petrinovich, L., & Patterson, T. L. (1981). Field studies of habituation: IV. Sensitization as a function of the distribution and novelty of song playback to white-crowned sparrows. *Journal of Comparative and Physiological Psychology, 95*, 805–812.

Pugesek, B. (1981). Increased reproductive effort with age in the California Gull (*Larus californicus*). *Science, 212*, 822–823.

Reiter, J., Panken, K. J., & LeBoeuf, B. J. (1981). Female competition and reproductive success in northern elephant seals. *Animal Behaviour, 29*, 670–687.

Richdale, L. F. (1955). Influence of age on the size of eggs in the Yellow-eyed penguin. *Ibis, 97*, 266–275.

Richdale, L. F. (1957). *A population study of penguins*. Oxford, England: Oxford University Press.

Rosenblatt, J. S. (1965). Effects of sexual experience on sexual behavior in male cats. In F. A. Beach (Ed.), *Sex and Behavior* (pp. 416–439). New York: Wiley.

Rosenblatt, J. S., & Aronson, L. R. (1958). The decline in sexual behavior in male cats after castration with special reference to the role of prior sexual experience. *Behaviour, 12*, 285–338.

Rozin, P., & Kalat, J. W. (1971). Specific hungers and poison avoidance as adaptive specializations of learning. *Psychological Review, 78*, 459–486.

Schein, M. W., & Hale, E. B. (1965). Stimuli eliciting sexual behavior. In F. A. Beach (Ed.), *Sex and behavior* (pp. 440–482). New York: Wiley.

Seligman, M. E. P. (1970). On the generality of the laws of learning. *Psychological Review, 77*, 406–418.

Seligman, M. E. P., & Hager, J. L. (Eds.). (1972). *Biological boundaries of learning*. New York: Appleton-Century-Crofts.

Sevenster, P. (1973). Incompatibility of response and reward. In R. A. Hinde & J. Stevenson-Hinde (Eds.), *Constraints on Learning* (pp. 265–283). London: Academic Press.

Shapiro, L. J. (1980). Species identification in birds: A review and synthesis. In M. A. Roy (Ed.), *Species identity and attachment: A phylogenetic evaluation*. New York: Garland STPM Press.

Sheffield, F. D., Wulff, J. J., & Backer, R. (1951). Reward value of copulation without sexual drive reduction. *Journal of Comparative and Physiological Psychology, 44*, 3–8.

Shettleworth, S. J. (1972). Constraints on learning. In D. S. Lehrman, R. A. Hinde, & E. Shaw (Eds.), *Advances in the study of behavior* (Vol. 4, pp. 1–68). New York: Academic Press.

Shettleworth, S. J. (1983). Function and mechanism in learning. In M. Zeiler & P. H. Harzem (Eds.), *Biological Factors in Learning, Advances in analysis of behaviour* (Vol 3, pp. 1–39). Chichester, England: Wiley.

Silberberg, A., & Adler, N. (1974). Modulation of the copulatory sequence of the male rat by a schedule of reinforcement. *Science, 185*, 374–376.

Siniff, D. B., Stirling, I., Bengston, J. L., & Reichle, R. A. (1979). Social and reproductive behavior of crabeater seals (*Lobodon carcinophagus*) during the austral spring. *Canadian Journal of Zoology, 57*, 2243–2255.

Snow, D. W. (1958). The breeding of the Blackbird, *Turdus merula*, at Oxford. *Ibis, 100*, 1–30.

Stern, J. J. (1970). Responses of male rats to sex odors. *Physiology & Behavior, 5*, 519–524.

Timberlake, W., Wahl, G., & King, D. (1982). Stimulus and response contingencies in the misbehavior of rats. *Journal of Experimental Psychology: Animal Behavior Processes, 8*, 62–85.

Tinbergen, N. (1960). *The herring gull's world*. New York: Harper.

Trivers, R. L. (1972). Parental investment and sexual selection. In B. Campbell (Ed.), *Sexual selection and the descent of man*. Chicago: Aldine.

Valenstein, E. S., & Goy, R. W. (1957). Further studies of the organization and display of sexual behavior in male guinea pigs. *Journal of Comparative and Physiological Psychology, 50*, 115–119.

Walter, M. J. (1973). Effects of parental colouration of the mate preference of offspring in the zebra finch, *Taeniopygia guttata castanotis* Gould. *Behaviour, 46*, 154–173.

Warriner, C. C., Lemmon, W. B., & Ray, T. S. (1957). Early experience as a variable in mate selection. *Animal Behaviour, 11*, 221–224.

Whalen, R. E. (1963). Sexual behavior of cats. *Behaviour, 20*, 321–342.

Wickler, W., & Seibt, U. (1981). Monogamy in Crustacea and man. *Zeitschrift fur Tierpsychologie, 57,* 215–234.

Wilson, E. O. (1975). *Sociobiology: The new synthesis.* Cambridge, MA: Harvard University Press.

Wilson, J. R., Kuehn, R. E., & Beach, F. A. (1963). Modification in the sexual behavior of male rats produced by changing the stimulus female. *Journal of Comparative and Physiological Psychology, 56,* 636–644.

Wooler, R. D., & Coulson, J. C. (1977). Factors affecting the age of first breeding of the kittiwake *Rissa Tridactyle. Ibis, 119,* 339–349.

Zamble, E., Hadad, G. M., Mitchell, J. B., & Cutmore, T. R. H. (1985). Pavlovian conditioning of sexual arousal: First- and second-order effects. *Journal of Experimental Psychology: Animal Behavior Processes, 11,* 598–610.

Zamble, E., Mitchell, J. B., & Findlay, H. (1986). Pavlovian conditioning of sexual arousal: Parametric and background manipulations. *Journal of Experimental Psychology: Animal Behavior Processes, 12,* 403–411.

12 Some Comments on the Adaptationist Approach to Learning

Michael D. Beecher
University of Washington

What conclusions can we draw from the burst of research on evolution and learning of the last 25 years or so? If we take the papers of this volume as reflecting the state of the area, it appears to me that there is a clear consensus on several points and, in addition, a growing awareness of some new directions that research will have to take. The consensus has been forced by the cumulative impact of studies showing that there are great differences among species as to what an animal will or will not learn. This diversity in learning is now taken as a given, not only by the researchers who revealed it, but by those students of learning processes who, in the beginning, may have regarded it more as a nuisance than as a fundamental observation. Reviewing the chapters in the present volume, I identify two points of consensus and two points of concern regarding the study of evolution and learning. My general theme is that while the adaptationist approach to learning has substantially changed our thinking in this area, further evolutionary insights will come only if we recognize and adjust to inherent limitations of the adaptationist approach.

POINTS OF CONCENSUS

Point 1: What an animal learns and fails to learn may be as viewed reflecting an adaptive strategy

Animals tend to learn some things quickly, others things slowly or not at all. In the laboratory environment these inclinations and disinclinations may look quixotic, but when extrapolated to the context of the animal's natural environment, they generally make adaptive sense. For example, in laboratory foraging situations, hummingbirds are inclined to learn to shift from the rewarded target to a new target (*shift learning*), but disinclined to learn to return to the previously rewarded target (*stay learning*). This evidentally reflects the logic of their natural foraging strategy, in which previously rewarding targets are eschewed for the simple reason that they will have been depleted by the bird on the previous visit (Cole, Hainsworth, Kamil, Mercier, & Wolf, 1982; and see Kamil & Mauldin, this volume). In this view, these inclinations and disinclinations to learn are seen as *adaptive learning strategies*. There are certain contingencies that are likely in the environment, and certain that are not. Natural selection will therefore favor any mechanism that promotes learning of the likely contingencies over learning of the unlikely contingencies. Thus learning becomes more constrained but more efficient, more fail-safe. Twenty years ago, the difficulty our hummingbird has learning the *stay* task would probably have been attributed to the animal's limited capacity for learning (compared to mammals). These days this difficulty is seen instead as an *adaptation* to the animal's particular ecological niche. This view is reinforced by our relatively recent realization that even humans—learning experts *par excellence*—have their own learning constraints, as in taste aversion learning (Logue, this volume).

Point 2: General process learning theory is compatible with the evolutionary approach to learning

Not long ago the view that a unitary learning process underlies all or most instances of learning (and failures to learn) was anathema to researchers looking at learning from an evolutionary perspective. Now the question of the nature of the learning process is seen by most as orthogonal to the question of the adaptive value of particular learning strategies (a notable exception is Johnston, 1981). This trend is well illustrated in the work of John Staddon and John Garcia. In Staddon's chapter in this volume (see also Staddon, 1983) he argues forcefully for both the adaptive viewpoint and for a form of general process learning theory. He suggests that all learning (excepting simple processes such as habituation and sensitization) follows essentially the same rules, the rules of Bayesian inference. He includes here not only classical and operant conditioning (which many learning theorists now regard as a single type of learning), but also cases such as imprinting and song learning, types of learning usually thought of as perceptual learning, as occuring without reinforcement, and as having distinctive developmental characteristics (such as a sensitive period).

The evolution of John Garcia's position is even more illustrative of this trend. In his early studies, Garcia took the facts of taste aversion learning as evidence for the failure of general process learning theory. In his newest work (Garcia, in press) he argues instead for a new bipartite classification, which he believes can accomodate the various kinds of associative learning including taste aversion learning.

Thus the nature of the underlying learning mechanisms, on the one hand, and the adaptive value of learning strategies, on the other, are now perceived as separable, logically independent problems. This view is simply one instance of the recent trend to clearly distinguish explanations in terms of function (ultimate cause) from those in terms of mechanism (proximate cause). Whether two instances of learning reflect the same underlying process is a question of mechanism and is logically independent of the question of their adaptive value.

For this reason, the researcher primarily interested in the process of learning and the researcher primarily interested in the adaptive value of learning have been able to pursue their primary interests with little concern for the other question. It is becoming apparent, however, that we have reached a point where the interesting questions about evolution and learning can only be answered by explicit efforts to integrate these two approaches. Although it is sometimes said that the ultimate-cause and proximate-cause approaches are truly independent approaches, this is true only in the sense that a particular mechanism does not necessarily imply a particular function, nor vice versa. The ultimate-cause and proximate-cause approaches, I believe, are like two different perspectives on a scene which can be reconstructed only by integrating the two perspectives. The need for this sort of integrated viewpoint is reflected in points *3* and *4*, which identify two shortcomings of the adaptationist approach to evolution and learning. These two shortcomings, which are noted at several points in this volume, are in fact inevitable in any adaptationist approach to behavior. Our ability to deal with them constructively will be crucial, in my opinion, to future advances in the study of the evolution of learning.

POINTS OF CONCERN: DIFFICULTIES
WITH THE ADAPTATIONIST APPROACH

Point 3: Constraints on adaptation pose a problem
for the evolutionary approach to learning

While learning is generally adaptive, there is a growing realization that it is not always perfectly so, that there are limitations or *constraints* on the evolution of learning adaptations. Indeed constraints on adaptation are now widely recognized as presenting special problems for application of the adaptationist program generally (e.g., Maynard Smith et al., 1985). In the present volume, Galef points out that observational learning would certainly be adaptive for many animals, yet there is at present no hard evidence that it is found in any animal (excepting, presumably, humans). Similarly, Kroodsma points out that song learning is wide-spread in oscine birds but, apparently, absent in the closely-related suboscines. Kroodsma identifies no ecological variables that would favor this learning ability in oscines while disfavoring it in suboscines. Instead, he suggests that this ability appeared in phylogeny at the time of, or after, the divergence of the two groups. Thus whatever adaptive value there is to song-learning and related phenomona such as song dialects and song repertoires, presumably the suboscines could reap much the same benefits as the oscines, but have been constrained from doing so by phylogenetic inertia. These two examples illustrate the problem: We cannot always safely assume (whether via a carefully reasoned prediction or a post hoc just-so story) that learning will be adaptive in all respects. Nor do we presently have any simple way of predicting constraints on learning adaptations in any particular situation.I return to this point below.

Point 4: We must distinguish between adaptive uses of learning and adaptive specializations of learning

I consider this to be one of the most important issues in this area. It is stated clearly by Sherry in this volume. He states that while we now know of many distinct adaptive uses of learning, in no case can we make a case for adaptive specializations of learning. The problem does not seem to be appreciated by some researchers who regard any impressive demonstration of learning in an animal (or a failure to learn that can be construed as making adaptive sense) to be an adaptation. As Williams (1966) has convincingly argued, however, adaptation is a special and onerous concept that should only be used when strong evidence can be marshalled that the mechanism in question has been shaped by natural selection for the function postulated. Yet, to date, there is probably not one case of a learning difference—either intraspecific, as in the preference for shift-learning over stay-learning in hummingbirds, or interspecific, as in the incredible feats of learning and memory displayed by the bird species that specialize in storing food—where the mechanisms underlying the difference have been identified. Indeed, in most of the cases it has not even been shown—often it is merely presumed—that the difference really reflects learning, as opposed to some other mechanism (while it is widely recognized that simple sensory-perceptual differences have to be excluded, beyond this there is generally little attempt to identify the mechanisms responsible for the difference). For example, consider one of the food-storing specialists discussed by Sherry. Clark's nutcracker returns to caches where it stored food many months earlier, locating these caches from memory. In doing so it unquestionably is making adaptive use of learning that few other animals can match. But what exactly is the adaptation? Has there been an adaptation of the learning mechanisms per se? Or merely of the mechanisms that switch in the ubiquitous general processes and focus them on the particular problem? Or, simpler yet, in the mechanisms that cause the animal to decide to store food and to decide to look for it 9 months later? Some students of evolution would not particularly care about the specific nature of the adaptation, pointing out that food caching is adaptive in this species (it allows the animal to exploit a rich food store at a critical time of food scarcity) and the bottom line is that the bird can do it. But a student of the evolution of learning is concerned precisely with the nature of the adaptation—it is quite crucial whether a Clark's nutcracker accomplishes this very impressive feat via specialized learning mechanisms or via generalized mechanisms, which any animal could tap if it were moved to store food and go back to find it 9 months later.

AN ILLUSTRATIVE EXAMPLE: PARENT-OFFSPRING RECOGNITION

In many species parents learn to recognize their offspring. This learning, which usually takes place shortly before the young become mobile, is conceived of as a process like imprinting (though because of the difficulty of replicating this situation in the lab, the details of the learning process have not been studied). In many species, parents never show any signs of learning heir young's identities. In several cases, a comparison of two closely related species reveals the occurrence of recognition in one species and its failure in a second. Beginning probably with Cullen's (1957) description of apparent differences between herring gulls and kittiwakes with respect to parent-offspring recognition, such differences have most often been taken as examples of the evolution of a *learning* capacity. I use this natural class of learning to illustrate the two major difficulties with the adaptationist approach to learning discussed earlier.

Adaptive Specialization of Learning?

It is generally true of species in which parents fail to recognize offspring that young do not intermingle to any significant extent, hence recognition simply is not needed (for an exception to this rule, see the next section of this paper). For example, among the swallows, in two colonial species—bank swallows and cliff swallows—parents recognize young, but in two noncolonial species—rough-winged swallows and barn swallows—they do not (Beecher, Medvin, Stoddard, & Loesche, 1986). This striking contrast among these closely related species undoubtedly reflects the fact that young intermingle extensively in the two colonial species but very little in the two noncolonial species. For example, in both bank swallows and cliff swallows newly fledged young are left behind in large, temporary, tightly packed groups (*creches*) while the parents forage; on returning to the creche, a parent must pick out its young from many other similar-aged young. Barn swallows and rough-winged swallows, however, do not creche, and so this pressure for recognition is not present in these species.

We know that the species difference in recognition involves learning. In bank swallows this learning takes place around Day 17. If bank swallow young are cross-fostered between nests before this day, foster parents learn their identities and accept them. Alien young cross-fostered on or after this date, however, are rejected by their potential foster parents. Moreover, young cross-fostered before this critical age (and so accepted by their foster parents) will be rejected by their true parents if they return to the natal nest later. In comparable cross-fostering experiments, rough-winged swallow parents accept any young bird, related or unrelated, at any time. So, clearly, we have an adaptive use of learning in the bank swallow, where recognition is most definitely needed. And the rough-winged swallow's evident failure to learn is understandable given that this capacity would rarely if ever be needed.

But do we have a learning *adaptation?* Because it is almost certain in this case that the colonial species evolved from noncolonial ones, it is likely that there have been some adaptations in the colonial species for parent-offspring recognition. Yet, while this recognition clearly represents an adaptive use of learning, the adaptations for recognition need not be of the learning mechanism itself. There are several possible alternative adaptations that could produce this species difference in recognition. For example, one adaptation would be an increase in interindividual variability of the *signature* traits that are used in recognition. That is, perhaps bank swallow young are more individually distinctive than are rough-winged swallow young so that individual recognition is possible for bank swallow parents and difficult (or impossible) for rough-winged swallow parents. In fact, we have gathered strong evidence for such a *signature call* adaptation in bank swallows (Beecher, 1982). This call, which is the mechanism by which parents recognize their young in bank swallows (Beecher, Beecher, & Hahn, 1981), is much more elaborate and individually distinctive than is the homologous call in rough-winged swallows. (We have made a parallel finding for the colonial cliff swallow and noncolonial barn swallow; Beecher et al. 1986.)

Although we believe the signature call adaptation is *one* of the adaptations facilitating parent-offspring recognition in the colonial bank swallows and cliff swallows, other experiments have indicated that additional factors underlie the species difference in recognition. In particular, experiments in which one or a few alien chicks are added to the parents' brood, have shown that not only do rough-winged swallow parents fail to discriminate between related and unrelated conspecific young (which might well be a difficult discrimination), but they fail to discriminate between their own young and heterospecific (bank swallow) young, despite the clear difference between the conspecific and heterospecific young. Bank swallow parents, on the other hand, reject cross-fostered rough-winged swallow young (Beecher, 1981). So, clearly, an inability to distinguish between own and alien young is not all there is to the species difference in recognition. Another factor is suggested by a different sort of cross-fostering experiment, which makes use of the rough-winged swallow's habit of sometimes nesting in bank swallow colonies. In this experiment, bank swallow and rough-winged swallow broods from adjacent or close burrows are interchanged: Both the rough-winged swallow parents and the bank swallow parents will shortly begin to feed their chicks at the new location, suggesting that when *forced* to make a hard choice, the rough-winged swallow parents can indeed discriminate conspecific from heterospecific chicks (Beecher & Beecher, in preparation).

Taken together, these two cross-fostering studies suggest another hypothesis for the species difference in recognition: Parents in the colonial and noncolonial species may employ *different decision rules* when confronted with recognition problems. It seems likely that in the colonial species, where parents are often confronted with discriminations between own and alien young in which contextual evidence is lacking (say all the young are in the home nest, or are in the creche), parents have been selected to base their decisions on individually distinctive cues, while in the noncolonial species, where discriminations between own and alien young are almost never required, the criterion of "feed any chick you find in your nest" would be a generally reliable, conservative rule. A chick's presence in the home nest is, of course, strictly circumstantial evidence as to its relatedness, but in rough-winged swallows it is a virtually fail-safe criterion; in bank swallows, however, it is an unreliable predictor of relatedness. According to this hypothesis, in the chick substitution test, on finding a bank swallow chick in its nest, a rough-winged swallow parent gives priority to the chick's location in the home nest over the chick's unusual look and sound and so accepts it. In the close interchange test, on the other hand, the rough-winged swallow parent is confronted not only with an entire brood of transplanted heterospecific chicks in its nest, but also its brood of chicks calling vociferously at the mouth of a burrow a foot or so away. In this case the very large difference in calls and physical appearance is pitted against a small difference in location, and the parent gives priority to calls and appearance. Even in species where recognition occurs, we have evidence for a decision rule of this sort. Caspian tern parents will accept young substituted for their own in the first week of life, yet when given a *choice* between their own and alien young, in nest scrapes either side of the original nest, they will unfailingly choose their own (Shugart, 1977).

In summary, while learning is clearly involved in parent-offspring recognition in these species, we have no real evidence that the difference between species that recognize and species that do not actually reflects an adaptive specialization of learning. Moreover, we have strong evidence that it does involve adaptive specializations of the signature traits by which offspring identify themselves, and we have suggestive evidence that the adaptations may involve the decision rules by which parents decide whether to accept or reject young at the nest. Thus it is clear that these species differences in recognition *need not* involve any adaptive specializations of learning at all. Indeed, we probably need not contemplate testing the learning specialization hypothesis until we unequivocally show that the species failing to show recognition is incapable of learning the identities of its young, or is clearly inferior in this regard to the species showing recognition. I rather suspect that a number of species differences in learning that have been described in the literature do not involve any specialization of learning per se, but instead reflect other adaptations which permit learning to occur and be manifest.

Constraints on Learning Adaptations?

While certain failures of parent-offspring recognition can be interpreted as adaptive—as in the failure of the noncolonial swallows considered earlier—other examples resist this interpretation. For example, although it is widely stated that parents in the colonial herring gull recognize their chicks a few days after hatching, recent evidence indicates that they do not (Graves & Whiten, 1980; Holley, 1984; von Rautenfeld, 1978). Any *recognition* that does occur appears to be based on the frightened behavior of alien chicks: Any transplanted chick that stays at the nest will be accepted by the parents. Parents seem unable to recognize their young on the basis of calls, visual appearance, or any other such cue (though young do recognize the calls of their parents). Numerous cases of natural adoptions indicate, in fact, that failures of recognition may be fairly common in this species. It must be emphasized that any straightforward adaptationist argument predicts that in a colonial species like the herring gulls, where intermingling of young is demonstrably present, parents should recognize their off spring. Thus, this failure of parental recognition—which may or may not reflect a failure of learning per se—is difficult to explain. While there is no favored hypothesis at the present time, it should be clear we would have to consider hypotheses that posit constraints on the adaptive expectations. For example, Holley (1984) has suggested that the herring full until relatively recently was a cliff-nester (like the kittiwake; Cullen, 1959), a habit which eliminates chick movement and hence the need for recognition for approximately the first 4-weeks-of-life. Holley suggests that ground-nesting is a recent innovation for herring gulls, and that they do not yet show this necessary adaptation to it.

It is not a simple matter to develop a plausible adaptive hypothesis for the lack of parental recognition in herring gulls. As of this writing, none has been proposed despite considerable interest in the question. This illustrates another limitation of the adaptationist approach to behavior in general, and to learning in particular. Once one gets past the very obvious adaptive predictions—an animal ought to learn readily what it needs to know, and learn slowly, if at all, what it does not need to know—it is really quite difficult to develop good adaptive hypotheses. Basically this is because we generally do not have all the information we need to develop these predictions.

CONCLUSIONS

The study of evolution and learning has moved into a new phase. Originally the research and the debate were fueled by two questions. (1) Is learning diverse or uniform across species? (2) Underlying the specific instances of learning, are there a few or many basic learning processes? On the first question, there is now wide agreement that species do differ, often in extreme ways, in what they will learn.

On the second question, there seems fair agreement that the diversity of learning need not reflect different learning processes. In fact, there is no evidence that it does, and persuasive arguments have been made for a small number of basic learning processes (e.g., Staddon, in this volume). Thus the questions in the area have shifted, and I would suggest that they have shifted in the following way. It is now widely accepted that the behavior of animals is adaptive, in the Darwinian sense, and that whether we study this behavior in the field or in the lab, it will always reflect the animal's ecological niche and natural history. Yet, the adaptationist approach to behavior can only take the investigator so far. For example, it is fairly easy for me to predict that a species whose natural environment demands recognition ability will in fact have that ability. Yet, it doesn't enable me to predict exactly what adaptations natural selection will have shaped to this end. Mechanisms are the interface between natural selection and the adaptive behavioral outcome; theory can usually allow us to make predictions about what natural selection *should do* (i.e., what the behavioral outcome should be) but it can rarely predict the mechanisms by which the bottom line is achieved. Evolution is opportunistic. We cannot expect to predict, purely on logical grounds, what opportunistic solution evolution will have seized upon in the particular case we are looking at, nor what limitations (*constraints on adaptation*) this solution may have.

Learning is a mechanism—it falls in this grey area where evolutionary theory cannot make very compelling predictions. Yet it has surely evolved, and the study of the evolution of learning is certainly a reasonable enterprise. I close with two suggestions for this enterprise. First, I think it is essential that researchers be exceptionally cautious with the implication that they have an instance of the evolution of learning. As already indicated, an adaptive use of learning need not imply any action of natural selection on any aspect of learning. We could be looking instead at adaptive modifications of decision rules (affecting performance but not learning), of sensory systems (affecting sensitivities but not learning per se), of attention, or whatever. Just because they result in a learning difference does not allow us to imply that learning itself has been the target of selection. Second, I think the key to success will be to make the learning mechanisms as tangible as we can. This is what students of mechanisms have always done. The clever designs of experimental psychology are a start, but they are indirect. I believe that we will have to tie learning mechanisms to neural correlates if we are to gain any truly new insights into the evolution of learning. (To say again, or in some slightly different way, that learning is adaptive is not a new insight in my view). This research will have to be truly comparative of course. Recent work on neural mechanisms of song learning and of classical imprinting in birds are precisely the sort of work I think will be fruitful (e.g., Bateson, 1984; Konishi, 1985; Nottebohm, 1985). Already we know that these instances of learning utilize dedicated parts of the brain. Thus while we cannot yet speak of specialized learning processes, we can speak of specialized neural sites for particular kinds of learning. While it is too early to extract any broad generalizations about learning from this research, I predict that this type of work will pave the way for the next major conceptual advances in the study of evolution and learning.

REFERENCES

Bateson, P. P. G. (1984). The neural basis of imprinting. In P. Marler & H. S. Terrace (Eds.), *The biology of learning* (pp. 325–340). Berlin: Springer-Verlag.

Beecher, M. D. (1981). Development of parent-offspring recognition in birds. In R. K. Aslin, J. R. Alberts, & M. R. Petersen (Eds.), *Development of perception* (Vol. 1, pp. 45–66). Orlando, FL: Academic Press.

Beecher, M. D. (1982). Signature systems and kin recognition. *American Zoologist, 22,* 477–490.

Beecher, M. D., Beecher, I. M., & Hahn, S. (1981). Parent-offspring recognition in bank swallows (*Riparia riparia*): II. Development and acoustic basis. *Animal Behaviour, 29,* 95–101.

Beecher, M. D., Medvin, M. B., Stoddard, P. K., & Loesche, P. (1986). Acoustic adaptations for parent-offspring recognition in swallows. *Experimental Biology, 45,* 179–193.

Cole, S., Hainsworth, F. R., Kamil, A. C., Mercier, T. & Wolf, L. L. (1982). Spatial learning as an adaptation in hummingbirds. *Science, 217,* 655–657.

Cullen, E. (1957). Adaptations in the kittiwake to cliff-nesting. *Ibis, 99,* 275–302.

Garcia, J. (In press). Unification of classical conditioning and taste aversion learning. *Psychological Review.*

Graves, J. A., & Whiten, A. (1980). Adoption of strange chicks by Herring Gulls, *Larus argentatus. Zeitschrift fur Tierpsychologie, 54,* 267–278.

Holley, A. J. F. (1984). Adoption, parent-chick recognition and maladaptation in the herring gull, *Larus argentatus. Zeitschrift für Tierpsychologie, 64,* 9–14.

Johnston, T. J. (1981). Contrasting approaches to a theory of learning. *Behavioral and Brain Sciences, 4,* 125–173.

Konishi, M. (1985). Birdsong: From behavior to neuron. *Annual Review of Neuroscience, 8,* 125–170.

Maynard Smith, J., Burian, R., Kauffman, S., Alberch, P., Campbell, J., Goodwin, B., Lande, R., Raup, D., & Wolpert, L. (1985). Developmental constraints and evolution. *Quarterly Review of Biology, 60,* 265–287.

Nottebohm, F. (1985). Birdsong as a model in which to study brain processes related to learning. *Condor, 86,* 227–236.

Shugart, G. W. (1977). The development of chick recognition by adult caspian terns. *Proceedings of the Colonial Waterbird Group, 1,* 110–117.

Staddon, J. E. R. (1983). *Adaptive behavior and learning.* England: Cambridge University Press.

von Rautenfeld, P. B. (1978). Bemerkungen zur austauschbarkeit von küken der silbermöwe (*Larus argentatus*). *Zeitschrift für Tierpsychologie, 47,* 180–181.

Williams, G. C. (1966). *Adaptation and natural selection.* New Jersey: Princeton University Press.

Author Index

Subject Index